Women at Work
Perspectives and Experiences

and

Tips for
Women at Work
Kick-start your Career

Women at Work
and
Tips for Women at Work

Edited by Professor Anna M. Maslin
PhD, MSc, BA (Hons), RGN

International Officer for Nursing & Midwifery,
The Department of Health, England

Professor, School of Health, Community and Education Studies
Northumbria University, UK

Chair, Commonwealth Health Ministers Steering Committee
for Nursing and Midwifery

Published by Northumbria University Press
Trinity Building, Newcastle upon Tyne NE1 8ST, UK

First Published 2005

Copyright © Anna Maslin

All rights reserved. No part of this publication may be reproduced or transmitted in any form or by any means, electronic or mechanical, including photocopy, recording, or any information storage and retrieval system, without permission in writing from the author. This book is sold subject to the condition that it shall not, by way of trade or otherwise, be lent, re-sold, hired out or otherwise circulated without the author's prior consent.

British Library Cataloguing in Publication Data. A Catalogue Record for this book is available from the British Library.

ISBN 1-904794-10-6

Designed and printed by External Relations, Northumbria University.

Typeset in Garamond.

Northumbria University is the trading name of the University of Northumbria at Newcastle. ER_24959.

For
my daughters
Sarah, Charlotte, Victoria
and my niece
Antonia

Special thanks to

Stephen, Alex and Mabel

Each one of the Contributors

also

Beverley Akwara

Glenda Bailey

Maeve Binchy

Honor Blackman

Cherie Booth QC

Heather Cawthorn

Professor Tony Dickson

Sarah Doukas

Countess Patricia Mountbatten of Burma

Dame Sarah Mullally

Andrew Peden Smith

Sharon Saber

Dr Marla Salmon

Dame Cicely Saunders

Saxon Bampfylde Hever

Ann Towner

Derek Webster

Andrew White

for taking this project seriously and for their support and encouragement.

Contents

Part One: Women at Work

Foreword xiii
Introduction xvii

Chapter 1 1
Facing the dilemma
Professor Anna M. Maslin

Chapter 2 19
Who are these successful women and what drives them to succeed?
Kathleen McCourt and Susan Miller

Chapter 3 27
The Profiles*

Professor Anna M. Maslin with:

Professor Heather Angel 27
International Wildlife Author and Photographer

Dame Margaret Anstee 31
International Consultant, Author, Lecturer

Ms Rosie Barnes 37
Chief Executive, Cystic Fibrosis Trust

Ms Valarie Bragg 40
Principal Chief Executive, The City Technology College, Birmingham

Ms Darcey Bussell 44
Principle Ballerina, The Royal Opera House, Covent Garden

Professor Sandra Dawson 47
Master Sidney Sussex College also Director,
The Judge Institute of Management Studies Cambridge University

Dr Qling Qling Dlamini 50
Special Advisor, Commonwealth Secretariat

Ms Sarah Doukas 56
Storm Model Management, London

Professor Judy Dunn 59
MRC Research Professor, Institute of Psychiatry at the Maudsley,
Kings College London

Dame Rennie Fritchie 61
Commissioner for Public Appointments and a Civil Service Commissioner, England

Ms Kegalale Gasennelwe 67
Deputy Permanent Secretary, Health Manpower, Ministry of Health, Gaberone, Botswana

Dr Victoria Harrison 71
Executive Secretary, The Wolfson Foundation

Dr Margaret Kartomi 73
Head School of Music, Monash University, Victoria, Australia

Professor Christine King 76
Vice-Chancellor and Chief Executive, Staffordshire University

Mrs Glenys Kinnock MEP 79
Member of the European Parliament, Brussels

Dr Yvonne Lau 81
Consultant Surgeon, The Breast Centre, Kwong Wah Hospital, Hong Kong

Ms Sonia Lawson 83
Royal Academician, Royal Academy of Arts

Ms Zoe Congo (see under Ms Sonia Lawson R.A.) 85
K. P. Plastics

Ms Prue Leith 88
Business Executive, Food Expert and Writer

Countess Elizabeth Longford 90
Social Reformer, 1930's Labour Party Candidate, Writer

Ms Virginia McKenna 93
Wildlife Conservationist/Actress

Ms Sally Magnusson 96
Television Journalist and Writer

Professor Jane Manning 99
International Concert and Opera Singer

Mrs Barbara Maslin 106
Nursery Nurse

The Rt Hon. Dr Marjorie Mowlam MP 108
Minister for the Cabinet Office

Dame Lorna Muirhead 109
President, Royal College of Midwives

Rabbi Julia Neuberger   112
Chief Executive of the The King's Fund, London

Ms Susan Brookes Parker   115
International Labour Office (ILO), Geneva, Switzerland

Mrs Lisa Perry   123
Housewife and Mother

Dr Jan Peters   126
Head of the Promoting Science Education and Technology for Women Team, Department of Trade and Industry

Ms Nyree Dawn Porter   130
Actress

Ms Anita Roddick   132
Entrepreneur and Human Rights Activist

Dr Nafis Sadik   134
Executive Director of the United Nations Population Fund (UNFPA)

Professor Marla Salmon   136
Dean and Professor of the Nell Hodgson Woodruff School of Nursing and Midwifery

Dame Cicely Saunders   141
Chairman, St Christopher's Hospice

Ms Monica Louie Sims   143
Director of Production, Children's Film and Television BBC, since 1985

Ms Ruth Sims   146
Chief Executive, Mildmay International

Dr Rita Sussmuth   152
Politician, Prasidentin des Deutschen Bundestages, Bundeshaus, Germany

Dame Helen Suzman   154
South African Politician and Human Rights Activist

Ms Joanna Trollope   157
Novelist

Ms Catherine Walker   158
Fashion Designer, Chelsea Design Company Ltd

Ms Lynn Wallis   161
Artistic Director Royal Academy of Dancing

Dr Hanna Gronkiewicz-Waltz 165
President of the National Bank of Poland

Baroness Mary Warnock 167
Philosopher and Life Peer

Mrs Rosalind Wright 169
Director of the Serious Fraud Squad, Serious Fraud Office, London

Chapter 4 173
What qualities and coping mechanisms do these women have to achieve?
Professor Andree Le May

Chapter 5 179
Is success worth it?
Professor Anna M. Maslin

Part Two: Tips for Women at Work

Chapter 6 193
Preparing yourself
Professor Anna M. Maslin

Chapter 7 199
Cracking the CV
Tom Storrow

Chapter 8 213
Interview intelligence
Tom Storrow

Chapter 9 225
Salaries and individual performance review
Jennifer Parr

Chapter 10   239

Personal presentation

April Brown and Professor Anna M. Maslin

Chapter 11   247

Managing time

Professor Andree Le May

Chapter 12   255

What about the kids?

Sue Harrop and Sue Miller

Chapter 13   271

Dealing with the unexpected, stress, and bullies

Catherine Gaskell

Chapter 14   289

Work-life balance – flexi-time and working from home

Professor Anna M. Maslin

Chapter 15   293

A personal view

Heather Angel	293
Dame Lorna Muirhead	299
Rosie Barnes	303
Linda Conlon	306

Chapter 16   309

Conclusion

Professor Anna M. Maslin

Contributors' Profiles*

NB. The details given in the profiles were correct at the time of writing. Due to the inevitable passage of time, specific notes, dates and times, etc., will have moved on.

FOREWORD

Sarah Doukas

I first met Anna a few years ago when she approached me for an interview and contribution for her original book *Women at Work*. I thought it was a valuable tool for today's working women, and I was delighted to be asked to write the foreword for her follow-up book. I have been a working woman since I was 17, and have a wealth of experience gained from many years in business, but Anna's book provides practical and informed advice to make achieving success in the workplace easier.

It's not easy being a woman in today's workplace. Women's roles have changed dramatically over the decades and today's modern woman has been programmed to believe that she should be a high achiever professionally, an amazing partner and a perfect mother. Anything less is viewed as an under achievement of sorts. Personally, I think all women should set their own agendas and recognise and applaud their own levels of success. Whether they are in the boardroom or the playroom.

I have been the Managing Director of the Storm Model Agency for the past 15 years. I never set out to become a model agent, and somewhere along the way, I ran an antiques business at Clignancourt Market in Paris, and managed a punk band in London during the mad mid-1970s. I have always known that I wanted to be my own boss and work for myself and I left school before sitting my A Level's. Up until that point I had been privately educated — but I then rebelled against my academic father, who had dreams of university and a more traditional and professional career for me, and I set off on an amazing adventure.

I actually modelled for a while, moved to Paris, married my first husband — a musician, and moved to San Francisco for a few years where I managed a punk band. When I finally returned to the UK I had a young daughter in private education to support and bills to pay. I managed to talk my way into a job with a top modelling agency. Although I didn't have any fashion experience, I had learnt a lot managing the band, and I was organised, efficient and confident — all valuable qualities.

I started at the bottom of the ladder, making tea and trips to the dry cleaners for my boss. The hours were long, the atmosphere stressful, and there were frequently problems with model bookings. At the beginning the majority of my salary went on paying my childcare costs. Though I was commuting across London on public transport with my daughter in tow, I had finally found a profession I loved, and I was determined to learn as much as I could. After a few years I had worked my way to the top and was running the agency, and after seven years I was ready for new challenges. I left to pursue my dream.

I was bursting with ideas and put them into a detailed and comprehensive business plan. I foresaw a gap in the market, a need for UK-based models to be represented and marketed from the UK, to clients all around the world. I had established a valuable network of agents in various influential markets that I still work with closely, and I wanted to open up the UK market to more lucrative and creative opportunities. I wanted to establish the first international model agency that operated from the UK.

I have always been very proactive about achieving my ambitions and realistic about my professional strengths and weaknesses. I have a talent for recognising and realising the potential in people, whether staff or models. I'm also good at spotting talent, 'new faces' that may be interesting, edgy, beautiful but ultimately photogenic. I'm a great motivator, organiser and multi-tasker and I'm calm under fire too. My financing experience was limited then, and knowing I needed some expert help, I enlisted the services of a really good lawyer and a fantastic accountant who both decided to support me in my efforts to find financial backing for my fledgling company. They warned me it would be difficult to find backing, but they liked my drive and determination and my fresh ideas for the business.

I met with several 'city types' to discuss finance and partnerships. These included Adam Faith and Miles Copeland who had managed the band The Police and several financial controllers and bankers who had little or no understanding of fashion or the modelling business. There was lots of offers but none of the interested parties felt right and I didn't want to sign a deal with the wrong partner.

Ironically, I never once thought about failing, and this ultimately kept me focused and strong. At the eleventh hour I signed a deal with Richard Branson whose sister I had gone to school with. He was happy to accept the terms I offered and backed me through his private company, Voyager. We signed a deal that allowed us both to be equal partners. I would be allowed autonomous control and support from Richard if I needed it. These conditions allowed Storm to flourish and I managed to repay Richard his start-up loan within the first 3 years of the company trading.

I now employ 30 staff and run the agency with my brother Simon, who came on board in the early days. I was travelling with Simon in 1988 when I struck gold and spotted Kate Moss at JFK airport in New York. She was 14, 5'6" tall and had a different look to any of the 'supermodels' that were gracing the pages of all the glossies at the time. I didn't care, Kate had something about her, an attitude, an individuality, a look and I thought she was great. I couldn't have predicted then how famous or successful she would become but I still represent her today, nearly 15 years later.

I now have three children whose ages range from five to 23, and the company has expanded quite organically to include a Men's Division, a New Faces Division and a theatrical agency — Storm Artists' Management. I also have two model agencies in South Africa, one in Johannesberg and another in Cape Town that specialises in Sports Management and Production.

Life can be stressful and I am incredibly busy, but I surround myself with a good team of predominantly female staff who provide a solid support network, and they allow me to get on with the business of running and developing the company. It's important that everyone works well together and gets on with the models, and I make great efforts to get the chemistry right at Storm. While I also employ male staff and I think mine are incredible, I find that more women in general have the necessary qualities to be good bookers. Women are born organisers, very intuitive and able to spot potential problems, calm under stress and naturally emphatic when it comes to dealing with people. I also look for strong characters who can 'nurture' the young inexperienced models but also 'manage' the more recognisable 'supermodels' we represent.

Today, I'm still as motivated and enamoured of the business and the models I represent as I was 15 years ago. If I was asked to offer advice to women in employment, or looking for employment, it would be to find a career you like, work hard, and don't be afraid of getting down to the business of making your plans a reality.

INTRODUCTION

Professor Anna M. Maslin

There continues to be huge interest in the role of women at work globally. For example, many of the United Nations (UN) agencies are hoping to increase the number of women in key UN positions. The British Government is committed to sexual equality, to people friendly working policies, to flexible working and support for the working parent. We are all often fascinated to know what motivates another person especially if the other person has done something exceptional or faced huge challenges. Women in all walks of life perform daily miracles, in the care and work they provide for their families, society and the economy. Most of us acknowledge it is wise to learn from the mistakes and experiences of others. This book in a unique way allows us to glimpse into the lives of women who have successfully worked. Work in the context of this book may be paid or unpaid. Salary does not necessarily equate with value or status.

Women at Work is a combination of substantive chapters dealing with the relevant issues for women in, or hoping to be in, challenging personal roles and contributions from women who have achieved excellence in their own unique worlds. The contributions give personal perspectives, which are unique to each individual. The reader has an opportunity to evaluate for himself or herself the insights gained from each account.

The chapters aim to explore; the theory and practicality of the dilemmas surrounding the desire for success, however that is defined, who these 'successful' women are, what drives them to succeed, what qualities or coping mechanisms do they have to achieve success and finally is success worth it?

The profiles provide a brief snapshot in time presenting the views of a number of key women at an important time in history, the dawn of the millennium. The women asked for their views represent a cross-section of 'successful' women globally. They were all asked because they have a unique view to share. As we have already suggested the definition of success and work will be wide and therefore the women will reflect that breadth and diversity.

We hope *Women at Work* will be of interest to all women, but especially those women who are considering a life change or those who want to gain insight from women who have gone before them. *Women at Work* is a book which aims to increase awareness of the issues facing successful women, to increase understanding, to provide inspiration, to encourage women to achieve their own unique brand of success and to highlight the effectiveness of women in key positions.

Women at Work represented a journey for me as much as for the women who have so kindly taken part. They have been generous and candid. It has been a privilege to be allowed to share these experiences with them. This book is a unique snapshot sharing the perspectives and experiences of nearly a century of outstanding women.

Tips for Women at Work comes as a follow-up to *Women at Work* and moves on a stage. *Tips for Women at Work* is a practical resource focusing on areas that many women find a challenge. How do we actually get moving and start progressing towards the kind of work we would really enjoy? How do we crack the all-important CV? How should we present ourselves at interview? What are the skills and techniques involved? How do we address the salary issue? No one needs me to tell them that women generally speaking are not earning the same as men. Women sometimes lack the knowledge, skills and expertise in salary negotiation. What about personal presentation? Sometimes we are concentrating so hard on getting the qualifications or getting the job done that we don't realise the visual impact we make on people by not giving this aspect a little more thought. What about time management? Women are brilliant at multi-tasking but again sometimes there are principles and tricks we can learn to help us manage our day-to-day lives. What about the kids? For most women this is one of the biggest areas of concern. If we are working because we need to provide financially for our children and giving up work is not an option how do we ensure our children's health and happiness and our own sanity? What about stress and bullies? Sadly there are occasions often more frequently than we would choose when we are forced to deal with these unpleasant situations. How should we respond so we are not victims? Finally work-life balance how can we achieve a balance and a style of working, which is productive and sane?

There are many books on the market which deal with aspects of these subjects, many of which are excellent, but these books are different because they focus on a unique combination of areas that many women feel are vitally important and address these issues from a woman's perspective.

I hope this compilation of *Women at Work* and *Tips for Women at Work* will be of interest to all women, but especially those women who are considering a life change or those who want to gain insight from the knowledge and experience of others. *Women at Work* and *Tips for Women at Work* aims to increase awareness of the issues facing successful women, to increase understanding, to provide inspiration and to encourage women to achieve their own unique brand of success. I know I have learnt a great deal and enjoyed reading all the contributions. I hope you will too.

CHAPTER I

Facing the dilemma

Plus est en vous – *there is more in you*

Professor Anna M. Maslin

Success is a seductive concept. Power has a magnetic pull and adrenaline can be an all-encompassing aphrodisiac. Why do so many of us, male and female, want success so badly? Why do we have this need to be accorded worth and to be seen to have significant value? For some of us the desire for success is fulfilled by the ability to exercise a unique talent and to receive recognition for it. For many of us the desire for success is based on the need to react against the circumstances life has dealt us, for example because we have been born into poverty, suffered oppression, been devalued at some point in our lives. In adulthood the desire for success may be fuelled by the desire to prove something to others. Sometimes we want to show 'them', whoever 'they' are, that we are 'good enough', 'intelligent enough' or 'valuable enough' to achieve 'this', what ever 'this' is. 'This' can be rooted in material or psychological terms. We may want a good job, we may want money, or we may want the things money can buy. On the other hand we may want the respect, the sense of worth, the feeling of importance, or the feeling of security that comes with a perception of success.

Work is an interesting concept. At one time men were largely considered to be the 'workers' i.e. employers/employees working outside the home for 'pay' however widely that was defined. Women were thought to be the homemakers but not necessarily at work. Time has moved on. Work is now seen to be both in the home and outside. Men and women may interchange domestic and professional roles. Work may be paid for or it may not. The true value of the work is not necessarily quantifiable by the size of the paycheque. Interestingly though, other than in vocational work, size of remuneration or the size of budget controlled is often how an individual male or female's success is judged. Judging success and value in this way is dangerous because it means society will devalue work, which is creative or focused on the young, the poor, the vulnerable and the oppressed. Most of us would agree this work which involves a high degree of commitment and caring is important and yet society as a whole at times appears to only pay lip service to this.

In the search for personal success we need to ask ourselves a number of fundamental questions. At it's most basic level we need to know who we are? What has made us into the person we are today? Where are we going in life and why are we going there? Is our goal in life a 'good' one? If it is how can we achieve it? What is holding us back and ultimately what next when the goal is in our grasp?

Success is also a double-edged sword. There can be the win/win situation where our success brings success to others and everyone is happy, but, very often the success of one leads if not to the failure of others, at least to their disappointment. Success can also attract emotions like envy and jealousy, which are destructive to everyone. People who are significantly in the public eye often have to deal with being the target of cruel or abusive criticism being used against them. There is also the knock on effect. You may develop a tough skin to weather attacks made on you but you may feel much more vulnerable when people you love particularly, children or parents, are drawn into a frightening or unpleasant situation.

Success can also be difficult in relationships. The prominent success of one partner can lead to the feeling of impotence on the part of the other. On occasions one partner will sacrifice their goals and hopes to support the other. Sometimes this works out well but on occasions the supporter is lost along the way and a replacement relationship whether of a more equal or trophy partner is pursued. How can you ensure you spend enough time working on a personal relationship when you may be working 14+ hours a day and weekends? Another important area is compromise? Where does this feature in the relationship of two very driven individuals?

There is also the difficult issue of what constitutes success? Material success without professional satisfaction can be empty. Professional success without personal happiness can be deadly. Success can be defined very widely. It can be whatever gives the individual personal satisfaction and a sense of achievement. It could be designing the millennium dome or it could be arranging your baby's first birthday party. It could be leading a Fortune 100 company or it could be nursing an elderly patient. Success in itself can be good or it can be evil.

It is important for us as individuals to understand what our concept of success is and what impact achieving that will have on our lives. I often feel sad when I think of a young woman I know whose marriage broke up because she needed more time to 'network' to help further her career. More time to 'network'? It's only my personal view but nobody needs that much time to 'network'.

Success also has a cost. Sometimes striving for this illusive goal means we have little time for the people who matter. One thing that impressed me, when I read it, was that, the Clintons as a family, throughout their time in Washington, used to sit down with their diaries and put their daughter's key events in first, like school plays, recitals, etc. Mr Clinton may have had his faults, but if the President of the USA is not too busy to put his child first, then there is hope for the rest of us. There are very few things, barring, war, the threat of war, a natural disaster, a major incident involving the threat of injury or loss of life that are actually so important that they cannot be rescheduled to make time for the people we love. If a person maintains they are that busy, with day-to-day work, then they really are too busy.

We cannot be all things to all people. Sometimes trying to please everyone simply means frustration and ineffectiveness. I admit we're all very different but prioritising and regularly revising your list of priorities can help to keep you sane. Many women do, in my opinion, still carry the burden of ensuring large proportions of the domestic responsibilities are met or at least considered. It is very hard to be the perfect wife, mother, partner, professional, etc. and most of us will crack up if we try.

It is impossible to please everyone and therefore realistically we do have to decide what is important to us and how we will define our own personal success. Another important fact is that there are phases in all our lives. There will be times when babies, children, parents, friends, relatives or even a sick pet will have an impact on how we organise our lives. These demands on us are legitimate, they will only be with us for a time but we do need to be sensible in how we handle them to avoid frustration and stress.

Children are a huge consideration. As women many of us now have a choice whether or not to have children. Their needs are important. They require love, nurturing and care. How are these needs going to be met when women work outside the home? For some working outside the home is a choice for others it is a necessity. For some their work fits in easily with family life, for others there is the constant pressure of unsociable hours, late meetings, travel, etc. How does a mother cope with the guilt of a plethora of research studies that tell her whatever she does is wrong? How can mothers admit that sometimes being at home with two toddlers is actually more stressful and harder work than being the chief executive of a major corporation? What happens when the 'mother substitutes' who ever they are start acting as if they are the woman of the house instead of you? These are all-important issues, which need to be resolved if working outside the home is to be a success. The ideal I guess is both mother and father working part-time and sharing equally in the care of their children but how realistic is this?

Even if we do prioritise our home and work lives successfully, keep our values and put the most important things in our life first, another trial can be the fact that there are any number of people who feel they have the right to judge or criticise. These can range from the 'mother/mother-in-law cliché' to the friend who hasn't got a clue. It can be very demoralising to feel we are being misjudged and to know that the offending person is basing their judgement on inaccurate or incomplete information.

Another interesting phenomenon related to success is that we can work so hard to achieve it that when it arrives it is an anticlimax. We need to be realistic. It may be wonderful to be the best, the most powerful, the most revered, etc. but it may also be lonely, stressful and empty. Achieving great success can also have an inherent problem in that once it is achieved, what then? If there genuinely is no further goal to aim for you could suffer from a reactive depression. The high you achieved by striving for your goal may be gone once the goal is in your grasp. If there is a step further you may want to go on but then you need to ask yourself why? Life is made up of physical, emotional, psychological and spiritual dimensions. True success will take into account the legitimate claims of all of these.

The accepted wisdom is that women have difficulty in gaining acceptance for senior roles, outside the handful of activities that are thought 'suitable for women'. But Saxon Bampfylde Hever's (SBH) experience as a top head-hunter suggests that reality is not that simple.

They have been involved in the appointment of many women to very senior posts in international commerce and industry and in the Government, Higher Education and voluntary sectors. Among these appointments were the first woman chief executive of a British FTSE 100 company, one of the few woman vice-chancellors to run a British university and the first woman regulator of a British privatised industry.

The women they've worked with at this level have encountered remarkably little opposition in climbing the ladder of success. Indeed, as head-hunters, they've found that the problem is not necessarily persuading clients to consider women; equally it is finding enough female candidates who are willing to compete for the top jobs – and who have the appropriate experience.

SBH asked Peter Wallis of SRU – who also writes as trend-spotter Peter York – to carry out qualitative research among a group of over 30 women who had convincingly proven their ability to reach the top of their chosen callings. They wanted to see what difficulties the women encountered in getting there, in the hope of finding lessons that would help able women to overcome career obstacles.

The findings contradict the accepted view that men invariably make it difficult for women to get to the top. Most of these women had been greatly helped in their careers by men. Less surprisingly, the research found that their success was rooted in supportive parents, high levels of education and a great deal of hard work. Most important was the discovery that these exceptional women had a simple trick for breaking through the glass ceiling: ignore it. Rather than staring at their own reflections, like Alice they appeared to have simply stepped through the glass into a world concealed from their sisters.

It would be absurd to imagine that there are no areas of misogyny and prejudice left in our society, but this sample of women leaders does show what is possible today – and how it can be done.

Background, objectives and method

There have been many studies of senior women in their working environment and of the glass ceiling effect. But what is little heard in the debate is the viewpoint of women whose careers have demonstrably not been limited by gender: the small group who are already at the very top in business and the public sector.

SBH selected respondents at the most senior strategic level. Their jobs are concerned with the direction of policy and management of their organisations. They are the thought leaders' in their spheres. The buck stops with them. These glass ceiling breakers include women who are CEOs of major companies, have reached the highest levels of the Civil Service, lead public boards and committees or have respected practices and policy responsibility in the law and other professions. They are exceptional individuals, but they have shown what is possible and how it can be done.

The focus of their study has been corporate and establishment Britain. They have not sought to include entrepreneurs who have built careers in structures of their own making (although as it happens one of our respondents started her career there), media stars, the police, the armed services or the medical profession. All these areas warrant separate study.

As the balance of the gender relationship changes, each generation faces a slightly different springboard and set of obstacles. This study looks at the current generation of senior women – for the most part in their late 40s and 50s, and educated during the 1950s and early 1960s.

Objectives

Their objectives were to determine the factors that have led to success for the present generation of demonstrably successful women; and, from their experience, to define pointers both for other women seeking to emulate them and for corporate Britain.

Method

SBH interviewed women who have reached 'Great and Good' status in the UK. They also talked to a small group of senior Human Resource (HR) directors who have experience of best practice in the employment of senior women. All respondents were drawn from major UK companies, the professions and the public sector.

The interviews were lengthy – typically between one and two hours. No formal agenda or questionnaire was used, but interviewers ensured that the core issues were covered and gave particular emphasis to history, both career and personal. This allowed respondents to reveal their own priorities, concerns and emphases rather than reflecting the researchers' preoccupations.

Findings 1: Glass ceiling?

Most of SBH respondents appeared at first not to acknowledge the glass ceiling phenomenon at all, leading us to ask: are they in denial? Have they forgotten? Are they exceptional? All three turned out to be true.

Even when pressed, they denied experience of active discrimination or harassment. Clearly, some had needed to make sideways moves or take initiatives to prevent becoming becalmed or ghettoised: 'I've never been harassed – just soft discrimination'. But these manoeuvres were no longer front-of-mind. Memories of past obstacles and irritations had become humourous with hindsight: 'A judge once told me to wear a skirt!'

They had 'forgotten' because the view from the very top appears to encourage geniality and reconciliation – particularly in women. Indeed, the ability to rise above problems was a key characteristic of our respondents. They saw dwelling on past difficulties as a waste of energy and a habit which could also erode the precious self-confidence, which, we found, has been central to their success.

They were exceptional. Their family backgrounds, education, sectors of work and personalities were very distinctive. They have talent and ability. There was a noticeable absence of bullies or bluffers. Respondents offered a range of possible explanations, including:

- Women may need to be better all round than men to be accepted/sought after.
- Men can give themselves permission to report to a woman if she is self-evidently a superior human being.
- Women are less likely to want success for its own sake and therefore their substantive worth is all there is.

Very successful women are unlikely to see their careers as a battle or a campaign. What drove them upward was the matter in hand, the enjoyment and sense of achievement that came from addressing challenges and opportunities. In no case had there been an ambition or strategy for self-advancement for its own sake.

'No grand design – I like to be in the thick of things, where things happen... part of it is that I wouldn't be a good No 2: I can't take orders.'

Findings 2: Traits of senior women

Despite the variation in individual histories, a few themes emerged so consistently that they seemed to characterise almost all their respondents: self-belief, a high-quality education, a well-balanced disposition and the ability to work hard and pay attention to detail.

Belief in me, myself and I

Very noticeably, these women have very high levels of self-confidence – which appear to stem from an ingrained belief in their abilities and their judgement, rather than a thick skin or insensitivity. This tended to produce a 'walking on water' effect: if you have sufficient faith, difficulties will be overcome. 'I am a woman, you are a man – so what? ' is the unspoken message of this confidence, and male colleagues appear to understand it.

Respondents typically said that it had never occurred to them that as women they would have to take a lesser place in any traditional man's domain. Some actually felt they had an advantage, because of their ability to deal with emotional issues. They had expected no trouble and encountered none.

'I am never conscious of being a woman unless it is drawn to my attention. You should operate on the strength of what you have to offer. I am effective by being me.'

For a minority this self-belief was hard won, especially in cases where family and education had not been so solidly character forming. In some cases, their own talent – spotted by others – had opened their eyes to opportunities and carried them forward. The trick, and these respondents were aware it was a trick, was to keep your head and learn 'not to look down':

'Don't let them see you are thrown'.

Self-belief, it would appear, can be an exceptionally powerful and effective tool in countering other perceived disadvantages, too. For instance, two respondents had Asian origins; both said they had experienced almost no racial discrimination at work or anywhere else in the UK.

Education + education = freedom

This was a highly educated group. They saw education as central to their success. They were, at very least, as well educated as their male peers and in some cases better.

They had enjoyed learning. Many recalled their enjoyment of being tested and discovering they could excel, uncovering their power and building their self-belief. Most had had a traditional general education: History, Maths, English, Philosophy, Modern Languages, Law, and History of Art for their first degree. Perhaps unsurprisingly for this generation, there were no business studies degrees or MBAs.

Oxbridge in particular had propelled them into a man's world. Some had become honorary men, for instance through a doctorate, which freed them from the more limited social world of traditional women's circles in the '50s and '60s.

We came across only two people who had missed out on education: one from a truly working-class origin who had later scrambled through night school and an external degree; and another whose parents and teachers had set their sights too low and simply denied her a crack at Oxbridge – to her lasting regret.

Steady as she goes
The third essential characteristic both cited and displayed was the ability not to take things personally – to maintain a positive outlook and to move on quickly after setbacks. Variously described as 'generosity of spirit', 'courage', or 'the ability to accept that you may sometimes be wrong or mistaken', this resulted in seemingly well-balanced individuals who would be hard to blow off course. There was not an obvious neurotic among them.

Make light of hard work and details
Several respondents claimed that attention to the matter in hand rather than personal status was an advantageous female trait. Many said they had had to work harder, particularly by ensuring they had covered all the detail, but suggested that it would be unwise to make this a problem for male colleagues: 'You can work harder than men, but don't talk about it and don't ever whinge about it."

None of the respondents combined working hard with playing hard. Almost all agreed that it was natural for working women to have two lives – work and children. Among those who had decided not to have children earlier on, most had done so in order to devote more time to work, not to indulge themselves with, say, a second home or long holidays. None had become keen racehorse owners or become hugely 'social' beyond duty and close-ish friends.

Findings 3: Women what it takes
No factors guarantee success, but seven elements are clearly crucial:

Mum and dad matter

What do they think of women?
The respondents often said the start came from their parents. Typically, the view that they could do anything they wanted came from both parents. Their mothers, whether graduates or not, valued education for women and encouraged their daughters to be as academic as they chose. Parents were almost universally described as believing strongly in education for both boys and girls. Barriers and ceilings for girls were not acknowledged: 'It never occurred to me that I couldn't' was the norm.

'I never really thought about being a girl: I never thought there were any limits'.

'I did no work at university – I don't think my generation thought about careers or how to keep yourself for the rest of your life... Once I'd got the job I loved it, I was very happy, I became a noticeable person... but if I'd been a man I'd have had it years earlier.'

While their parents had been inspiring, many of their friends had grown up with more traditional expectations and had failed to fulfil their potential. For two respondents with less visionary parents, the first suggestions of possibility had come from friends and contemporaries: 'Abstract ambition is a male thing, it's only when someone you know does it...'

The feminist movement in the US was influential: 'It gave a name to some of our dissatisfactions'. Individual American women appear to have been ahead in aiming for the top and have been able to command senior posts here in the UK. 'Americans get senior positions because they're feisty and tough in a way that's not acceptable in an Englishwoman... English men buy the American brand.'

Parents' occupation

SBH respondents' parents were not hard-bitten go-getters. Mostly they were academics, civil servants and members of professions – people who believed that to serve and contribute was as important as money making.

They found very few top women could claim inspiration from parents in industry or commerce. Self-made entrepreneurs of that generation were not particularly interested in educating their daughters: they often came from backgrounds where education was little valued, and were unlikely to encourage or even welcome highly educated girls – who might even seem threatening to them.

Parental influences had also led to a certain modesty about money: none of these women was in any way anxious to mention any form of grand lifestyle. They expressed satisfaction that they 'had enough' but made it clear they were not from backgrounds where conspicuous consumption was encouraged.

Class issues

All SBH top women except one came from middle-class backgrounds – primarily the 'professional' rather than the 'commercial' sub-group.

Upper-class girls, from families where for several generations neither father nor mother had worked in the traditional sense, were less likely to have been encouraged to have a 'real' career. It wasn't thought necessary – just an optional extra, a bluestocking tendency – and in many cases was actually discouraged as unfeminine and a distraction from catching your man.

Working-class women hardly featured in their sample. In the '50s and '60s working-class girls, even with a grammar school education, could look no higher than local government or the public sector. Our one working-class respondent had been brought up in a foster home where education was not a consideration and had gone straight out to work from school. She had caught up with spare-time learning as she saw the opportunities open to her and, as an entrepreneur, had made her own structure in a 'new' sector.

Sector selection

It has been and still is important to pick your sector carefully.

Gender-blind sectors

Some sectors are more gender-blind than others. Among the favourites are media organisations and the civil service (which has clearly defined requirements and an examination tradition). Sectors with strong software and intellectual property components tend to be more used to women and more able to value women's traditional strengths – such as the 'soft skills' of interpretation and intuitive insight. That said, none of their respondents claimed to have moved from a less gender-blind sector or to have deliberately selected a softer option than they would have chosen if they had been a man.

New sectors

Fast-growing new sectors like IT, with few established hierarchies or recruitment patterns, are hungry for talent from wherever they can get it. They cannot afford to select by gender: they simply need the best and must constantly create new opportunities. Their management tends to be young and less gender prejudiced.

SBH's sole entrepreneur had set up her own software company in the '60s. She was convinced that if she had wanted to set up in a traditional, male-run sector – such as manufacturing – she would have had no chance of attracting backing at all.

Roles

What about 'girlie' jobs – in areas like HR and Public Relations (PR) – that are supposed to require touchy-feely female qualities? Most of SBH respondents had shunned such roles as limiting; others admitted using them opportunistically as a stepping stone to more senior status.

Reputations count

Looking back, SBH respondents said that a key success factor had been the development of their reputation. Once established, it had proved a potent tool – in effect, a marketable brand. While few had set out to manage their personal brand or their networking in a calculated way, they all now realised the value of making a name for themselves.

A well managed personal brand or name has great benefits. Best of all, it tends to be offered jobs while a 'candidate' has to compete for them. Over and over, we heard respondents say: 'I've never gone after a job… I was just asked to do this'. Personal PR, networking and brand management really do change perceptions and get people saying: 'We must have her, because she's a good candidate'. The moral: don't be a token woman – be a celebrity woman.

Brand champions

Having champions proved key for many respondents. While none had actually sought such a person out, many had acquired one by instinct and circumstance. Champions among the established Great and Good who 'put your name about' among the right people in the right way had proved very important, and many older people proudly parade their young 'discoveries'. For women with less robust academic and family backgrounds, talent spotters had proved crucial in the first phases of achieving confidence and visibility.

Packaging

Most of SBH sample dressed in a businesslike, plainish style – wearing obviously good quality clothes but with no attempts at 'power-dressing'. Very few of them wore evident makeup or jewellery. Their appearance ranged from elegance and smartness to a cheerful, scrubbed untidiness. Being in the public eye had often been a trigger to upgrade the wardrobe and haircut – but on the whole they were not that interested, beyond the desire to look respectable and undistracting. They were not so much sexless as safely distanced by age, marriage, family or seniority and respect. Nevertheless, several pointed out that being a woman gets you noticed and can be exploited in the later stages of a career. Above the glass ceiling, being a woman confers an intrinsic celebrity status, which is frequently an advantage.

Start at once

Few of SBH respondents were late starters – almost all got into the fast lane straight away. Making yourself useful from the start can open up avenues, particularly in the public service sector: for example, a good job in race relations at 25 could take you to a major appointment in your early 30s.

Being noticed early has its celebrity value, too: a female `bright young thing' tends to have a high profile from the start. Visibility can be vital in lifting a woman out of junior line management, if insecure immediate superiors are too nervous to promote a women: 'Only top men are able to take a risk on a woman'.

In short, it's wise to take the long view: show yourself to be useful, avoid making enemies, and start to be part of it all as soon as possible.

No room for role-play

Not for high calibre women

All SBH respondents said they had no time for role-playing; they had simply been themselves. Conscious role-playing was associated either with an earlier generation of 'spinsters and male impersonators' or with second-raters. Historically, they were told, women have related to men as kittens, mistresses, lovers, wives, nannies, mothers – or one of the boys. But role-playing has proved more trouble than it is worth: 'If I have used any "tactic" it's been my analytical ability'.

Role-playing with clients is a different matter. Respondents whose careers depended on client relationships said they assessed the role they needed to play man by man. If they needed to play the nanny or mother they did so. A senior woman in consultancy pointed out that the client relationship was so false and expedient that role-playing was a natural part of the ambience.

Wearing your gender lightly

The respondents mainly said that they played it straight, acknowledging their gender/sexuality/femininity as a matter of course while wearing it very lightly.

The subtext of confidence is all. Most said they certainly weren't 'professional women': they tended to be highly critical of groups and ideologies focused on gender, describing them as for losers or the 'professionally aggrieved': 'I've never been involved in a women's group – they're irritating and unreal. Men and women should mix.'

Discontinuous careers

Several respondents had created an entrepreneurial stage in their careers – often to facilitate child-rearing. Starting and growing a company or brand that is eventually bought by a mainstream business had proved an effective strategy to break the ceiling: 'If I'd worked my way up I wouldn't have done it – I'd have made too many enemies. I couldn't have done it by their rules. It wasn't worth fighting through the male hierarchy'.

Equal measures

Men at work

Men, according to the respondents, sense nervousness.

SBH respondents were to a large extent fearless, secure in their self-belief, transmitting the soothing subtext of confidence. When working with men they had consciously avoided any impression of stridency or nervousness through a combination of assiduous homework and realistic objectives – braced by the mantra that if you don't expect trouble it is less likely to happen. The repeated refrain was: 'I'm not conscious of any problems – I don't seem to have had many/any'.

'Psychologically, men are on the back foot with a successful woman.'

When gender problems did occur – male resentment of women affecting business decisions, fear of women leading to aggression – their effective methods of dealing with them had included:

- Brushing the problem aside – making it 'his' problem
- Rising above it – refusing to acknowledge irritating behaviour
- Moving the goalposts and dealing with it as a business issue rather than a gender matter.

What they did not do was:

- Declare a foul head-on
- Appeal to others to become allies
- Allow it to achieve corporate problem status.

Gender problems had rarely, if ever, included sexual harassment. This was seen as more often the fate of more junior non-graduate-intake women. Any early tendency to uneasy encounters evaporated with seniority: 'It's easier now I'm out of the realms of sexual possibility'.

Mentors

Mentors were less public than champions but nevertheless had played a vital role as coaches and advisers as well as gateways to the critical networks. Several respondents said their husbands had been their greatest mentors – but for most, mentors had been quite distinct from lovers. Many men derive genuinely disinterested pleasure from encouraging clever young women whom they feel deserve their help. Typically, what colleagues had assumed was a sexual relationship was in fact based on something more important: 'He saw something in me and was pleased and proud to develop it'.

Gallantry

Among successful women there is a growing acknowledgement that equality with men brings a responsibility to behave with gallantry towards them – to be gentle with the male ego and not to use sexual weaponry to unfair advantage, either to persuade or to hurt. We heard much about the insecurities of middle-aged middle-management males threatened by a changing world and inexplicable new kinds of success, particularly that of women.

The man at home

This generation of successful women described their husbands as not quite in the traditional mould for their generation. These 'flexible friends' provided emotional support, mentoring and encouragement.

A number of respondents had had early broken marriages and chosen better the second time around: a commonly used word when describing current marriages and partnerships was 'comfortable'. Many had husbands or partners with complementary work patterns, who had taken a substantial share in childcare. A less aggressively career orientated husband provided a happy resolution for many of these women because:

- They did not need to spend time propping up their husband's career
- They needed to devote less of their time to domestic matters.

Mother of all mothers

'Women have two agendas – it must be possible to work that out'.

Motherhood presents the greatest career problems for ambitious women. The respondents often said their contemporaries saw motherhood as 'an excuse to give up' – yet they seemed to manage their own children with apparent success. Their techniques for success included new career patterns (see below) and helpful husbands: 'It's pointless to try and fit your career into male patterns.'

Self-belief

They approached motherhood with their customary confident attitude to questions of guilt or neglect. They did not envisage problems – and believe their children have grown up just fine. As far as they are concerned, if the parents don't feel guilty or project anxiety the children don't pick up on it – the fact that mum works is simply accepted by all as part of the way things are: 'If you have the ability the rest is a matter of faith. If you believe in yourself you can do it.'

New career patterns

Many of these women had coped with child-rearing by pioneering new career patterns. Some, for example, had started their careers in traditional structures – and by gaining a partnership or achieving early seniority and strong personal branding in an organisation, they had been able to make good contacts and start their own businesses or practices while their children were young.

This transitional self-employed phase allowed them to have their children with them in the office and use their time flexibly. Once they were in their 40s and the children were older, they could typically sell themselves and their brands back into the mainstream at a very senior level.

Strikingly, though, everyone in this category said they now felt unable to extend the same flexibility to employees. Although they felt bad about this, they were adamant that it was a necessary business decision in all cases.

Findings 4: Today's day and age

Things are not the same

The traditional working environment was based on a model in which a public/grammar school educated 'officer class' led unwilling men'. This has now been almost entirely superseded by the more co-operative style of a generation untrained for battle. Hierarchies and disciplines have been replaced by a culture of encouragement and 'empowerment'. Women have contributed to this change and continue to benefit from it.

SBH heard much comment about women's natural concern for doing a job well, contrasted with men's need to be competitive and combative or to show off. But their most senior respondents tended to be unimpressed: 'Leadership is not gender based. There are ruthless, heartless women as well as men. All this empathy and warmth is complete rubbish.'

The HR angle

The HR chiefs want women...

SBH's sample of male HR directors was small but highly experienced, speaking for large organisations with diverse workforces. In their view, the case for more senior women in the workplace is won. Modern organisations recognise and need women's talent: 'The quality has drifted dramatically towards women, in terms of professionalism, ability and fit'. HR directors say that they want more senior women to enhance organisational effectiveness – unfortunately the practical implementation remains imperfect.

... but not their children

All our HR respondents wanted to recruit the best young female talent, but acknowledged that children were the main obstacles to retaining them: 'If your middle layer of management is likely to leave or become part-time in significant proportions, it makes running a business very difficult'. Several of our top women respondents also said that they will sometimes recruit a man in preference to an equally good woman for this reason – in such cases women really do have to be better than men.

In the professions, the big London law firms for instance, there is a race for partnership within six years of recruitment. Once they've secured a partnership and built their personal 'brand', many of the best women leave to begin child rearing and a softer job out of town.

Firms want to offer recruitment packages that give women space for child-rearing later on, but the perfect formula has not been found.

Part-time working

Part-time working in this group had not proved a viable route to the top. Work spills over into non-working time and clients demand weekend attention: 'That's when deals are done'. There are three main areas in the UK:

- Job sharing does not work at senior levels – learning curves and intellectual property that develop over time do not lend themselves to being passed back and forth.

- Mornings or afternoons only are difficult, as meetings and work inevitably spill into the afternoon or evening.

- The 3- or 4-day short week has proved workable for some, but weekends may be annexed at short notice for anything from a customer pep-talk to an M&A deal.

Findings 5: Rising to the future
Up-and-comers take note

Are you ready to rise?

Senior women have high hopes for the upcoming generation, but do not appear to identify closely with them. They see three problem areas:

- Young people in general are better qualified, better educated, more focused and more dedicated than the current generation in power... but seem a little dull. They come across as anxious and intense. And the girls seem worse than the boys. One respondent said she often favoured men because the women were so intense: 'Their first interest is themselves and their future, not the matter in hand'.

- Related to this is the tendency of both sexes to disappoint. The most driven and ambitious get the good jobs early, 'because they want them so much', but often lack the intellectual qualities to fulfil their promise. Ambition *per se* is not enough in corporate structures: 'Intellectual horsepower is essential over the long haul'.

- Young graduates who step in above the dogsbody level may 'have it all' too easily and too early. If they miss out on the character-forming struggles, they may lack the necessary rigour and toughness for more senior roles.

Are you mad enough to rule?

Will women ever lead the creation of complex, Murdoch-scale networks, or is empire building likely to remain a male initiative? Some respondents argued that only men had the form of madness that empire building requires.

A word in your ear

Your own career

The next generation of women have two perspectives on the future: building their own careers, and guiding their children's ambitions. Respondents thought today's young women should:

- Play it straight – or ensure feminine wiles are completely invisible
- Avoid 'in your face' dressing-up
- Tread lightly over rough ground, recover quickly from failure, keep their nerve
- Always ensure a dialogue of equals
- Never let people see their fear, and keep heartache and headaches out of sight
- Focus on the matter in hand
- Acquire authority and be known for it
- Deny the gender issue!

What shall we tell the children?

In bringing up their children, the new generation should:

- Instil faith and all-round self-confidence in their daughters, teaching them the benefits of independence
- Assume equal opportunities for brothers and sisters
- Bring up their sons in complementary ways to fulfil themselves and relate well to women
- Educate, educate, educate.

Captaining corporate Britain

Organisations should nurture their female alumnae:

- They should take pride in their women employees and claim credit for them. Providing a stimulating environment and a springboard for the brightest and the best is a key recruitment tool.
- They should stay in touch with past employees as a way of regaining access to fully developed talent. To recoup their investment in the best young women they have trained they should be inventing ways to retain female talent beyond and through child-rearing. This may include accommodating or acknowledging the fact that women will be with their young children in mind, though not in body, for part of their working lives.

- As they recognise the advantage of women's influence and contributions, they should find ways to identify the aspects of female thinking and behaviour that represent best practice- and disseminate them to men.

- And finally, if corporate Britain is becoming more female-friendly, it should also recognise men's response to this and ensure that men, too, can find fulfilment in the new environment.

Discovering more

SBH acknowledge this study is only a snapshot. They admit there are fields where hostility to women is still rife. For example, as one of the sponsors of WHERE, the Women in Higher Education Register, they are aware that there is a long way to go before a representative number of women are holding top jobs in Higher Education. Yet other fields – such as PR or HRs – appear to be almost disproportionately staffed with women. Is either imbalance smart? SBH would like to find out. And what about able young women at the start of their careers? Are things really so much better for them now?

They intend to commission a continuing series of studies and publish the results periodically. Women's comments and suggestions are welcome: please call Paula Alexander at their Westminster office or email your thoughts and comments to glassceiling@saxbam.co.uk.

By sponsoring research and encouraging debate SBH hope to establish that able women of all ages are competing on an ever more level playing field and that in pursuit of top jobs they are increasingly likely to be judged on their abilities and not on their gender. That said, they have found that – all other things being equal – the odds these days usually favour the female candidates who feature on their shortlists.

*Reproduced by kind permission of Saxton Bampfylde Hever, October 1999

CHAPTER 2

Who are these 'successful' women and what drives them to succeed?

Kathleen McCourt and Sue Miller

'My expectations – which I extended whenever I came close to accomplishing my goals – made it impossible ever to feel satisfied with my success.'

Ellen Sue Stern

How familiar this description can be! Looked at in the cold light of day this is recognisable behaviour for many of us. The old saying 'Good, better, best, let it never rest, till our good is better and our better best' means that being 'good enough' be it in our professional or personal lives is simply not an acceptable position to adopt. The refusal to give up, to walk away, to shrug metaphorical shoulders and 'lie down and take it' is a strong feature in those who achieve success in their chosen fields. They are starter-finishers who refine what 'finished' means by adding new challenges and standards for themselves and others. They can be variously described as single minded, selfish, driven, visionary, pains in the neck. But they make their mark, they get the job done, they make a difference.

This chapter provides an opportunity to reflect on what might be the personalities, temperaments and shared psychology of successful women. We can all bring our own suggestions and perspectives to this. After all, most of us will know women who have managed amazing achievements. Some, like those in this volume, will have demonstrated skills and abilities that have brought them to the public's attention.

There will be other women who have successfully overcome enormous challenges that exist purely within the private worlds of their own homes and families: coped with personal tragedy, found ways to deal with traumatic emotional and physical abuse, lived with poverty and disease. In many ways it could be argued that these women are the truly successful, for success may be more easily measured not by the position that a person has achieved in life than by those obstacles that have been overcome in getting there. Elbert Hubbard said: 'God will not look for medals, degrees or diplomas, but scars.'

All the women who have shared their stories in this book have told these histories as they see them. Each contribution reflects the insights gained from the experiences of women from a range of backgrounds, but the majority all have one thing in common. These women have achieved in ways that have brought them recognition beyond their immediate family circles.

This recognition has come in a number of forms, and the narratives variously refer to these. Some are external and visible rewards such as fame, accolades and awards, status, titles, promotions. Success is often a phenomenon in the public realm as external evidence used to validate achievement, other rewards are internal and invisible such as self-esteem, a sense of pride or inner peace.

In reading these contributions we will all look for different things, consciously or unconsciously. Some of the perspectives will resonate with our own. This may be because we recognise the role described or the job undertaken, or the relationships within this, or the characteristics and temperament of the writer. Some common themes will emerge that seem to carry these particular women through and these may also remind us of ourselves. Belligerent optimism, dogged determination, fear of failure, sheer bloody mindedness, personal conviction, they are all there in these women. Some of these characteristics are to a greater or lesser degree in us all.

We do not, in a work of this nature, have the opportunity to enter into dialogue with the contributors. None of them are in a psychiatrist's chair. We cannot probe their accounts with them, or check if our understandings of them accord with what they were seeking to communicate. They are simply offering us their story, as they see it and as they want us, an unknown audience, to hear it. As women used to living their lives in the public eye they will be well used to projecting images of themselves, but they will know that many people who know them well will be reading these accounts.

What motivates anyone to succeed will reflect their beliefs and values about what is important. Aiming for communal rather that individual achievement inevitably leads to a greater need to gather as well as drive forward. There has been an increasing awareness in recent years of the importance of seeing a team as comprised of individuals with different strengths but also needs. Effective managers are being recognised as those who see 'the person' as well as 'the role'. People like Daniel Goleman have drawn attention to the additional energies that can be released by working with what he calls emotional intelligence. The public realm is reshaping itself to incorporate values which might in the past have been seen as being more rightly kept to the private domain – empathy, flexibility, compassion, understanding. Rather than always being viewed as getting in the way of success, their place in the world of work is being acknowledged.

'What does it profit the man if he gains the world, but loses his soul.'

There is the story of the successful businessman whose company held a dinner to honour his lifetime of achievement. All the most important people in his work life were there, together with his wife and four children. After all the speeches in recognition of his achievements, his tireless energy, his loyalty and commitment, his 17-year-old daughter stood up and took the floor. She explained to the assembled audience that this person was also her father – but she barely knew him and he certainly didn't know her. As far as she was concerned there was one area of his life where he was a singular failure.

There are risks involved in pursuing success, clearly, and for women those around the family can still be seen as primarily creating guilt for them to bear. Very few people, if any, reach the end of their lives without some 'if onlys' and a few 'too lates'.

The issue of image is very important to success. Their public roles are very significant in how these women are defined. Self-presentation has been a central issue for women long before it appeared as a career factor. Women have consciously constructed and managed their image to the outside world as a way of coping with the conflicting demands of the public and private realms – they have for instance worn cosmetics in different societies from early times and one function is to mask the individual with a protective colouring. The geisha's face paint eradicates from the features not only imperfections but idiosyncrasy and personality, presenting not an individualised identity but an image determined by its social context.

Make-up seems to have served as protection from most ancient times. It seems that kohl rimmed the eyes against brilliant sunlight in ancient Egypt and still does in Asia. Some women are condemned for their style and cosmetics they use. Make-up has been seen as subversive, the more usual adjective is 'immoral'. Clothes and cosmetics are indicators of identity and have grown in importance with the advancement of individualism.

Although the women in this volume convey a positive self-image, their accounts do not suggest that they have all had a problem-free route to success. There are many references to challenges faced and difficulties, both personal and professional arising from tensions experienced in marrying the various roles undertaken both at home and at work. The tone is candid; the accounts are reflective and insightful.

One of the aspects of this process that is, therefore, particularly relevant for us is what seems, to these women, to have been the factors that have contributed to their success that they are willing to share in this way. We may not always agree with their analysis of these factors, but their validity arises in part from the relevance ascribed to them here by the individuals involved.

A strong feature of successful women is that they look to have their activities validated or sanctioned by some external significant other. Even Margaret Thatcher when talking about her success says of her husband Dennis, 'He was a fund of shrewd advice and penetrating comment. I was never alone, what a man, what a husband, what a friend.'

Rather than identifying internal drives as fundamental to their achievements, women instead externalise many of the reasons for their success to the support of others and to what are occasionally described as 'lucky breaks'.

These women have in many ways shown themselves to be extraordinary individuals. But as their accounts unfold they describe many contributory factors that the most ordinary woman will recognise.

Over and over again, these contributors identify that they perceive their success as being completely inseparable from the support of significant others in their lives. If no man is an island entire of himself, then no woman appears to be either. None of these women perceives themselves as having succeeded alone.

Success requires the harnessing of the skills ands resources of others and successful women, if these are typical, appear to focus overwhelmingly on relationships and values. Women are sometimes described as being more ready to vocalise and share these than men and as becoming more unsettled when these relationships and values are being challenged (ref). These women appear to be comfortable with an image of themselves in the centre of a network of support. They have the confidence to acknowledge their need for others on their journey. They look to others to support them and are not afraid to move on to other networks when they find this is not forthcoming. They see themselves as having something important to contribute and are driven to do so. Although this frequently involves great pain, they will take difficult personal decisions to 'move on' from a destructive personal relationship if they feel this undermines their capacity to be who they were meant to be. Although people are very important to them, so are tasks.

It is absolutely impossible to talk about what drives women without talking about what drives men. We know that we are living at a time of enormous economic and social change in the Western world. The definitions of male and female roles, the types of employment opportunities for men and women, the effects of family planning and improved health have all contributed to the different ways in which men and women are now being defined by others and by themselves. Society in the past expected public success for men, whereas women were defined primarily by the achievements of their husbands and their children.

One wonders to what extent this has actually changed. One of the features of these particular narratives is the way in which they tend to focus on the positive, contributory factors in each person's life. Hardships and difficulties are described often with great candour and honesty, but they have been presented at times in a way that is tempting one to perceive these almost as 'blessings in disguise', events and experiences that actually strengthened resolve and quickened the spirit. Whether one would describe this as snatching victory from the jaws of defeat, it is a capacity not to give up when things go wrong and retrospectively at least to view the glass as half full rather than half empty that pervades these accounts.

One should not let this feature pass without consideration. It seems likely that successful women, will at times have been isolated, different, accused of selfishness, unreasonableness even. Some may even have had to contend with accusations of unnaturalness if, in order to achieve their goals, they did not follow society's expected female path leading to marriage and motherhood. Over and over again these women focus on the conflicts that arise from trying to juggle the joint responsibilities of family and work. Yet all of them had sufficient help to carry on regardless.

In the context of a consideration of who these successful women are and what drives them, this seems to be an absolutely fundamental feature that has to be explored. It is not, in all fairness, simply a trick of their personal perspective that creates this sense of support around them. We can see also that they all, to various degrees had help. For some there was considerable material advantage, for others there were parents that had influence and enormous wisdom. They had access to education, travel, scientific advances, health care, family and friends.

The issue though seems to be that lots of other women similarly have these features in their lives, but choose very different ways of using these opportunities. Faced with what is often an overwhelming tide of doubt and negativity, from others and from within, they find it very hard to give themselves the necessary permission to take risks, to step out in faith. It was Shakespeare who said: 'Doubt is a thief that often makes us fear to tread where we might have won.'

So, without the constant combination of encouragement from others, practical support from people with whom we can share the workloads and that quiet, but persistent inner voice that says 'You've got this far, you can't give up now,' many of us settle for something akin to second best. We find excuses. We refuse to risk what we have for what might be. Rather than to challenge, which would draw attention and make us responsible, women learn to accept, which creates disempowerment and conformity.

Lack of confidence seems to inhibit women from engaging in activities and pursuing occupations in which they are interested. This is something on which women's groups and networks focus. Success is one of the chief aims of the public world in a society that places a high value on individualism. This creates a tension for women torn between wanting to be part of a group but also wishing to achieve as an individual.

Balancing success and satisfaction clearly represents a major challenge in the public and private spheres of women's lives. Women are aware of the tension between family and work commitments. Although fulfilment is an acceptable goal for women it is difficult for them to pursue this outside of the home environment. It requires courage to dare to be different.

Like all successful people, all women have had to take risks. Anyone who breaks out of the mould, stands against the crowd, acts with the degree of single-mindedness that is evident in the narratives that follow will be likely, at some point or other, to court unpopularity. 'I don't know the key to success, but the key to failure is to try to please everyone,' said Bill Cosby. These women appear to have taken this on board, but to have carried on anyway.

From where have they got the courage to do this? Their situations combine self-esteem and inner confidence arising from incremental successes achieved over time with real, demonstrable acceptance, love and respect from people whose good opinion these individuals valued. These twin characteristics appear, again and again, in these narratives. Their stories reflect lives that have been tested, skills that have had to be honed, and understandings that have been developed from experience and reflection. Whether because of family, friends, faith, or a combination of all three, these women have, in each instance, described themselves as not having to face these alone.

Rather than being driven from within, these women describe themselves as being supported from without. They seem to have developed the 'knack' of sharing uncertainty and vulnerability in ways that have actually made them stronger. If they have been successful in anything it is in asking the right questions and harnessing wise counsel when they needed it most.

Many of these contributors have children. Several comment that their children represent if not their greatest 'achievement' then, without doubt, the most important people in their lives. One has a strong sense that there is no comparison between the significance of family life in these women's minds and any success they have had in work. Although family life is regularly identified as requiring an enormous commitment in terms of time and energy, this strong investment in the family actually allows these women to take greater risks at work. The bottom line is that, should everything at work go pear shaped, it is not the end of these women's worlds, for their personal life means more than anything to them. It is not simply that they have a family, to fall back on, but they are significantly defined as people in more than one role.

It is interesting therefore that so many of these women comment on the value that they place on 'personal space'. It is as if, subconsciously they are recognising that having another world apart from work is not only a lifeline, and a way of 'recharging batteries', but actually a source of power and energy for being able to take chances and rise to challenges at work.

This is clearly a deeply felt belief in these women. In itself, the fact that they have been able to maintain these dual constructs of their family lives as both relationships to which they contribute and sources of their empowerment gives them an incredibly significant launch pad for their activities. Potentially it frees them and allows them some room to view their paid roles alongside their roles as daughters, sisters, wives and mothers.

Clearly this is not easy. Women in our society have been overwhelmingly viewed as the people holding the underpinning infrastructure of family life together. The presence of those traditionally 'female' qualities of sensitivity, understanding, empathy and care have been subtly, and not so subtly identified as essential for sound psychological development and women have been blamed in the past when they have been missing in children's lives. We have a whole raft of feminist literature that would testify to this.

But these women have succeeded in articulating to themselves and others why they are doing what they are doing. They have done this in an often-hostile world unused to constructing women in these new roles of leadership, management, authority and power. Most importantly, they have also had to articulate this to themselves, to give themselves permission to be successful in new ways.

Eleanor Roosevelt once said, memorably of men, when she could have just as easily have said it of women:

> 'If at the end one can say, "This man used to the limit the powers that God granted him; he was worthy of love and respect and the sacrifices of many people, made in order that he might achieve what he deemed to be his task," then that life has been lived well and there are no regrets.'

These women's success is derived from the combination of two very familiar features: an interaction between the innate qualities these women possess and their personal circumstances as created by their particular social contexts. Together these have created the necessary soil for them to sow the seeds for their success. One suspects that, as with so many aspects of human achievement, they have only become aware of this on reflection and had a sufficiently flexible (if any) game plan to be able to be responsive to the throw of the dice.

Sue Miller MSc (Educational Psychology)
Senior Lecturer

Division of Childhood and Family Studies, School of Health, Community and Education Studies, Northumbria University

Currently undertaking significant work in policy and practice development in parenting.

Kathleen McCourt MEd (Educational Development)
Principal Lecturer/International Co-ordinator

School of Health, Community and Education Studies, Northumbria University

Currently working with governments of China and Egypt on health issues and professional leadership development.

CHAPTER 3
The profiles

Professor Anna M. Maslin

The interviews/profiles in this chapter provide a unique glimpse into the world of a number of women some of whom you may know well some of whom you may not. These women come from all walks of life and have been generous enough and brave enough to share a private part of themselves. These women are all facing the issues of being women at work. They are different women so their perspectives will reflect that diversity. I will not be commenting or analysing the views they express. They are personal. I will leave it to the reader to consider for themselves the lessons and implications of these accounts.

Heather Angel BSc (Hons) MSc DSc (Hons) FRPS FRIPP
Professional international wildlife photographer/author

Heather manages her own stock photo library (her website was launched in December 1999: www.naturalvisions.co.uk) with four staff supplying magnificent colour photographs to world-wide clients – national press, major publishing houses, corporate companies, etc. She is a Hood Medal recipient for 'her contribution to the advancement of nature photography through her books, her teaching, her exhibition work and her encouragement of other nature photographers'. She has received the Société Française de Photographie – Medaille de Salverte. *Heather was appointed a Special Professor within the School of Biological Sciences at Nottingham University and also received the Louis Schmidt Laureate (Premier annual award of BioCommunications Association of USA).*

Heather had never used a camera – not even a box Brownie – until after she graduated. Before she went on an underwater expedition to Norway in 1962, her father gave Heather her first camera, which she used as a tool to document the marine life they found, researching for her MSc.

In 1985 Heather was commissioned by an Italian magazine to photograph the vegetation on Mt. Ruwenzori in Uganda. It was a tough trip involving up to 12 hours trekking a day. As she staggered into the penultimate hut 16,500 feet up she thought she was seeing double she stumbled over a Benbo tripod. An elderly man emerged from out of a dimly lit room extending his right hand saying "Heather Angel, I presume"! The gentleman was a retired vet, Guy Yeoman, Neither of them knew the other would be there but he recognised her from her tripod (a tripod she repeatedly promotes.)

For a quarter of a century, wildlife photography has been an all-absorbing profession which has drawn me repeatedly to the poles and the tropics. It gave me the impetus to try my hand at writing, which now fuels my ideas for photography. Not least, it has opened my eyes, so that I have become a much wider communicator of the natural world by developing a more artistic eye. Yet, the evolution of my natural vision came about by accident.

My fragmented education (I attended 14 schools in as many years because my father was in the RAF and we were constantly on the move) was not ideal grounding for any profession. What it did give me, however, was the ability to integrate and make friends quickly, plus a gritty determination to pursue any quest relentlessly to the end.

In my early twenties I was a budding scientist lacking any atom of creativity and without any ambition whatsoever to be a photographer – indeed I never used any camera before I was 21. After graduating in zoology, I took part in an underwater expedition to Norway working twice as hard as the other (all male) participants as the cook/marine biologist. By a curious twist of fate my husband-to-be (an ex-Cambridge graduate) was not enthusiastic about having a female on the expedition, but when I volunteered as cook he was outvoted! Whilst working in Norway, I took my first pictures – all of marine organisms.

Back in Britain, in between researching as a marine biologist and lecturing, I sold a few illustrated articles on marine topics. These labelled me as a source for marine pictures for several years to come, so I remain forever thankful to the picture researcher who not only asked me for a picture of a daisy but also gave me enough lead-time to go out and shoot it! I soon realised that if I was going to make my mark and sell pictures in the international market place, I had to think beyond daisies and robins in my back garden. Only by being prepared to travel to remote corners of the world – where the most productive wilderness areas are situated – could I broaden my horizons.

Two factors helped me achieve my goal. First and foremost, a wonderfully supportive husband, whom I had married whilst I was completing my MSc. Martin was also a zoologist who became a peripatetic oceanographer; which meant that we often travelled in different directions, but on our return we had a multitude of experiences to share. Secondly, the demand for stock colour photographs of wildlife grew continuously throughout the late 1970s and the 1980s.

In between visiting remote oceanic islands – such as the Galapagos, the Seychelles, Madagascar and New Zealand – to document their endemic flora and fauna; I worked in Britain, always aiming to develop an approach combining scientific accuracy with an artistic eye.

The publication of my first book *Nature Photography: Its Art and Techniques* in 1972 changed my life overnight. The photographic press had discovered a nature photographer who could also produce a complete photo and text package. Soon I wrote regularly for *The British Journal of Photography*, I had my own column in *What Camera?* from 1989–90 and in *Amateur Photographer* from 1990–97.

When I married, my father gave me some EMI shares as an investment. After struggling for several years with barely adequate equipment, I discovered that realisation of the shares would enable me to purchase the Hasselblad camera of my dreams. My father was furious with my 'frivolous' purchase. Years later, after I had become established, he did a complete u-turn and admitted it was the best decision I ever made!

Having been trained as a scientist to observe and record, initially I found popular writing was a chore. That was until one winter's morning when sitting in a hide waiting for the rising tide to push waders closer towards me, I peered out of the rear flap and was rewarded with a glorious spectacle of the changing light on the Welsh hills. That moment was infinitely more memorable and inspiring than the few oystercatchers, which eventually moved in closer. From that day, I learnt how to savour 'unproductive' moments, regarding them as a bonus instead of a waste of time. Instead of f-stops and apertures, my field notebook became peppered with notes about the light, the atmosphere and even the sounds. Now, I never travel without my notebooks so that any downtime at airports, in planes and on boats can be utilised to outline ideas for articles and books.

Joining the Royal Photographic Society, I gained my Associateship and Fellowship and became the founding Chairman of the RPS Nature Group, which opened many doors to unexpected places. During my spell as President of the Royal Photographic Society (only the second woman in the entire history) from 1984–86, I thoroughly enjoyed being an ambassador for the Society, leading a small photographic delegation to China in 1985. However, at the time my own photography had to go on the back burner.

I regard myself fortunate in having found a niche I could exploit relatively early in my working life. Through my books (47 published to date), lectures and workshops, I get a real thrill conveying my enthusiasm for photographing the natural world to others. I was particularly delighted when Nottingham University appointed me a special professor in 1994 (the first British wildlife photographer to be so honoured) so that I could put something back into the academic world.

When our son Giles was born in 1977, my husband and I arranged our work so that one or other of us was always at home or else we took him with us. It is a great delight that Giles after completing a science degree, is back home and working alongside and inspiring me with his enthusiasm for digital imagery.

A family home creates a permanent – and vibrant – base to return from abroad. Everyone wants to hear about the trip and to see the pictures. I could not image returning to an empty flat. Children not only provide the link with the past and the future, they also provide a purpose and impetus for continuing to work.

Nowadays, any woman with a computer connected to the internet has instant access to a vast source of information and has greater scope for working from home. Even basic food shopping need no longer be a chore – it can be done online.

My career as a professional wildlife photographer came about by accident, but if I had my time over again I would not hesitate to follow the same rewarding path. Whether seeing polar bears in Canada, giant pandas in the snow in China or lemurs in Madagascar, it has been one long voyage of discovery: discovery not only about life in remote locations and extreme climates, but also about my own artistic inclinations that otherwise might have remained dormant forever.

Admittedly, crouching for hours in a mosquito-infested swamp or enduring temperatures of -30°C could never be described as pure enjoyment, but the thrill of the quest – to distil a moment of time within a still image – spurs me on. Had I remained a biologist I would neither have travelled so extensively nor have been able to appreciate at first-hand the problems of man's impact on sensitive habitats.

There are times when I cannot cope physically and I have to find alternative ways to solve an impasse. For instance, strapping it to a child's sledge solved carrying heavy camera equipment over miles of snow-covered ice in Antarctica. When working up at altitude in India or China I simply hire a porter – although it was rather embarrassing when my Chinese porter in Anhui Province turned out to be a slip of a girl even shorter than my 5' 1".

I cannot recall ever having been disadvantaged because I am a woman. On the contrary, time and time again it has proved to be an advantage. Whenever a new book of mine is published or an exhibition opens, it is featured not only in the photographic press but also in women's magazines. People are intrigued to learn how a woman survives – and succeeds – in a male-dominated profession. After I was featured as one of only two women in a landmark book *World Photography*, a Japanese television company approached me to make an-hour-long documentary about my life and work. This turned out to be the first of many fruitful links with Japan. The recent launch of my website now makes my work accessible to anyone – irrespective of distance or time zones.

The important criterion is to have a vision and to follow it through. Do not falter along the path. If, however, the opportunity arises to make a more interesting or rewarding detour, grasp it and enjoy it. You never know to where it may lead.

Margaret Joan Anstee DCMG BSc (Econ) (London) BA MA (Cambridge)
International consultant, author, lecturer.

Margaret Anstee retired from the United Nations (UN) in July 1993, with the rank of Under-Secretary General, after 41 years of service, during which she lived and worked in some 15 countries and visited over 120 countries on official missions. She made her home in Bolivia, on the shores of Lake Titicaca, in sight of the Andes, but she spends part of the year in the Wales and continues to travel widely all over the world. Since her retirement she has engaged in many activities, almost all on a pro bono publico basis (i.e. without pay). Margaret lectures and writes on UN peacekeeping, UN reform, economic and social development, including a major book on her experiences in Angola, Orphan of the Cold War. *She has advised the President and Government of Bolivia on economic and social policies, and has negotiated on their behalf with international financial institutions and bilateral donors, including substantial work relating to debt relief. She has led missions for the Inter-American Development Bank leading to a report on socio-economic reform in Bolivia and for the UN Conference on Trade and Development. She advises the UN Secretary General on post-conflict peace-building and helps train troops in the UK, Sweden, Denmark, Africa, USA and Latin America in peacekeeping techniques.*

I feel my main achievement has been as a pioneer in fields that women had not previously entered: the British Diplomatic Service; the first woman UN field officer, the first woman UN Resident Representative (an ambassadorial level function, in charge of UN development operations in a given country that cover a wide spectrum of economic and social matters, from mining projects to education:); the first woman UN Assistant Secretary General having line functions; the first woman UN Under-Secretary General; the first woman appointed to head a UN peacekeeping mission (Angola), comprising military and police elements as well as civilians (and still the only one to have commanded such a force in combat conditions).

I took up my career quite by chance. I embarked first on an academic career; then, when the Foreign Service was opened for women I became one of the first few women to enter the Foreign Office at the diplomatic level. As a result of this, and personal circumstances too long to recount here, I found myself in the Philippines when one of the first UN offices providing assistance to developing countries was being set up. I had always wanted to be a diplomat but now realised that my real vocation was to work in and for poor countries, on practical programmes to raise living standards. I believe I am the only locally recruited UN staff member, male or female, to have risen through the ranks to the highest level of Under-Secretary General.

Many aspects of my work here given me satisfaction, particularly when some project has transformed prospects for a community or a country like helping to locate the first natural gas well in Bolivia; setting up the first rural hospital in Bolivia; well-drilling in sub-Saharan Africa, not only providing water to villages, but training women in well maintenance, thus improving their status as well as lightening their water-carrying duties; alleviating the suffering of people in the Bangladesh disaster (1973–74), the Mexican earthquake (1985), the aftermath of Chernobyl – and many more. On the career front it has been a great satisfaction to see other women following in my footsteps and to have been able to help a number of them who were on my staff to develop their potential and go on to have highly successful careers.

My most difficult professional experiences occurred in life and death situations notably Chile after the Pinochet coup in 1973 when I was head of the UN programme there and over 1,000 people sought refuge in my office. With an ecumenical religious group, we managed to negotiate, with a government that obdurately refused at first to recognise that there was a problem, a safe haven under the UN flag. I had to rescue people who had been tortured from the notorious Stadium and saw many scenes of horror and violent death. Even worse was Angola in 1992–93 when, heading a UN mission that had been given a shamefully inadequate mandate, and even more pitiful resources by the Security Council, we managed to pull off successful, free and fair elections against all the odds, only to have the loser unleash renewed, and even more horrendous, war while the internal community stood on the sidelines and provided no support to my desperate efforts to mediate a cease-fire and a new peace agreement. The horrors of that war, and the sufferings of the Angolan people, are still going on 7 years later, largely unnoticed by the outside world. It was almost as hard to write about my part in these events (in my book *Orphan of the Cold War*) as to experience them but I felt obligated to do so.

I have had to face many other traumatic experiences besides Angola and Chile. Entering the Chernobyl complex, where one sensed being enveloped by an insidious invisible menace, felt almost more threatening than the palpable danger of bullets and bombs in other circumstances, various revolutions, real and attempted, (Colombia, Bolivia, Morocco) each brought their own scares and challenges, as did the Mexican earthquake and the burning oil wells in Kuwait after the Gulf War.

My parents were my greatest influence. They were both intelligent people who were determined that their child should have the education they had been denied, despite criticism from the rest of the village that it was a waste of time and money, since I was a girl. My mother, in particular, was indomitable in surmounting all obstacles, ranging from lack of money to serious childhood illnesses that early scuppered my chances of sitting scholarship exams.

At Cambridge my Spanish professor significantly influenced the course of my career. He instilled in me a love of Spanish language and literature and an understanding of Latin American culture and history that was to stand me in good stead when I went to work there, albeit in a completely different field, as a 'UN experiment' to see how a woman would fare in that macho environment. (When I was left in charge of the large UN programme in Colombia, not yet 30, there was a military government in power and women did not yet have the vote). Later in life a significant personal and professional influence was the late Sir Robert Jackson, a logistics genius (as a young Australian naval officer he persuaded the powers that be, against all the conventional thinking, that Malta could be defended and prepared the master plan). Together we worked on a major reform plan for the UN in 1968–69 that is still quoted today, and undertook the disaster relief operation in Bangladesh in 1973–74 that is considered to have been a model of its kind.

Since my career took me all over the world, to many remote places, and often in peculiar circumstances it abounded in comic incidents (not always funny at the time!) especially in travel. For example when I was transferred from Montevideo to La Paz, a combination of floods and incipient revolution turned a four-day train journey turned into a two-week nightmare, during which I stayed in the most primitive places and spent one night on top of a lorry that broke down, in torrential rain at 14,000 feet, in the Andes. A frequent source of mirth arose throughout my career from the fact that no one could believe that a woman was the boss so that, even as a very senior official, I was always being taken for the wife or secretary of men working on my staff. This confusion became embarrassing (and almost career-threatening) when I was assumed to be the wife of the current Secretary General: of Dag Hammarskjold in Uruguay in 1959, when I had been warned that I must be inconspicuous; and in Peru, sometime in the 1980s, when I was accompanying Perez de Cuellar and his wife on their first state visit to their home country. On that occasion a major newspaper published a long article on Mrs Perez de Cuellar, extolling her beauty, unique gifts as a hostess, philanthropic bounty, prominence in Peruvian high society and generally unmistakable and unforgettable personality. The only problem was that the photo accompanying the article was of me...!

On another occasion, just after the major revolution in Bolivia in 1964, it was rumoured that I was about to be declared *persona non grata*, because I had worked closely with the ousted (elected) government. Shortly afterwards I had to accompany the new, military President to the inauguration of a gas well deep in the jungle which my geological experts had helped to find. He was well known for his predilection for the fair sex (in fact, had two wives) and insisted that I should sit in the jeep beside him. In vain I tried to engage him in a discussion of the importance of the gas discovery for Bolivia. He simply enthused about the beauty of the surroundings, far and near, snuggled up, and fell asleep on my shoulder, his head sliding down on to my bosom, under the conspiratorial glances of the accompanying generals and ADCs, while I tried frantically to shore it up to a more decorous position. From being a potential *persona non grata* I had suddenly become all too *grata*! When we reached the clearing with the gas well flaring and a brass band blaring, I had to wake him up, dust him off, find his cap and usher him out just in time to salute the last strains of the national anthem.

In reflecting on the ups and downs of my career I find it hard to dissociate the person from the professional. In both senses my greatest challenge was, as a pioneer, to break into fields that no woman had entered before and demonstrate that women could perform as well as men in areas traditionally regarded as exclusively male preserves – and this in places where macho dominance was unrivalled, such as Latin America in the 1950s (I went there for the UN – the Foreign Office refused to send women diplomats there at that time as a matter of policy). I was also the first woman to represent the UN as head of mission in an Arab country – Morocco – and led several missions to Saudi Arabia, where I was declared an 'honorary man', as well as to other Moslem countries. Even when I had a respectable body of experience reflected in my CV, governments always had to be cajoled into accepting any appointment as Resident Representative in their country because they did not want a woman. The first months were always difficult as I had to work much harder than a man to show that I was up to the job, both professionally and in coping with the hardships and dangers that went with it in most of the places where I worked. I was very conscious that it was not just my own career that was at stake but the prospects of other women who would follow on, or not, according to my prowess. The UN told me when they sent me to Latin America, that I was a 'pilot experiment'. When, 7 years later, I was still the only female UN Head of Mission anywhere in the world I asked if I was 'the light that failed'! Eventually the number increased and there are many more today, though still not as many as men.

On the more personal front perhaps two challenges are relevant: (i) remaining a 'woman' (i.e. feminine) while striving to survive in a man's world, rather than becoming a surrogate man, (ii) 'not having a wife': my job entailed many official representational functions, usually at a high level, but, unlike most of my male colleagues, I had to find and furnish my own house unaided, on top of a more than full-time professional job, organise diplomatic luncheons, receptions and dinners and be both host and hostess. This was a very considerable burden, especially as a bachelor in my position would be judged leniently on any entertainment or housekeeping shortcomings, for which a woman like myself would be heavily criticised – especially by other women.

In personal terms it was enormously important to me to fulfil my parents expectations. Sadly, they did not live long enough to see all my achievements but they visited me in South America when I was already a successful Chief of Mission. Through me they were able to travel abroad (my mother had never been abroad, my father only on active service) and I was able to provide for the material comfort of their later years. I know that they felt that their considerable sacrifices on my behalf had been worthwhile.

Others are better placed than I to judge my professional achievements. I can only say that I have felt privileged to show that women could work in high-profile diplomatic, political and complex operational functions, including command of military and police operations before in countries where no women, local or foreign, had ever discharged such functions and while it was galling that governments consistently balked at giving agrement (agrement with accent = correct diplomatic term) to my appointment, despite a lengthening CV, I derived considerable satisfaction from the fact that all were sorry to see me go when my tour of duty came to an end.

As will be clear from what I have said already a happy childhood and supportive parents were key factors in my later development, as was the fact of being an only child – had there been more children it is doubtful, given my family's very modest circumstances and rural background, that I would have been given the chances that I had.

In my generation it was virtually impossible for a woman to combine a highly peripatetic career such a mine (I moved to some new part of the world on average every 2 years and was constantly on mission travel) with marriage and a family. Apart from the practical difficulties, until as late as 1971 it was strict Foreign Office policy to insist that a woman resign irrevocably on marriage no matter who the prospective husband might be, or whether he was ready to follow his wife to the ends of the earth. The UN had no such ruling but did not make any accommodation for married women and made it unequivocally clear that single motherhood would not be tolerated. Now things have gone to the other extreme in both institutions and elaborate arrangements are made to accommodate the career aspirations of couples and the Foreign Office even pays travel and support costs for 'partners' of either sex. While in some ways I regret not having children or a companion for my retirement I cannot regret the extraordinarily full and varied life that I have led (and still lead) one which was virtually unique for a woman of my generation. It is part and parcel of the inescapable fact that women who wished to pursue professional careers had to make far harder choices than their male counterparts. Fortunately things are vastly easier for today's young women, but the choices they face are still harder than men's. Though their lot is easier than mine was I do not envy them. Nothing could equal the good luck that I had to explore untrodden paths in parts of the world that were then much more inaccessible than now.

If I could change one thing for women it would be access to education, including the higher levels, according to ability, such as I had, for all girls, especially those born, like me in rural areas with less facilities, and, even more particularly, for girls in poor, developing countries. Not only they, but their countries, would benefit enormously. Women's education is the key to the advancement of societies.

My advice to other women would be work hard and make the most of every opportunity that comes your way. Don't hide your light under a bushel as so many women do. In my experience most men will claim to be able to do a job with the flimsiest of qualifications, while highly qualified women will be at pains to spell out why they can't. When I was young I was suddenly thrown in at the deep end and found that I could swim. It is the best way to discover your potential. Nothing ventured, nothing gained!

It's very hard to prophesy what will happen in the future. With so many old barriers thrown down the way should be clear for educated women in developed countries to find fulfilment in both their personal and professional lives and to combine the two according to the wish of each individual. In other words, the sky's the limit. There is the danger of a backlash, though I do not think this could be lasting in these countries. Much will depend on the attitudes of the women who reach the topmost rungs of politics, diplomacy, business, etc. My hope would be that, now so much of the struggle against prejudice and discrimination has been won, women can concentrate showing that they have their own approach and contribution to make to policy formulation, government, management, etc. rather than simply competing with men on the same well-worn ground.

The outlook for women in developing countries is much more sombre; especially as long as disparities in income continue to widen both within and between countries and grinding poverty constitutes an insuperable obstacle to women's education and advancement. As for Moslem countries, while recent developments in Iran give cause for hope, prospects for women in countries where fundamentalism is rife look very bleak, Afghanistan and the Taliban regime being the extreme example.

Were I at the start of my career would I choose the same path? Yes! Yes! Yes!

Starting from the rather inauspicious beginnings of a rural working-class family in a village where the schoolteacher drummed into us that country children were not as intelligent as town children and girls were not as intelligent as boys, I have gone on to have a life full of excitement, adventure and accomplishment, living and travelling all over the world, including many very remote places, a life of infinite variety, working and negotiating with world statesmen and leaders as well as some of the poorest people on the planet. Surely a heady and intoxicating enough cocktail for anyone!

Just before I first went to South America I had the chance to go into politics. I was terribly torn at the time. A dozen years later I could have revived that possibility when I worked for a year as Senior Economic Adviser to the Prime Minister in 10 Downing Street but by that time I knew unhesitatingly that I wanted only to get back to international work with developing countries.

Rosie Barnes
Chief Executive, Cystic Fibrosis Trust

Rosie Barnes is 54 years of age. She has three children, aged 27, 24 and 15 years. She worked virtually continuously since leaving university in 1967. She has had three quite different jobs over these years.

The first years were spent largely in qualitative market research, currently known as 'focus' groups, followed by 5 years as the Social Democrat Party Member of Parliament for Greenwich.

Having lost her Parliamentary seat in 1992, she then moved into the charity sector and is currently employed as the Chief Executive of the Cystic Fibrosis Trust.

I often thank my lucky stars I was not born earlier, because I would not have thrived as a housewife. Whilst I love my children, my dog and my home, my talents do not lie in the domestic arena. I marvel at what Chris, my wonderful cleaning lady can do in three hours, and know that had I spent three weeks at it, it would not look nearly so good. My energies and enthusiasms are better directed elsewhere and I am pleased to have had three quite distinct careers in my working life.

By accident rather than design, I became a Qualitative Market Researcher during my earlier working years. There also seemed to be a lot of chance and luck in my having the opportunity to become a Member of Parliament (MP) some 13 years later, although the workload involved reminds me that luck alone was not enough to win and retain the seat. After 5 years as an MP, I found myself unceremoniously jettisoned back into what seemed rather like 'civvy street' and had the opportunity of making a third fresh start. So here I am, with the job that probably satisfies me most of all, that of Chief Executive of the Cystic Fibrosis Trust.

When at work, I am happy, dynamic, motivated and enthusiastic. I feel as though I achieve a great deal and pack a lot into each day. Whilst like most people, I have my 'off days', I usually arrive home with a sense of accomplishment and a feeling of a job well done. Time at home is relaxing and pleasurable, but too much of it, for me leads to lethargy, boredom and a lack of a sense of significance. That is not to say I underestimate the value of domestic life and interactions. I find my immediate and extended family fulfilling and fascinating. But it is not enough.

My energies and aptitudes are more suited to tackling other problems with broader horizons. However, combining work and motherhood has not been without its stresses. Coping with small children whilst meeting deadlines, grappling with the practicality of getting everyone up, fed, dressed and out of the door in the morning, steeling oneself against a seemingly inconsolable toddler who does not want his mum to go to work, all took their toll.

Erica Jong once said: 'Show me a woman who does not feel guilty, and I will show you a man'. I would modify that to say 'Show me a working mother who does not feel guilty, and I will show you a robot!' I thought I had talked this issue through with myself and had accepted that my working was in everyone's best interest. My complacency in this area was challenged recently when my 14-year-old son was writing an English composition on his earliest memories. The essay began with a lament about being in floods of tears because his mother was leaving for work. I was so agitated and distressed by this, and challenged his recollection so vociferously, that being the obliging and tactful boy he is, he rewrote it, using poetic license to steal another incident that has become a family legend from his sister's childhood and transporting it into his own. But it forced me to re-evaluate my sensitivities on the subject and I have had to give myself another good talking to on the theme of my children being better with a happy, fulfilled working mother than with a depressed, discontented, non-working mother.

As little children, they probably would have preferred me to be fulfilled and at home, but as they have become older, I think they appreciate my lack of dependence on them for fulfilment. Mothers hovering anxiously at home, waiting for the return of lively teenagers whose horizons have also expanded can be something of a liability.

So what do I like so much about working? I do like waking up in the morning with a purpose, I like to have something to get dressed up for, I like a sense of urgency, with a 'places to go, things to do' zing to life. Here at the Cystic Fibrosis Trust we have a clear mission, to fund medical and scientific research aimed at understanding, treating and curing Cystic Fibrosis. It also aims to ensure that people with Cystic Fibrosis receive the best possible care and support in all aspects of their lives. As Cystic Fibrosis is a life threatening disease with an average life expectancy of 31 years, we deal mainly with children and young adults and their families who are coping, usually very bravely, with the hand that life has unexpectedly dealt them. A hefty part of my job revolves around ensuring income is robust. If I did everything else wonderfully well but our income plummeted, I do not think I would be deemed a great success. So whilst I am not a fundraiser by profession and training, ensuring we maximise our income to enable us to fund research, provide better hospital care and to offer direct support to families is my number one priority.

People often ask me if it is not depressing dealing with children and young adults with a life-threatening condition. Whilst it is often very sad and I find myself deeply affected by the deteriorating health of those I have come to know, I have found it exhilarating to work with young people who show such courage, fortitude, wisdom and humour in the face of the constant pressures of poor health and fear of what the future might hold. Although I know they have their sadness and black days, they remain cheerful, often funny, down-to-earth and never precious. They recognise their own mortality in a way that those of us with good health often neglect to do. I have learned a great deal from working with those with Cystic Fibrosis and they have my respect, admiration and deep affection. In terms of this being my job, I recognise that a sense of social purpose is important to me, and whilst I cannot take on all the problems of the world, I can and will take on the problems of those affected by Cystic Fibrosis, and I will help to make a difference.

At the age of 54, I have around 6 years left of my working life, and I hope and expect to see a real breakthrough in the care of those with Cystic Fibrosis during that time. A cure via gene therapy is very possible, and whilst it will not eliminate Cystic Fibrosis once and for all, it may take the 'life-threatening' out of the description of this disease. To give these young people and their families hope and the chance of the future they so desperately want and deserve is a worthy objective and one I am proud and pleased to be involved in.

I know I will always be best remembered for my time as an MP and whilst it might eventually be superseded by helping to find a cure for Cystic Fibrosis, my greatest public achievement to date must have been winning the Greenwich by election in February 1987 and then retaining the seat in the General Election later that year. As a Qualitative Market Researcher, I had worked largely 'behind the scenes'. To find myself totally in the public eye, faced with banks of journalists and teams of cameramen, could have been daunting and intimidating. I regard it as one of my greatest achievements that I was able to rise to the challenge and not only to cope but to excel in the spotlight. It was a period of my life when I worked harder than at any other time in my life. I would get up at the crack of dawn to meet commuters at the various railway stations in Greenwich, go on to a briefing session for the morning's press conference where the combined efforts of the media included the tripping up and humiliating of the candidate when possible, followed by endless door knocking throughout the day, monitoring of campaigning literature and planning, public meetings or yet more canvassing in the evening, followed by a drink with the team, back home for dinner, a couple of hours sleep, rudely broken as a gnawing anxiety about what might be thrown at me the next day penetrated my consciousness, prompting me to get up in the early hours to ensure I was up to speed on all aspects of Social Democratic Party (SDP) policy. Then back to bed for another hour or two, and then up again, showered and dressed for the world, because as a female candidate, it was not enough to have the right answers, I had to look the part as well. Any dreariness in my appearance or repetition of outfits would surely be remarked upon and it was!

I applied myself to the task in hand with a dedication and a tenacity that I did not know I had. My reward was in victory, and in retaining the seat out of the spotlight a few months later. In the longer term, I learned a lot about life in the public eye from that experience, not least how short or fickle the public's memory can be, or perhaps more accurately how misguided a politician's perception of what the public thinks is important can be. This leads me to one of my greatest disappointments that of the demise of the SDP, at least as a party in its own right and under its own banner, because in many respects the SDP is alive and kicking as New Labour. But I digress. In the 1980s, the SDP commanded the media heights, it was heralded as a likely conqueror, set to annihilate and replace the Labour Party and to challenge the Tories, in conjunction, of course, with our partners, the Liberals. Those of us who resisted the attempts of the Liberals to subsume the SDP in their merger plans stood proud on a matter of principle and policy. As the 'rump' of the SDP, we had some spectacular near misses, including running a young Mr Hague rather ragged in another famous by-election in Richmond, Yorkshire, where a Tory majority of over 30,000 was reduced to a mere 1,000. Eventually the SDP disbanded, but we saw ourselves as having made our stand, changed the face of British politics and made our mark on history as well. Perhaps we did, but I now come to the rub of another key lesson in life. The SDP is now largely forgotten, other than by the stalwarts who defended it to the end. As I go about my daily business, I am often stopped by a well wisher or a 'passer-by' who says good naturedly something on the lines of 'You must be pleased, your lot did well last night'. I smile wanly and move on because, of course, they are referring to the Liberal Democrats, who I so passionately resisted.

All forgotten! What was so important to me and my colleagues has been submerged in the passage of time. But again, I digress. And could I not have been politically active and done my share of voluntary work without getting paid for it? No, for me, the disciplines and rewards of being a working woman have kept the spring in my step.

Valarie Bragg BSc PGCE FRSA
Principal/Chief Executive, The City Technology College, Birmingham.

Valarie is the Principal of the first City Technology College, set up by the Government in 1988 in an area of Birmingham blighted by high unemployment, rife crime and easily available drugs. She is proud to say that the Kingshurst City Technology College (CTC) has succeeded in replacing a culture of hopelessness with one of excellence, preparing children for a high-achieving future, instead of the dole-queue.

The CTC was founded as part of a pilot network of new schools in urban areas pioneering a partnership between business and education, the CTC has had a massive impact on the local community, the children in particular. In 1988, 83% of students in its catchment area would leave school at 16 – if they bothered to stay that long – with few, if any, qualifications. The majority would become 'dole-queue-fodder'; seemingly destined to perpetuate the cycle of despair which had trapped their families before them. By 1998 the situation had been reversed with more than 83% of Kingshurst students continuing their post-16 education. Today the CTC's 1,350 students – aged 11–19 – regularly achieve examination results well above the national average and about 40% go to Higher Education, as opposed to 2% in 1988. A powerful 'can do' culture has replaced despair and helplessness and expectations have risen dramatically.

After winning the Midlands Quality Award in 1999, the CTC beat almost 100 public sector organisations to collect the first TNT Modernising Government Partnership Award in April this year for dramatically increasing standards in academic achievement by working with parents, local businesses, charities and other educational establishments. The CTC's achievements were further confirmed in 1998 by a glowing report from Ofsted, the national school inspectorate. Ofsted assessors did not indicate any significant weakness, which meant the CTC had 'no key issues for action'. Valarie says when they are recognised from outside it gives them a real sense of pride.

Valarie also set up a commercial subsidiary company in 1990 because the College is a charity and a company limited by guarantee. The Commercial Company is called 3E's Enterprises Ltd, Valarie is Chief Executive and surplus profits are covenanted back to the College.

Valarie acts autonomously as the Chief Executive of both the charitable organisation and the commercial company and is responsible for ensuring that the students gain an outstanding education with raised standards of achievement. She tries to satisfy the needs of the students – her customers, and also the parents and in addition provide an input into the local community by linking with Business, Industry and Commerce, using the latest information communications technology.

I had no idea what I wanted to do. I decided in the sixth form at school that university sounded very interesting, so I went to Leicester University, more or less plucked a subject out of the air, decided to read Zoology Special Hons. I had a great time and enjoyed the experience. I had been going to do geography or chemistry, so it was very much a case of not being certain of where my career was going. I then decided it would be rather interesting to do some research in to getting more food out of the sea, so I applied to the Ministry of Agriculture and Fisheries. Then in the middle of my finals when I was 21, I was told that all I would be doing is sitting behind a table doing the paper work because they don't have facilities to take ladies on trawlers. I really had no idea about what I wanted to do. The Professor at University spent a long time talking to me and he said 'well, why don't you teach?' I said 'I can't do that because I vowed all my life that I will never ever teach. I haven't enjoyed school particularly, it has never switched me on and I don't want to go back.' Cutting a long story short, I think in desperation I said to him 'OK then I'll try it.' I thought I don't want to spend time doing a year's training, I'll just go straight into teaching and see what it is like. To my surprise, I thought it was absolutely fantastic and from that moment on it's been so exciting and stimulating, the best career possible, I've thoroughly enjoyed it.

In my professional life interaction with the students has been most satisfying – talking to them, listening to them, earning their respect, treating them as young adults, watching them grow and mature, and leave for exciting careers ranging from entrepreneurs, business people or on to Higher Education. Also being able to watch young teachers come in enthusiastically and develop and enhance their training and skills. I also enjoy innovating – I am not a maintenance manager. I have been fortunate that I have been able to innovate in all the schools I have worked in.

It has been disappointing for me that teaching doesn't seem to be a very attractive career for people and that the right entrants don't seem to be motivated to enter it. I mean, even I got there by a fluke. I think often some of the best, outstanding teachers got there by chance, rather than anything else. It is such a pity that we can't really show people what a wonderfully rewarding career it is.

I don't really know who has influenced me as a person. I think possibly when I was in the sixth form I had a range of teachers, some of them were not terribly good, and I know once I did start teaching I always said I would make it more interesting than they did and more enjoyable. I've always said that whatever I've been doing in education it has got to be fun and something that people enjoy, putting their heart and soul into.

I actually think I have been more influenced by people not from education but businesses, I think each organisation, although different, has similarities, and you can learn and pick up ideas and skills from everybody. During my career I've realised that you go on learning forever and it is really exciting that the more you learn the more you want to learn.

When His Royal Highness the Duke of Edinburgh visited the College in 1989 I had arranged a tour of the College for Prince Philip to see various classes. I walked the route prior to his arrival and noticed that there were all boys in the Electronics Starship Enterprises room. I did not want to convey a stereotype view even though it was pure coincidence that there were no girls in this group on that day. I therefore arranged for four girls to join the boys and 'true to form' Prince Philip went straight to the girls and asked what they were doing there. The students being very honest said 'Oh – we can do electronics so we were told to come here so that you don't just see all boys'!

Probably the most traumatic incident is when in a school or a college you have a tragedy such as a student who dies. The first time this happened to me it was particularly traumatic because of the impact it had on the students and their friends. When you have a child of 13 knocked over in a road accident it is particularly upsetting and disturbing.

Just after I had my second child, when I had a son aged one and a half and a baby, my husband was promoted and commuted backwards and forwards at weekends. We had to sell the house, we had a burglary and I was still in a responsible job working full-time. I remember thinking to myself, if I can cope with this, I can cope with anything.

Setting up the first CTC from scratch was a huge challenge. It was highly political and had been an idea of Kenneth Baker, announced at a Tory conference. There was an enormous amount of animosity and of people saying 'You're selling your soul' 'How can you do this?' I just maintained that it was because it was an educational opportunity. It was a time when if you didn't believe in what you were aiming to do you could have felt isolated and very much on your own. I think because I had a vision and ideas I just did it and was very single minded.

Having only had one day off in my whole working life due to sickness or childbirth has been my greatest personal achievement!! To switch children on and help them to learn is a great professional achievement. To help them believe in themselves and have the confidence to achieve. The same for teachers as well, and giving them the opportunities to develop and go on to greater things.

I did get married, it didn't work out. It didn't work out because I got married for the wrong reasons. All my friends were getting married and it was just the done thing, I'd had a boyfriend and it just went on, and each year a different friend got married and until everyone was saying its your turn next, its your turn next. So it just happened, and I had this rather idealistic view of marriage and the fact that my husband would look after me in my old age and then I think I just developed in a different way, I grew up and I matured, I was very young for my age. I was extremely ambitious, and although I had children I didn't give up work at all, in fact I only had one day off when I had my daughter. I was very focused on wanting to really achieve in teaching. I didn't want the children to miss out so I took them to a day nursery and then tried to spend the evenings and weekends with them, but I think that once I got my first headship, then the children perhaps missed out a bit and I expected my ex-husband to do quite a lot. Since then, I've remarried and found my soul mate. We are both in education and we both just clicked and I think it's a pity in a way that we hadn't met much earlier, so that we wouldn't have had to go through the traumas of divorce.

I like being a woman. I think women have a lot of advantages. What I'd like to change is that it's expected that the woman look after the child. It would be rather nice if it could be anybody, male or female whatever and that the husband doesn't automatically say it's your job.

My advice to other women would be 'believe in yourself' – 'you can do it' – 'go for it'. But you've got to have a very clear view in your mind of what you are going to achieve.

In the future I hope clubs and boardrooms for 'men only' will become a thing of the past. There will not be the distinction or differentiation of whether a job is suitable for a man or woman. More women will rise to the top in the 'men only' professions on their own merits and be confident in what they achieve. More women will be able to combine a high-profile profession with having children.

We are currently preparing and encouraging our girl students to become good leaders – so – who knows!

I am not sure if I would still choose my current profession. I could do because I've really, really enjoyed it and found it fulfilling and rewarding and exciting in every conceivable way, I really believe the job I've got at the moment is the best there is, that I've had an opportunity given to one in about 20 million – to be able to set up something from scratch, put into practice all your philosophical thoughts and beliefs about education and then to see it working, and to see your actual vision working. Even after 14 years very few changes except for the fact that you've had more and more people getting involved in it and adding to it in real partnerships. I sometimes think I should have gone more directly in to business, or management or so on, but it might just be a case of what would it have been like if you'd done this or what would it have been like if I'd set up my own business. I mean certainly now towards the end of one's career you have all sorts of opportunities and job offers and you are head-hunted and its very exciting, but nothing has been as exciting, in spite of some very attractive offers, as the job I have at the moment. Its absolutely wonderful and all the time one is thinking about it, living, eating and sleeping it and coming up with new ideas. I'd like to live my life again though. That's one thing I would like to do.

Darcey Bussell OBE
Principle Ballerina, The Royal Opera House, Covent Garden

Darcey is one of the most famous ballet dancers of our time. She was born in London and attended the Arts Educational School studying all forms of stagecraft before moving to The Royal Ballet Lower School at the age of 13 to concentrate on ballet. She graduated from the Upper School in 1985, staying for 2 years before joining Sadler's Well Royal Ballet for the 1987/88 season.

The late Sir Kenneth MacMillan had noticed Darcy's exceptional technique while she was still a student and cast her in the principle role of his ballet Concerto *for the 1986 School performance. During her first season with Sadler's Wells Royal Ballet he chose her for the leading role in* The Prince of the Pagodas, *his new work for The Royal Ballet and she subsequently transferred between the two companies in September 1988. She joined The Royal Ballet as a Soloist, becoming a First Soloist in September 1989 and, just three months later, on the first night of* The Prince of the Pagodas *being promoted again to the rank of Principle. Darcey was aged just 20 at the time.*

Darcey was to create two major roles for MacMillan before his death: Princess Rose in The Prince of the Pagodas *and Masha in* Winter Dreams. *The final farewell* pas de deux *had been created in advance of the full ballet and was performed at the Queen Mother's 90th birthday tribute at the London Palladium in July 1990.*

Her classical repertory includes Odette/Odile in Swan Lake, *Princess Aurora in* The Sleeping Beauty, *the Sugar Plum Fairy in* The Nutcracker, *Nikiya and Gamzatti in* La Bayadere *and the title roles in* Giselle *and* Raymonda Act III

Darcey has won a significant number of awards and has appeared on television on numerous occasions. A full-length portrait of her by the artist Allen Jones RA, commissioned by the National Portrait Gallery, was unveiled on the 23rd May 1994 and now hangs in Number 10 Downing Street. She was created an Officer of the Order of the British Empire (OBE) in the 1995 New Year Honours List.

Like many other young girls I loved to dance and enjoyed going to dancing classes with my friends every Saturday. My mother also thought dancing might help strengthen my legs because I seemed to have slightly knocked knees. It obviously worked because not only did my legs improve but also I enjoyed the lessons and seemed to have a natural talent. By the time I was 13 I began to concentrate on ballet.

My career has given me many challenges but also huge opportunities. I have really enjoyed being able to travel and to be able to perform abroad. It's fascinating to work with colleagues overseas and meet new Companies. Each Company has its own unique style and atmosphere. I've found it extremely hard work but immensely satisfying to be able to perfect my career, to be able to work for a top Company and to aim for the highest standards.

Being in this unusual position has also brought me some special responsibilities. I've appreciated the opportunity to be able to support the work of Cancer Relief Macmillan Fund.

I have found it is essential to be able to learn from your mistakes and maintain a sense of balance and perspective. In my work my body is very important. I have to treat it with respect to try avoid injuries if at all possible. To be able to keep going and to be able to perform are only possible if the body and the mind are at one. I do think it's important to be able to laugh at mistakes. My work can sometimes feel so intense and disciplined. If you can't laugh at yourself and life at times it would be virtually impossible to survive.

It was a huge personal achievement to be a Company Principle at the age of 20 but it was also an enormous responsibility. Looking back I really was very young. My mother and my family have been a great support. My mother gave me confidence when I thought things weren't possible. She encouraged me, supported me and always believed in me. My family are very down-to-earth and they help me maintain a sense of perspective and balance in what can be a very rarefied atmosphere.

Sir Kenneth MacMillan had a profound influence on my professionally. He noticed my ability and he nurtured it. Like my mother he gave me the confidence to work to develop the talent I had. He also gave me very unique opportunities to perfect my technique. I have always been conscious of how lucky I have been. It has also been a privilege to work with so many excellent partners. Each one has made an impression on my work and on me.

It was very difficult for me about 5 years ago when I had to have an operation on my foot. It happened at a crucial time in my career and I was unable to perform for eight months. The whole experience at the time dented my confidence somewhat and I didn't have the luxury of slowly coming back up to par. As soon as I was back on form I was in the Principle role once more. The whole experience was hideous, it felt totally impossible, I was struggling hard to overcome my physical injury and at the same time as trying to build up my confidence. I lost the opportunity to make the *Sleeping Beauty* film, which was very important to me. Although no one can deny it was awful at the time, in some ways, the experience became one of the best things that happened to me. I had to come to an understanding of who and what were important to me and to reflect on what being able to perform meant to me.

Another challenge in my career was when I was still young and I was taken out of the role of Manon although I did go on to perform it successfully the next season. I had been working hard with a Russian colleague and we didn't seem to quite gel. Two weeks before the ballet was due to open he came to me and said he felt it wasn't working between us and because I was the younger artiste I was dropped from my role. The main reason it was so hard at the time was the totally disproportionate press attention I received. The front pages of a number of the newspapers had stories on the Gulf War on one side and me being dropped from the role on the other. It was surreal. How could a 21-year-old ballet dancer equate with the Gulf War! To add to the bizareness of it all was having to deal with the fabrications some people dreamed up. I felt very alone and I really didn't feel my Company was supporting me in the way that they could. No one seemed to want to help me and I was very aware of the injustice of it all. I was young and vulnerable. I was so disillusioned I felt like leaving the Company. Handling negative and inaccurate press is a learnt skill and I think I would have felt better about the whole experience if proper support had been in place.

There have been some tremendous moments in my work but one or two unusual ones stick out in my mind. I attended a banquet at Buckingham Palace and it was awe inspiring to see the work that goes into these events and to be a part of it all. I was really impressed seeing diplomats in action looking after the guests from overseas. Another unique moment was receiving my OBE from Her Majesty the Queen in 1995. It was a tremendous honour and I was really touched. On the professional side it has been incredibly satisfying to play Juliet in *Romeo and Juliet*. It is a beautiful story and Sir Kenneth MacMillan's music is magnificent. It is a role where you are working on so many different levels. You have to be a technically competent character actress as well as a skilled dancer. It is not a part where just your body is pushed to its limits the whole of you has to be absorbed in the part.

I think it is important in life to be conscious of where work fits in, even in a career that is as all encompassing as mine. I am still young but I am very aware of the importance of meaningful relationships. I've only recently married so I don't think its right to comment on my private life but I do feel very strongly that when all is said and done what you have once a career has come to its natural conclusion is your enjoyment of life with your partner. In my view there needs to be balance. We are holistic beings and we need to have contentment in the emotional, psychological and physical dimensions of our lives.

Thinking about the world generally and the way women are treated I am conscious that the experience of women varies enormously not only within a country like our own but also between women living in the developing and more developed countries. My strong wish would be that women everywhere would be treated with the respect accorded to men. I am a romantic at heart I appreciate the well-intentioned kindness of a gentleman opening a door or taking a coat but I do feel that cannot replace the genuine respect men and women should share for each other. Although I feel there has been considerable progress over the years I still feel women can be disadvantaged at times because of their gender.

If I were able to pass on one piece of advice to other women it would be to have confidence in yourself. Don't let other people put you down. Believe in yourself. You can and you will make a difference. If you really want to do something you can. It is important to be proud and to have a sense of humour.

What will happen over the next 20 years? Who knows? I do expect though that we will all want more out of life. Men and women will want more balance. There will be a conscious desire to work hard but to spend time on relationships and with children. At the moment you could get the feeling work has taken over everything in people's lives. I think there will be a swing in the other direction. Women, for example, will be given the support to spend more time with young families and options will be more readily available to combine a career and family life.

Sandra Dawson

KPMG Professor of Management Studies
Director of the Judge Institute of Management Studies University of Cambridge
Master, Sidney Sussex College Cambridge

Sandra moved to the University of Cambridge as KPMG Professor of Management Studies, Director of the Judge Institute of Management Studies and fellow of Jesus College in 1995, having previously been Professor of Organisational Behaviour 1990–1995, Senior Lecturer and Research Associate 1969–1990 at Imperial College, London University. In December 1998 she was elected Master of Sidney Sussex College, Cambridge, a position she took up in July 1999. She continues as Director of the Judge Institute of Management Studies.

From 1992–1995 Sandra was Chairman of Riverside Mental Health NHS Trust and is now a Non-Executive Director of the Fleming Claverhouse Investment Trust and Cambridge Econometrics. She also serves on the Senior Salary Review Body.

Sandra is the author of numerous articles and three books writing on organisational behaviour, health management, innovation and technology transfer. Sandra favours an interdisciplinary approach in her studies, frequently working with engineers on matters of operational safety and with medical doctors on health management. She acts as a consultant to a wide variety of organisations in the public and private sectors.

Although my family were supportive of my education and encouraged me to develop ideas and strive to achieve there was no real expectation that as a woman I would pursue a strong career. I was the only daughter in our family, a middle child with a younger and elder brother.

I had no long-term career path in mind when I went to university but I did want a course that I felt would be stimulating and challenging. I opted for an excellent 4-year degree at Keele, which began with a study of Western Civilisation and developed these ideas through a range of disciplines. Later I continued my studies in history and sociology.

My first job was as a civil servant working for the Government Social Survey. Due to the fact a number of people were unwell and there were vacancies I was able to gain a breadth of experience, which was unusual. I worked with the then Minister for Employment Mrs Barbara Castle on the incoming Industrial Relations Legislation. I was able to conduct a thorough investigation into disciplinary procedures, which marked me out for special attention.

Although I enjoyed the work I somehow felt I wasn't being stretched enough. I was fascinated by the work of the industrial sociologist Joan Woodword and the opportunity arose for me to take up a 1-year research project with her, which I did. Serendipity followed and I stayed at Imperial College taking on a variety of challenging projects. My role developed with additional teaching, management and research. I was able to work in both the public and private sectors, which was immensely satisfying.

I married relatively early at 23 in 1969. My husband who has been very supportive pursued his own career as a quantity surveyor. One theme throughout our married life has been how do a couple pursue interesting work and locate together. This partially answers the reason why I was at Imperial College for so long. We took the view not to have our family until I had got permanent tenure at the University. When I had my first child in 1976 there was no maternity leave provision but we were allowed to take it as sick leave. The general expectation was that as a 30-year-old woman that had, had a full career I would stop once a baby arrived.

Imperial College had very few women and even fewer mothers but there was a very farsighted senior tutor for women, Lady Anne Thorne. She realised women would not be able to afford childcare as individuals but together they could employ a trained nanny to care for their children. That was how the Imperial College nursery came into being in 1970. I used this excellent facility for all three of my children.

I went back to work officially after five months with each child and was able to continue to breast-feed them until they wished to stop by popping into the nursery. By the time I had the second child we had someone at home to help out but the main care during the day was in the nursery where I was free to go back and forth. I did find it strange when my eldest daughter started school and she became not only geographically distant but also subject to an external time-table.

Although the children have on whole been fit and healthy we did have a serious scare with each one. I noticed virtually at birth that our eldest daughter had something wrong with her hips. I expressed my concern but no one seemed to take it on board. After three weeks they discovered she had bilateral dislocated hips. The problem was the test at the time looked for a difference in one hip to the other and obviously in this case they were the same and both were incorrect. Hannah was in plaster for many months. My husband devised a number of aids to help her during this period and we kitted out the nursery so she could be cared for easily.

When our last child was a baby our second child had a serious playground accident and a major head injury. The hospital informed me we could go home but I wasn't convinced. I felt something was still amiss. My feeling was confirmed she had suffered a massive bleed, which required neurosurgery. As a result our whole family set up camp in the hospital and she recovered well after the surgery. This incident made me reconsider my work/home priorities and for a period I worked part-time so I was able to be there to collect the children after school.

Last but not least my son. My son suffered from a severe asthma attack, which resulted in a collapsed lung. These incidents demonstrate clearly that however driven one is at work nothing compares with having health and happiness at home.

After a year of the part-time working I returned to full-time with no ill effect. I enjoyed my work at Imperial tremendously but I wanted to accept the fresh challenge here in Cambridge. Being Director at the Judge Institute means I must rise to all the demands, including business pressures, student's aspirations and university requirements. Being elected the Master of Sidney Sussex was a wonderful honour. Although Oxford has had a woman elected as Master of an all-male college this is the first time for Cambridge.

It's strange but now all the family is here in Cambridge and it's almost like an old-fashioned family group. The children are happy and settled, which is very satisfying.

Many people in my life and career have influenced me. My mother demonstrated a strong commitment to family. She was an angel. My grandfather taught me the love of books and learning. Joan Woodword obviously had an impact on my professional development.

It is only my view but work issues cannot compare to the emotional joy of having a baby. I have enjoyed work-related achievements enormously but it is the human side of the piece of work, which adds the unique dimension. I feel my greatest achievement on a personal level are my children but on a professional level I believe my greatest achievement is still to come. I enjoyed becoming a professor. I want to do a good job and to be recognised for having done good work.

I believe one should never regret. Never regret anything, learn from the past and look forward from the day. I would hope women in the future will have access to good-quality, affordable childcare. I hope childcare costs will be tax deductible. I hope the range of choices available to them will encourage women. I hope women will have the courage to believe what they would like to do is possible. It is important women don't underplay their contribution if they are returning to work. Women who have been at home have many skills which are valuable, parenting, volunteering, teaching and administration to name but a few.

Finally I believe women should have a choice as to whether they marry or not and have children or not. Life can be full and productive whatever the choice. I chose marriage and children as well as a full and satisfying career. I hope women who choose a similar path will be encouraged to choose their life partner carefully. It can make all the difference.'

Qhing Qhing Dlamini MB ChB MPH
Commonwealth Secretariat, London
Special Adviser and Head of Health Department

Qhing Qhing's current role and responsibilities involve the provision of professional and technical advice on health matters in general and health programmes in particular, to the Secretary-General of the Commonwealth and to Secretariat Divisions. This includes the provision of technical guidance on the preparation, implementation, monitoring and evaluation of the Secretariat Health Programme. She is also responsible for professional and technical involvement in the delivery of programmes/projects for the benefit of the 54 Commonwealth member states and on occasion undertakes short-term technical assistance consultancies as requested by governments and partner agencies.

Her other responsibilities include pursuing an Advocacy, Brokerage and Catalytic (ABC) mandate of the Secretariat Health Department by continuing to liase with partner agencies and organisations (UN, bilateral and NGOs). This involves the raising of extra budgetary funds for the Secretariat Health Programme. Qhing Qhing represents the Commonwealth Secretariat at policy meetings of partner agencies including attending WHO Governing Body meetings in an observer capacity, that is, the Executive Board, the World Health Assembly and Regional Committees.

When I completed High School in 1971 in my home country, Swaziland, I wanted to study for an Engineering degree. However, my teachers and family all thought that I should study Medicine. I still put down Engineering as my first choice and Medicine as my second choice, when applying for a scholarship from the Government of Swaziland to pursue my university studies. When I went for an interview for the scholarship upon obtaining my High School graduation results, the all-male Scholarship Selection Board was simply appalled that a female could think of studying Engineering. Without even giving me an opportunity to justify my first choice of studying Engineering, they emphatically informed me that they are granting me a scholarship to study Medicine, which is what I did.

I have spent most of my professional life working in public health, which I enjoy tremendously, and find to be professionally fulfilling and rewarding. After qualifying in Medicine and Surgery, I worked briefly as a Clinician, and shortly after studied Public Health, specialising in Maternal and Child Health, where I worked for about 5 years in my home country, Swaziland. Still working in my home country, I then broadened into general Primary Health Care, particularly Family and Reproductive Health and Health Systems Development and Strengthening, where I have worked for the past 12 years. I have enjoyed these aspects of my profession and found them to be most satisfying, having been prompted early on in my professional career by the old and wise saying 'Prevention is better than cure'.

What I have found most difficult is not in the profession as such, but the efforts of my professional contributions in assisting countries to shape their health systems and the delivery of health care. This applies to my country, where I can proudly say I gained my professional experience, other countries and organisations where I have worked, and in my current position where I work with 54 Commonwealth countries. Despite many of these countries' efforts at delivering basic health care to their populations, obstacles and challenges still face these countries, some obstacles more difficult to overcome than others. The HIV/AIDS epidemic is a big challenge and a nightmare for many Commonwealth and non-Commonwealth countries, and for me professionally, the most difficult challenge, yet extremely urgent.

My parents, both my mother and father influenced me enormously. My mother is still alive, but unfortunately my father passed away when I had just started at Medical School. He had a cerebrovascular accident (stroke), just like that, and it was a dense CVA. I had never seen him ill even for a single day in my whole life, such that when he had the stroke, I could not believe it. He had been a very active, dedicated and hard-working civil servant. One minute he was leaving his office and getting into his car to drive off to attend a meeting. The next minute he had collapsed in the car as he was about to drive off. He was in a semi-coma for one year, one month and one week. He eventually passed away after suffering a great deal. My mother took leave of absence from work and stayed with him in hospital initially in Swaziland, and then in South Africa to where my father had been referred.

My parents were both educators and they instilled the value of education in all their children. It was reading and studies first, before anything else. When my siblings and I were still young, my parents taught us to think ahead, plan carefully what we wanted to do and grow up to be, and to work towards that. They would set small rewards depending on how well each of us performed in our examinations. Of course each of us wanted to get the "best price" and we would all work hard towards that, and so my parents had to be ready with a number of these prices when our examination results come out.

I can think of two people who have influenced me most as a professional, particularly in my work in public health. One of them is my mother and the other person is a former Minister of Health in Swaziland, a Swazi woman, Dr Fanny Friedman with whom I worked for 6 years in my capacity as Adviser in MCH/FP/PHC, with overall responsibility for these services in the country. She is now retired. She was a physician who also specialised in public health.

Upon graduating from Medical School I worked briefly in the clinical area in South Africa, and shortly after decided that I wanted to branch into public health. Whilst still working in South Africa I felt that I needed to undertake training in public health. I could not get a fellowship at that point, despite sending out applications to all the agencies that I knew of at that time. My mother knew my passion for public health, and had always encouraged me to move in that area despite criticism from many people that I would be a "wasted physician", by leaving clinical work. She offered to secure a loan against one of her properties to obtain the required amount needed for my tuition at the London School of Hygiene and Tropical Medicine where I had been accepted to study public health. I thought that it would not be fair to her and to the rest of my siblings. I eventually obtained a fellowship from UNFPA and studied Public Health at the University of California, Berkeley in the USA, a year after joining the Ministry of Health in Swaziland.

Dr Fanny Friedman not only influenced my professional career but also contributed to shaping my career in international health. To my knowledge, she is the first female Swazi physician, who in addition specialised in public health. She held a number of senior positions in government, eventually ending up in politics and becoming the first female Cabinet Minister in the history of the country.

I worked very closely with her while she was Health Minister. I accompanied her as Adviser whenever she attended policy meetings of various organisations. These included WHO Governing Body meetings, that is, the World Health Assembly and Regional Committee, UNICEF policy meetings, OAU Health Ministers Meetings, Commonwealth Health Ministers Meetings. The exposure and experience I gained during these policy meetings of Health Ministers has shaped my professional career. During her term of office my government designated me a member of the Executive Board of WHO from 1992 to 1995, where I learnt a lot about the organisation. I thus became familiar with international health issues and got to meet and know a lot of people in that field.

A funny thing happened in February 1994 in Douala, Cameroon on our way to Yaounde to attend the 16th WHO/AFRO Regional Programme Meeting (RPM 16c). It was a planeload of us nationals from African countries in East, Central and Southern Africa and WHO Representatives in these countries, all travelling to Yaounde to attend RPM 16c. We had boarded the Ethiopian Airlines from Nairobi to Douala, where we were supposed to change planes and join the Cameroon Airlines to connect to Yaounde. In Douala we were each issued boarding passes, except that it was free seating. The unfortunate bit (not funny, actually) is that the ground staff issued more boarding passes than the actual number of seats in the plane.

When one of my colleagues, who had travelled in that part of the region more frequently than the rest of us, realised that the boarding passes did not have pre-assigned seats, she shouted at us 'free seating, let us rush quickly to the plane and locate seats'. You should have seen the marathon across the airport tarmac to the plane, which was parked some distance away. Senior government officials and WHO staff members were all racing to reach the plane in time to secure a seat. I did manage to secure one, but some colleagues could not get onto the flight despite possessing valid confirmed tickets and a valid boarding pass for that particular flight! They eventually arrived in Yaounde a day later, missing the first day of the meeting.

Another funny incident during one of my official travels was in 1987 after I had been attending a Seminar in Niamey, Niger on Immunisation in Africa. Our plane took off from Niamey bound for Nairobi, and landed in Ougadougou, Burkina Faso to pick up

The profiles

passengers. In came a lady who was accompanied by a goat. I got such a shock at seeing a live goat get on a plane that I screamed. I never realised before that day that some airlines allow goats on to their aircraft's!

The most traumatic situation I have had to deal with was when I was on a long weekend call working in Casualty at Edendale Hospital in South Africa, over the Christmas weekend of December 1982. I was the only doctor covering Casualty, another doctor was covering the Intensive Care Unit (ICU) and the Registrar on call was busy full-time in theatre. Over two successive days (and nights) on call that weekend I attended predominantly to patients who had sustained stab wounds mostly either in the chest or abdomen. They would seem to come in floods, most of them needing urgent attention, in the late afternoon, early evening, and late into the night. Many of them had been drinking, which was when they would sustain the injury.

Being the only doctor in Casualty, working with the Sister-in-charge, nurses and orderlies, I had to attend to each and every patient. Some patients needed to be sutured, others needed an intercostal drain (ICD) inserted in their chest because most stab wounds on the chest resulted in a pneumothorax or haemothorax, and still others had to be assessed and prepared for theatre, that is, those who had been stabbed on the abdomen, resulting in disembowelment.

I recall my second evening on this particular weekend call, after not having slept for over 36 hours since Casualty was busy day and night. People were having Christmas celebrations, and indulging in alcohol a bit too much, ending up in arguments or fights, resulting in stabbings.

I had been to ICU to check upon a patient I had admitted whose condition was critical. I returned to Casualty after about 30 minutes. Before leaving for ICU I had been working non-stop for almost two hours, attending to patients (mostly with stab wounds) and had cleared all the patients, and had left Casualty empty. As I was approaching, I found the corridor and waiting room packed with people. For a minute I thought that there might have been a bus accident or something like that, that some people had been injured and the rest were accompanying relatives or friends.

Unfortunately for me that was not the case. Instead most of those people were patients who needed attention, urgently for many of them. There were at least a dozen, ranging from those with stab wounds needing suturing, stabs resulting in pneumothorax or haemothorax, to those with disembowelment. One guy actually had his entire intestines out through a large gaping abdominal wound, and held his bowel in his T-shirt, which he had taken off. He was very drunk and I guess could not even feel any pain at that point. The other patients with pneumo and haemothoraxes were at that point gasping for breath, since the collection of air or blood in the lung cavity severely affects breathing.

I was hungry and exhausted, and had come downstairs from ICU looking forward to a short 15 minute or so break when I could sit down and rest my aching feet, and have a quick cup of tea and whatever there was to eat in Casualty – a sandwich probably. At the sight that met me, I quickly and quietly went into the Duty Room, closed the door, and started sobbing in frustration. The Sister-in-charge quickly followed me inside the Duty Room with a cup of tea, which she offered to me, gave me a tissue and gently informed me that there were patients in the corridor all of them needing my urgent attention. I gulped down the cup of tea, wiped my face, and followed the Sister. I quickly attended to those patients needing insertion of an ICD and completed the job hastily but efficiently. We inserted ICDs to patients so often at my hospital that we were now "experts" in the field, compared to other hospitals in the country that did not experience so many trauma cases.

I spent the rest of that frustrating night battling with the guy with near total disembowelment. I admitted him to the ward and tried to prepare him for theatre with the assistance of ward staff. Because he was drunk and violent, he did not even want us to touch him. Eventually he sobered up, which was when we got him ready for theatre and he was then whisked off into the operating room. I never slept that night, the second night in a row, because at some point I had to assist the Registrar in theatre and then return to Casualty to attend to even more patients with stab wounds.

The greatest challenge I have faced was when I left my country, Swaziland and my family for the first time upon graduating from High School in the seventies, and went to study in a part of the world which is quite different in many respects, (culturally, weather-wise, the food, etc.) to where I come from. This was to Nigeria, in West Africa, where I spent 3 years at the University of Ife, in Ile-Ife. I eventually left Nigeria to continue with my studies in South Africa, at the University of Natal Medical School, which was the only medical school for blacks at that time. I started there in January 1976 and shortly after that there were the Soweto uprisings and things in South Africa got politically heated. I saw many of my colleagues at Medical School thrown into jail, some having to flee the country and go on exile. At our residences security police from the apartheid racist regime continuously harassed us. At one point, on a Friday, during the nation-wide demonstrations against the apartheid regime, 90 medical students were arrested. All 90 of us (18 females and 72 males) ended up spending the weekend in prison. I had never been in prison before then. The conditions were very bad. All 18 of us were squeezed into one tiny cell, sleeping on the concrete floor. The food was terrible. The female warders kept all the food, chocolate and cigarettes our colleagues brought for us. We appeared in court the following Monday and were eventually released on bail. Our colleagues outside had spent the whole weekend raising funds and contacting lawyers for our release.

As a professional I was adamant and pursued my career in public health in my country at a time when the general public, also fellow medical colleagues, regarded that a physician working in public health was a wasted human resource, since there was 'such a serious shortage of doctors in the country'. Hopefully today the importance and relevance of public health has now been realised and recognised by all concerned.

I feel my greatest achievement has been pursuing my dreams, and seeing many of them turn to reality. It has been tremendous, the feeling and realisation that I have made some contributions to public health in my country and internationally.

I value and love my family a great deal. They are a positive and needed influence to my life. I value the relationships I have had during my life because in a very special way each and everyone of my friends and or colleagues has contributed to shaping my life. I feel that I have given and gained something from each and every relationship. I married and had twins, a boy and girl who are now 18 years old. I am not married at present.

The world and nations should give the opportunity and supportive environment to women to excel themselves, to exhibit and utilise their inborn and inbred potential. Then the world will be a better place for all of us. I am referring to all levels in society, where women play, or are supposed to play an important role, given the opportunity.

Women are great. They are wise, clear and level headed, loving, caring, dedicated, hard-working, can withstand a lot of stress, are managerially sound by nature and when it comes to household management, they are the best. Even in the poorest of families, with very limited resources, they are still able to feed and clothe every member of the family.

Given the opportunity every woman can make it to the top, can do and accomplish every thing they wish for. Dreams do turn into reality.

Over the next 20 years, women at work will continue to face some of the biases, which come their way. However as they unite and start to speak in one voice, support each other and begin to or continue to bring across the biases and injustices they face, I believe that the situation will improve and women will soon overtake men. The fight for equal opportunities will have to be sustained, and should be well orchestrated. We know that men will feel threatened and will not like this, but who cares? Women have been excluded for far too long from developmental issues, especially their participation in senior positions, and redress of this is long overdue.

Yes, I would still choose my current profession. I believe in the contributions of my profession to overall economic and social development amongst nations. And I do enjoy my professional work, and find it most stimulating and fulfilling.

Sarah Doukas
Founder and Director of Storm Model Management

Sarah oversees a team of 14 booking agents and continues to act as a booking agent herself, sitting at a round table in front of a computer terminal with 8 other people. She represents over 500 models, marketing them to hundreds of international clients in the fashion and advertising industries and is responsible for the long-term potential of their careers. More than that however; she feels it is her responsibility to represent them in a professional and ethical way. Sometimes she is their business manager and at other times she is a shoulder to cry on. Sarah also works with fashion designers, art directors, casting agents, commercial directors, photographers and editors. At Storm Sarah liases with her IT and accounts departments and generally guards the welfare of all her 30 staff. Sarah famously discovered the then unknown Kate Moss at JFK Airport in New York, when Kate was a teenager, bringing her to the world's attention as one of the new global supermodels.

I left school in the middle of my A level course to the horror of my parents and went straight to London and started working in Kensington Market. Then I modelled, ran an antique stall and went to Paris for 3 years where I modelled, acted as a photographer's agent and had a weekend stall in the flea market at Clignancourt in Paris. I returned to London and managed a punk band for a year. After that I moved to San Francisco with my husband for 4 years and had my first child. Finally I returned to London where I worked for another London model agency for 6 years.

Initially I took on my present career because there was a lack of money and because I have always done my own thing. Working for someone else made me feel like a rat in trap. I felt I was always having to prove myself because my father had always told me that I was bound to be a failure and this made me more determined than ever to prove myself.

Learning to be a decent boss has been challenging and satisfying. Trying to establish that fine line between being one of the crew and being respected by the employees, and also being a boss that can shoulder the burden of running a company and ensuring it's a success on many levels.

It has been difficult on occasions having to act as a highly skilled psychotherapist when problems arise among the people I deal with whether it's staff or clients and certainly with the models the problems can be traumatic. Sometimes I can be trying to help someone with an eating disorder or some serious emotional crisis. Several problems can and do arise from dealing with the numbers of people that I am responsible for.

My grandmother who had a very strong and unusual personality was the person who influenced me the most in my personal life. She was an eccentric who always threw caution to the wind and paved her own path in life and who at the same time was very good-natured. She was uncompromising, fascinating and very non-conformist.

My father in many ways acted as the spur to my professional success – I didn't achieve academic success and my father always told me that I would find no path in life without a university education.

The world of modelling has its humourous moments like the time we lost, top model and UN Ambassador, Waris Dirie, in London. She had been flown in especially by a top director for a highly prestigious and very lucrative TV commercial, where she would be dressed in over a million pounds worth of diamonds. She had been collected by limo from Heathrow airport and the chauffeur confirmed he had dropped her off outside the hotel, and from there she just vanished. She was due to catch a connecting flight in hours and no one including the hotel had any idea where she was. The police were called to interview the chauffeur to establish whether he was involved in a possible abduction. We drew a blank and in desperation I despatched my brother Simon, also a director of Storm to find her. And he did, fast asleep in a bunk bed in a dormitory in the YMCA next door to the hotel, spluttering about the quality of the hotel the client had booked her into.

One of the most difficult experiences I have had to deal with was when Colleen – one of my younger girls witnessed her father being murdered. Trying to help in her recovery was perhaps the most traumatic thing I have done. Another dreadful experience was the death of one of my most loyal and brilliant staff who had worked here for 7 years, the lovely Gregory, who was also my friend. Dealing with the impact his death had on me personally and all of my staff was very difficult.

For me as a person the greatest challenge I face is my responsibility towards my family to provide for them now and for their futures. In a way that responsibility led to my greatest professional challenge i.e. taking the risk of setting up my own business 13 years ago.

I have worked hard to try to see everybody's point of view whether it's a member of staff, or a client, or one of a hundred different models, and then trying to deal with the industry pressure, and managing to deal with the many different issues that frequently arise when you are working in such a fast business. It's difficult – sometimes I have to play politician, being diplomatic, sensitive, business minded, and tough without alienating people.

I feel my greatest achievement is probably running my company Storm to the best of my ability while having a successful married life and three children. It's the hardest thing in the world to have a very demanding career and juggle a home life. I never discuss work at home unless it's amusing or of great importance.

I have been married twice. My present marriage is a very successful one simply because I want it to work and I put a lot of effort into it. I wouldn't be a happy person alone, I'd definitely feel there was something missing from my life, I get great enjoyment from my children. Also, most of my closest friends date back to my childhood and I've made an effort to keep these friendships intact. My early relationships are important as they keep me level headed. I don't really socialise within the business and this gives me a more balanced outlook about the business and prevents me from being obsessive about it.

If I could change one thing in the world for women I'd change a gene in women's heads that makes them feel they have to be the emotional providers for everyone in their lives. I feel we've come a long way as women and we can achieve anything we want from becoming prime minister to being the head of MI5, but at the same time, we are still the emotional providers and we still deal with every aspect of the home life. I take over the children's welfare, I look after my husband, the cooking, the household shopping, it's a burn out situation – and it's something I do completely subconsciously. It must be my role in life, something that just happens. It helps me deal with the human element of my work and gives me a greater understanding towards my relationships with the parents and their children, and just generally dealing with everybody.

I think it's important for women's general stability to earn their own money and to know that she provides equally financially. It's still hard for women to operate in a man's world and they need to have more confidence to go out and do it. You must have absolute confidence and grim determination and never think that you're not capable. Tenacity and determination win out and it's such a wonderful feeling trying to achieve something, it's liberating.

In the next 20 years I can see more women taking over as heads of industry and more women attaining even more erudite positions, and perhaps increasing numbers of women will opt to not have families and will just focus on these careers. Children are such a big issue for women who want to have both a career and a family and I think if there were more Government initiatives for employers, women might be able to find a greater balance between being happy mothers and fulfilled career women.

If I were at the start of my career would I choose the same path? Yes undoubtedly because I love it. It still makes me happy, and I still find it stimulating and greatly fulfilling and fun.

Judy Dunn PhD
MRC Research Professor, Institute of Psychiatry

Judy is a psychologist, carrying out research on children's development and relationships. Her current role is as an MRC Research Professor, directing several research programmes. At a general level, her chief responsibility is to carry out excellent scientific research – focused on increasing our understanding of risks and protective factors in children's development, on the significance of their early experiences etc. At a practical level, this means Judy is responsible for the organisation of several research teams, for the development of the team members as scientists, for the smooth collaboration between scientists of different disciplines. She is also responsible for making the results of the research available to others – academics, parents, policy makers, etc.

Judy read Natural Sciences at Cambridge University, and got a first class degree in Zoology and the Frank Smart Prize (for the top biologist). She was an undergraduate at New Hall (then a college for women undergraduates). Judy intended to go on to do a PhD at Cambridge, but found she was pregnant (Judy had married in her second year as a student), and interrupted her academic career to go to the US where her husband was a graduate student, and then had three children within 18 months (a daughter followed by twin sons). It took Judy a while to get back to work, and she had an extended period of working part-time, because of the children. Judy finally got her Cambridge PhD through submitting 17 published papers, from the research she started carrying out in Cambridge in the 1970s. She had a research post at Cambridge (with the MRC), where she was a Fellow of King's College between 1978 and 1986, when she took a university post in the US, then returned to England for the position she now holds at the Institute of Psychiatry. Judy was made a Fellow of the British Academy in 1996.

It was really the experience of having three children so close together, and so different in personality, that prompted me to become a developmental psychologist: I wanted to understand why the children were so different from each other, what factors influenced the way they grew up, how they influenced the people around them. I had been interested in development and behaviour as a student, and especially in the approach of ethologists – who emphasised the importance of studying animals in their own environment. Psychologists were at that time very narrow in their ways of studying children, and I thought that their strict 'experimental' approach had led to a misrepresentation of what children understood, and the way they related to others. I was very keen that we should not 'throw away' what we knew as people and members of families, in our approach to the scientific study of children's development.

I have hugely enjoyed watching children, talking to them, and learning from them and from their parents – chiefly from their mothers. It's been a privilege to be able to do so. I also find writing very enjoyable and satisfying, and giving talks about the research to both parents and academic audiences.

Among the aspects of the job that are least satisfying for me I would say the most difficult is managing very large projects (such as my current study of 13,000 families), in which much of my time and energy is taken up by 'managerial' issues that seem very distant from the real life of the families we study, and from the central scientific questions we want to answer.

I think the most important influence on me, as a person has been my mother – a wonderfully loving, tolerant, sensitive and intelligent person – a lovely mother and grandmother. Her influence was not only in her loving relationships with others, but much broader: if I get pleasure from looking at paintings, listening to music, it is through growing up with her.

Probably the most important people in my education and professional training have been Professor Robert Hinde, a splendid scientist, who taught me as a student, and has continued to be a mentor, as well as a close friend and my husband who is an enormously impressive scientist from whom I continue to learn.

One funny incident among many that occurred during my observations of children involved a mother saying to me that she'd noticed her 2-year-old walking around with a funny posture and a shrugging of her shoulder; when asked what she was up to, she explained she was being Judy Dunn (the shrugging of the shoulders was to keep her portable tape-recorder on her shoulder while she wrote in her notebook – a crisp capturing of my own action). Another involved a mother saying to her 2-year-old 'Who have you got in the cupboard?' And the 2-year-old blushed as she opened her cupboard and whispered 'Judy Dunn'; she pulled out of the cupboard a giant teddy bear, who was, since my last visit to the family, me. Apparently she took 'me' to bed with her every night.

As a person, taking a decision to leave my first husband, and worrying about the consequences for the children was a challenge and a source of major anxiety.

As a person my greatest achievement is probably in my role as mother of three and as daughter during my mother's 10 years of tragically increasing disablement, as she aged from 85 to 95 years, staying at home. As a professional: two sorts of achievement have been important to me: First, transforming the way people think about children's development, through the sorts of observational studies I've done, and my books and papers about what they show; Second, repeatedly arguing against the 'mother-blaming' orientation of clinicians, who automatically assume that if a child has problems, the first person to see as the cause is the mother.

I've already noted the importance of my relationships with my mother, and the huge significance to me of my three children – both in my family life and in my professional life. I have been married three times: the first time, too young, as a first year student. I've been happily married to my present husband for 10 years.

If I could change one thing about the world for women it would be making their lives as mothers easier – more supported if they want to work, by decent, reliable childcare, happier in the sense of less guilt and pressure and anxiety that any problems their children have are bound to be 'their fault'.

My advice to other women would be to try to relax as a mother/parent: children are very adaptable and resilient: Enjoy them. It's not all your fault.

I don't feel very optimistic about the world of work for women in the next 20 years within academic institutions, women have a very tough time, especially if they have families, and I don't see things changing quickly. I was the only woman professor at this institution when I was appointed. The contrast with the US was very bad. Cambridge has a poor record too, especially at the higher levels; many medical institutions do too. And it is specially hard for women who don't have either financial resources or family support,

Would I have chosen the same career if I were at the start of my working life again? Yes probably, though I sometimes wish that I had got a medical degree, so that I could be more immediately and directly useful to people.

Rennie Fritchie DBE
Commissioner for Public Appointments and a Civil Service Commissioner

Dame Rennie has adopted a 'portfolio' approach to her career and has a number of jobs and positions which include Consultant on organisation change and management development, working out of Mainstream Development; President of the Pennell Initiative, focusing on the health of women in later life. Dame Rennie is also a Visiting Professor with a Chair in Creative Leadership at York University. She is also a Non-Executive director of the Stroud and Swindon Building Society and Chair of Council and Pro-Chancellor of Southampton University.

On March 1st 1999 she was appointed Commissioner for Public Appointments and a Civil Service Commissioner. In addition she is a Fellow of Cheltenham and Gloucester College of Higher Education, a visiting Faculty Member of the Health Service Management Unit at Manchester University, and a visiting Fellow at the NHS Staff College in Wales. Dame Rennie is also Patron of 'Headway' Gloucestershire a centre for work for those recovering from long-term head injuries, Patron of Art in Health and Patron of the Meningitis Trust.

Her work in the area of conflict resolution has involved action research over 5 years. She is co-author of a number of books and publications; most recently Resolving Conflict in Organisations *co-authored with Malcolm Leary and published by Lemos & Crane.*

I have long been grateful to Professor Charles Handy who, some years ago, invented the titles of 'Portfolio Worker' and 'Portfolio Careers' to describe a way of doing several jobs or holding several different roles simultaneously. This conferred a legitimacy to having that kind of career which had until then been treated in a dismissive and patronising way.

As a person with a long-standing Portfolio Career style, I've thought about it and lived it for many years.

My current Portfolio includes:
- Commissioner for Public Appointments
- Consultant on Leadership and Personal Development
- Non-Executive Director of Building Society
- Hon. Visiting Professor with a Chair in Creative Leadership
- President of the Pennell Initiative for Women's health
- Patron of five charities.

This, together with my personal roles and relationships – mother, grandmother, daughter, sister and friend keeps me pretty busy.

I know that I am not alone and that more and more people have this style of career and are endeavouring to juggle their many interests and demands on their time. In my experience more and more women, for a variety of reason are 'Portfolio People'.

Some of us select portfolio or flexible careers because of preferred style of working. Either we have a range of disparate interests which we wish to follow simultaneously or our character and temperament suit this style of working.

Some of us by virtue of the organisation structure may elect to have a portfolio career. That is the organisation decides that only two days a week of a person's time should be spent on a particular role. Therefore we elect this, often reluctantly, as a way of working because we believe in the need for the different roles and accept the limitation of two days a week on one thing and three days a week on another.

Some of us by force of life circumstances, reject full-time working and take on part-time roles for a limited time. This may be due to health, family circumstances or wider responsibilities. So we have very different motives, very different juggling capacities and a very different reception and support within our different organisations for us to undertake a flexible career.

Number 1 likes to duck and dive, enjoys networking and may well link the strands. Number 2 believes in the cause or reasons for the different roles and manages to do the two separately. Number 3 often feels apologetic, guilty, frustrated, keen to do a good job but may not have the wide range of support that the other two have, or the personal conviction or confidence.

Over time as a portfolio worker I have learnt a number of lessons and would like to share 12 of them with you.

Lesson One: Time

It takes longer than you think to do each job. We underestimate the entry and re-entry time into each of our work and life interests. There is only so much time available for paid employment and therefore I suggest you overestimate the time required and build in breathing space.

Lesson Two: Meeting challenges

Those of us who work in a flexible way are regularly challenged with the clever put-down comments like, "When are you going to do a full-time job?" and "Aren't you just part-timers or butterflies?" or a whole range of other fairly negative things. Every put-down needs a response. Have your own one-liners ready.

I like to use what I have come to call the 'Haight Ashbury' response. In the '60s there was quite a bit of unrest in California with some student rioting. The National Guard was called out to deal with it. There is a famous picture of a young man with a crew cut and fierce face pointing a gun at a young hippie in an area called Haight Ashbury. She had just placed a rose, with the long stem into the barrel of his gun, which completely disarmed him. This picture has stayed with me for a very long time and when challenged aggressively I generally try to disarm rather than attack back. It is usually very successful.

In meeting challenges we need to be assertive. Also it can be helpful to answer a question with a question. If someone says, 'How could you possibly do a good job working in such a part-time way?' or 'How can you expect to develop your career and get promoted when you are not here working like the rest of us?' then answering that with 'What an interesting thought! What makes you think that that might be the case?' or 'Tell me more about how you draw these conclusions...?' puts them on the back foot, rather than you.

Lesson Three: Accentuate the positive

Anyone who works in a flexible way offers a range of additional benefits to an employer and to colleagues and sometimes it is important to make sure they recognise it. For example, making statement like 'Because I'm not here all the time I bring objectivity to this issue' or 'Because I do a variety of jobs, I don't get stale and keep my energy and enthusiasm up' and so on. There are many many good things that happen as a result of working in this way.

We need to recognise them; then we need to draw them to the attention of others in a positive way.

Lesson Four: Being perfect

Many years ago I came across a wise saying which said, 'Not everything worth doing is worth doing well'. This absolutely true.

There is a danger when doing a range of jobs and being in them for limited period of time means that we try and do everything perfectly so that no one can point a finger and say that we aren't doing a good job. Learn to prioritise and to be discriminating about what needs to be done excellently and what just needs to be done.

A poem on failure which has helped me over the years I'd like to share with you:

'Last night I dreamt, marvellous error!
I had a beehive in my heart and golden bees were making sweet honey
from my old failures.'

Antonio Machado

It is alright to make mistakes. It's alright so long as we learn from them and don't keep making the same mistakes over and over again. Trying to be perfect tends to lead to mistakes all over the place and a great amount of stress on you and others. Failure can be powerful learning and development – sweet honey in fact!

Lesson Five: The best of you

When you are doing a range of tasks you are bound to get stressed from time-to-time. Who gets the short end of the stick when you get ratty and are under pressure? Is it the organisation? Is it the family? Or is it you? The best of you and the rest of you should be shared amongst them all.

Lesson Six: Pace the changes

We can take pressure, change or problems in one area of our lives but not in all simultaneously. Be realistic in your goals; don't try to do everything at once. And if you are under pressure in one area, take the pressure off yourself in the other areas. Look to see what can be done to give you the kind of support you need in order to manage change or difficult times.

Lesson Seven: Find new names for things

Part-time working sounds like part-time commitment. As a portfolio worker I endeavour to be wholehearted and fully present for the whole variety of my life and work interests. Therefore, I'm not partial in any way. So, perhaps the new name for part-time working should be 'flexible working'.

How often are women asked if they work? It's the wrong question and the wrong name. If you are at home looking after a family or caring for relatives you're working extremely hard. So perhaps we should rename work 'paid employment'. Find more positive names and don't have negative labels stuck on you or the work that you do.

Lesson Eight: Have a support network

I belong to a learning set that meets for half a day, six times a year. I bring my whole self, that's my personal self, my professional self and my range of interests to this set. Each of us discuss what is going on in our lives, what's going on in our work and address the themes and challenges that arise and in this way work together on our development. It's been immensely important to me and I can recommend a learning set. Or at the very least have a support network where you can go to say 'Ain't it awful?' and 'How would you tackle something like this?' These networks should also be fun and developmental – not just there for times of difficulty.

Lesson Nine: Learn to say no

So many of us in order to be seen as helpful, committed and competent say "Yes" to just about everything. Learn to say 'No' early on. Not 'I'm sorry I'd like to' but just 'No'. Say it loud, say it clear, say it in a kindly way and don't get bulldozed into saying, 'Well, No'…'Yes, maybe'… 'Okay'.

Lesson Ten: Speak up loud and clear about what you do well

Modesty is an admirable quality. However if you are over-modest about the work you do and the contribution you make you'll be underestimated.

I remember an American poem I came across many years ago which typifies this. It says:

> 'If you whisper down a well
> About the goods you have to sell
> You will not make as many dollars
> As the one who climbs a tree
> And hollers!'

So many people, particularly at interview are over-modest about the their contribution and end up not getting the job. So don't whisper down a well. Climb a tree and holler occasionally.

Lesson Eleven: Balance

Balance is a deservedly popular word today and we tend to concentrate more on work-life balance which is important. However, having a good balance between different jobs, using a variety of skills and abilities is also important. For many of us, this also means balance between paid employment, giftwork and public service. Balance also translates to the different shifts over time within our whole life experience, as the following poem demonstrates:

If Life's a Circus, Who's Laughing?
As a girl I played the clown
Always sunny, even funny, jumping up and falling down.
In my first job I rode the unicycle, new and on my own
Wobbly, uncertain, getting better, look no hands, throw this dog a bone!
Early married, I learned to walk the tightrope,
Trying to stay upright, learning how to cope.
With the children a juggler I became
Kids, work, home, no two days the same.
Faster and faster I never dropped the ball.
But where was I? I wasn't there at all.
As a single parent, life grew so much harder
Always running, jumping, tumbling and replenishing the larder.
At work a manager, at home a Roadie mum,
Planning, linking, shifting, moving till the setting of the sun.
Now in my fifties I finally hold the ring
In my three ring circus, balance is everything.

RF April 1996

Lesson Twelve: Reliance

As a woman typical of my age (57) I spent my early life expecting to be a dependent wife and looking for Prince Charming. I wasn't very successful at either of these and only much later came to realise that self-reliance was a positive goal. Of course I recognise that I am also part of the community and I am interdependent on a wide range of other people. As a portfolio worker, developing inner self-reliance has been one of the most positive attributes gained.

Some day my Prince will come
They said when I was small.
Brave and true, kind and strong
Handsome, dark and tall.
I'm only a woman doing my best,
Waiting for my turn.
Supporting, listening, smiling and nodding,
Knowing I have much to learn.
Only men could do the tough stuff,
Telling others what to do.
I just ran the home, the kids, my job,
Filled the larder, cleaned the loo.
Along the way I met some stars,
Pretenders who didn't tarry.
And then one day I realised
I'd become the man I wanted to marry!

Rennie Fritchie May 1996

Kegalale Gasennelwe MSc RN RM Dip Adv Nursing
Deputy Permanent Secretary, Ministry of Health, Botswana

At the time of writing Kegalale was dealing with the devastation left by massive flooding in East Africa. Mozambique, and Botswana were profoundly affected. Her main task was trying to help those that were left homeless as well as planning for their social needs. During this traumatic period Kegalale found the time to write this piece.

Kegalale was promoted to the post of Deputy Permanent Secretary at the Ministry of Health in 1997 one and half years after graduating from the Hubert Humphrey Fellowship program at the University of Washington. The main goal of the Ministry of Health is to provide quality health services to all of Botswana in order to enable each individual to attain a level of health that will enable him/her to lead an economically and socially productive life. Kegalale's responsibility is to participate in the development of health policy for the country and for the SADC Region by participating in the committee of senior officials. She ensures that there is equity in health by providing infrastructure, human resources and financial resources to enable officers in all their facilities to achieve the goal of health for all. She represents the ministry in high level decision-making committees, conferences and meetings. She also has to ensure that there is efficiency and effectiveness in the delivery of health services.

There was no career guidance during my time and when I left school I was not very sure about what I wanted to do. I did teaching for a secretarial course for one year but realised that was not what I wanted to do. I wanted to go to university to do social work but I did not know where to apply, let alone how to get a scholarship to do the course so I decided to apply for nursing at Athlone Hospital.

I have enjoyed my work particularly teaching year one students where one has to help them deal with a new role in life and all the personal conflicts that this entails. It has been satisfying helping them become involved in the development of projects where they have to deal with the families and communities they serve in the promotion of health and delivery of health services. Students unlike adults are very frank and open with their views. They are also keen to learn and change. I have found there is a lot one can learn from them. Students are not as defensive as other colleagues are. In teaching one can see the results both positive and negative at the end of each course and this helps one to either replan or modify strategies.

In administration targets are sometimes nebulous and poorly defined. It is only now that the Government is implementing a performance management system. This is a particular challenge for me and other managers to reorient all our colleagues into this new concept.

For me as an individual and a professional the concept of death and dying is a very difficult one to deal with emotionally. Since the majority of us fear death because we don't know much about life after death it is difficult to grapple with. 'The undiscovered country from whose bound no traveller returns puzzles the will' as Shakespeare puts it in

Hamlet seems to sum it up well. It has been difficult to deal with families where one member is dying. Religions have different beliefs about death and dying which compound the mystery.

My father was a very interesting man who I feel has influenced me most as a person. He had a mind of his own and would not give up on what he believed was right even though the world did not necessarily understand. He was born in 1901 but the actual date is not known since the parents could not read and write. One example of his own unique worldview that I remember vividly, was about when the date of births are calculated. He believed we calculated age incorrectly. He was convinced the actual date of birth should be calculated from conception. By the time a baby was born he said, that person was already nine months old, because a woman is pregnant nine months and therefore counting should start from 9 rather than zero. He urged that the months of pregnancy were counted. He argued that even when one has an abortion people are very clear about the number of months when the abortion happened and this is proof enough that the months mean a lot to the age of an individual on earth. He was very clear about his beliefs and he believed it was him and him alone that had the responsibility to let other people know what his beliefs were. It was his determination and orientation, which has enabled me to survive to this level. In my nursing life I always requested explanations before embarking on anything.

As a professional the other person who influenced professionally is Professor Serara Kupe/Mogwe. She taught me when I was a student and we worked together as colleagues. She has a strong personality and is visionary. She is the first nurse in Botswana to be the Chief Nursing Officer and to get her a doctoral degree in Nursing. She made a lot of changes in nursing and the image of nursing was enhanced.

The most traumatic experience I have had to deal with in my career was when the students nursing, dental therapy, pharmacy, medical laboratory and midwifery joined other students during a political demonstration leaving their lectures or examinations. Since this was a political demonstration it was difficult to discipline the students as some of the politicians sympathised with them.

The greatest challenged I faced as a person was when my parents died when I was at University of Washington in Seattle. I had to deal with the guilt of leaving my beloved parents to pursue my studies. I had to imagine the pain it caused them when they wished in their hearts to see, or talk or touch me before their last breaths! This has been in my mind for some time and has been difficult to get over!

My greatest challenge as a professional was to assist my country in the transition to operationalise the primary health care model in the nursing education system. Since 1990 the nursing education system was restructured and the new entry level into nursing practice changed from enrolled nursing to registered nursing. The curriculum was revised to make it more primary health care oriented in all nursing programs from registered nursing to Masters degree. One Institute of Health Sciences was designated to upgrade the current pool of enrolled nurses to registered nurses either through distance learning or formal learning and upgrading of diploma nurses to degree was also to be through distance learning and generic bachelor's degree for those coming from the secondary schools. Involvement and participation of all stakeholders and the community accomplished this achievement at large. This approach has provided a positive foundation for leadership mobilisation and community education as we face the challenge of HIV/AIDS scourge in our country. The challenge has also provided my other colleagues and me with an opportunity to communicate with other colleagues on an international basis. One of the recognition of my efforts in dealing with this challenge is the Award of Excellence during the 10th International Conference in Teaching and Learning at Jacksonville in April 1999.

As a person coming from a family of two (my brother and I) I have managed to raise a family of five. One electrical engineer and the first Botswana woman to do electrical engineering to get an academic award after a long time from 'Ryerson' in Canada. The second daughter is an Interior Designer and the first Botswana who is merging the modern design with our traditional designs and is currently is South Africa. One daughter is studying medicine in Ireland and is finishing this year. The only son is an Industrial Psychologist and is working with a private company as a strategic planner. The last daughter is finishing her matriculation this year and is going to do Architecture. Besides these five children I have one boy who was our gardener through his education and he is married, and is running a transport company. I have also educated three of the children of one of the gentleman who was looking after our cattle in the farm. I have organised the community this gentleman was coming from so that they can have access to health and education and other social needs. There is a school, a clinic and a community development office now in this village of Magotswhane.

As a professional I have risen from a position of registered nurse to a clinical instructor, a lecturer, Head of Department, Principal, Director of Human Resources for Health and currently Deputy Permanent in the Ministry of Health, the first nurse to get this position. I am currently reading for my doctoral degree with University of South Africa.

I had very supportive and understanding parents particularly my mother who was always ready to come in to help me with the upbringing of my children. I always believed that I managed to have this large family because my mother was the one who took the responsibility of helping me to bring my children up. I did not have to employ anybody to help me in the house or with the children. My family were always there to help. My father was also always there to help support us financially. My husband is a wonderful man and very accommodating. He is the one who raised the children with my mother while I was at Universities of Nairobi, Manchester, and Washington. I would not have been able to manage the demands of my current job had it not been for his support and encouragement.

Women must learn not to be submissive and carry everyone's burden except their own. They must learn to be assertive when needed. Women must be kind without sacrificing wisdom. People tend to think that women because of their motherly love have to bear almost all the problems in the family, at work and in the community. Women do have a special love but they must also have a special wisdom.

We need visionary leadership for women. We need a vision about the attributes and roles women can take on in all different professions and occupations including the church, politics the army and so forth. Women must learn to develop clearly defined goals and strategies to operationalise their vision. What is very important for us is that we support each other rather than compete to out do each other. Women must join politics and influence decisions that have a negative impact on women. Those in high positions must lobby for others to be put high echelons of decision-making in the country in order to alleviate poverty, illiteracy, sexual abuse and unemployment.

I believe women will become more educated and as such will be more critical thinkers and visionaries. Women will occupy higher positions than now and be involved in decision-making at high levels. Because of their foresightedness they will develop programs to alleviate poverty and enhance the health status of their families and communities and the world at large. Because of their kindness and wisdom women will use of rational thought rather than physical strength. As a result there will be fewer wars and prosperity will abound.

If I were at the start if my career again I would still choose the path I took. I am convinced my career in nursing at the start was an invaluable asset. It is a noble profession that aims to help humanity rather than exploit the people. I would always want to encourage nurses to be more loving and help improve their conditions of service so that they do not displace their frustrations on the sick people. People need to be given/shown love in this cruel world. Somebody must be empathetic rather than sympathetic to the needs of the suffering. Nursing helps women give women an opportunity to demonstrate their femininity by showing love to their husbands if married, their children, their patients and their communities.

Victoria Harrison MA DPhil
Executive Secretary of the Wolfson Foundation

Victoria is responsible to the trustees for running the Wolfson Foundation, one of the major UK charitable foundations, which makes grants in three areas: science and medicine, the arts and humanities, and education. She organises the expert assessment of applications and the monitoring of how the grants have been spent. She liases with fund-managers and accountants over investments and management of finances. Victoria's duties include managing a small office in the West End of London, and travelling within the UK and Israel to discuss potential new projects and to see grant holders.

I like the varied nature of my job, and the wide range of contacts involved, while at the same time remaining in touch with important advances in scientific research. I came from a home where I was encouraged to make the most of my educational opportunities. It wasn't an academic home, but my mother taught me numbers and the alphabet, so that when I was in hospital for a fortnight at the age of four, it was discovered that I could write letters (of a kind) to her before I went to school.

During my school days my parents encouraged me: taking an interest in my homework, testing me on factual information, and paying for extra tuition in areas which the school didn't cover. I was better at learning anything involving a logical sequence than at memorising things, and I remember my mother drumming history dates into me to ensure that I did better in the next examinations in history, one of my less good subjects, though I later married a historian. My father was also ambitious for me, and encouraged me not to drift away from the natural sciences – though at that time it might have been easy for me to move, as so many girls then did, into the arts and humanities. I was not pushed unduly: my mother's exhortations to 'think, Vicky, think', among my earliest memories, were not designed to further my academic attainments, but rather to correct my mispronunciation of words beginning with 'th'.

The fact that my first grammar school, in West Cumberland, was co-educational – where boys and girls learnt science in the same classes at the same pace – led me into studying science. I also thrived on the competitive atmosphere, which this school generated, and feel that it gave me a good grounding and toughened me in useful ways; having survived school dinners in there, I can now eat almost anything. When at the age of 14 I moved south to a girls' grammar school, the approach to teaching science was quite different ('now, girls, you may find this difficult, so do try hard'). My interest in science survived only because of the firm foundation I had earlier received during my co-educational years. My experience of course conflicts with what is now the received wisdom: that girls do better in science in the context of single-sex education.

My second grammar school was better known than my first, but suffered from being in an area where Girls Public Day School Trust schools offered free places at the 11+ stage, so that the brightest children were creamed off at that point. Two of the four of us who gained Oxbridge places in my school year had moved in later.

Of course I enjoyed Oxford, but I now see that an Oxford education also offers opportunities for making 'contacts'. Some of my contemporaries eagerly grasped these, but I did not – though I made a number of friends for life. And Oxford gave me more self-confidence and an analytical approach. One of my Oxford tutors (male) gave me freedom to write my weekly essays on subjects that interested me, instead of cramping me into an inflexible programme of teaching, and this increased my enthusiasm and helped me to do well in my final examinations: a first-class Oxford degree in physiology then obviously opened doors. At that time, the mid-60s, it was not a foregone conclusion that the wife of an Oxford don, which I had by then become, should have a career of her own. There was also no problem about staying on in Oxford to do research for a DPhil. degree, and doing that was in a sense a way of keeping my options open, but in the course of researching into neurotransmitters I realised that I wanted to use my scientific qualifications. However, I wanted to use them in a broader way than a life dedicated to scientific research then seemed to offer.

During my 2 years in scientific publishing after completing my doctoral thesis, I acquired experience of recruiting, training and managing staff, and discovered that I had a taste for organisation and administration within a broad scientific context. That led me, in 1972, to become a scientific administrator in the public sector (the research councils and Whitehall). I was involved with the assessment of grant-applications, science management and policy for national and international research programmes, and learnt from on-the-job experience rather than from formal courses. I was in regular contact with key British scientists, especially in the medical and biological areas, and later often found myself in Brussels. I had several business trips to Japan, and was involved in negotiations that were as much diplomatic as administrative and scientific.

My understanding of how the Government operates gained much from a 2-year secondment from the Medical Research Council to the Science and Technology Secretariat of the Cabinet Office. There I had first-hand accounts of discussions on Mrs Thatcher's sofa and was involved in drafting some of the documents that got into the handbag. I joined the public sector at a time when it was a highly regarded profession, with high morale. By the late 1980s, however, I regretted the politicians' growing tendency to depreciate the skills of the profession, as evidenced by the arbitrary cuts and the elaborate monitoring procedures that were increasingly being set in place. I am disappointed that this attitude to the public sector has persisted and even intensified beyond the Conservative Governments of the 1980s and 1990s into the present Labour administration. It is now fashionable to brand Government administrators as 'bureaucrats', but without their skills and dedication in what is a complex and demanding occupation, Governments cannot hope to deliver effective policy. The status of the profession has for some time been falling, and the consequences will be damaging to the public. I was doubly interested, therefore, when in 1997 I was invited to move from the public sector to the private charitable sector, to run a Foundation more than half of whose resources support projects in science and medicine, with the added bonus of being involved with projects in the worlds of the arts and education. Here it is my experience that there is generally a better balance between on the one hand accountability in the use of charitable funds, and on the other hand the manager's freedom to manage.

I am pleased to have reached my current destination, but I cannot say that I arrived in it as a result of particular ambitions or sustained or coherent planning; it was more a matter of taking opportunities as they presented themselves. I believe that it is important to be flexible, to be prepared to change tack, and sometimes to do something completely different particularly if trying to co-ordinate two careers in a family. I love my work, but I have never regarded the pursuit of any particular career as overriding. I hope that in future it might be made easier for women (and for men) to achieve a better balance, and to pursue interesting careers without the current macho pressures to work exceptionally long hours to the exclusion of other interests and family life.

Margaret Kartomi AM FAHA DPhil B Mus AUA
Head, School of Music, Monash University, Victoria, Australia

Margaret is the Head of the School of Music, Monash University. As Head of School and Professor of Music she is responsible for all School activities, building up the School's reputation and sharpening its 'competitive edge' within Monash, in the local and national community, and internationally. She is spokes-person for the School and host for official visitors to the School. She chairs staff meetings, School executive meetings, concerts committee meetings, studio teacher allocation meetings, auditions/student selection committee meetings and meetings of other committees. She is a Member of the Faculty (of Arts) Executive and of the Faculty Board, and an Executive Officer of the Board of Studies in Music. She is responsible for the School's curriculum and timetable, for the allocation of duties to all staff and or supervisors to honours and postgraduate students. Margaret is Editor of School handbooks, the School of Music Newsletter, School brochures and other printed material such as distance education work and study books. She is the Liaison Officer with Monash Malaysia and YAAM Malaysia. Margaret is also responsible for fund-raising, including working with Public Affairs toward setting up the Monash Music Foundation. In addition to all this she still carries out extensive research, publishes widely, teaches classes and supervises MA/PhD students.

I had a strong interest in Western classical music from earliest childhood on. My parents were amateur chamber musicians (violin and piano) and played together and with other musicians nearly every night, both at home and in public. I learned piano from the age of five. In 1959 I went to Indonesia, fell in love with it, and decided to research Indonesian music. I met my Indonesian (Javanese) husband at the Adelaide Mosque in 1955 (the Yugoslav Imam [cleric] lived in our home as a boarder for 20 years and invited us to Muslim feasts at Idul Fitri and Idul Adha). So I wrote my BA thesis on the influence of gamelan music on European composers.

I was determined not to follow in my mother's footsteps and be a housewife – a thankless task, it seemed to me, that gained one little respect. I decided on a career as an academic musician and scholar, with a primary research interest in ethnomusicology.

I have enjoyed research enormously particularly fieldwork with my husband Dris between 1961 and 1999 in 25 provinces of Indonesia, Malaysia (four provinces), the Philippines (Mindanao) and a little in China in 1977. I am the only person in the world to have recorded the traditional music of Indonesia so extensively– annotated copies of my recordings have been deposited in the Monash Music Archive and the National Library, Jakarta. I love writing, analysing and presenting fresh insights in published form, which is very rewarding.

I did not expect to find administration fulfilling, but when I was appointed to the Monash University Chair of Music in late 1989 after 15 years as Reader in Music at Monash, I had a challenging task of rescuing a deteriorating Department of Music (renamed School in 1999). Only 60 EFTSU (equivalent full-time student load) were in the Department at that time. So I expanded our musicology and ethnomusicology offerings (we were the best-known department in Australia for ethnomusicology) to include performance and composition. Having been a Visiting Professor at the Department of Music, University of California and Berkeley in 1986-87, and heard the wonderful inter-faculty orchestra there, I decided to start such an inter-faculty orchestra at Monash, with ancillary orchestras and later choirs, and to invent a new degree of Bachelor of Music. Now student enrolments are about 320 EFTSUs – i.e. very healthy, and we have three orchestras, one gamelan, two choirs, a Wind Symphony and we will restart our Big Band next year. I also raised two million dollars for Monash and fought successfully for the establishment of the Monash Arts precinct (given the five magnificent music and drama venues we have at Monash Clayton). I also fought to obtain a new building; called the Monash Performing Arts Centre (the architect won a prize for its design). Though administration is so all consuming, it brings its own satisfactions and rewards.

There are of course difficulties at times. Having to compromise between the interests of some staff and the changing needs of the Department of Music, which resulted in several staff leaving to allow appointments in our newly developing areas of performance and composition (essential in any Music School). Also, time factors, how to fit research and teaching and a personal life into a hectic administrative job as Head.

As a person I have been most influenced by my husband, Dris. My husband, being Indonesian and very ambitious for me and proud of me, was a positive influence in (1) encouraging me to do higher degree work in Germany and (2) accompanying me there and on about 35 field trips, mainly in Indonesia. I chose to marry him and it worked better than most marriages I know, despite some difficulties.

As a professional my greatest influence has been Prof. Georg Knepler (historical musicologist and my doctoral supervisor in Berlin). I still correspond with him, and with his colleagues and my other teachers Prof. Reiner Kluge (systematic musicologist) and Prof. Juergen Elsner (ethnomusicologist) about aesthetic, Marxist interpretative and other aspects of musicology. I still enjoy long and fascinating conversations when meeting them in Germany or at conferences elsewhere. They have a different approach to understanding music from most Western European musicologists, expressing themselves in terms of Intonations theory and dialectical theory and emphasising social and class issues in interpreting music history.

Another area of my professional life I have found very satisfying is supervising post-graduate thesis students: I get as excited about my students' research as I do about my own.

One of the funniest things that happened to me was standing on the stage of the Alexander Theatre in 1999 as Producer of an Indonesian dance drama to make a grand speech introducing the Vice-Chancellor of the University – and forgetting his surname! The audience and the Vice-Chancellor were hugely amused and the VC's first words to me were 'When did you say your contract comes to an end?'

The most difficult situation I had to deal with was undoubtedly having to tell some long-term members of staff that their output had been found to be not up to scratch and that, as the Department was changing direction, they should consider leaving.

My greatest challenge personally has been bringing up a beloved daughter and my greatest achievement has been being a good wife and mother.

My greatest challenge professionally has been balancing research output with heavy administrative demands and teaching and my greatest achievement professionally has been becoming an internationally known and respected scholar-ethnomusicologist.

If I could change one thing about the world of work for women it would be that they be given the respect they deserve for their enormous gifts and potential and be allowed fully to realise that potential. Especially until the 1960s, men and some brainwashed women constantly put down women in Australia too. It was good for men's jobs, but wasted most of the potential for half the population. The one thing women most need are educational opportunities.

Women must believe in themselves and aim high. We can do anything we want to do. There are ways, if you stubbornly pursue your goal, of doing what you want to do, even though you may not – e.g. due to poverty – be able to aim very high, relatively speaking.

Over the next 20 years more women will enter the workforce and obtain a high level of success – even now in New Zealand, the Prime Minister and Opposition Leader are both women. Many will find their work straining their marriages and relationships, so it is important to find tolerant partners. Most importantly, we must educate the next generation of boys to be full, proper human beings, with their 'feminine' side as well developed as their 'masculine' side, and avoiding the 'macho' idea of manliness.

If I were at the start of my life and career again I would still choose my current profession. Research, performing music, supervising other researchers and recreating/reinventing a Department/School of Music successfully is very satisfying, like all creative work.

Christine King PhD MA BA(Hons)
Vice-Chancellor and Chief Executive Staffordshire University

Christine is Vice-Chancellor and Chief Executive of Staffordshire University in England. The University has some 17,000 students and 1,600 staff. They offer undergraduate and postgraduate study in a wide range of academic areas and undertake research, scholarship and consultancy with business and industry. This is Christine's fifth year as Vice-Chancellor and in this role she is responsible for the leadership and management of all aspects of the University's work. In her capacity as Vice-Chancellor she also sits on a number of national and regional public bodies. In addition to her academic qualifications Christine is Deputy Lieutenant, Staffordshire, has an Honorary Doctor of Letters, is a Professor of History, a Fellow of the Royal Historical Society, a Fellow of the Royal Society of Arts and a Companion, of the Institute of Management

My career has been an unfolding tapestry. Until a year or two before I applied for, and was appointed to my current post, I did not even consider such a position. I have been involved in education of some kind all my working life and have remained a researcher throughout. I chose my early teaching posts as a way of exploring whether I wanted to work in education and if so, in which part of it. Thus I have worked in a school, in Further and, for the bulk of my working life, in Higher Education.

What led me into the education profession was the opportunity to work with students. They always have been and remain my greatest satisfaction and reward. I have tremendous respect for all the individual achievements by students I have worked with, in one capacity or another, whether they are school leavers or working parents studying part-time. My students have never ceased to amaze me with their ability to think around corners and with their humour and grasp on life. I have a particular commitment to offering opportunities to people who might otherwise be excluded from Higher Education, whether because of physical disability, social and educational background, age or any other barrier. What is so thrilling about working in Higher Education is that we see our students develop intellectually and personally and know, as they graduate, that one way or another they will make a difference to the worlds they enter. Because of the nature of our jobs, working with colleagues is also a great privilege. My experience at Staffordshire University is that the staff there, academic and professional support staff of all categories, share a commitment to students and have that same creativity that we see in our students. Thus we are a community and membership of this is the very best aspect of my current job.

Difficulties that I have faced have changed as my position has changed. An abiding factor of my experience, however, and one which has never changed, is the vast amount of time the job takes. Whether supporting students directly, as in the past, or attending national or regional business meetings and dinners as at present, I have always worked well over the odds. All my working life I have expected to work long days, most evenings and often at weekends. Whilst this has its own reward, there are obviously great risks to such a pattern.

There has been a dearth of role models, particularly female, and mentors during my career so far. Colleagues and friends have helped me, both personally and professionally. Apart from having wanted to be Margot Fonteyn when I was a child, and an ongoing desire to perform like Tina Turner, I am not aware of any one person influencing me, other than, perhaps, my parents. Whilst they are not part of my professional world, they have always and continue to listen to and support me.

When I worked in Further Education I taught a large number of the infamous 'liberal studies' classes. On one occasion I was in the midst of a series of classes on 'life education' as the syllabus coyly called it. I had survived the session with a class of 40 or so day release apprentices on birth control and we were now ready to move on to 'the birth of a baby'. The students, all male were all aged about 22 and I was only a couple of years older. I set up the film *To Janet a Son* on the ancient Bell and Howell projector, gave an introduction and warned the lads that I wanted no silliness. If anyone felt the need to giggle or felt faint, I expected them to leave the lecture theatre. Most, I later discovered, were, unlike me, already parents and had witnessed at least one birth. I started the film, Technicolor and graphic in its images. All went well until there was a terrific thud as I fainted and awoke surrounded by highly concerned students. I never have had children and I often wonder if Janet and her midwife were to blame.

The most difficult situations I have faced in my professional life have always been around the internal politics of organisations. As a result I have a very strong commitment to try to build my own organisation as an open community where people can understand what is happening and why and where they are listened to. We don't always get it right, but that is the intention and aim.

My greatest challenge, as a person, has been the same one that faces all of us; to work through what happens in life and to make sense of the journey. Apart from issues of health, my traumas in the past have all been around relationships, starting with a divorce, which I found very painful.

My greatest challenge as a professional has been to find the balance between knowing when and where I needed to learn and when and where to trust my own judgement and way of doing things. This is, I believe, particularly difficult for women as we often do things differently and have few role models or peers to check with.

My greatest achievement as a person has been to move into the professional world in which I now work from a basis which was a million miles away. I grew up in a family and community where university, let alone anything further, was unheard of. I like to think that, whilst I have moved professionally, I stay close personally to those roots which I value and which taught me a great deal, often the hard way.

My research and publications on Nazi Germany represent my greatest professional achievement. I write and speak extensively on the work on the fate of a number of Christian minority groups in the Third Reich, in and out of the concentration camps. The work brings me many wonderful contacts, including survivors, as well as other scholars in the area. The work also allows me to touch an area which is, I believe, vitally important for us, as a society, to try to understand and learn from.

As I have said, I do not have children and I am divorced. These decisions were made before I got to my current dizzy heights so I do not think that there are necessarily any connections. I have always had, and continue to have, a great relationship with my Mum and Dad, who are amazing and lovely people. I'm relaxed about what has happened and where I am now.

When thinking about what it would be good to change for women in the world, then the first on the list would be some action to help alleviate the poverty in which so many women live in all over the world. More locally, I'd like to see women in key positions in critical mass so that we need no longer feel under such a lonely spotlight.

If I were able to give one piece of advice to other women in a professional context, it would be around believing and trusting in yourself. It's very easy, in my experience, since many women are very open to new ideas and others' opinions, to wonder if the original idea and gut feeling about what is right is valid. Test it, by all means, but accept that it may be different and go with it. Enjoy the diversity that we bring to organisations and relationships.

I hope that women in the professional world in the West in the next 20 years will see an increase in their numbers in positions of power. I believe that this will happen, albeit slowly. We have, for example, only five women vice-chancellors out of over a hundred in the UK. Once in such positions, I hope also that we will 'keep the faith' and change the ways in which we work for the better.

I would choose my career if I were starting again. For all the tensions, lack of funding and hassles, we do, via education, help people change their lives and go on to change the world.

Glenys Kinnock MEP
Member of the European Parliament, Brussels

Glenys Kinnock was educated at Holyhead Comprehensive School in Anglesey and graduated from University College Cardiff. She was a teacher at secondary, primary, infant and nursery levels for almost 30 years before being elected to the European Parliament as Labour MEP for South Wales East in 1994. She was re-elected as MEP for Wales under the new proportional representation system in 1999. Glenys Kinnock is a member of both the European Parliament's Development and Co-operation Committee and the Foreign Affairs Committee. She is Vice-President of the EU/ACP Joint Assembly, and President of Steel Action in the European Parliament.

'Life, strife, these two are one!
Naught can ye win but by faith and daring.'

These are words from the Suffragette anthem. As the granddaughter of someone who talked to me as a child about women and 'the vote', these words still send a tingle down my spine.

Women in the UK have seen great changes to their status in society during the twentieth century. My own grandmother was denied the right to vote purely because of her gender – the debt we owe to the Suffragette movement for their determination to achieve women's emancipation is incalculable. Gaining the vote paved the way for women to increase their profile in society, and take their place in the world of work. The presence of women in the workplace changed dramatically as a result of the world wars, and the 1960s and '70s – with the women's movement's impact on the profile of women generally – saw an increase in the number of women pursuing Higher Education and a career. However for millions of women the progress was not translated into changes in their day-to-day lives.

Whilst the entry of women into the world of work is welcome, we are still vastly under-represented in all spheres of influence and authority. Just 18% of management positions in the UK are held by women, and this drops to less than 5% for women holding executive directorships of UK companies. To illustrate my own European Parliamentary constituency, 74% of clerical staff in Wales are women whereas 69% of the managers are men. In the sphere of education, women comprise 46% of head teachers in primary schools, but this drops to 11% in secondary schools, and in 1998 only 42 of the 384 principal officers in Welsh local authorities were women. There are those who preach about 'trickle up'. But it is time we all stopped analysing why women are under-represented and get on and just do it.

In most industrialised countries women's work is characterised by part-time jobs, and unemployment levels are higher for women than for men. The gender pay gap is a serious issue. Women's hourly earnings are only 80% of those of men, and it is a worrying factor that the decision to start a family is the most significant factor affecting women's income and earnings opportunities. For many working women, having a child means a reduction in personal income, a loss of momentum on the career ladder and can often mean leaving employment for several years.

There is still much to be done to ensure conditions are conducive for women to combine work with family commitments – after all, working mothers, rather than fathers, still bear the primary care responsibilities of their children, and 9 out of 10 lone parents are women. Many more men are of course taking a full role in the home – although I have never met a man who has complained about the difficulties of combining a family and a career!

Mothers of young children who wish to restart work after maternity leave must be offered the necessary measures to facilitate their return to the workplace. It is to be hoped that the gradual moves we have seen recently, towards the provision of crèches and family-friendly policies, gain momentum.

The UK's membership of the European Union has undeniably had a favourable effect on women's position at work, and has provided the UK with a backbone of equal opportunity law and rights. This includes equal pay and equal treatment of women and men at work, social security schemes, rights for self-employed people and the crucial Maternity Leave Directive which, for the first time, gave part-time women employees in Britain the right to maternity leave. This, coupled with national measures such as the New Deal and Working Families Tax Credit has made a demonstrable difference to the lives of women and their families.

But there is a great deal to be done. We all know that just as we think we have made progress, some blatant act of misogyny hits us and reminds us that we have a long way to go.

It is time we learned about the true history of women – like the women of Wales who have kept up the struggle for a decent standard of living for their families.

I am reminded regularly that, in spite of the enormous contribution of women, the national anthem of Wales is called 'The Land of my Fathers'!

Many Welsh women remain severely disadvantaged – socially, politically and economically – at home and at work. It is not just attitudes to women that need to change. Women need better training, comprehensive childcare and improved rights. Great strides are being made but we have a long way to go.

In this quest our feminism should not be demonised by those who want to hold those who espouse it with responsibility for the emasculation of men.

Women are able to get together and act together. Mary Wollstonecroft said, "It is justice, not charity that is wanted in the world". These words have a resonance for us now and for all those young women who try to make sense of their world.

The fact is that there isn't a country in the world where women enjoy and exercise their full entitlement to rights. No amount of fashionable writing about post-feminism can make the inequalities acceptable. That one cruel chromosome, as UNICEF says, continues to guarantee an apartheid of gender across the world. Moving to gender equality is a political process and not a technocratic goal.

Women are not looking for favours. We are not the 'second sex' and we are certainly not prepared to accept second best. As Barbara Castle said, 'If you go for little things then men will give you little things – never the big things. Never mind the trivia – go for the jugular!'

Yvonne Lau MB BS FRCSEd FCSHK FAMHK
Consultant Surgeon
The Breast Centre, Department of Surgery, Kwong Wah Hospital, Hong Kong

Yvonne works as a General Surgeon with special interest in Breast diseases. She was responsible for the setting up of Hong Kong's first Breast Centre which is still probably the most established of such centres in Hong Kong. She is responsible for the everyday running and continuous development of the Breast Centre. Apart from the provision of high-quality clinical service, she is heavily involved in the promotion of breast education amongst colleagues and in the public sector. In addition, she also participates in general surgical work and oversees the training of junior surgeons.

To become a medical doctor was like a 'calling' I had since childhood. Within the medical curriculum, Surgery is a highly logical and practical discipline. This was attractive to me.

I have found it particularly satisfying being able to help those who are sick whether this is to cure a disease, improve symptoms or simply provide psychological support. It has also meant a great deal to me personally to know that what I have done has meant something important to the patients I have treated. Being able to educate and assist junior trainees in establishing a meaningful career in medicine is a great honour. Success in setting up the Breast Centre and the achievements of the Centre has been very rewarding.

It has been difficult for me as a professional to have to deal with the increasing mistrust between patients and the medical profession. There are also the increasing, excessive and unrealistic demands from the public on the medical profession. Medicine is a human science. There is no perfection. Medicine cannot provide for immortality. Medical professionals can only try their best. Medical care is also expensive. Unfortunately, there is heightening discrepancy between patients' expectations and the doctors' ability to provide quality health care within the capacity of limited resources.

The person who has been the greatest influence in my life has been my husband, Dr Kin Wah Fung. He has been a major support to me in many aspects and in many important decisions in my life. As a professional I have been deeply affected by Professor Michael Baum's vision, his sincerity and devotion to medicine and patients, his honesty in scientific research, as well as his humanity.

Breaking bad news (serious illness, deaths, etc.) to relatives of young adults in the prime of their lives is very difficult and as a result I have fully supported the emphasis on empathetic communication and psychological support for patients.

To impart an appropriate attitude towards breast cancer screening in Hong Kong has been a very challenging exercise. There is a general feeling within society that 'the more screening, the better'. In Hong Kong where privately funded medical care has a very prominent role, there is a tendency towards 'relentless' screening activities, such as, checking blood for breast cancer genes without informed consent or support from genetic councillors or surgeons; mammography screening in young women in their twenties with no bad family history. It is most important to remind society that any screening activity must be evidence-based, have a proven value, and must be undertaken with the strictest attention to quality assurance. I have found it very challenging to try to convince the public, the medical colleagues and the relevant health authorities on this issue. It is an area I am still working on.

I feel, as a person to be what I am now is probably the greatest achievement. I believe that I am essentially an honest and kind-hearted person who is eager to help those in need of my expertise. I am able to pursue happiness in life and in particular, have not fallen slave to 'power' and 'money'. As a professional I believe having the vision and success in setting up Hong Kong's first Breast Centre within a rather short period of time using limited manpower is probably my greatest achievement. The Breast Centre was established with the following aims:

1. Providing a focal point for women with breast problems.
2. Promoting quality diagnostic services and treatment for women with breast problems.
3. Promoting breast education in the public and in medical and para-medical workers.
4. Providing a reference point for clinicians who require information or assistance regarding breast issues.
5. Promoting rehabilitation service for women with breast cancer.

The Centre effectively concentrates expertise and effort. All the aims set out have been fulfilled and the Breast Centre continues to work along these directions. Amongst the educational programs, the Breast Centre successfully produced the multimedia interactive program on breast diseases in both kiosk version and on CD-Rom. We also successfully organised an international breast conference with the ESO in 1998. These could be considered some of our major achievements.

I married just after my intern year. My marriage has been an immense success. My husband is without doubt the most important person in my life. Our characters have matured through the years of our marriage and we feel that we are much better persons than before. We have however chosen not to have children and do not regret this decision at all.

If I were able to change one thing about the world for women it would be that they should have the right to be treated as a human being equal to men. This does not necessarily mean equality in everything but it does mean the right to choose to be equal, the right to enjoy equal rights.

Women should have confidence in themselves, in their own abilities. Women should not consider themselves inferior to men. Women should endeavor to fulfil their desires and dreams.

A woman's role will become more important in the years to come. The situation is already changing for the better in many countries where women used to be inferior to men. Women will find themselves contributing more to the betterment of our world. As women become more active contributors in society, it is likely that marriages and child-births will be delayed to fit busy schedules. This may bring about significant changes in society.

I have enjoyed being a doctor, in particular, a surgeon. I have no regrets in choosing this profession. It has given me much satisfaction and a strong sense of worthiness. However, I do not think that I would pursue the same profession for the rest of my life.

Sonia Lawson MA RA
Royal Academician, Royal Academy of Arts

Sonia is a renowned artist who paints symbolic and poetic figurative works that allude to mythology and memory. Modern and narrative, her paintings suggest an interest in the fundamentals of life: love, destruction, death and particularly the personal experiences of a person undergoing change. Her images are powerful and bold, influenced by her upbringing on the dramatic Yorkshire Moors. Sonia is a Royal Academician performing certain duties for the Royal Academy of Arts on a rota basis for 2 years at a time. She also works as a visiting lecturer at the Royal Academy Schools.

I studied at the Royal College of Art, London and gained an MA and a travelling scholarship to France. I taught part-time in various art colleges until the birth of my daughter. I am now 60 years of age and have spent a great deal of time looking after my parents. My father was 22 years older than my mother was and so this period of 'looking after' spread over about that many years.

Both of my parents were artists of real calibre but my mother had Graves disease in the 1930's which was not attended to early enough and led to her having some heart damage and mental difficulties which recurred intermittently during my lifetime. In 1989, aged 78 she had a major stroke. She couldn't write, speak, nor walk, but her mind remained totally alert. I looked after my mother and we communicated quite well, we even had a number of laughs together. She lived with us for 5 years until she died. My husband was at work and my daughter at university during this time.

Irrevocable loss is a terrible thing but now I am freer than I have ever been in my adult life.

I am an artist commanding some respect, with works in many municipal/national collections, but have not in my own opinion, because of domestic duties, (parents and child), had good runs at sustained effort. Now I am involved in keeping this up and feel I'm on track.

My mother remains my biggest life influence. She taught me to 'see' that understanding is not limited to visuals alone but the entire gamut of history of art, social and intellectual dimensions.

As a child I wanted to have a farm like my uncle, (we lived in the Yorkshire Dales). To others and to me he praised my practical common sense while working on his farm, helping out with the various tasks. But revelation comes with a flash of light and this happened to me at about 16 when I told him I finally 'understood' what art was about and wanted to be an artist. He was unhappy about this and said, 'you'll end up like your mother, all artists are mad.' Needless to say I went to art school, first in the provinces and later to the Royal College of Art in London.

My husband's business is in plastics, light manufacturing. He and a partner run a small factory. I would choose to have the same career again and the same husband but with a farm! The land, the animals, the plants, the skies and the weather give 'nutrient' for my reason for working so I go to Wensleydale every few months – however London and its frenetic 'charge' is of equal importance to me. The countryside is to do with foundations; London is about things coming hot from the oven of creativity and ideas.

Given justice women have been allowed to fulfil some ambition but having children and being family nurse, (though willingly), are things hugely extra that women alone have to shoulder.

I still believe that not being one of the boys is in general something of a drawback in the art world. Male artists are clubish, they remember one another, and (women don't). Many women run art affairs but favour (fancy) men, while those art things run by men – frequently homosexuals, I am told often favour men. The road for women is there but a bit narrow, a bit bumpy.

That girls/women in Afghanistan are not allowed schooling, not allowed most things is evil and of the dark ages. The men of Afghanistan are breeding nation female slaves, pure and simple. Amnesty International, all people concerned with freedom and justice should be making one hell of a stink but they're not. It's only women and girls.

It would seem women have to be constantly vigilant, if not, things will be taken away either by stealth or by overt brutal man-made laws: laws made by men with men in mind.

In the West in 1970 women's lib took off. Only 30 years ago yet men moan about it as if their 10,000 years of imbalance and rank injustice, if that was their fancy, should not be put to a fairer balance.

If I were able to change one thing for women in the world it would be that babies could be incubated outside the womb. In my view no pain, plenty of gain.

A lot of my past work was social/political comment but these days I'm not inclined to rant in paint. Instead I belong to Greenpeace, Friends of the Earth and Compassion in World Farming.

Currently as an artist I do not interpret nor copy but 'make' something that is a presentation, a work standing for itself, a created, wrought 'special' thing with its own inherent, abstract principles, poetic surfaces and integral imagery.

'Energy is Eternal Delight' said William Blake.

How true.

If I can't paint I'm like an exile.

Zoe Congo BA (Hons) MA
K. P. Plastics (Bletchley) Ltd

Zoe is the daughter of Sonia Lawson R.A. Together they thought it would be good to have a mother and daughter perspective. The women have chosen quite different career paths both working hard to succeed and to make an impact in highly competitive fields.

At the age of 30 I find myself working for a family owned plastic injection moulding company. My job has no distinct title, partly because, depending on what is required, I adapt: Office Supervisor, Wages Clerk, Financial Director, Maintenance Supervisor, Web Site Designer, Purchase Manager, Sales Manager, First Aider, Van Driver *et al*. The company is small enough to allow me and my colleague Simon to function at all these levels, (Simon is the other director's son and the same age as myself, therefore we hold joint responsibility in the company).

I have worked at the company for 5 years, and made a role/roles for myself. As indicated it is not a simple office job: we have 28 workers and 28 injection moulding machines manufacturing items ranging from golf spikes to supermarket shelves and I am often called down to inspect, or advise on them. Over the Christmas shut down, myself, my colleague Simon and another man employed by us, scrubbed clean the concrete floors and laid a special epoxy resin paint, a backbreaking and tedious job. I was the only one of the three who could use the scrubbing machine effectively as it required not just muscle to keep it in the correct place, but balance. Some days therefore I work physically as hard, if not harder, than the lads.

As the daughter of Sonia Lawson I have been incredibly lucky to have been brought up in an environment where one parent works from home. Looking back I realise now how difficult it must have been for her to get any serious work done when I was around. My father, as a self-made businessman, must have valued her work, but I feel that his appreciation of her worth as an artist and her role as a working woman grew as their marriage grew. Now they fully respect each other's roles, but I surmise it was not always thus. Perhaps respect must always be earned from both sides, although as an artist not in full-time employment it may have been more difficult to gain that respect in comparison to my father's self-made and salaried role.

As an only child being brought up in that environment I felt no restrictions on what I could do and was confident that, as a woman I had many choices. I chose first to study English Literature at King's College London, than after gaining a BA (Hons) became an au pair in Italy, partly to learn Italian and partly to further my choice of studying for a MA in art history at the Courtauld, which I completed in 1994 (and during which I worked part-time at Sothebys). I then chose to work at the Plastics Injection Moulding factory, although Simon had already established himself there. That was very difficult at first as I had no defined role and I sensed he felt I was an upstart, and artistic to boot!... even worse! (he had studied business studies and accountancy). Those were troubled times for the first few months and I had to resolve what I was searching for at the company. I realised it was partly a need to prove to myself and my parents that I could succeed at this line of work, and that I had always fought shy of working there because of my own fear of failure/rejection.

Five years later Simon and I are good business associates and can rely on the other for back up and sound business sense. We each have a role to play in the company, but I am very fortunate in being able to work for a family run small business that allows a fluidity. My role is never restrictive, instead it is self-defined for Simon and myself. Having said that I do still appear to be a rare breed in the manufacturing industry and, of course, none of this could have happened without the full support of my father who part owns the company. 'Whoever' & Sons is common place but 'whoever' & daughter(s) is looked on as a curio.

Many people are surprised to find a 30-year-old female in such a position, and often ask questions that they would not dream of asking Simon, who is the same age as myself and of equal 'rank'. The most common question is 'how did I come to work at the factory?' Sometimes I do confide that the business is family run, and then a light of understanding appears to flood their eyes and they nod sagely as if the mystery is revealed. However if I give no other explanation than I was simply chosen at interview, they often go away perplexed and confused, especially if they learn of my arts background... something is awry they think! I have even had one man ask when I was thinking of giving it all up, getting married and settling down with kids. I didn't get cross with him, (at least outwardly,) but calmly replied that marriage and children may be on the agenda one day, but I wouldn't necessarily give up the job. After that I then felt at liberty to ask him if he had given up his job after having children! His reply was no, and the conversation went on from there. We get on fairly well now, although I think him rather naive... to have said what probably many other reps only wondered.

The difficulty is this need to go through the whole process with each new sales rep. Perhaps I should get a c.v. printed to ease their curiosity!... I must be a great rarity in the small company manufacturing community.

Another difficulty is that I do feel the need to side step the issue of role and my presence in the company. I dare not let myself be pigeon holed in case that becomes the accepted norm, when in fact there is no accepted norm. I am often wary of doing or saying something that could be seen as reverting to female 'type'. Perhaps I am too guarded, but I want to be accepted as a female doing a good job in the manufacturing industry, not type cast as a good or bad role model.

The challenge of being a female at work is if you have children. Many of our female workers are called away from work by school if children are poorly, or have to stay at home when the children are unwell. Perhaps it is lack of infrastructure in the family, no grandparents or siblings nearby that could ease the burden?

I am 30 and as a working woman must think seriously if I want children and a career. The answer is yes and I hope to continue working at the family firm and have children. My father still works at the firm but is semi-retired, however my mother, Sonia is working very hard, with several major exhibitions planned. I do not want to encumber them with my children while I work, or miss out on looking after my children. I am lucky enough to be in a job where my role is partly self-defined and I have the support of my partner and my parents, however I must not let the company or my colleague Simon down, similarly I don't want to let myself, or my partner, or my future child, or my parents down... does this mean something has to give? Or can I define another role that encompasses all these and probably more? Only time will tell.

Prue Leith OBE
Business Executive, Food Expert, Writer

Prue was born in Capetown in 1940. She was educated in Haywards Heath, Sussex; St Mary's Johannesburg; Cape Town University; the Sorbonne, Paris; Condon Bleu, London. Prue is married with an adult son and daughter.

*Prue has had a very full professional life. In 1960 Prue started a small business supplying lunches for director's dining rooms, which grew rapidly into Leith's Good Food Ltd with contracts for such prestigious venues at the Queen Elizabeth ll Conference Centre in Westminster, the Edinburgh International Conference Centre, banks and large corporations. She has been a Non-Executive Board Member of a number of companies including the Argyll Group plc, Halifax plc and Whitbread plc to name a few. She has been a cookery correspndent, a TV presenter, and an author, including, cookery books and most recently a novel (*Leaving Patrick, *1999). She has chaired many notable bodies including the Royal Society of Arts, Manufactures and Commerce (RSA) 1995–1997. Her accomplishments and achievements are too numerous to list including many honorary awards, fellowships and degrees. Prue won the Veuve Clicquot Business Woman of the Year award in 1990 and was appointed Deputy Lieutenant of Greater London in 1998.*

I came into the world of good food after considering other career choices. My mother was an actress so drama held a certain attraction. I was at University in Cape Town but never completed. I went to Europe instead. Living in Paris I became more interested in food. It was at that time a working au pair that was a great cook inspired me. My father had a huge influence on me and I must admit I am a little sad he never saw what we were able to achieve. He died when I was only 21. He was Director of the African Explosive Corporation and had got to the top of his tree by the age of 54. Although he was exemplary in his business life I must say work was not that important to him. Family was the most important thing in his life especially his relationship with my mother. He was a very straight man with very clear values. I think he would have been proud of what we have been able to achieve.

I have found my life and career to be very satisfying. If I was asked which aspect of my professional career was most rewarding I would have to say it varies depending on which time of my life I consider. Obviously opening my first restaurant was hugely satisfying. I loved driving by at night and seeing the buzz and lights. I enjoyed the tendering process in the catering world. I am highly competitive by nature so preparing a good pitch and winning the contract was satisfying. Latterly my passion has been promoting good education in its widest sense. Education is not about learning facts and figures for an exam only to be forgotten as quickly as possible. It is about learning skills for life, transferable skills and competencies, which can be demonstrated. Communication skills, team-working and problem-solving are all key skills which education should be addressing. Personally I have also enjoyed chairing the RSA. For me it is a 'think and do' tank. There are tangible outcomes and benefits.

My greatest achievement I guess has been having the luck to keep all the balls I am juggling in the air at one time and having the great privilege of being happy. I feel relationships are one of the most important aspects of life. I guess I learnt that from my parents. I have enjoyed my life with my husband and children. I enjoy spending time with them. I was very keen my children should complete university, as I hadn't. It wasn't so much wanting them to get a certain grade but wanting them to apply themselves to the course of study and complete it. I promised them both if they did they could choose any travel experience as a reward, the down side being that they would have to take Mum. My son, Daniel, and I went to Hong Kong for the handover and had a wonderful time. My daughter, Li-Da, is taking me to Argentina, which should be equally exciting. The key for me though is having the opportunity to spend time together with each of them on a one-to-one basis.

Probably the most distressing business experience I ever faced was taking on the catering contract at Hyde Park. It seemed such a good idea but it went so terribly wrong. We lost a great deal of money. It represented three horrible years. Things were constantly going wrong, everything from relations with the park authority, to geese landing on tables and vandals throwing the tables into the serpentine. When the weather was bad no one came but when the weather was good you could have thousands angry because they couldn't get a table.

Another traumatic experience in my life was selling the business, it happened in two phases, the first in 1993 when I sold the catering business, the conference arm and the cookery school. I kept the restaurant because I felt if I had no business to run I would suffer from withdrawal symptoms but by 1995 I did sell it to my business partner and friend Caroline Waldegrave. Passing on what I had worked so hard to achieve was a huge wrench but it was made easier though by the fact I was selling to friends. I have been touched over the years that in business I have managed to have good relationships even at times in difficult circumstances. We have a regular dinner of 'Leith's Old Soldiers' where all my old managers and I meet. These relationships have been important for all of us.

One quality, which has helped me to achieve success, has been the ability to find good people and delegate responsibility to them. It is important to hire people who are better than you are and not to feel threatened by them. You do need to keep control and know exactly what is going on but staff need the freedom to grow, to solve problems and to surpise you. It is important to be fair, to be honest and to be up front. I feel it is vital to be part of the solution not just the person who finds or creates the problem. For me it was important to develop family-friendly working policies so I was able to keep the best staff. Flexibility and good maternity leave arrangements at work is important. Companies need to concentrate on what is essential. Companies need to concentrate not only on client's needs but staff needs. Companies are organic living creations. If all the company stakeholders, including staff, are not content the company will become unhealthy. We need to think laterally, to take controlled risks, to motivate and encourage. By doing these things I think we will become more successful.

It is important to me to plan for the future to have a life strategy. I am at a stage of life now where I want to concentrate my time and efforts on what I feel is important. I have begun to weed out the activities, which although they may be laudable do not necessarily need me at this stage. I have enjoyed writing the novel. I want to be an even better novelist. I am aware that life has a limited span and I want to concentrate my time on key pieces of work and on the relationships, which are of vital importance to me.

The late Elizabeth Longford MA
Wife, Mother, Civil Rights Activist

Lady Longford was 93 years of age at the time of writing this contribution. She has seen a period of tremendous social and political reform and has been very much at the centre of the debates. She felt that her views on 'Women at Work' have changed somewhat since she first made speeches on the subject as a young Labour Candidate in the early 1930s. She was a writer and the mother of eight children.

I think I can safely say I grew up with very little consciousness of prejudices against women. The eldest of five, two girls and three boys, I idolised my next brother, regarding him and myself as way above all my other siblings, of whichever sex. I had known about the Suffragettes and Mrs Pankhurst since our nurse shook her fist at a burnt-out red letterbox in Regents Park. 'That woman did it!' No mention of the reason why. But our parents told us afterwards.

I was born in 1906, my mother was a qualified doctor, though she never practised after marriage. My father, at least in theory, believed in equality of education for the sexes, but could not forget that he had taken his first at Cambridge, and it was to Cambridge his three sons must go. Oxford was good enough for girls – and my sister and I went to Oxford.

Oxford was going through a transitional period in my day. We still enjoyed the blessed privacies of 'women only' colleges. I was permitted to spend the day in mixed company without chaperonage, but would return to my essay secure in the knowledge that there would be no interruption. Unlike my eldest daughter, who was to come up when women's colleges admitted male visitors, so that she could not even wash her hair without someone bursting in. Nevertheless all colleges eventually had to become fully mixed, before there could be a reasonable chance of equal work opportunities afterwards. In my day, a vast majority of us women intended to be schoolteachers. My own secret aim was archaeological research, then virtually a male preserve. Luckily for me, my future husband directed my imagination on to the burning question of education for deprived women and men – through the Workers Educational Association (WEA).

The profiles

Here in this admirable institution for adult education there were no traces whatever of old fashioned sexual prejudice. We took it for granted that if a woman wanted to be an electrical engineer of minister of religion and was adequately qualified, then technician or church leader she should be. But for most of us women the battle had shifted on to other ground. Not what a woman worked at but what conditions she worked was the question of the day. I well remember the sad affliction of one of my brightest WEA pupils. She was a painter in one of the pottery companies of North Staffordshire. The companies liked to have women to paint their exquisite china because of their artistic gifts and delicate touch. But my friend, like many of her colleagues had contracted a horrible skin disease from the paint on her hand. Her all too philosophical attitude augured ill for recovery, and I felt from then on that conditions in women's work were even more important that its equal availability to women and men.

This linked all women together, whether they were working at the paint-pot in a factory or over the stew pot at home. Conditions among women out at work and women working at home as mothers were often equally appalling in the potteries before the war. When I came to be adopted as the Labour candidate for Kings Norton, one of the Birmingham parliamentary seats, I hardly mentioned the traditional battles of the sexes, though valiant old ladies would protest now and then that the sex war was only half won. Apart from the slogan of 'Equal Pay for Equal Work', my campaigns were on behalf of the workers as a whole at the bottom of the pile. My main demand being for the outrageous luxury of 'one weeks' paid holiday a year. All workers would benefit, but mothers who went out to work most of all.

After the war, with eight young children, I transferred from active politics to journalism. My subjects were chiefly family and social affairs. This was when 'Women at Work' again came in. I evolved a slogan, which has focused my social thinking for the rest of my life. 'A Full Life and a Family Life'. That is the dual ideal. Women must be able to have both. Woman's dual nature, as mother and career-worker, should both be capable of satisfaction. Like all slogans, mine has to use language somewhat crudely, in order to obey the twin laws of brevity and emphasis. Why a 'full' life? By 'full' I mean a woman's need to all their individual gifts, special capabilities, and even oddities, beside the recognised feminine talents for child-raising and home-making.

An example of a modern woman who leads a full life is my brilliant niece Harriet Harman MP, daughter of my eldest brother already mentioned, and whose mother is a solicitor. Harriet has found a solution to the problems of combining her parliamentary life with the demands of three children and an active husband. She has written a book whose title immediately gives away her solution: *Twenty-First Century Man*. Man is the answer. In the new Millennium mothers and fathers will share equally in running the house, raising the children and going out to work. No more of Mum's coming home dead-beat from the office to refresh herself by hoovering the carpet, mopping the lino and cooking the supper; while Dad, whose feet are killing him, rests on the bed.

The slogan is to be 'Share and share alike'. The mop is no longer purely a female weapon any more than the website is a purely male one. When I put this new future for the twenty-first century man to some young peers in the House of Lords, they replied with one voice. We're doing it already! Of course this solution does not rule out the traditional stand-ins; nannies, aunties and grannies when available. Nevertheless Harriet's idea will probably not be generally adopted in the near future.

Meanwhile, long before Harriet was writing, my own slogan about a full life and a family life was suddenly called in question by implication. John Bowlby, a distinguished psychiatrist and friend of ours, wrote a seminal book about mother love in the early stages of a child's life. All crimes, all failures he discovered could be traced to a critical deprivation of mother love. So women at work, listen! Come back to your homes! Let your full life be full of nothing but family for those first few years, admittedly Bowlby was brought round in the end to the use of mother substitutes when necessary. But his book had been a shock.

Today I have come to realise, reluctantly, that another factor tends to make the slogan, 'A Full Life and a Family Life', less than obvious. Some professions and forms of work are more suited to combination with family life than others. The suitable ones usually include authorship, the arts, journalism, medicine, the law, farming and with some reservations the media. Some of these professionals can generally work at home. But if you are inspired to do social rescue work in Kosovo or Sarajevo for weeks on end there are difficulties. I myself worked entirely from home with occasional breaks for research abroad or in the British archives. None of my daughters – all of them writers, too, of one kind or another – went to work outside the home.

My final conclusion goes somewhat against the grain. I would certainly have rejected it 30 years ago. It is that on the whole it is better for women to choose professions compatible with family life. Thirty years ago a 'full life' meant everything and just as there were no boundaries to the 'march of a nation', so there were no boundaries to the march of a sex. I hate to set limits to women's aspirations even now, any more than to men's, yet in the end happiness probably depends as much on selection and rejection as it does on limitless freedom.

Virginia McKenna
Wildlife Conservationist – Actress

Virginia McKenna was born in England. After spending the war years in South Africa she returned to England to lay the foundations for her acting career at the Central School of Speech and Drama.

Her first professional engagement was at the Dundee Repertory Theatre in 1949 and six months later she appeared in A Penny for a Song *at the Haymarket Theatre, London. A season with the Old Vic, television, films and theatre occupied the years that followed.*

Classics such as The Cruel Sea, Carve her Name with Pride *and* A Town like Alice, *for which she won a British Academy Award for Best Actress have been highlights in a long and successful career, as was her role as Mrs Anna in* The King and I, *for which she received the SWST Award, opposite Yul Bynner. She is perhaps best remembered and best loved for her roles in* Born Free *and* Ring of Bright Water *starring opposite actor husband Bill Travers. For* Born Free *she won The Variety Club Best Actress Award.*

These films marked a turning point in Virginia's life. The dedication, which had given her such a varied and interesting career, found a new path in her passionate concern for animals and the environment.

In 1984, she co-founded Zoo Check with her husband and eldest son, William, a charitable trust dedicated to preventing the suffering of captive wild animals and striving to protect and conserve them in the wild. Zoo Check grew to become a major force in the animal welfare movement. The organisation was renamed The Born Free Foundation in 1991 and Zoo Check became one of its projects together with Elefriends, Big Cat, Orca, Wolf, Primate and UK Wildlife campaigns.

Whilst she still finds time to work occasionally as an actress, her leading role is now within the conservation movement. In addition to her work on behalf of wild animals Virginia is also committed to human charities like Children of the Andes, raising funds to rescue, look after and educate the sewer and street children of Bogata in Columbia.

I can honestly say that, in the whole of my life, I have never been bored. Whatever I do, and that continues to embrace a huge variety of activities, I never cease to enjoy the challenges, excitements and sometimes, over the past years, the office disciplines, which are a necessary part of working in an organisation.

Work has never seemed just that and I realise more and more how lucky I am to feel this. Although the acting profession was not my first choice, (I had wished to go to university to read English but did not have the requisite Latin), I was fortunate to be accepted by the Central School of Speech and Drama. So, on leaving school at 17, I enrolled, combining acting with an academic Diploma Course, which fulfilled the more studious side of my nature.

Perhaps my career as an actress, portraying a never-ending assortment of characters, coping with failures as well as successes, learning to work with a diversity of people in both welcoming and indifferent environments, prepared me for the other 'work-hats' I was to don in later years. It taught me to be adaptable and flexible – and yet to be true to myself. For, whatever road one follows, I believe that is one of the most important tenets to hold fast. Not being an ambitious person, I never yearned for international stardom and, indeed, refused several opportunities to work in America, as it would have meant leaving my family. The job in hand was what I cared about, and that has never changed – including cooking a meal or working in the garden!

Some people would find the uncertainty and unpredictability of an actor's life hard to handle. Weeks or months of 'resting', waiting for your agent to phone. Yes, it is difficult. I remember one year when I hadn't worked for about eight months and I felt my brain was atrophying. So, I decided to ring an actress friend Elizabeth Counsell, a talented musician and composer and ask her if she felt like 'putting something together'. Poems, songs, readings. By lucky chance she was free too and we devised a programme which we then managed to perform in several venues. I think that was the moment when I realised one could be pro-active in life. *The Lily and the Tiger*, our little show, was my first step along a path I would follow increasingly as time passed. Pick up your suitcase and travel, take up a cause and spread it abroad. Be courageous. Not easy for actors who generally conceal much of themselves behind the parts they play.

From 1949, starting with a wonderful 6 months at the Dundee Rep., until 1964, I led a full and deeply satisfying life, both in my career and personally. I married Bill Travers in 1957, worked with him in theatre and films several times and then, in 1964, we were both invited to take part in the film of Joy Adamson's extraordinary book *Born Free*. What made the producers ask us? What inner voice, simultaneously in both of us, led us to accept? Whatever the reason it was our destiny as that decision, that film, that experience marked the beginning of the rest of our lives.

Two actors – ignorant of lion-matters, wildlife issues, life in the bush, acting with wild animals – were plunged into ten and a half months of learning by trial and error, how to understand and deal with all of these.

The *Born Free* experience wrote its story in a very particular way on our hearts and minds and almost immediately after we returned home Bill made the first of his wildlife documentary films *The Lions Are Free*. His new career had begun.

Mine started to branch out in different directions as well. Participating in his films when it was appropriate, narrating, writing a little – but never completely giving up my work as an actress.

Nevertheless, our rapidly growing interest in wildlife made us thirsty students of animal issues and our exposure to the nature and behaviour of lions during our stay in Kenya endorsed our already existing concerns for the welfare of wild animals in captivity.

It was the death of a young elephant at London Zoo (one we had worked with in a film in Kenya and gifted by the Government of Kenya to the Zoo in 1968) that truly launched us into the work which subsequently dominated our lives. In 1984, together with our eldest son Will, we founded Zoo Check (now called the Born Free Foundation). Primarily to investigate conditions in zoos; to reveal the inadequacies of many and, in certain cases, the truly shocking circumstances in which thousands of animals are incarcerated for our so called pleasure and education.

It is true to say that actors never retire. Even when one can't remember the lines one can still read them on the radio! And I suggest that this refusal to give up applies also to anyone who has a cause, a purpose, and a crusade – if that's not too strong a word.

Bill worked tirelessly for the cause he believed in until his death in 1994. His purpose, he passionately believed, was to show on film and in photography, the wasted, sad lives so many captive animals endure and, by telling their story, to try and influence the crowds who visited zoos for 'a good day out'. I believe, as a pioneer, he was successful; he was indeed an extraordinary communicator, and the work we continue to do at the Born Free Foundation is building on the foundation stones he so graphically laid down.

I am a great believer in natural timing. Things and people evolve, and now wildlife matters occupy my life virtually full-time. I travel a great deal; I see many beautiful places; I see many heartbreaking sights; I meet people I respect and others I could never call a friend; I rejoice when we manage to give an animal a better quality of life; I am desolate when we fail.

If I flip through the pages of the picture book of my mind I see the stages at the Old Vic and the Palladium, the film sets of *A Town Like Alice*, *Carve Her Name With Pride*, the location of *Born Free* and *Ring of Bright Water* – as vibrant and fascinating now as all those years ago. But they are years ago and the later pages of my book are a kaleidoscope of the open plains of Africa, the barred cages of lions, the forests of India, the chains of elephants, the white baby seals on the ice, performing seals in the dolphinarium. There are still some empty pages and I hope to fill those too – although I have to say that the pages that will fall open first will be of my greatly loved family, whose kindness and patience provided a constant cornerstone of encouragement, humour and affection in both the difficult and the happy times of which most lives are made.

Fulfilment is a very personal thing and, I suppose, depends on ones expectations. I have found it in the light of an African dawn, the hand of a friend, the love of my family, the eyes of a rescued animal, a walk in the wood in winter, beautiful music. It just needs an open heart and an open mind. In a world with so much to see and wonder at and try to understand, how can one ever be bored?

Sally Magnusson
Television Journalist and Writer

Sally was born and brought up near Glasgow in Scotland. After starting as a reporter on the Scotsman, *she later moved to London and to television journalism presenting BBC* Breakfast News *among other programmes. Since her return to Scotland, she has anchored the BBC's* Reporting Scotland, *and is a busy writer, broadcaster and author. Her books include* The Flying Scotsman *1981,* Clemo-A Love Story *1986,* A Shout in the Street *1991 and* Family Life *1999.*

Sally is the mother of five children. She says, 'One of the hazards of bringing up five children while carrying on a career in broadcasting and writing is that there are simply not enough hours in the day for all the interesting invitations that come your way – not least this one.' Sally didn't have time to write an original contribution, but was happy to give us permission to reproduce a chapter from her 1999 book, Family Life.

Some time ago, mother-of-five Nicola Horlick sensationally resigned from her high powered job in a merchant bank and entertained us vastly for a few days. The newspapers were quick to dub her Superwoman, although since she has been struggling for years with a desperately sick child along with everything else, I suspect her life is less dauntingly efficient than it appears and she would probably be the last to call herself a superwoman.

For the fact is, nobody with a secretary to answer phones and letters, two domestic helpers a day to cook, clean, wash clothes and iron and a full-time nanny for the children needs many specialised skills beyond being good at her job, a flair for organising staff and the ability to sink into her chair at the end of the day and say 'Come to Mummy, darlings.'

It is a fallacy that the more children and the more demanding the job, the more of a superwoman the mother must be to manage it all. The truth is once you start paying someone else to do everything except actually have the babies, it's not very difficult at all.

I know plenty of real superwomen. They're the ones who spend two hours trailing a wailing toddler and a fractious three-year-old all the way to the supermarket and back for one item they forgot when they did the same thing yesterday, and who do it without losing their temper.

They're the ones who teach other people's children all day, then go home to make the tea, mark the jotters, supervise their own children's homework, turn out for the football club, put the kids to bed and prepare for tomorrow's class.

They're the ones who run up a costume for the school concert with one child on their knee, another under their feet and a husband asking why nobody has fed the dog.

They're the ones who would like nothing better once in a while than to get up in the morning, bid a cheerful goodbye to the children as they breakfast with the nanny and head off to do a spot of investment fund managing. Stress? You tell me anything as stressful as trying to get a howling two-year-old into his coat while ordering another for the fifth time to brush his teeth, and another to try looking for his shoe down the toilet because that's where the baby put it last time.

I do have some help these days, and while my doughty au pair is not exactly staff on the Nicola Horlick scale, that support makes all the difference. It is the sheerest luxury to be sitting here toying with this word or that on the computer while she shivers her way around the garden, enthusing manfully over every blade of grass, every minuscule puddle that the toddler see fit to inspect.

Since I find it infinitely easier to present television programmes than manage the ironing competently, I'm lucky to be able to do the one to avoid the other. So when people hear how many children I have, reel back in some sort of horrified admiration and stutter, 'But how on earth do you manage everything?', the answer is actually quite simple. I don't.

The hardest times were when I had fewer children and no help. I have never known days which felt so long as in the months after my first child was born. Having embarked on motherhood with the quaint notion that babies spent most of their time sleeping and the rest gurgling contentedly while you whisked round with the Hoover and then got down to a good book, the birth of a child who simply cried unless he was being nursed, carried or shoogled was a terrible shock.

I used to bump him round the village in his pram for hours on end, day after day. I knew every gravestone in the churchyard off by heart; the big decision of the morning would be whether to go round the path clockwise or anti-clockwise. We visited ducks the baby was not remotely interested in. We wandered past the village hall and I wondered how old he would have to be for us to qualify for the mother and toddler group, the acme of my social aspiration.

OK, so I was no superwoman in the Nicola Horlick sense, but I do know that these early months and years dug into reserves of patience, stamina and imagination that I never had to tap before.

It was easier when the second one came along, because I knew what I was doing and at least had a two-year-old for company. But I still contend that no investment manager in the hurly-burly of a stimulating job has it remotely as tough as the mother of two grizzly under-threes facing the long hours between lunch and teatime. What will it be today? You ask yourself after clearing up the devastated table and wiping Heinz apricot dessert off the wall. Swing-park? Shops? Phone up a friend and hope she invites you to visit? Go for a drive on some pretext you can figure out later?

The friend's not in, a drive will send the children to sleep at the wrong end of the day, you can't think of a single thing you need at the shops, so you choose the swings. Getting them ready to go out takes half an hour, a couple of tantrums and a dirty nappy – which means you have to start all over again just when you've finally zipped the snow-suit up and enticed the gloves on with the help of a biscuit that's now plastered all over his face. It uses up your entire stock of patience, which has never been large.

You push them the half-mile to the swing-park in the double buggy – and there should be a superwoman award for this achievement alone – straining a muscle in your arm as you try to control the side that's got the thumping great two-year-old in it to stop all three of you careering into the gutter. And at the park you nearly pull a muscle in the other arm, trying to push two swings at the same time.

And then you look at them, squealing with delight, their faces ruddy and their eyes bright, and you think there is nowhere else in the world you would rather be, and its worth it, and you don't care that the biggest decision you make today is whether to have eggy soldiers or Dairylea sandwiches for tea. This is it. This is life.

And that was, indeed, a very special time. The current toddler has scarcely seen a swing-park and it's a loss for us both. But make no mistake. Those were the days when superwomanly qualities were required by the sackload. But no one ever said then, 'How do you do it?'

Jane Manning OBE D UNIV FRAM FRCM GRSM LRAM ARCM
International Soprano Singer, Lecturer and Teacher specialising in Contemporary, Classical, Music

Jane is now in her 36th year of singing professionally and still enjoys an active international career, appearing mainly in London and abroad. Her work is mainly (although not exclusively) in the field of new music, and she continues to work closely with composers. Her tally of premieres is approaching 400. Jane has an ensemble of young musicians, Jane's Minstrels *which she formed in 1988, and is still going strong.*

Jane gives private lessons intermittently, mostly to students from abroad who come to her for a specific period. She is currently a Visiting Professor at the Royal College of Music, which involves her in giving a Master Class once a term and an Honorary Professor at the University of Keele, visiting twice a year to give classes and demonstrations.

Jane enjoys academic visits, and short residencies have long been a favourite part of her work. She frequently visits campuses here and abroad (especially the USA) to give lectures, workshops, and master classes for composers as well as singers.

Jane has had two books published: New Vocal Repertory – An Introduction *(Macmillan 1986 – re-issued as a Clarendon paperback by OUP, 1994) and* New Vocal Repertory 2 *(OUP 1997). She is also author of the chapter on Song Cycles in* A Messiaen Companion *(Faber & Faber, 1994)*

Jane is also involved in Committee work and is; a Vice-President of the Society for the Promotion of New Music, Chairman of the Nettlefold Festival Trust, and a Member of the Executive Committee of the Musicians' Benevolent Fund.

I took up my present career largely on impulse! Weary and alienated by the pressures of school (Norwich High School GPDST) although successful academically, I sought refuge in music lessons. From a non-academic background, I envisaged university as an even more tedious extension of schooldays with the constant strain of examinations. Against the school's' advice, but, luckily, supported by my family, to whom music , especially singing had a special glamour – (many family members sang in G & S, oratorio and Cathedral music locally, and I had recently made my debut as a soloist), I rejected the idea of university in favour of a Music College. The fact that this did not go down well with my teachers added to its appeal! My voice was still very immature, and I hadn't sung much in school, being the school's leading pianist, and having to play for the school choir. I was accepted at the Royal Academy of Music (RAM) (I am certain I would not have passed the audition, had the Panel not discovered, at the eleventh hour, that I possessed absolute pitch). After four decent but undistinguished years at the RAM (where I'm remembered more for my high marks in Aural Training than for my singing) I spent three rewarding years teaching music in a mixed secondary modern school back in Norfolk, and conducting my own choral society as well as singing as an oratorio soloist locally. Each summer I attended Dartington Summer School, where several people urged me to develop my singing further, and I was introduced to the world of new music. In summer 1963 I was befriended by a group of singers who were studying at a small private international singing school in Ticino, Switzerland, with the renowned German Professor Frederick Husler. They told me of their idyllic life there, and the opportunity for intensive vocal work daily. I experienced a 'blinding flash' and the way ahead seemed incredibly clear. On the spot I decided to give up my 'safe' teaching job and become a student of Husler's, and this I did, for the whole of 1964, supported by a Grant from Norfolk Education Committee, my ex-employers. I still recall the horror of my parents at my sudden decision – I had no experience of travelling abroad and had never met Prof. Husler, who accepted me on recommendation. I never had a moment's doubt about the step I was taking, despite tearful farewells at the school where I had taught so happily.

My voice developed very fast in these perfect conditions – to be a student again after having earned my living was a particular privilege, and I learned to speak German and Italian in addition to acting as coach for other singers, expanding my knowledge of the operatic and lieder repertoire. After that I moved to London to throw in my lot with the other young professional singers. I made my London recital debut in the Easter holiday of 1964, and that and the Dartington contacts led to more engagements, and I was able to support myself by session singing in professional choirs, until solo work began to predominate.

The most rewarding and constantly fascinating part of my work has been collaborating with composers, especially those that are young or unknown. There are a never-ending variety of new styles, ideas, challenges and experiences. The performer feels genuinely useful, in being able to contribute to the future of music and even have some influence on the creative process. Less-known composers are dependent on sympathetic performers. A bad first performance could give an erroneous impression and mitigate against further hearings. I have always found this responsibility both stimulating and calming – an antidote to stage nerves. There is less opportunity to be self-centred, and one feels needed by someone specific, often present on the occasion. Unusually for a singer, I find that most of my close friends are composers and instrumentalists rather than other singers, although in my occasional forays into the opera world, I have enjoyed the camaraderie backstage (but not some of the competitive rivalries and, worst of all, the political/sexual manoeuvres often lurking in opera companies.) The other great joy in my working life is my young ensemble Jane's Minstrels. Most of the founder members are still with me, and it's a rare pleasure to work alongside soul mates. Since I picked each member individually for their personal as well as their musical qualities, my choice has been most happily vindicated, and the special warmth and cohesiveness of the group is always remarked upon, inevitably enhancing the musical results, of which I am very proud.

By far the most aggravating aspect of a freelancer's life is the phenomenal increase in the amount of unpaid paperwork and administration one has to do, much of it totally unnecessary, mainly to give work to the ever-expanding numbers of salaried management personnel, whose jobs depend upon what we, the practitioners, do. This transference of power from those who make the music to those who administer it has gathered pace over the last ten years, and one is now required to keep to a nine-to-five working week, with only evenings and weekends left free to practise our profession, once those administrators who take so much of our time have left their offices. One has only to glance at the front of an opera or orchestral concert programme, to see that the number of managerial staff often runs close to the number of artists appearing during a whole season. In addition, one is often judged on the quality of one's publicity material than on one's attainments, and this leads to a deplorable lack of discrimination, since some of those now 'in power' have little experience or judgement.

Many people influenced me in my early life and their memory continues to inspire me. One was my Aunt Flora Manning, at one time my primary school headmistress. The family 'intellectual' she had an independent, lively mind and was fiercely idealistic and prepared to argue her case. She died before my career burgeoned and I know how much she would have enjoyed supporting me as she did everyone. Her moral uprightness was a great example. I also had a godmother, known as Auntie May, who was not a relative, but my mother's school friend. She had the wonderful gift of simple goodness and humility, and I think she would be genuinely astonished if she knew how much I cherish her unfailing sweetness of nature in the face of provocation. My paternal grandfather J. J. Manning was an amazing character, flamboyant and egocentric. He sang as a baritone and was a member of Norwich Cathedral choir from the age of 8 to 80! I only knew him when elderly but he was enormous fun. When at the Academy a fellow lodger and Academy student, Peter Stevens, shamed me into a belated love of learning and fine arts, especially poetry. My husband Anthony Payne has of course had a great influence on my general attitudes – his generosity of spirit tempers my tendency to be hyper-critical, and his comprehensive knowledge and enthusiasm for literature, poetry and art have been a great boon.

While still at school my sympathetic music teacher, Barbara Coyle, played me a record of Dietrich Fischer-Dieskau singing lieder, and from that moment he became my ideal singer. His meticulous attention to detail and articulation, and the incredible variety of nuance, shading and colour in his voice inspired me. Its wide range and beautiful quality seemed awesome, and he became the yardstick by which I judged others. Some time after that I heard Janet Baker in a recital in Norwich, which included Schumann's *Frauenliebe und Leben,* and I found her commitment and deep spirituality most moving, as well as her technical command and palette of colours and dynamics. Clever imitators of these influential figures have appeared, but none has for me come anywhere near their profundity and idealism as artists. I resolved to emulate them as far as I was able, and strove at least to vary my voice according to the style and language of the music. These days, perhaps influenced by the record industry, there seems to be a vogue for artists who make just one unvarying sound, and I don't find this very satisfying. My husband's wisdom and unrivalled knowledge of the repertoire has been of enormous benefit of course. I might otherwise have become entrenched in the world of vocal music only.

Humour has been a part of my career, once, when I was giving a recital in California, a large Alsatian dog mounted the platform, ran along behind me and exited through the stage door! Another time in Australia, on a very hot day, I was giving a lunchtime recital in a university chapel. The doors were open and a fly became attracted by my stickiness. It buzzed close to my face, occasionally landing. The audience were becoming distracted by my having to flick it away. Finally, during a particularly rapt passage, it settled on my upper lip. Fearing to break the atmosphere I let it remain there until, needing a sharp, deep breath for a strenuous phrase, I sucked it into my mouth, swallowed and sang on! The audience watched in horrified fascination!

I've occasionally had to deal with supreme tactlessness from agents and opera companies whom I feel misjudged my work woefully, often from an ageist and chauvinist perspective. When young and inexperienced I was crushed and dispirited, but there came a time when I received a particularly hurtful and dismissive letter from an opera company, when already well-established and receiving excellent notices for my concerts and recordings. I took my courage in my hands and wrote back attacking them for their insensitivity and said I wouldn't wish to work with anyone so lacking in judgement or humanity, and I felt that I stood up on behalf of so many singers who are treated in this patronising way and dare not answer back. Luckily I had a full diary and a large network of eager employers to fortify me against this kind of nonsense, and I regarded the whole episode (they had asked me to audition) as a complete waste of my valuable time. I never regretted writing the letter, even if it made me unpopular in places where power politics count. I received quite an abject apology, but learned the lesson that working with people who don't understand you is a soul-destroying waste of energy. I have often suffered (as in this case so I believe) from being labelled 'clever', being able to cope with difficult contemporary music, and this singles one out for special punishment, especially from insecure male conductors who prefer their sopranos to need help and play up to them!

On a more light-hearted note, I was singing under Pierre Boulez in one of his own works at the Festival Hall – the concert was being broadcast live. Suddenly, one of his conducting gestures inadvertently swept a central portion of the score to the floor by my feet, right in the middle of a passage when I was desperately counting beats in order not to lose the place. In what seemed like a long time, but was only a few seconds, I gathered it up in a heap and flung it back onto his music stand, thereby losing my place, and hoping I'd be able to re-enter correctly. All was well, thankfully, and I'd saved the performance.

Personally, privacy has always meant a great deal to me. I never had it as a child or young adult. I spent much time at home, my every movement monitored by caring parents, especially my mother, whose relationship with her own mother had been exceptionally close. I was expected to conform and never really did. I suppose it was inevitable that I should end up in a profession where eccentricity is the norm, and I always felt more comfortable with individuals who were a little out of the ordinary. At school, I was deemed to be so lacking in public-spiritedness that I was never made even a sub-prefect – the only person in my form to be overlooked. I was a late developer and now realise this to be an advantage. To be allowed to be myself was quite a battle, but when I spread my wings and went to Switzerland, I discovered that I could function very well in the world at large, and that unnatural regimes such as school or college are not the real thing! My freedom was hard-won but I treasure it.

One of my most challenging tasks, early in my career, was to cope with the demands of Schoenberg's masterpiece *Pierrot Lunaire*. I had to evolve my own version of 'Sprech-stimme' (half-singing, half-speaking) at a time when there were no satisfactory recordings and hardly any performances to guide me. Even now, no conventional singing teacher will help with this work. Its musical and dramatic difficulties are also immense – the rhythmic and ensemble problems alone require tremendous concentration. I have now performed it over a 100 times with more than 20 ensembles world-wide and still find it exciting and stimulating. More recently I gave six consecutive staged performances of Peter Maxwell Davies's solo monodrama *The Medium*, lasting 50 minutes – a great test of stamina apart from anything else.

I suppose I'm thankful that I seem to be reasonably adaptable to circumstances, and am now ready to accept the limitations of growing older. Ageism is rife in attitudes to female performers, and I am now finding this. I've always believed that if one door shuts, another will open, and this has been true throughout my career. I think I am fortunate in having been able to recognise key moments for change: for instance when I suddenly decided to form my own ensemble. I am extremely glad that, early in my career, I obeyed the urge to promote the cause of contemporary music, and took the opportunity to collate my thoughts in regular lectures and written articles – this was unusual for a young singer and remains so. Many of today's top artists are merely concerned with accepting engagements as they come in, but not troubling to initiate projects or follow a special interest (or even create new repertoire by commissioning new works)... I believe the relevant terms are 'pro-active' and 're-active'. I've always had a bit of a crusading spirit and don't hesitate to give my opinions! It has become more of a battle to remain a freelance self-employed person in these times of increasing bureaucracy, and far fewer opportunities for work now present themselves. A great many people have opted for security in regular jobs well below their level of attainment, just for economic reasons, and good fees, except for the very few 'star' names, are even harder to come by. I'm grateful to have managed thus far. I've never prized security very highly, believing it to lie within oneself rather than depending on external trappings, and I am happy that 'lifestyle' means virtually nothing to me. I wouldn't want the kind of friends who would be attracted by possessions. Being appreciated for the wrong reasons is very depressing!

I am proud of the fact that I have read all of Proust in French – a task I set myself to atone for a misspent youth reading pulp novels and film magazines. A love of culture came relatively late to me.

I have been very happily married for 33 years to the composer, writer and broadcaster Anthony Payne, after a whirlwind romance of only three months (another happy impulse!). We have no children, a mutual decision. My career blossomed at just the time when a family might have been planned. I'd also had some rather off-putting experiences with badly behaved toddlers! We put off thinking about it until we realised we didn't really wish to change our lives so radically. Although aware I have missed many important experiences, I don't regret this – one can't do everything, and our ensemble of young musicians, Jane's Minstrels are a happy alternative family – with much more in common with us, I think than our own children might have had. So I haven't missed out on close contact with young people. (I was in fact engaged to a local man when I left the Academy, but discovering that my teaching job meant rather more to me than the relationship, broke it off just in time.) I can honestly say that I never experienced the overwhelming maternal urge described by friends, and, despite having many close friends whose children are a joy to them (and whom we also enjoy) I've never wished to change places with them.

For many years I was the main breadwinner during the most lucrative portion of my singing career, and travelled abroad constantly. We both thereby fulfilled our need for privacy. Our marriage works well because we are diametrically opposed temperamentally and have stimulating arguments – no settled 'Darby and Joan' existence, but a volatile combination of two independent spirits, probably regarded as eccentric by our large network of friends. I found out rather late in the day that, after childhood (in our case wartime, which engendered a strong community feeling) family life was not the be-all and end-all, and that not all members of one's family were destined to be soul mates, and very importantly, one should not feel guilty about this. Our friends are special because we chose them freely. I believe firmly in obeying one's instinctive feelings about people. Earlier on, colleagues would gush enthusiastically about some agent or promoter about whom I had 'bad vibes'. I invariably discovered later that my first impression was correct!

Our lives are somewhat chaotic and disorganised, since we are both freelance and self-employed, but it is wonderful to have the freedom to go to our country cottage or go to the cinema (a shared passion, evoking old memories of 'forbidden fruit' in one's teens!) at odd times. I think we are very fortunate to have found each other, and cannot imagine being married to anyone else. I personally found the prospect of spinsterhood rather attractive! Have never cared for small babies, and disliked the idea of the process of motherhood, although I love young people and identify strongly with their need for privacy and dignity. We also find young children very sweet now that we're the grandparent age – I don't think we are a typical childless couple!

Women are still not represented strongly enough in the top-level jobs. Ageism seems to apply much more to women than to men, and this should not be so. Mature women are a great asset in the workplace. For things to change, men have to have more grown-up attitudes to women, and must not exploit or patronise them . The idea of legislation to ensure that top positions are shared equally between men and women seems an impossible dream. If I could wave a wand...

If I could pass on one piece of advice I would advise women not to be their own worst enemies. They should support each other and not play games from the male point of view. I've noticed that the service one gets from other women often leaves a lot to be desired, especially when travelling alone. Female airline staff and waitresses can flirt with male customers, and leave women unattended, and a woman seldom gets an upgrade. And mothers should not spoil their sons... I think that, in addition to flirting, other ways of 'flaunting' femaleness can be counter-productive – I am personally highly suspicious of the motives of some women, who, formerly quite retiring, seem to need to breast-feed in as public a situation as possible, when more discreet alternatives are available, and when those around are not close family or friends!

I believe that things are still quite bad for women in the workplace, especially those trying to bring up families at the same time. Men simply do not do their fair share in running the home and looking after the children. Stereo-typed attitudes still prevail, and equal pay remains a pipe-dream. Hopefully, effective legislation will bring a gradual improvement. Also, the elderly will soon dominate our population as more and more people live to a ripe old age. Since statistics prove that women live longer, it is to be hoped that the wisdom and insight that older women have to offer will at last be properly appreciated. Our youth culture (a phenomenon first noticed when I was a teenager) is now concentrated on younger and younger age groups – children are targeted as prime consumers. I do believe that everything goes in circles and there must be a return to an appreciation of mature adults and a response to their needs – this will now seem a fresh approach! One has only to look at the major films of the '40s and early '50s to see that they pre-supposed a certain level of culture in their viewers and were not geared to teenage tastes. The number of all-male casts in 'action' movies has increased considerably. Women must get in on the media to have more influence, not just as decorative presenters. Men should become used to being secretaries to female managers where appropriate! The fact that 'secretary' conjures up a female image illustrates this point.

I have only one major regret – that I didn't take the opportunity to go to university, and if I had my time again I might do that, but perhaps to study Philosophy and Languages rather than music. However the urge to perform would probably have surfaced. My year in Switzerland was a perfect substitute for university, but a little too brief, although my career has enabled me to travel extensively and I've continued to learn and develop my cultural tastes, aided indispensably by my husband. I would, if time allows, love to take an Open University Degree. Had I remained a teacher, I would have been quite happy – a sense of mission is in-built, and I always felt the need to communicate my enthusiasms and interests to others. My patience rarely runs out. Many family members are or were teachers and I feel it's in my blood.

It was, I think, inevitable that I should gravitate towards the more intellectually-challenging areas of the music profession, since I was aware that a routine round of traditional repertoire. did not engage my brain enough. It is important to retain a zest for new experiences, and I await the next strong impulse. I have strong leanings towards social work...

In conclusion; every time a tenor, good or bad, ends an aria on a high note, a roar of applause ensues, in which male voices predominate – the sound is very similar to that which greets a goal at a football match. I have an uncomfortable feeling that the worship of the tenor voice (unabated since the early days of Radio's Family favourites, which invariably featured either Gigli or Bjorling singing *Nessun Dorma* – nothing changes!) represents a primitive form of male power, even triumphalism. There seems to be no female equivalent.

Barbara Maslin NNEB
Wife, Mother, Nursery Nurse

Barbara is a wife, mother and part-time classroom assistant in a local Primary School. She is active in her local community and church. She has taken the decision to work largely part-time to enable her to be available to her children.

As a working mum, I often feel that my home is being run like a military operation. My evenings, during term-time, take on a routine that if not adhered to can cause chaos the following morning. School uniforms hang expectantly on the back of bedroom chairs. Full lunch boxes, polished shoes, games kit, finished homework, all positioned by the front door, in an endeavour not to be forgotten. For the following morning takes on a life of its own and its every person for themselves.

I launch out the door at 7.45 (on a good day!) leaving my husband Keith and our two children, Ryan, 10 and Antonia nine, to fend for themselves until such time as they leave for school. Even now, after 4 years back at work, I still get that pang of guilt, that perhaps I should stay at home to be the one to take the children to school, or take care of them when they're unwell, a job that is under taken by my parents. I don't have to work for financial reasons, although my money certainly makes things a little easier. Should I feel guilty for working, doing something I enjoy?

I have a job it's not a career. That is one area that I felt I could not follow when I decided to have a family. I felt I needed to compromise. I am not in a unique position, there are plenty of women who do what are sometimes described, and looked upon, as fairly menial work because it fits in with the family. I am sure that employers take advantage of this and the pay is often low. I could work and be paid in a way that reflected my qualification and my experience but positions can be difficult to find when you want to work, and be the main carer of your children. I work in a reception class as a classroom assistant at a small village school. And contrary to belief do more than sharpen pencils and mix paints. Some schools do employ Nursery Nurses, for that is what I trained as, but tend to go for the cheaper option of classroom assistants. But if a more experience person applies then what the heck, they've got the job!

Money aside, I do love my job, 4 year olds are usually so receptive and keen to learn and your hard efforts are often rewarded. It is hard work but life is never dull when you're with young children. A sense of humour is a must.

I've always been a fan of the late Joyce Grenfells. Her monologues always make me laugh no matter how many times I hear them. They are so true even today though they were written 40 years ago. My favourite has to be *The Nursery School Teacher*. The only thing that dates it is some of the names. Just a few weeks ago I even found myself sounding like her when I said to a child 'Isobel, I think you need to wipe your nose. Go and get yourself a tissue.' 'Isobel you still need to go and get a tissue but now to wipe your sleeve!' I found myself having a little chuckle.

Dressing and undressing for PE is often a time of great amusement. And laughing out loud at a child is a definite no no, however funny they appear to look. The child who comes to you for help having manage to force their head through the armhole of their vest mistaking it for the neck and there seams to be no obvious way of prising it out. Lost socks, shoes on the wrong feet and clothes on inside out are a weekly occurrence. The art is in spotting the offending articles and helping to correct it before the child leaves at the end of the day. You don't want the parents to think that they have uncaring teachers! Parents can't always understand why we don't dress their children, after all they do!

Which is usually the problem, and they haven't got 28 of the little darlings!

It has been known for a child to walk out of school at the end of the day wearing their trousers inside out! Pocket linings flapping in the wind and all the teacher and I could do is look on in horror, too late to rectify the error. Everyone looking on in amusement having noticed straight away. How come we didn't? You have to laugh.

At the end of the day I like my family to all eat dinner together. Although I grew up being allowed to eat my dinner in front of a television it is something I have never let my own children do. I know that as they get older it will become more and more difficult to achieve. So I treasure it as long as I can but it is the one time in the day when we are altogether and can talk. It's when you find out how the spelling test went or the game of football. How the boss's hunt for a new secretary is going. I wonder what my contribution to the conversation would be if I didn't work? 'You should have seen the queue in Sainsburys' or 'I had to replace the Hoover bag today' instead I tell them about my day at work. They know my class almost as much as I do. It's the funny things they like to hear about best!

Marjorie Mowlam MP
Minister for the Cabinet Office

Mo Mowlam was educated at the University's of Durham and Iowa. In 1987 she was elected Member of Parliament for Redcar. Mo worked tirelessly for the Labour Party and was appointed Secretary of State for Northern Ireland at a crucial point in history. Mo now holds the appointment of Minister for the Cabinet Office sometimes known as the 'Cabinet Office Enforcer'. Mo courageously carried on working whilst dealing with treatment for an operable brain tumour. She is married with children.

Government isn't about telling people what's best for them and how they should live their lives.

Government is about listening to people's concerns and hopes, and then acting to make sure that as many people as possible have the opportunity to make the most of their lives.

For women, there can often be specific barriers preventing them from reaching their true potential – education, home life, and even confidence.

As a Member of Parliament in a House of Commons which was male-dominated for a very long time, I feel I can relate in some way to the difficulties people face when trying to fulfil their potential.

I'd like to see the day when we have as many women as men active in politics – at all levels. Women make up 51% of the population of this country. Their voices should and must be more influential in shaping our country.

The Welsh Assembly recently made headlines by having the first executive in Western Europe with more women in it than men. And although the House of Commons now has a record number of women MPs, there are still five times as many men. So there's plenty of room left for improvement!

When it comes to the town hall or serving on public bodies, the situation is poor – so we're committed to getting a 50:50 balance in quangos and NHS trusts.

Why? The reason is simple. Women have so much to offer and there is real value in greater diversity in public life.

In the last 25 years, women's lives have undergone a revolution. Nearly 8 out of 10 of all mothers now work. More women are graduating than ever before.

My job as a Cabinet Minister means I am in a privileged position to help influence these priorities and make them a reality.

That said, I believe it's a two-way process. It's not just about what the Government is doing. It's about what you yourself can do.

One of the most important assets you can have is confidence. The confidence to set yourself goals, and the determination to meet them. The confidence to take the future into your own hands.

Confidence in yourself and your abilities – and also in the people around you – is essential, whether it's when you're starting a new job, growing a business, doing the next stage of exams, or even getting into the House of Commons.

If you believe in yourself it can make all the difference.

Lorna Muirhead
President, Royal College of Midwives
Practising Midwife

Lorna is the President of the Royal College of Midwives the oldest and largest midwifery organisation in the world. She is also a practising midwife. She has worked as a clinician predominantly on a labour ward in a teaching hospital, which does in excess of 6,000 deliveries a year. Lorna has had a long and distinguished career. She lectures frequently and maintains a passionate interest in promoting clinical standards. Her most recent published work was as a member of the working party on the joint Royal College of Midwives/Royal College of Gynaecologists document Towards Safer Childbirth.

In common with women throughout the ages I live a busy life, juggling the competing demands of being a wife, mother, daughter, homemaker and citizen. As a woman living in the latter half of the twentieth century I also pursue a professional life practising as a midwife on a labour ward of an inner city hospital. Three years ago I was elected to be the President of the Royal College of Midwives which is the oldest and largest midwifery organisation in the world. In this role I act as an ambassador for midwives and the midwifery profession representing them at both national and international forums.

I originally trained to be a nurse in the early 1960s and was drawn to the profession because I was attracted by the uniform, the order and discipline which then was part of being a nurse, coupled with the desire to be of use to people when they most needed it. Nursing fulfilled all of these things, but like many nurses I then went on to become qualified as a midwife and became totally fascinated and absorbed by pregnancy and childbirth and decided that midwifery was the profession for me. I briefly left the clinical area to become a midwife teacher but decided that clinical practice was the area in which I wanted to work. I like to have my sleeves rolled up and be actively involved in caring for mothers and babies.

In the 30 years I have spent working on a labour ward and have delivered many babies and witnessed the births of many more. I regard the birth of a baby as the Christmas Day of pregnancy and continue to be fascinated, excited and in awe of the process.

The aspect of my profession, which I find most difficult, relates to the increasingly political framework in which it operates. Over the last decade there has been increasing political impingement invading the caring professions, and a new philosophy which has changed the National Health Service (NHS) from the service which it has been since it was introduced in the middle of the twentieth century into the business it is now, a consequence of which has been to denude the caring professions of the power and influence they once had, handing it to the bureaucrats. This has not in my opinion been to the benefit of patients, nor indeed staff within the NHS.

There is nothing original in my saying that the person who has influenced me most in my life is my mother. Mature reflection of her qualities do not diminish the influence she had on me nor indeed on the lives of many others whom she meet. She represented all that is good and loving. Encouraging and supportive, she never once let me down in any way physically or emotionally. Only now that I have adult children of my own do I realise just how difficult is the role of being a successful mother. My mother had a great gift of hospitality to everyone and anyone whom she met and was a true Good Samaritan. She has been dead for 9 years now but I still strongly feel the power and influence of her love surrounding me from wherever she is.

There are many other people who have had a positive influence on my life and I count myself fortunate to have met people at key moments in my life who have been forces for good and who have influenced me. Possibly the most influential was Chloe Thomas, my head mistress at senior school, a musician and mathematician who convinced me that I was capable of doing anything I chose to do with my life – but thought I could do a lot better than becoming a 'nurse'.

The most traumatic situations I have had to deal with professionally relate to losing a mother in childbirth. Death in childbirth in the late twentieth century is not a common experience in our society although in the developing world every minute of every day a woman dies as a consequence of it. My practice has taken place on a busy labour ward of a teaching hospital which deals not only with the majority of women for whom pregnancy and childbirth is a normal life event but also deals with women for whom childbirth is a difficult or dangerous process. During my practise as a midwife I have been aware and sometimes involved when 14 women have lost their lives. This is exceptional, especially if I tell you that many midwives and doctors nowadays thankfully will never see one. I particularly remember a young woman with four children coming into the labour ward on Christmas morning. She was not established in labour. Without any warning she collapsed in front of us. Extensive resuscitation failed and she died. In order to try and save her child a post-mortem caesarean section was performed. This was a horrible experience. The child was born alive but was severely brain damaged and tragically died on Good Friday of the following year. We washed the dead mother and made the room as lovely as we could leaving it bathed in soft lights. I cannot begin to tell you how devastated all of us involved were. The poignancy of the date was not lost on us. We had come on duty in fancy dress to the great amusement of all the other women in labour. The Christmas decorations were up and it was 4 a.m. in the morning when everyone is at their lowest ebb. The woman's husband paced the sitting room floor; their other children were at home in bed with their Christmas toys. All the staff involved, some of whom I had worked with for many years enjoying a close relationship with them, stood round the bed whilst the priest offered prayers for the dead. The silence, which followed, and the darkness reflected how we all felt. It was a grim reminder that birth is not always about life.

The biggest challenge I have faced as a person was caring for my mother who suffered for a number of years with dementia whilst at the same time trying to keep my professional life going. This is of course what many modern women have to do. She was quite young when it happened and I found it excruciatingly painful to watch my once strong supportive mother becoming more and more dependent, and because of the medication necessary to make her comfortable she became mentally estranged from the family. For me she died many years before she actually physically died and my family and I had to deal with a stranger in our midst that looked like our mother and occasionally behaved like our mother but for most part was a stranger. I was beginning to feel that I could not cope with looking after her and dreaded the day when I would have to admit failure and let someone else care for her. One morning I found her dead in bed. Typically I thought, mother knows I cannot go on much longer, and with characteristic goodness has saved me from the guilt of letting her down when she needed me most.

My biggest achievement as a professional is to have been involved in thousands of births where mothers and children have been alive well and happy.

Without doubt family life has been the bedrock on which I have built my life. It is the single most important thing to me. The proverb 'to be happy in the home is the ultimate aim of all ambition' is my mantra. I acknowledge that my experience of family life has been very fortunate and that in spite of the best efforts some families and some marriages break down and that is a tragedy. I am extremely fortunate to have married a scientist whom after 35 years I respect and love and hope to spend a long retirement with.

One piece of advice I would pass on to other women were I to be given the opportunity is sit down and decide what it is you want from life, do not take on too much, and leave some time for yourself. I realise that this is a privileged woman's view and that not all women are fortunate to be able to make those choices but nevertheless all of us have some choice and control over our lives. Over the next 20 years I hope women will take my advice and if they pursue a professional life I hope they will be paid enough to employ someone else to do part of their domestic role.

If I were to start my career again I would choose to be a midwife but I am not sure that I would remain at the bedside for such a long time. Although I love caring for women in childbirth and indeed this is central to what midwives do and I like to think that I have handed on some of my skill and knowledge to the rising generation of midwives, I have realised since I became President that you cannot influence things as effectively in the 'ranks' as you can from the top.

I am thankful to have lived in the latter half of the twentieth century and hope to survive the first half of the twenty-first! When I look back at women in history I am glad of being a woman today who in no way feels subordinate to men and has had in the main the benefit of equal education and opportunity.

Julia Neuberger BA MA (Cambridge)
Chief Executive of the King's Fund, London

Julia is Chief Executive of the King's Fund. The Kings Fund is an independent health care charity, which works to improve the health of Londoners by making change happen in health and social care. She was educated at Newnham College, Cambridge and Leo Baeck College, London. She became a rabbi in 1977, and served the South London Liberal Synagogue for 12 years, before going to the King's Fund Institute as a Visiting Fellow, to work on research ethics committees in the United Kingdom. She then became a fellow at Harvard Medical School in 1991–1992, having gone to the United States on a Harkness Fellowship.

Julia became Chairman of Camden and Islington Community Health Services NHS Trust in April 1993 and finished in November 1997. She is a member of the General Medical Council and the Medical Research Council, and a trustee of the Imperial War Museum. She was formerly a trustee of the Runnymede Trust and is a member of the Board of Visitors of Memorial Church, Harvard University. Julia holds honorary doctorates from eight universities, is an honorary fellow of Mansfield College, Oxford and has been Chancellor of the University of Ulster since 1994.

Julia has also had several books on Judaism, women, health care ethics and on caring for dying people published. She broadcasts frequently and writes articles on a variety of subjects. In her spare time she likes swimming, gardening, family life, opera and Irish life.

My present role requires keeping a general overview of the activities of the King's Fund. In the past 2 years, I have totally re-organised the King's Fund reshaping it around five key 'themes', and collapsing what had been a federal structure into one structure, so that we were able (and are able) to conduct research, do policy analysis, develop ideas on the ground, give grants to drive an agenda, conduct leadership development and educational programmes, run a public affairs programme – all around our five 'key themes'. My job now is to see that all this works, and that we have a clear corporate direction, with a clearly defined strategy that allows us to influence health and social care in London and effect change as much as possible within our financial and human resources.

My career started as a rabbi, and I came into it, at least in part, because I could not continue with my original planned career of being an archaeologist working in the Near East. I was refused entry to Iraq in 1969 and Turkey in 1970 – my future as a budding Assyriologist (which is what I read at Cambridge with Hebrew as my second language for part I, changing to Hebrew as my main subject for Part II) looked less than hopeful. I then thought I would become an academic in Jewish studies, but my then tutor,

The profiles

Nicholas de Lange, suggested I look at going to rabbinic college, which I did. From there my career has just mushroomed. I had 2 years at the King's Fund after 12 years as a pastoral rabbi, then a year in the US at Harvard, followed by 4 years as chairman of a NHS Trust, before coming to my present job.

I love being able to give a grant from the King's Fund plus some people to help on the ground that effects real change or improvement for ordinary people in London. We have achieved that, I think, in some mental health projects at present, and we hope to do so in a health and homelessness project in the future.

The down side is running a large-ish organisation – and certainly a very complex one – and having to do some of the most horrible of management tasks – such as firing people. I moved 50 people on in my first year – with no compulsory redundancies – but I felt awful about it even though it was the right thing to do. Most of them, ultimately felt they had moved at the right time, but a few remain angry.

So many different people have influenced me – but I believe that Dame Cicely Saunders has probably influenced me most professionally, though mostly not directly. Privately, I suppose the greatest influences have been my father and my paternal grandmother, because of their clear value systems and their belief that you have only got a short life and you had better do what you can for others within it.

I think the funniest incident I ever had to deal with in my career was when I stood in my student pulpit in Nottingham and a blind woman, who was not Jewish, but married to a Jew, used to come with her husband and sit in the front reading a Braille edition of the *Church Times*, which in those days had a very large dark printed title which I could see clearly – and it seemed so hilarious – and perverse – to be reading the *Church Times* in a synagogue service.

There have been many traumatic situations I have had to deal with in my career, amongst which have been some of the most difficult funerals (suicides, babies), and one minor attack on the synagogue when I was conducting a service and I had to persuade everyone to stay calm.

The greatest challenge is always the next one – the one you don't think you'll be able to meet. Personally, the greatest challenge was ensuring my father had a good death at home which he wanted, when my mother would have been happier if he had stayed in hospital to the end.

My greatest achievement has been to have two children, apparently reasonably well adjusted, who as adults seem to like spending time with their parents, despite our busy and chaotic life styles. As a professional, I think my greatest achievements have lain in moving on to the next thing without – I hope – leaving the people I worked with before feeling I had simply abandoned them.

Family is hugely important to me. I have been married to the same man, Anthony, for the last 26 years, and we have a close family relationship, close also to our two mothers and my three brothers-in-law and their wives, and we live near the two mothers who were both widowed 3 years ago. I have a strong sense of family – and a strong sense of familial duty as well as pleasure.

If I could change one thing for women it would be the extent of the isolation many elderly widowed or single women experience, after the deaths of their spouses or siblings. I think the fear and loneliness of so many women – and men – in old age is what I would like to change if I could.

The one piece of advice I would give other women is that you can have it all – but that it requires absolute determination and the clear thought in your mind that you only have the one life, so you better make use of it.

I don't believe there will be great change in the world of work for women in the next 20 years. There will be a gradual shift towards greater equality in terms of rank and position, and some closure of the pay gap. I suspect women will still be working as they do now – and that they will retire at 65 or after, as retirement ages shift for society as a whole.

My current profession is such a mixture that it's hard to say whether I would choose it again. I'm not sure I ever chose it at all. But I would still want to do what I have done – and I still look forward to whatever's next, and I don't have a clue as to what that might be.

Susan Brooks Parker BS MSP
International Labour Office (ILO), Geneva, Switzerland

Susan was recruited in late 1998 by the ILO for the express purpose of initiating the development of new policy for the ILO's constituency; specifically, to build a Code of Good Practices on Disability Management in the Workplace *for use by employers, workers' organisations, and governments. The Code's basic construction, occurring primarily in 1999 with the support of one part-time consultant under her supervision, has required original compilation of secondary source data available from the world's developed countries. Because of the dearth of actual enterprise management practice data, a sub-project was conceived, designed and implemented between July and December, 1999, yielding new primary data deriving from over 30 case studies on actual good practices now occurring within small, medium and large enterprises in developing countries. The Code's scheduled publication date was 2001.*

Concurrent with the above responsibilities Susan was appointed in March 1999, as the Officer-in-Charge of the ILO's Disability Program immediately after the appointment of the new Director General. Additional responsibilities included the usual personnel and administrative management tasks associated with day-to-day activities in Headquarters and the field. The third activity cluster concerns design and development of 'employment for peace' programs in countries just emerging from armed conflict; in December, 1999, a fact-finding mission to Sierra Leone is, as of this date, generating prototype development. As has been the case for all the appointments Susan has had the actual tasks undertaken exceed any terms of reference officially associated with the job slot.

My academic degrees are all from the USA, specifically the New England region where I grew up, the older of two children born to parents who themselves are from families who emigrated from England and Scotland (by way of Holland in two instances) to the "New World," before 1660. My father influenced the growth of an enduring curiosity about the natural world, reinforced from early childhood onwards by him providing a role model who, with his friend who owned a flying service, flew hunters and fishermen into the State of Maine's backwoods of the 1950s. I have early memories of flying with him in a Piper Cub, riding on his shoulders as he skied down a mountain, or canoeing with him in heavy fast water. He taught his children and our friend's outdoor sports: camping, mountain climbing, swimming and alpine skiing. My participation in organized sports, notably skiing, honed a competitive spirit having a spillover effect to all life areas. My mother greatly encouraged and reinforced intellectual and artistic pursuits, especially reading, music, and creative writing. In May 1968 I graduated from the University of Vermont with four areas of major and minor study: English Literature and French (majors); music and psychology (minors).

Although certified upon graduation to teach English and French in the State of Vermont, I chose instead to have two children (1968 and 1970) after a May, 1967 marriage to the owner of Vermont Hotels, consisting then of a country inn, two seasonal resorts, and a year-round commercial hotel. I used parenting skills I thought I remembered from my own family plus trial and error. I recall reading Chapter 1 of *Dr Spock's Baby Book*, wondered what the fuss was about and never re-opened it. I do not regret for a second having had two children by the age of 25; in fact, in many ways we 'grew up' together. The hotel business demands meant that my two sons and I spent an uncommon amount of time together, especially when they were small. I have thoroughly enjoyed passing along to another generation my love of the outdoors, sports, and life in general. I learned hotel management from my husband's parents who were acknowledged and respected masters in the art, according to their New England and national contemporaries.

Like my father in the early 1950s in our northern Maine community and his sister (my Aunt Virginia) who started ski teams in the late 1940s and early 50s (she is now a member of several Halls of Fame for her achievements in organised American women's sports of the 1950s, '60s, and early '70s), I started a community ski program as a volunteer in 1971, obtaining public school district funds benefiting the many children who have since participated. As a volunteer president of a parent-teacher organisation in 1972 I led an initiative to establish a publicly funded kindergarten; our little group did house to house voter registration. The opponents were the town's old guard who scared older voters living on fixed incomes by saying that the property tax rate would go up if the measure passed. The measure passed in our favour by one vote at the Town Meeting. The opposition called a second town meeting. We won by nearly 20 votes on Round Two. My main opponent went to the newspapers using tactics relying on false information, which called on me to write editorials, stating the facts. This was my first (and not last) exposure to public campaigns that turn personal. My opponent (a community leader) died of a heart attack after the first vote; members of the loyal opposition went around our small town saying that the 'young Mrs. ***** ' killed him. The kindergarten is now an institution within the school.

However, the pressures of simultaneous roles, not entirely compatible when acted out in the crucible of a small family dominated by a patriarch, stimulated me to consider various alternatives to the hotel business. I recalled my earlier interest to pursue medicine, which had first found expression in early undergraduate academic work. At the nearby Dartmouth Medical School in 1972–73 I qualified for certification in the field use of Advanced Emergency Medical Technology. Testing further my level of interest, I did additional medical fieldwork in 1973 in the St. Ann Parish Hospital on Jamaica's North Coast. With no regrets I ruled out a medical career which would have required an additional 4 years of intensive academic work plus several years of residency. At the time I was the primary parent raising the two boys; the hotel business and my husband's parents' expectations on him left nearly no time for family life. I returned to Vermont in 1974, the seeds sown for leaving the hotel business in favour of building a more balanced life for at least the children and me. The decision meant that I would establish my own career.

In September, 1974, I found the 'needle in the haystack' job 10 minutes from my home, enabling me to balance home and family. This was an entry-level psychiatric social worker position in the fledgling Vermont community mental health movement. I was a liaison person between the State's only Psychiatric Hospital and my rural geographic region for a caseload of 50 chronically mentally ill people. Six weeks into this job I felt a natural fit between my interests and abilities and the needs of the patients. A gifted psychiatrist who was then well ahead of conventional national practice in his work with mentally ill people mentored me. He singled me out after a trial by fire first day in the hospital wherein he assigned me to two patients, one in the morning, and one in the afternoon, with the elliptic instruction to find out what's going on. There I was on a locked ward with Geneva in the morning and Tom for the afternoon. His guidance allowed me to progress rapidly through case analysis and problem-solving; after 18 months I knew that the next step was more academic work in the area of social service systems. I felt inadequate not knowing how to solve the system's problems for my patients.

This 2-year hands-on position (1974–76) formally launched the present career of 25 years whose trajectory has now included ministerial-level appointments at the State and Federal levels in the USA and two international appointments, noted below. After two and a half years of additional academic work to obtain a Masters in Social Planning (MSP) with an additional concentration in Psychiatric Clinical Social Work, I graduated in May, 1978 from Boston College. The MSP degree, unique for its time, used urban planning principles course work taught at MIT, combined with community organising as a method to get the job done. The coursework and practica also utilised developmental planning applied to so-called third world countries. Our planning class contained only 25 people, over half of whom were from developing countries, speaking English as a second language. As a team leader I was responsible for editing our reports. The over 2-year cycle had me spending 10 days in Boston and four in Vermont with the children.

The degree enabled me to assume economic independence after graduation, an essential given that the divorce from my husband became final at the very same time. The terms of the divorce granted a small lump sum settlement, no alimony and very modest child support. These were, even for the time, astounding terms if one considered the amount of my contributions to the family business. In fact, the house that we had designed and built together (albeit using business funds in the customary way) was sold, along with the adjacent hotel property, without my prior knowledge during my first year in graduate school. No one ever asked whether I wanted the curtains I had made for the lake-facing windows; I mourned the loss of those kitchen curtains in the 'Red House' for at least 3 years. The principle of 'equal pay for equal work' was not extended to me as a working wife of the son. Following the tradition of six-day workweeks in the seasonal resorts, I learned most jobs in the departments. I belatedly started actively advocating for my own rights in 1973, causing considerable family conflict. The level of the conflict and the resistance galvanised me to think about other vocational alternatives. The manner in which I was treated completely convinced me my values were not meant to lodge in my husband's family.

In fact, I started my adult life over in 1978 amid considerable opposition, building on internal strengths and new skills. Thankfully, my parents and grandparents emotionally supported me. They, too, I am sure, wondered from time-to-time whether or not I knew what I was doing. While the marriage and the relationship endured for about 15 years, I can now clearly see that the extreme opposition forced me to make difficult choices and move on with my life according to my life values. I was determined to give my sons a choice of which values to use as guides to living their lives, and even more resolved to honour my own.

The pattern of 'finding the needle in the haystack' at the right time continued after graduate school. As a new single parent, I needed a job within commuting distance of our new family home, which I managed to purchase as a single woman. The divorce's terms decreed that I continue to live in the same town as the hotel business and the children's father. I question to this day why the Judge was persuaded to rule this way. Two weeks out of school a wonderful Quaker woman who, as chairperson of the Board, became my professional mentor for several years hired me. She herself, a retiree from years of running a large program for psychiatrically disabled youth living outside New York City, was in one of the first graduating classes of the Columbia School in the late 1920s (the present day Columbia School of Social Work). Out of over 50 applicants, the Search Committee hired a newcomer to the field of community planning to start up a human services planning agency responsible for program planning, evaluation, and budget allocations for services in 10 towns. The job was a 30-minute drive from our home, the children's school and their friends. In 1980 the pattern repeated itself; I was invited to apply for a state-wide position as the head of a quasi-governmental planning agency charged with overseeing the state's work with persons with developmental disabilities.

A considerable promotion (everything is relative), I obtained this job also by competing with others who had more practical experience. Two years out of graduate school, I was then directly on the track leading to successive appointments to positions of ever-increasing responsibility. The 1980 move to a new city in the neighboring state of New Hampshire (my birth state) permitted me to build a new life over the next 9 years for our small family, done entirely as a single parent. I petitioned the New Hampshire Probate Court in 1981 to take back by own family name of 'Parker.' My only hesitation concerned the fact my sons would have a different family name. The next three appointments, briefly summarized, occurred between 1987 and 1998:

(1) 1987–1989: Commissioner, State of Maine's Department of Mental Health and Mental Retardation. Appointed by Governor John R. McKernan to the Cabinet-rank post, the Department's $228 million budget paid for 2,500 staff spread across three acute and long-term care hospitals plus two service delivery systems serving those with mental illness and mental retardation. Managed contracts, facilities, and personnel in addition to directing union negotiations and legislative hearings. Conceived and directed initiatives to reform two hospitals and build community services.

(2) 1989–1993: US Associate Commissioner, Disability, US Social Security Administration (Washington) President George Bush's Administration appointment required the management of central office staff and, indirectly, another 13,000 employees in each state. The program had a budget of over $one billion. The job required policy development and marketing of new policy to elected decision-makers, management of constituency relations, Congressional committee work representation of the US Government to foreign governments and to international organisations. Implemented the US Supreme Court's Zebley *v.* Sullivan decision through the design and development of historically significant childhood disability regulations liberalising the adjudication process to benefit disabled children in the United States.

(3) 1993–1998: Secretary General, Rehabilitation International (RI, New York). Chief Executive Officer to an international board of directors representing the five world regions containing the membership from 90 countries and 200 organisations in this 75-year-old Non-Governmental Organisation (NGO). Consultant expert on disability policy to the United Nations' ECOSOC on behalf of RI Organiser of the Disability Caucus for the World Summit for Social Development, Copenhagen, 1995, with the resulting inclusion of significant text in the Copenhagen Declaration and Program of Action. Management of international staff, numerous initiatives, including technical seminars, conferences and policy development.

Career choice, satisfactions and frustrations

Since childhood I have been conscious of 'being of service to others' as a value that underpinned living a life. As a middle-aged child growing up in a small town in the northern Maine woods, I was aware of others less fortunate than me, especially the little friends who had moved over from Canada, speaking only French in the English-speaking schools. The teachers and other students who blatantly harassed them treated them as inferior. By age 10 I was a spokesperson within my peer group, confronting teachers or other authority figures as the need arose. The leap was not large to progress to work with mentally ill and mentally retarded persons. Such work was based on human rights, principles of economic and social justice, including equitable access to education and services. The advocacy practiced within the United Nations framework springs from those values.

The satisfactions have been many, great and small alike. To summarize, the theme has been to contribute positively to improving the life situations of those who were born, or have become, disenfranchised. The continuing challenge is to identify work situations in which the application of my time and skills can make a positive difference. My level of felt satisfaction obtained from helping a patient adjust successfully to community living situations is the same as that deriving from the successful building of public policy, management of an agency, or establishing effective community services. I have found that working within a team of good people with similar values and goals is a work environment yielding by far the greatest satisfaction. It is also one of the most elusive situations to maintain in today's work life.

The greatest frustration continues to stem from people who, using politically correct words, have no intention of contributing to progress on any front unless the progress benefits them personally. I have had considerable experience expending energy to analyze and dissect layers of organizational behavior for the purpose of identifying blockages to action. Many very good and sensitive people understandably develop cynical layers in order to protect themselves. I have found that all organizations have good people with positive values; in new job situations I make it a point to find them as quickly as possible, a fact helpful to maintaining an optimistic outlook. However, I highly value my colleagues who from time-to-time temper my sometimes-unbridled optimism with strong checks of reality, a reminder of the importance of working in a balanced team.

The funniest event in my career so far? In late October 1990, President Bush detailed me with two days notice (a government-wide travel freeze was on) to represent him in Beijing at an all Asia meeting of Rehabilitation International. My sole function was to deliver his and Mrs Bush's personal greetings to the Chinese people, especially important to him given his prior relationship with the Chinese people and the political situation of the day. I found out during the course of the trip that the Chinese wanted in the worst way to know the content of the greeting which I was not personally carrying as it was to be faxed from the White House directly to my hotel. The machinations applied by operatives to my luggage on route and in my hotel room to try to locate this piece of paper were extreme; even the China Airlines plane made an unscheduled stop in Dalian, still they persisted in asking questions as if I was hiding a State Secret. The to'ing and fro'ing delayed the Beijing arrival until the wee hours. My head at 2 a.m. after over 24 hours of direct travel from Washington, D.C., was practically in the teacup at the VIP Lounge Ceremony. I had to work hard to maintain a sense of humor; the details in the Briefing Book prepared by my talented staff had long since faded into the jet's contrails. The event has become quite funny over time: I call it 'killing a mosquito with a bazooka.'

The most traumatic? Getting beat up for political reasons for months on end in the State of Maine's popular press for taking on the challenge of improving the patients' living conditions at the Augusta Mental Health Institute (AMHI) in the wake of five untimely patient deaths in 1988. I was part of a Republican Administration with a democratically controlled House and Senate; the 'D's' fiefdom had been the mental health system which they had elevated in preceding years to star status, especially AMHI. In fact, the conditions were less than positive, despite the fact that national accreditation's had continued to be awarded to various of the facility's services. Our administration called a 'spade a spade' and I was the one out in front taking the heat as the Cabinet Officer. I was outraged that, despite the evidence painfully presented in extended public legislative hearings, the press (fueled by the political opposition) and the medical community never acknowledged the hospital's deficiencies, including incompetent high-level staff. Fortunately for the patients, an advocate organization successfully brought legal action against the state, forcing improvement of the conditions for mentally ill people. The justice was sweet when in 1989, just before leaving to take up the Washington appointment, the patients of the second hospital, the Bangor Mental Health Institute (BMHI), voted to award Commissioner Parker a commendation for improving conditions at their facility.

Achievements, challenges, relationships

Balancing the activities of my personal and professional life by tuning into physical, mental, and spiritual health needs is the ongoing challenge. While I have been gifted with a strong body, from time-to-time I have let work overly dominate, neglecting to exercise which in turn affects my mental and spiritual well-being. Fifteen years ago meditation and yoga entered my life. Music has always been present, especially classical and rock. My piano at the moment sits unused in New Hampshire but it lived with me through the jobs in Washington and New York. Raising my sons together with career development during the 1980s had a strong sports component as we often skied, hiked, or played tennis. Relationships with men friends whom I met through our mutual work during the 80s usually included sports activities and travel. I found it relaxing with my sons to be the 'baseball mom' who transported team members and attended games, sometimes with papers to read and memos to draft on my lap. I have made a priority of ongoing communication and quality time spent with my sons, their new families, my parents, and the 'significant other.' A newer priority is taking the time to do for myself, an activity that comes with some difficulty. Writing the very words is a good reminder.

Maintaining healthy relationships in the face of the career challenges is a personal achievement forged by conscious decision-making about how to spend scarce non-work time. In the last year I have decreased drastically the amount of emotional emphasis on work in favor of certain relationships. A better balance is evolving. I now consciously take time off with no elaborated scheme of how the time will be spent. Time for reflection is time well spent. The old love affair with the French language is rekindled thanks to living in Geneva and taking classes. Yes, there is a special man in my life whom I greatly respect.

Throughout my career phases I have kept up with outdoor sports, though until moving to Europe the performances were confined to weekends or vacations. Alpine skiing is still the personal favorite. Here in Geneva, I delight in the nearness of the Alps. Extensive US and world travel during the Washington and New York years severely challenged the ability to regularly exercise and maintain healthy balances. The interest in artistic pursuits is returning. I have maintained since 1980 a home in New Hampshire despite traveling the world and carrying out work based in distant cities. Through the years I have maintained a ski house (used two out of the 9 years of ownership), and successive apartments in Washington, New York, and now Geneva. The base represents a nest and ties to immediate family, friendships that age along with the rest of us, and now a new generation of children. Relationships since the 1978 divorce had to fit in with the dual priorities of raising sons and an active career that involved significant job-related travel. A primary relationship during the Maine and Washington years was not strong enough to permit the continued growth of each of us. Our values turned out to be quite different when the heat was turned up. I have learned one or two things about equality in relationships.

Through the years as many friendships have developed with men as have with women. I find now that men and women who have attained some measure of achievement in their careers have many of the same problems as they reach career apogees. This I say knowing that the routes we have taken to the top, and often the help in getting there, has greatly differed. How much easier it would have been during the 80's if I had had another adult 'helper' at home. I feel good to have shed during the last few years a mantle of anger stemming from the sheer degree of adversity encountered as I have challenged the various institutions putting up roadblocks to living my life and doing my work. To have developed bitterness would have signaled death of my spirit. Today, I can only feel sorry for the people on my life's pathway who place a higher value on money than family, act for short-term political gain before doing the needful to benefit people who merit the help, and execute personal manipulations as opposed to genuine expressions of loyalty, either to me or to the larger cause. The problems are theirs and theirs alone.

The downside of this state of mind is a greatly diminished ability to waste any time through activity that won't make a difference. The upside is damn the torpedoes, full-steam ahead, let's see what's next. Were I at the start of my career again, I would choose sooner the same field, indulging in diversions of shorter duration which would have allowed more time to play and work.

Wishes, advice and predictions

Women today still have to make extra efforts to prove their worth, despite evident equal prowess on the playing field, in the class and boardrooms. Often, women identify one another as the enemy, applying competitive zeal to vanquishing someone or something that is not the root problem. Care needs to be taken to seek jobs yielding the widest perspective; seduction into a well paying dead-end, velvet ghetto will insure occupational obsolescence at an early age. Vigilant pursuit of 'wide angle' jobs will assist women to operate more effectively in the big picture.

Globalization of the economic and social market place has intensified the competition for the increasingly scarce good jobs. In the next 20 years, the ability to be mobile, flexible in location, realistic about the rigors of raising children within a structured family life, and consistency in the expression of personal values will provide the necessary ballast critical to holding up under complicated, institutionalized pressures.

I foresee renewed emphasis on working with people – teaching children, transferring capacity building skills, learning new skills as older adults – as part of a larger effort to re-tool our information-laden environments to cope with actually making practical use of the information. For much of the 90s we have been preoccupied with tools rather than applications. The New Millennium is here, the apocalypse is not in view, and our environments are in sad need of repair. Women with Big Pictures, maybe even wearing Big Hats, will be instrumental in the re-building.

Lisa Perry BEd (Hons)
Housewife and Mother

After 10 years of teaching, counselling, disciplining, encouraging, and caring for other people's children, I am now endeavouring to do the same for my 18-month-old twins Jonah and Isabelle. At first it seemed an overwhelming task and I like many new mothers wondered if I would ever again have time to take a relaxing soak in the bath or drink a hot cup of coffee. But as these two tiny, helpless, demanding babies have grown into little people with very different needs and characteristics some structure, routine and enjoyment has once again returned to my life. We begin each day determined to eat, explore, play, rest, clean at least one room in the house, and survive intact until bedtime. Ah bedtime, that wonderful, peaceful, precious time. And I thought teaching was hard work!

I finished my degree studies in the summer of 1989 and brandishing my BEd (Hons) I marched into my first teaching job. On the first day, sitting, less than confidently, in the staff room it seemed like no time at all since I was stood on the other side of the staff room door as it opened mere inches and a disgruntled teacher peered through the clouds of smoke. It wasn't the last time that term that I wondered if I had made the right decision to become a junior schoolteacher.

When I was very small I dreamed of a life on the stage, with the bright lights, colourful costumes and rapturous applause. When I became older and 'wiser' I realised that such dreams were just that and as I was particularly enjoying being in Mr Jones' class, top year of Junior School I decided that teaching was for me. After a very short time at my Senior School, remembering the halcyon days of Junior School, I refined my option to junior schoolteacher. I much preferred the thought of book corners, powder paint, and nativity plays to large, rough, rude children and grim-faced teachers.

Over the next 10 years I had the privilege and the huge responsibility of being one of the major influences in many children's lives. In September, instilling discipline to enable self-discipline to flourish. In November, insisting on high standards to enable everyone to achieve their best. In January, encouraging our small classroom community to support one another and respect one another to prepare them for the larger communities around them. By March, learning and growing and having fun. It is a wonderful feeling to compare a child in September to the child who leaves you in July – all she has achieved socially, emotionally, intellectually and to have played a part in helping her get there. I now enjoy the privilege of my own children. I share in the excitement of their achievements, such as Jonah's first hand clap and Isabelle's first few steps.

It is only now, as a mother, that I more fully appreciate what a loving, selfless and dependable women my own mother is. As a child I knew safety, security and love. Happiness and laughter are my overwhelming memories. My parents have given me a belief in my own abilities and talents, a sense of optimism that the world can be a beautiful inspiring place, a knowledge that although bad things happen and people do bad things they can also be kind and caring. I also have the security of knowing that wherever life takes me my parents will always endeavour to support, encourage and love me. They are certainly the two people who have influenced me most.

I was greatly influenced by some of my senior schoolteachers. Their impatience, inability to communicate and inept delivery of the curriculum provoked in me an intense desire to do the job well or not at all. They encouraged me to be dynamic, charismatic caring and professional in the classroom.

Working with children can be exhausting and frustrating but it is frequently amusing. Such 'amusing incidents' include watching five children in an enormous, painted, cardboard Blue Whale costume shuffling onto a stage with fits of giggles; being aware that a cheeky, precocious 11-year-old is doing impersonations of me whilst all her friends are watching not knowing whether to warn her or laugh; listening to a 'bunch' of 7-year-olds giggling uncontrollably at jokes they only half understand 'What do you call a man with a spade in his head? Doug!'.

When a child is about to be excluded permanently from a school it is the culmination of a long process and it is always traumatic. To spend so much time on one child, one of 34 in a class, disciplining, encouraging and supporting, often being the stable reliable adult in their life and then to fail to enable them to remain in the school has to be the hardest part of teaching. To have failed one of the children in my care makes me feel angry and inadequate. Angry with parents who fail to give their children the love, structure and discipline they need and angry with a state system which is unable to cope with extreme individual needs. By expelling a child we protect the needs and rights of the many but add to the problems of the individual. The greatest challenge is to successfully meet the needs of all the individuals in the class.

I thought the greatest challenges I faced as a person were leaving home, beginning my first job and getting married but I have discovered how difficult and challenging it can be to be a parent. Each day has the potential to produce a greater challenge than I have previously known.

So to my greatest achievements – collecting my degree and being a good teacher. I hope to add being a good parent but that remains to be seen. Being able, as a teacher, to tell a parent that their child, previously unruly and disruptive, has turned things around, worked hard, settled down, been a joy to teach, and seeing the amazement, pleasure and pride on their faces is a wonderful achievement.

If I could change one thing about the world for women I would change the view, predominant in two-thirds of the world, that emphasises a woman's 'right' to an abortion without taking into proper consideration the human rights – the right to safety and protection and life – of the child. I would ask women (and men) to take responsibility for the life they helped to create by the choices they made.

The one piece of advice I would want to pass on to other women if I were given the opportunity would be the challenge, the encouragement to 'be true to yourself'. Amidst the bombardment of stereotypes and pressure to conform, be the woman you are, become the woman God made you to be. Mother, magistrate, model, mechanic – it doesn't matter. Who I am is much, much more important than what I do.

I am not sure what will happen to women in the world of work over the next 20 years but I hope there will be an increasing desire and demand for a greater integration between personal and professional life. I believe this would enable women to transcend the unhelpful distinction that is made between the world of work and the world of family and home life. This in turn would release many women from the guilt of having to choose between pursuing a career and bringing up their children.

If I were to start my career over again I would probably not choose teaching as a profession. The job of teacher, certainly within primary/junior education, has become all consuming. I would not want a job that took over my whole life to the detriment of family and friends.

Jan Peters BSc MSc PhD
Head of the Promoting Science Engineering Technology for Women Team
The Department for Trade and Industry

Jan at 35 years of age is a young working mother with an outstanding academic background. Her BSc was in Chemistry and Oceanography, her MSc in the Molecular Science of Materials and her PhD in the role of defects in the radiation damage of solar cells for space applications. Jan's current role is to co-ordinate government and national efforts to increase the participation of women in science engineering and technology: to increase the uptake of science and related subjects at GCSE, NVQ, A Level and degree; to stimulate and facilitate increased levels of networking and co-ordination between organisations promoting Science Education and Technology for women in the UK and world-wide; work across the public and private sector; to ensure the progression and promotion of women to senior levels and ensure that the UK benefits from the contribution of women on public committees and policy-making bodies.

My career to date has been a series of jumps from sometimes apparently un-related areas. In part this is because I could never have envisaged doing what I am doing or have done. As a sixth former or even a new graduate it is impossible to know the diverse range of jobs that are available. I have moved between jobs based on interests, skills and opportunities that presented themselves. In retrospect one of my moves came because I had encountered sustained harassment that I didn't recognise at the time. However, the enforced move has lead me to a new world of opportunity. Although I can put this experience down as the worst part of my working life it led me to a greater understanding of people, what motivates them, and to be more analytical of the interactions between people and how they can be mis-construed. As such it was a valuable experience.

- As a teenager I was put off engineering by among others my mother who told me it was dirty and not for a person with allergies. I was then stimulated to practice scientific journalism to pursue environmental interests following an article on marine biology in the *Sunday Observer*. I studied for a science degree, driven by the sense that one needed a qualification to be able to write with authority and careers advisor recommended general science degree, based upon the subject I most enjoyed at A level.

- I was driven to further study following my degree as the only job options appeared to be quality control; the sense that I still didn't feel able to write with authority on any specific subject; an interest in electronics, properties of materials and microscopic order of atoms in crystals. A Masters project on semiconductors proved to me that engineering wasn't about being dirty – in fact semiconductors are made in such clean environments that the scientists/engineers need to dress up to keep the environment clean.

- I applied for several jobs based around my MSc project in the medical research environment, after three rejections I found a research job looking at solar cells. I applied for a research position at Southampton University and held a series of short-term contracts and ended up studying for a PhD. This was interrupted by a short spell as a media fellow working on Radio 4 *Woman's Hour* as a science researcher. I was put off working as a journalist but committed to the public understanding of science and the responsibility of scientists to learn how to communicate their science. I completed contract research after 5 years and also received a PhD.

- I got a job in industry as an Applications Engineer working for the equipment manufacturer Bio-Rad Microscience whose product I had used during my PhD studies. I had a great time working, running a demonstration lab, helping customers solve problems, liasing with R&D, production and the sales team. Not to mention the opportunity to travel visiting China, Taiwan, Japan among other countries. Key elements of the job were: helping customers, writing manuals and working with a German university who had done the development work on the product.

- I moved to work in the technology transfer area working for a public body as technology transfer manager: looking at the interface between industry and academia, advising and training scientists on intellectual property issues. Part of my work involved helping set up new partnerships between industry and academia, looking at commercialisation opportunities and I was also involved in changing the culture of a public body to be more customer-focused.

- A secondment to DTI for a short-term appointment to promote Women in Science involved setting up projects between organisations working to promote SET for women; spreading good practice in the promotion of science, bringing marketing skills to bear in the development of materials; working internationally to learn from other nations; undertaking research to identify new ways of tackling the issues.

- I have found having the opportunity of helping others to achieve things, setting up new partnerships and getting projects moving personally satisfying. Professionally, having the opportunity to meet, interact and learn from some exceptionally bright and creative individuals has been a great experience.

Trying to single out one individual for their influence in my life is difficult if not impossible. I think I have used the ping pong model, bouncing off people, trying out ideas and looking at their lives and experiences and figuring that *mmm* that looks good or hey, that's not for me!

- My partner – in providing a level perspective on the world, acting as a sounding board and offering a pragmatic approach and the fact that a single solution is rarely the only solution.

- My friend Louise for opening up my eyes and mind to a totally different approach to life: one centred on the arts, on pleasure and the self. Helping me to look behind things, not for the practical approach to the reasoning why but the emotional forces driving why things are so.

- An ex-boss for his perspective on life and his approach to policy development.
- My mother for showing me how I didn't want my life to turn out.
- My stepmother for showing me that it is ok to stand firm or strike out and do what you want.

Many of the professional influences I have experienced are people I have encountered that I have thought 'I don't want to be there' or 'I don't want to be like that' – the Pinball approach. Often these encounters have stimulated me to realise that to move on one has to work at it and if there is something you don't like you have to make efforts to change it whether that be to modify a practice or process or to develop a new skill to enable you to make the change in career. There is no time like now for doing those things. If you don't like something now there is little chance you will like it next year.

The death of my sister when she was 20 from leukaemia has been the most traumatic thing I have had to deal with.

Dealing with continual harassment from low level subtle sexist jokes/teasing on a daily basis and not realising how much they undermined my confidence and how debilitating they were has been a professional trauma.

Digging myself out of a hole of despair and reconstructing my confidence and realising that I had skills that other people could value has been a significant challenge.

Working to prove that I'm not the lazy person I have always thought myself to be and waking up to find that actually I have a rather interesting CV full of lots of different elements and am generally thought of as a whirlwind has been a personal achievement! It still makes me laugh.

As a professional publishing a handbook on *Intellectual Property Management* was very satisfying. For someone who likes finding solutions to problems and getting things moving finishing projects off is hard work.

As a frustrated teenager of a strict father I couldn't wait to get to college. Unfortunately hours of socialising and writing to pen friends during sixth form meant a poor set of A level results. Persistence paid off and I managed to get a place at Plymouth to study Chemistry and Oceanography – my chosen subjects. My plans were no marriage and no children – I hated them. I saw no point in marriage and couldn't bear the concept of being pregnant – what a state to get yourself in – as it happens I met my partner and now husband during the first week at college and was delighted to find someone who didn't think that any girl who took their eye was theirs for the taking. Never meaning to stay together for long, early in the relationship we both wished we had met the other 'much later' in life. Never quite managing to find time to live and work in the same place we have had, as a friend once told me, the perfect relationship – a partner for weekends and freedom during the week to go out without permission to a film, theatre, dinner or just a drink. We have been an item for some 17 years and have both grown as people and as a couple. We married in 1998 – realising that actually we were content with the other and that it was about time we finally admitted to ourselves and the world that we were in love. Children – one – came along as a surprise and she has fitted in without too much difficulty. It is a fine balance staying sane, working full-time and commuting (4.5 hours per day) and keeping up with friends. The time that has gone is the time for 'me' and that is for both of us. Having a child is a decision I could not make. There was no right time and I couldn't bear the idea of being pregnant, giving birth or changing my life. But it happened and there is great value in it. The fun, laughter and love far outweigh any of the difficult moments (for now!). Images of constant tears and tantrums haven't materialised (yet) but maybe we have just been lucky. I have also realised that there are as many approaches to parenthood as any other activity and none of them wrong. I take the 'it can't be that difficult' pragmatic type approach and hence find that I do not spend my hours worrying whether my child likes or dislikes something, what kind of toothbrush to buy. I can still think for myself, It is important to keep brain space for interesting things in life and not lose perspective.

If I could change one thing in the world it would be to prevent men from making small seemingly innocuous comments about women and things women do 'women drivers', 'women's work', an old woman and also stop women from re-uttering the very same statements. Women are undermined by this continual reference to negative behaviours that have been assigned to us by men through history. I liken this to being jabbed gently with a pointed finger.

My model for keeping your life in balance consists of a triangle. For me the corners represent home life, work and my relationship. I have found that if I can keep two of these elements in perspective I have resources to deal with difficulty in the third. But more importantly, it allows potential courses of action to be identified and analysed. When two elements go out of balance the third element suffers and the whole world seemingly collapses. Perhaps this is the approach of the analytical scientist in me: strip away all the extraneous factors and bare things down to the core. I read a book written by a physicist once, describing the human body. He managed to reduce the body to a sphere on top of a cuboid. My model has helped me to identify ways of moving forward, of getting out of situations when everything seems stacked against me. It allows a problem to be analysed in terms of what if scenario planning.

The future for women in work? For too long society has muddled along with many mediocre men and few high-calibre women. The pace of technological change means that if we are to keep control of advances and harness them for the benefit of humankind then we must engage women more effectively in the workforce. The impact of technology must be made to work for us, to allow us ever more flexible ways of working and to allow us to reach the nirvana of work-life balance. The barriers to achieving this are high. Not least is the problem of working from home, even occasionally, being referred to by friends and colleagues as working part-time, thus undermining the credibility and contribution of the home worker no mater how senior. Further evidence of the gentle finger poking I alluded to earlier. Harmless banter that does a cool job of quietly discrediting the flexible worker. It is not until men start to adopt more flexible ways of working will it become credible. My future vision of work's one where men work more flexibly and appreciate the compromises that need to be made to enable all of us to be fulfilled. We are moving there slowly and I hope that things will get better.

Would I start again or would I do the same? If I started again with access to better knowledge and advice I could study more seriously at A level, but I probably wouldn't. I might have realised that all subjects are accessible and doable and the idea that one degree programme is harder than another isn't true. I might not have done a PhD. I might have done any number of things differently but I don't regret what I have done or achieved. Ultimately after my current secondment is finished probably a move back into the area of technology transfer will be my next move.

The late Nyree Dawn Porter OBE
Actress

Sadly, since contributing this profile, Nyree passed away on 10 April, 2001.

Nyree was born in New Zealand where she toured extensively with the New Zealand Players Theatre Trust achieving national acclaim in roles as varied as Juliet in Romanoff & Juliet, *Jessica in* The Merchant of Venice, *and reviews and musicals, before coming to live and work in England. She has made many West End appearances as well as numerous other successful roles. Nyree created the role of Julia in* Sweet William *and was Lady Metcalf in Jeffrey Archer's* Beyond Reasonable Doubt, *which she played in a 30-week sell out season in Australia with Frank Finlay. Nyree had a baptism by fire for television – 17 roles in 17 months, which was followed with the title roles in* Madame Bovary *and* Judith Paris, The Liars, The Protectors, Never a Cross Word. *Nyree is probably most famous for her portrayal of Irene in* The Forsyte Saga *for the BBC. She has also appeared in many variety shows and has been the subject of* This is Your Life. *Nyree's film roles include:* Two Left Feet *with Michael Crawford;* The Cracksman; Live Now, Pay Later *with Ian Hendry;* The Martian Chronicles *with Rock Hudson;* Jane Eyre *with George C. Scott. Most recently she played the role of Dame Margot Fonteyn in* Jackie *with Emily Watson and Rachel Griffiths. She has also frequently broadcast on radio both in the UK and New Zealand. She has been nominated for and won numerous awards. In 1970 in recognition of her services to television Nyree was awarded the OBE.*

For me taking a career choice was not really an option. I didn't really have a choice. It just happened. I was three years old.

The world of the performing arts has been very good to me. I have had the privilege of being offered many challenging roles both classical and contemporary. It has been wonderful to work closely with good directors and fellow actors. I have found the excellence of my colleagues, their comradeship, their kindness and their ability to give so freely of themselves one of the most satisfying aspects of my profession. For me one of the funniest incidents I can recall was misquoting a line in *The Provoked Wife*. I lost control of the laughter, my own, the leads and the audiences.

My grandmother is the individual who influenced me the most as a person. She is an exceptional loving human being.

Being a mother has been my greatest personal achievement. Like many other working women I have found it difficult balancing the needs of family and career. Acting has its own unique strains particularly in relation to having to be on tour, or being on location with a film.

It has been traumatic on a personal level facing illness, my own and more importantly my daughter's. It has been a tremendous challenge being a sole carer for 11 years. For me it has been wonderful to have the opportunity to take forward a professional life and still be able to marry, have a child and live a full life. I feel I have 'done it all' and don't regret any of it.

On a professional level I have been influenced by many colleagues, the Directors' Peter Brook and Annie Castledine were two key individuals. It has always given me immense satisfaction when people are kind enough to tell me a role, play, TV, or film role has done something for them.

If I were able to change one thing about the world of work for women it would be that women did really get equal pay, more work opportunities, and a firm place in society. Women should be valued for their unique gifts and abilities. I believe there is the 'wisdom of women' and a special brand of 'kindness', which should not be dismissed. For me it is important that as women we do keep faith and feel free to offer and receive unconditional love. I sincerely hope the contribution of women will continue to grow and be recognised.

If I were at the start of my career again would I choose to be an actress? Given, that I started this by saying for me 'taking a career choice was not really an option. I didn't really have a choice. It just happened. I was three years old.' My answer strangely would be 'yes', I don't know why, but I have had a great life and a wonderful career!

Anita Roddick OBE
Entrepreneur and Human Rights Activist

The Body Shop was founded by Anita Roddick who in 1976 identified a niche in the market for naturally-based products with minimal packaging. The Body Shop rapidly evolved from one small shop in Brighton on the south coast of England, with only around 25 hand-mixed products on sale, to a world-wide network of shops. Franchising allowed for rapid growth and international expansion as hundreds of entrepreneurs world-wide bought into Anita's vision. The Body Shop International Plc is a values-driven, high-quality skin and hair care retailer operating in 48 countries with over 1,700 outlets spanning 24 languages and 12 time zones. Famous for creating an entire market sector for naturally-based products, The Body Shop introduced a generation of consumers to the benefits of a wide range of best-sellers from Vitamin E Moisture Cream to Tea Tree Oil, from Banana Shampoo to Aloe Vera Body Lotion.

The Body Shop has always believed that business is primarily about human relationships. They take the view that the more they listen to their stakeholders and the more they involve them in decision-making, the better their business will run. The company's campaigns against human rights abuses and in favour of animal protection alongside its commitment to challenge the stereotypes of beauty perpetuated by the cosmetics industry have won the support of a generation of consumers. The company continues to lead the way for other businesses to use their voice for social and environmental change.

I started The Body Shop in 1976 simply to create a livelihood for myself and my two daughters, while my husband, Gordon, was trekking across the Americas. I had no training or experience and my only business acumen was Gordon's advice to take sales of £300 a week. Nobody talks of entrepreneurship as survival, but that's exactly what it is and what nurtures creative thinking. Running that first shop taught me business was not financial science, it's about trading: buying and selling. It's about creating a product or service so good that people will pay for it. Now 23 years on The Body Shop is a multi-local business with over 1,700 stores in 48 countries, trading in 24 languages across 12 time zones, via more than 40 distribution centres. And I haven't a clue how we got here! I was born in Littlehampton in 1942. As the child of an Italian immigrant couple in an English seaside town, I was a natural outsider, and I was drawn to other outsiders and rebels. James Dean was my schoolgirl idol. I also had a strong sense of moral outrage, which was awakened when I found a book about the Holocaust at only 10 years of age. I trained as a teacher but an educational opportunity on a kibbutz in Israel eventually turned into an extended working trip around the world. Soon after I got back to England, my mother introduced me to a young Scotsman named Gordon Roddick. Our bond was instant. Together we opened first a restaurant, and then a hotel in Littlehampton. We married in 1970, me with a baby on my back and another in my belly.

It wasn't only economic necessity that inspired the birth of The Body Shop. Women, when they want to earn a livelihood, usually earn it through what they are interested in or what they are knowledgeable about. I had a wealth of experience to draw on. I travelled, and I spent time in farming and fishing communities with pre-industrial peoples. My travels exposed me to body rituals of women from all over the world. Also the frugality that my mother exercised during the war years made me question retail conventions. Why waste a container when you can refill it? And why buy more of something than you can use? We behaved as she did in the Second World War, we re-used everything, we refilled everything and we recycled all we could. The foundation of The Body Shop environmental activism was born out of ideas like these.

I am aware that success is more than a good idea. It is timing too. The Body Shop arrived just as Europe was going 'green'. The Body Shop has always been recognisable by its green colour, the only colour that we could find to cover the damp, mouldy walls of my first shop. I opened a second shop within six months, by which time Gordon was back in England. He came up with the idea for 'self-financing' more new stores, which sparked the growth of the franchise network through which The Body Shop spread across the world. The company went public in 1984. Since, I have been given a whole host of awards, some I understand, some I don't and a couple I think I deserve.

The Body Shop and I have always been closely identified in the public mind, undoubtedly because, it is impossible to separate the company values from my own personal values and issues that I care passionately about: social responsiveness, respect for human rights, the environment and animal protection. But, I must point out The Body Shop is not a one-woman show, but a global operation with thousands of people working towards common goals, engaged in their own livelihood, and franchisees running their own businesses.

Since becoming a grandmother in 1994, I talk about entering a period in my life when reflection is as important as activism, however, that does not stop me being passionate about 'doing'. Travel is a journey of discovery, much like a university without walls. I question myself, how else can I bring values in to an industry that is certainly not values-laden. The only way I can do it, is to perhaps bring back an idea for a trading initiative with an economically impoverished community in Mexico or Africa, or find inspiration for a new company commitment, just as my 1990 trip to Romania spurred the Romanian Relief Drive (now called Children on the Edge, a project of The Body Shop Foundation, registered charity number 802757). And in 1997, I proudly launched The New Academy of Business, with the aim of reforming business education for the next century. But above all The Body Shop is always on my mind, in one way or another. Whether it be in a state of delight or frustration. The relationship I have with The Body Shop is one where I sometimes can't tell the difference between stress and enthusiasm.

Reproduced by kind permission of Anita Roddick, The Body Shop International plc. Littlehampton.

Nafis Sadik MD
Executive Director, of the United Nations Population Fund (UNFPA)

Nafis on her appointment as the Executive Director of the United Nations Population Fund (UNFPA) became the first woman to head one of the United Nations' major voluntarily funded programmes. She holds the rank of Under-Secretary-General and as Chief Executive of UNFPA, the world's largest source of multilateral assistance to population programmes with an income level of approximately $307 million in 1998, Nafis directs a world-wide staff of 800. UNFPA provides assistance for over 140 countries and territories throughout the world. Since its inception in 1969, cumulative pledges through 1998 totalled over $4 billion from a total of 171 donors. Nafis' contribution to improving the health of women and children of the global community has brought her many international awards and honours in addition to over 10 Honorary Doctorates from universities throughout the world.

I have always called attention to the importance of addressing women's needs and of involving women directly in making and carrying out development policy. This is particularly important for population policies and programmes. I am proud that at UNFPA, 44% of the professional staff are women. We have promoted more women to leadership positions than any other part of the United Nations system. It is my firm belief that when the essential needs of the individual are addressed, those of larger groups – the family, the community, the nation and indeed the planet are more likely to be kept in the right perspective. One of the challenges we face is to find the balance between individual rights and responsibilities on the one hand, and the rights and obligations of the wider society on the other.

I was born into a conservative Islamic family in Pakistan. I had wonderful parents. My father was a very capable and gifted man. He held the positions of Finance Minister and former Vice-President of the World Bank. He was unusual in that he did not share the common view that women must always marry and raise children. My father had great vision. He believed it was important to educate both girls and boys. As you will appreciate that was not a common view in our part of the world at the time. Our wider family was not pleased and voiced their concerns about my going to college and then my being faced with the prospect of work.

After high school I considered two professions – engineering and medicine but I concluded the world was not ready to accept women engineers so I entered the Dow Medical College in Karachi. I was profoundly influenced by one of my teachers who was an obstetrician and gynaecologist and so I went on to specialise in women's health completing my internship at the City Hospital in Baltimore.

I went to the United States because my father became Executive Director in the World Bank. I did an internship and research in Washington D.C. and at City Hospital in Baltimore. In May 1954 I got married to my husband Azhar Sadik who was at that time in the army and returned to Pakistan in July 1954. Because of his job we moved a good deal. As a result I was able to work in a number of diverse communities and see for myself the link between family planning and the status of women. I saw many things. I witnessed first hand the suffering of many women including very young girls. For many women the only value they had was being the mother of a son. Women were not given the opportunity to space their families to protect their own health. Many women felt the significant pressure to produce a son at all costs. This view is one that still exists in many parts of the world. The female child is there to serve, to produce children, to be obedient particularly to her male relatives. The male child is the master and the person who takes decisions.

Family planning was one area in which a woman could regain a little control of her life. It was important to me that men and women should work together to improve the health of their family unit and take responsibility for the lives they create. For family planning to be effective particularly where a condom was the method of choice it was imperative to get the husband's co-operation. I strongly believe there is a joint responsibility.

In 1971, I came to work with the UNFPA and in spite of the difficulties and relocation of our family my husband took view that it was his turn to follow me in my work. My husband has been a huge encouragement and has provided wonderful support. I do wonder at times if my life and work would have turned out the same way if I had not married him.

I found working within the UN a bit of a culture shock at first. In many ways I was coming across the same sexist prejudices I had experienced outside, for example; if I made a suggestion it may be ignored but if a male colleague made the same suggestion at the same meeting it was taken seriously. This obviously changed once I became the first woman director of a UN agency.

The subjects UNFPA deals with – family planning, reproductive rights, health and gender issues have caused some controversy over the years but I can honestly say we have always tried to work for the best for women and families. These issues will always be emotive, which makes progress slow but essential. We must slow the exponential growth of the world's human population, which will soon reach 6 billion and at current rates of increase, will climb to approximately 10.5 billion by the year 2050. To be successful, three conditions must exist simultaneously and globally to help reduce the population, firstly the education and empowerment of women so that they can participate in decisions about the family size and the shape and nature of society, secondly we must have appropriate accessible family planning services and information available and thirdly that parents will have the confidence that their children will survive.

Since 1971 we have seen many strides forward. There are family planning programmes in most countries. Worldwide, about 350 million couples have access to reproductive health services and more than half of all couples use contraception, up from 10% in the 1960s. In some East Asian nations the average number of children has dropped from between six and seven to less than three. Although I acknowledge there is still much to be done. There are still women who cannot take control of their reproductive health because they have no access to contraceptives or instructions for their use.

In my vision for the future women would be accorded equality with their male counterparts and there would be education for all. Education encourages a sense of control over personal destiny and the possibility of choices beyond accepted tradition. Women with seven or more years of education tend to marry on average almost 4 years later than those who have none and mortality rates among children of educated women are significantly lower than those whose mothers have no schooling. Women should have access to safe affordable contraceptive care and they should have the assurance that the children they plan to have will have a good chance of growth and survival. All individuals should have the options to make choices about their lives and their future and we hope to help to make that possible.

I have had a rich and varied life. I have enjoyed the benefits of my education, my vocation, warm stable relationships, and wonderful children. It is my wish that other women globally would also have the same experience.

Marla Salmon ScD RN FAAN

Dean and Professor of the Nell Hodgson Woodruff School of Nursing, Emory University, Associate Vice-President for Nursing Affairs, Woodruff Health Sciences Center, Emory University, Professor, Rollins School of Public Health, Emory University

Marla serves as the Chief Executive and Academic Officer for one of the top ranking schools of nursing in the US and also as the lead policy leader for nursing education, practice, and research in the Woodruff Health Sciences Center of Emory University, one of the leading academic health science centers in the US. Her overall role is to enable and ensure the vision, leadership and organisational context necessary for the continuing development of nursing's contribution to both the academic and service missions of the university and its health sciences center. Because Marla is a professor in two distinct disciplines, nursing and public health, she also has responsibility for integrating nursing and public health together in ways that promote interdisciplinary academic collaboration. Lastly, Marla functions daily in the role of living out the values and philosophic framework of her school: scholarship, leadership, and social responsibility.

My career path is a reflection of multiple forces, rather than a conscious decision at any one point in time. It has been profoundly shaped by my early rural childhood experiences in a family led by a general practitioner father and nurse mother who believed that people should be of use to others around them and their larger community. Enhancing the health of people – and enabling others to serve in these ways – became a compelling commitment for me and a way to 'be of use.' My actual career choices do not reflect a linear, planned path. Rather, there are themes that reflect my commitment to being of use, an evolving understanding of what is important to me personally and professionally, what I believe and value, what I am good at doing, and what I've wanted to learn along the way. These themes have expressed themselves through shaping the ways in which I have acted on the many opportunities that have presented themselves along the way.

I have been most satisfied when I have been involved in the development of people, organizations, and policy that are of benefit to others, particularly the community and society at large. During my career, I have played leadership roles in the actual provision of health services, development of national and international health policy, and the organisation and management of complex academic and governmental organisations. In each of these arenas, it has been the knowledge that some good is being done and that people are growing in the process that has been most rewarding to me.

Perhaps it is the flip side of what is most satisfying about my work that is most difficult. It is when the potential to be of use to others, whether by individuals, organizations, and policy, is not realized. I suffer from the 'what could be' syndrome. I can often see the possibilities for what could be in ways that make it difficult to accept for those committed to keeping the present intact without regard for how the future might be better for others and even for that individual.

I suspect that my parents were of greatest influence on me in terms of the overall nature of how I approach and manage life (not to mention their genetic contribution). However, my husband and my children have filled in this framework with lessons of love, humility, perseverance, simple joys, forgiveness, and sacrifice. In a sense, my parents gave me the gravity and the horizon of my world. My husband and children have given me the color, weather, flora, landscape, and changing seasons. Under all of this is the spirituality, sense of meaning that my parents, especially my mother, gave to me. She had the ways of her Native American ancestors and found great peace in the beauty of living things. This has been a wonderful gift to me.

I have never been able to easily separate out what is professional and what is personal (a blessing and a curse). I would again name my family as being a constant source of encouragement. However, I would also add Vernia Jane Huffman, the former dean of my undergraduate program in nursing. She gave me a chance to live out my potential and challenged me at every turn to account for my decisions. She somehow knew that I had more to give than I had prior to entering the university, and helped me learn to challenge and focus myself. Most of all she gave me the gift of believing in me and helping me believe in myself. In some odd ways, she and my mother worked together on me – helping me to take on a world in which women lived in conventional roles. My mother always told me that I could do whatever I wanted to and believed in (and should). Vernia Jane Huffman told me that I should do what I wanted to and believed in, and challenged me to do so. They also taught me to mentor myself. In other words, they helped me to learn that ultimately I was responsible for finding the kinds of people I could learn from, seek the support and help that I needed, and move on when it was time to do so. They valued independence for women and helped me understand how very important it is.

I should begin by saying that I believe in guardian angels and have come to believe that among their many practices, insertion of humor in difficult times is one of the most wonderful. I should also say that I am a tall, large woman who has been described as statuesque. I am not a small or thin person, nor have I ever approached Twiggy-like proportions.

My guardian angel of humor visited me during the early part of my tenure as the Director of the Division of Nursing in the United States Department of Health and Human Services, when I was still an 'unknown' to many members of my profession – particularly those in specialties not related to mine. Here is the scene: I was to give a major speech for a large audience at a national professional convention. There was apparently some confusion about who was to introduce me, which was not discovered until the moment that I was to go to the podium. The convenor of the session handled the situation by saying something to the effect of 'We are delighted to have our next speaker whom you all know. Please join me in welcoming her,' without mentioning my name or title. What was clear to me was that most people in the audience didn't know who I was or why the introduction had been so strange. Needless to say, this led to a rather spotty and uncertain welcoming applause. Since I was already a bit nervous about this group and the message that I was to give, the introduction and anything but warm welcome put me totally off balance as I walked to the podium. I had no idea how I would begin my presentation. Fortunately, the guardian angel of humor intervened. I don't know what came over me, but my first words to this audience were 'Hi, I'm Elle McPherson!' It was quite clear to everyone present that I was not Elle McPherson the famous swimsuit model, as was evident by the roar of laughter that overtook all of us. This moment broke the ice gave me a boost of confidence, and I then moved on to say who I actually was and the message I came to deliver.

There have been many other funny situations in my career. I work with people who live highly stressful and demanding lives. Humor and laughter are the great outlets and the stuff that brings us all together.

The most traumatic situation that I faced came at an early age when I was Director of a Patient Advocacy Program in an inner city emergency room. This department was the scene of care for victims of terrible assaults. It was also the place where police brought suspects when they were injured. This particular emergency room was called the 'war zone' and was known for the terrible things that were experienced by patients, families, and staff. My job was to help make sure that peoples' needs were being met in the face of great challenges to all. I was in my early twenties when I began in this role and knew when I experienced the situation. It occurred in a normally quiet back hallway away from most of the usual action. I happened upon several policemen beating a man, out of sight of everyone but myself. I was horrified at the cruelty of what was happening. Before I really figured out what I should do, I ran to the scene yelling for them to stop and telling them I would take their badge numbers and report them. I think that they were so shocked to see me that they stopped. Much of the rest is a blur – the

The profiles

beating stopped, those officers and many others became very hostile and made my life difficult for a long time after. While there have been many other difficult situations since, this one was perhaps the most important to me. Somehow, I did the right thing in the face of adversity – perhaps only by instinct. But it did help to reinforce my belief that acts of courage help to build character and *vice versa*. I became a stronger person through this situation.

My greatest challenge is the same one for both my personal and professional life. It is the challenge of keeping all of the balls in the air at once while riding a unicycle up a steep hill in the dark – the challenge that all working mothers and wives face every day. It is the challenge of knowing that I will never be able to do any of it as well as I would like and will always miss something important somewhere for someone I love or for those whom I serve. It is the challenge of knowing that my family has been generous with me in ways that I can't return, and that my work has asked more than it should at times. Most of all it is the challenge of knowing that women really can make choices about their lives – but they are truly the hardest choices of all. You can have it all, it just won't be quite how you envisioned it, and it will never happen easily. But, all of these things together are also what makes the achievement so precious, and so much a part of our whole family's life, not only my own.

I would like to be able to take some credit for my children as my greatest achievement – I cannot. They are truly remarkable people who have paddled through some rough waters as part of our little family 'raft.' I will take some credit for paddling along with the rest, and in that way, I feel a great sense of accomplishment. I don't know that I have yet achieved my 'greatest achievement.' I always have a sense that there is more to do and be lived, and through this will hopefully be of some service to others. If I can do this, perhaps a lifetime of doing some good will be an achievement in itself. Ask me this in another 50 years and see what I say then!

My greatest professional achievement is also likely still in the future. I think that I have been successful in helping the professions of nursing and public health to become recognized as important social goods through my work with other disciplines and in the policy arena. I am at a career stage now where I am thinking about how I might help to shape professional education and practice in ways that enhance the abilities of these professions to be of social benefit.

My family is the force that keeps me whole. I have been blessed with close and sometimes very complicated ties with my parents and siblings, and also my husband and children. I cannot imagine what my world would have been without these dear and wonderful people. So much of who I am and how I have grown over the years can be attributed to them. Would I do it all over again? Absolutely without hesitation! I don't know that I made well-informed decisions when I chose to marry and have children. In fact, if I had known how tough it was I might have chosen otherwise. But now having had the experience of loving and being loved deeply and knowing that I am not alone, I would not exchange it for anything. My family is the greatest gift I have ever received.

The one thing I would change about the world for women is that it would become a world in which differences are respected and valued, education and social opportunity extended equally, and that the need for both women and men to make the world whole and healthy would be understood and appreciated.

If women experienced even part of what I would wish for the world in which we live, I would advise each woman to be clear about your commitments, values, and what you love and enjoy. Use these as the frameworks for your decisions – they make life much clearer, I believe.

My profession is a little bit like my marriage and family – I didn't make logical choices to begin with but wouldn't change things if given the chance to do it over again. In many ways, nursing and public health are professions whose time has come. People are beginning to understand that services that are aimed at keeping people healthy – and those that provide skilled caring – are critical to the overall well-being of societies, as well as individuals and families. Nursing and public health are well positioned to enable movement in these directions.

I would like very much to pay tribute to all women as women at work. Whether paid or unpaid, the women of the world are both the 'warp and woof' of the fabric of life – our hands do indeed rock the cradle and shape the destiny of the world. The old phrase, 'a woman's work is never done,' is true and unchanging. What hopefully is changing is the sense that women's work is invisible, unappreciated, and unrewarded. There is no end to the work that women must do – and I am grateful for that because we do it so well!

Cicely Saunders OM DBE SRN BA MB BS(Hons) MA MD FRCN FRCP FRCS
Chairman, St Christopher's Hospice

Dame Cicely is acknowledged as the pioneer of modern day palliative care and the hospice movement. Her remarkable career has encompassed nursing, medicine and social work. She has been awarded at least 20 Honorary Doctorates, in addition to many awards including being the first woman to receive the Worshipful Society of Apothecaries' (London) Gold Medal in Therapeutics 1979, the Templeton Prize for Progress in Religion 1981, the BMA Gold Medal for services to Medicine 1987, the Aristotle Onassis Prize for Services to Humanity 1989, the Raul Wallenberg Humanitarian Award from the Swedish Council of America 1990, and the Order of Merit by Her Majesty the Queen 1989. She has worked tirelessly to improve the quality of living and dying with cancer.

Dame Cicely wrote her first paper entitled Dying of Cancer *in 1957. In this paper she addressed the issues which have influenced the hospice movement so greatly i.e. the concept of special homes to care for the terminally ill cancer patient, specialists to care for the distressing symptoms cancer patients face and special attention paid to pain management. In 1967 St Christopher's Hospice, which Dame Cicely founded, opened its doors in South London to patients. Many have suggested this was the founding moment of the modern 'hospice movement' which over the following 30 years grew to have a global impact.*

At the time of writing I am now in my 82nd year. I remain the Chairman of St Christopher's Hospice, which I founded. I still work at the Hospice every day, seeing staff and attending various meetings. I also act as a source of continuity and support to the current Management Team and have an interest in maintaining a spiritual awareness through out the organisation.

I was prompted to take up my work by an encounter with a dying patient who was isolated and distressed. This catalysed my existing interest in the problems facing patients with terminal malignant disease.

I have found enormous satisfaction from all my work, the whole thing – just being with patients, their families and the staff. It has been tremendous to be able to help them realise something of their potential.

The person who has influenced me the most personally was David Tasma, a Polish Jew. He was 40 years of age and was dying in January/February of 1948. As a professional I was profoundly influenced by Mr Norman Barrett, a thoracic surgeon for whom I worked as a medical social worker and who impelled me into medicine at the age of 33.

Even in a career such as mine there is humour. At present I find it amusing to hear the constant surprise of people being told, 'Yes the Founder is still alive and working here every day.'

Like everyone else I have encountered personal and professional challenges at times. It was hard facing fellow students at the first MB in St Thomas' Hospital. They were all so many years younger and astonished to find me in their midst. It was also hard work trying to cope with night calls and being a Houseman at the age of 38.

As a professional I feel my greatest achievement has been being the catalyst for a world-wide movement of care for dying people and their families and matching science with spirituality to do this.

Personally it was a challenge remaining single until 1980. I feel my greatest achievement as a person was to have been loved by three men from Poland, marrying the third and helping all to die fulfilled and at peace. My work did have a profound impact on my life. I did not find it easy to be single but I could not have done it all if I had been married. Nor would I have met so many people to love. I now have a stepdaughter and three step-grandchildren, which is all I need. I also have numerous Godchildren and so many friends.

If I could change one thing about the world for women it would be increased help for the oppressed in the developing countries. It is so difficult to choose a specific thing but perhaps ensuring women owned themselves and their earnings. That would be a start.

If I could pass on one piece of advice to other women it would be educate your children, especially the girls.

It is impossible to second guess what will happen in the next 20 years in the world of work for women because attitudes change constantly and rapidly. There is also the global perspective, which makes any generalisation impossible.

If I were at the start of my career again I would still choose my current profession because God has helped me make a difference to dying and to reveal the incredible potential that exists at the end of life.

Editor's Note:
Dame Cicely is a remarkable woman who has led a remarkable life. In her modesty she has mentioned extraordinary events very briefly including the importance and impact of the men she loved throughout her life. David Tasma was a polish waiter Cicely met when she was working at St Thomas's Hospital in London. She was in the position of having to tell a man, alone in a strange country, that at the age of 40 he had inoperable cancer. They became close friends sharing their thoughts and their perspectives on faith. David was an agnostic Jew, and Cicely a Christian. Ultimately David and Cicely shared a love and his death. Cicely was moved to want to ensure people like David could die in peace with their pain controlled. Cicely shared this dream with David. She vowed to find a home where the circumstances would be right. David said to Cicely, 'I'll be the window in your home'. When David died he left Cicely a legacy of £500. which was all he had. Cicley was true to their dream, it took 19 years, but she used David's money to pay for David's window. The window still exists in St Christopher's Hospice.

Monica Louie Sims OBE MA LRAM LGSM
Past BBC Radio Talks Producer, Producer BBC Television, Editor of Woman's Hour, Head of Television Children's Programmes, Controller Radio 4 and Director of Programmes Radio, Vice-President, the British Board of Film Classification until 1999, Director of Programmes for the Children's Film and Television Foundation

Monica has had a long and distinguished career in film, television and radio. She was the first woman to hold such senior positions at the BBC. Her responsibilities included, BBC Radio Talks Producer, Producer BBC Television, and Editor of Woman's Hour, *Head of Children's Programmes Television, Controller Radio 4 and Director of Programmes Radio. Monica was also a member of a number of committees including the Council of the University of Bristol when she was Chair of the Careers Advisory Board.*

Monica read English at Oxford from 1943–1946. She became a lecturer in English and Drama in the Department of Adult Education at Hull University. She later took the post of Education Tutor for the National Federation of Women's Institutes at Denmam College.

I grew up in the 1930s and 40s in an atmosphere where men were assumed to be the natural leaders and women the practical supporters and peace-makers. My role models were my parents who were both teachers, and some single women teachers at my local Grammar School. The school's motto is 'In Honour Preferring One Another' and, although academic achievement was encouraged, the idea of service was fundamental to our Christian background. I first became aware that women could be a positive force in the world of work when we had an inspiring talk in school by an elderly Suffragette who made us realise that we had a duty to live up to the ideals of those self-sacrificing women and the opportunities they had opened up to us.

I had no particular idea of a carer, nor any defined ambition. As a child, when asked what I wanted to be when I grew up, I said 'An ordinary lady, like Mummy'. I still regret not managing to achieve a good marriage and children. But I had always hoped that I might become an actress or work in the BBC where radio news and music had become a big part of our lives during the war. My schoolwork was made bearable with the help of background listening to *It's That Man Again* or radio drama.

Jobs were not easy to find when I emerged from university, and the closest I could get to the theatre was to work in adult education in Yorkshire which allowed for experience in the summers at the Windsor Rep. and the Bristol Old Vic. In June 1953 I joined the BBC as a radio talks producer and had my first day off to celebrate the Queen's Coronation. For the next 31 years I found it difficult to take any time off because I was lucky enough to work continuously on programmes which I found stimulating and thought were worth making.

My introduction to broadcasting was in *Woman's Hour* where disciplines of a daily pioneering magazine were guided by two outstanding editors, Janet Quigley and Joanna Scott-Moncrieff, who demanded intellectual rigour, originality, humour and empathy with the nation-wide audience two thirds of whom were women.

The BBC at that time had a civil service-like organisation with a formal hierarchical structure. There was no obvious discrimination against women who received equal pay with men for the same work. The two professional and much-loved presenters of *Woman's Hour* – Jean Metcalf and Marjorie Andersen – were both married and worked on part-time contracts. On the staff were several impressive older women who were still holding responsible posts, which reflected their indispensability during the war when they took over work previously done by men. When these senior women retired younger men, not women usually replaced them, and the atmosphere was of a civilised man's club in which women were curteously acknowledged, but not promoted to positions of real power in the organisation.

Woman's Hour was able to be daring and provocative with subject matter that had not previously been discussed on air but was of interest to women. Topics included health, mental or social problems, religious doubts, financial difficulties, sexual orientation and child care, all suggested by listeners' letters. The production team was left alone largely because few of the male 'bosses' heard the programmes which went out live at 2 p.m. on the *Light Programme* sandwiched between popular light music sequences. I had one disconcerting experience when producing a Doctor's talk about the symptoms of the menopause when an angry man's voice on the telephone demanded that 'this filth should be removed from the airwaves.' The explanation that the subject was often requested by women at home was met with – 'Don't you realise this is being broadcast on all my market stalls?'

Like other radio producers of my generation, I moved to the expanding television service in 1956. The culture shock of the relaxed show business ambience and the use of Christian names was striking after the formality of Broadcasting House. Women in responsible jobs were still in the minority and I felt privileged to have a chance of learning to direct film and television from the tolerant instruction of men who were technically experienced.

At that time most television was transmitted live and there were many unplanned mistakes which made directing a nerve-wracking experience. I shall never forget the bulldog in a romantic costume serial which was supposed to die on the heroine's bed. The dog was well rehearsed and lay down effectively, but my instruction to the vision mixer to cut to a shot of the heroine's sad face was not acted on quickly enough and viewers saw the pleased dog sit up and wag its tail waiting for approval.

Gradually during the 1960s more women found opportunities as directors and producers in addition to the more traditional female roles of secretaries, make-up artists, costume designers or graphic artists. There were some vision mixers, film editors and floor managers (though no camera operators or engineers). Two outstanding women had a great influence on me – Grace Wyndham Goldie in Current Affairs and Joanna Spicer in Planning and Resources. But when I became the Head of Children's Television in 1968, I was often the only woman at the weekly Programme Review meeting attended by Controllers and Heads of Department and initially I found it difficult to join in the discussion about the week's output. I did, however, feel worried about the amount of violence in some evening and weekend programmes and pointed out to my male colleagues the large number of children who were watching after the 9 p.m. 'watershed', especially at weekends. As a result of this I was asked to examine the depiction of violence on television and this led to the BBC's first guidelines on violence which are now regularly updated in the light of changing output and audience reaction.

Conversations with programme makers demonstrated some extreme differences of attitude. I had been used to the protective approach of the Children's Programmes department where both men and women were anxious to provide a range of entertainment in a safe environment which would inform, educate, stimulate the imagination and exercise the mind and body. Producers instinctively assumed the position of caring parents, so it was a shock for me to hear the views of some of the men who made documentaries or dramas for adults where exposing all aspects of reality, however unpalatable, seemed more important than any possible ill-effects on the participants or the audience. This made me think more carefully about the responsibilities of public service broadcasting and the need to tread the tightrope between over-protection and the integrity of a medium which can be a lazy time-waster but can also be an enriching experience which extends delight and understanding. That was our intention in the Children's Programmes Department and my challenge was to revive its flagging fortunes at a time when the output was undervalued and split between adult departments. I was glad to re-establish drama and to extend the range of a mixture of programmes so that they have now become an essential part of television output.

Nowadays, women work in all parts of the BBC, but when I joined most of us were in the women's or children's or educational departments, so in 1978 I was pleased to move back to radio to become the Controller of Radio Four and to ensure its survival amid the onslaught of wavelength changes, the expansion of commercial radio and swinging budget cuts. Whenever I read accusations of extravagant overspending at the BBC I think ruefully of the continual cutbacks that I experienced. I was used to working on shoestring budgets, and relied on dedicated women clerks and secretaries who ran a tight ship and were devoted to their areas of work. Their replacement by highly paid consultants and intrusive management practices has destroyed a unique strength in the organisation. As in other large companies, ambitious men have instigated bold reforming measures, which have often ignored the prudent housekeeping skills inherited by women.

When I left the BBC in 1984 I was asked to investigate the shortage of women in BBC management. My report was based on conversations with BBC women throughout the country, and its 18 recommendations were all accepted except one that was thought to be impracticable. This was a suggestion for parental leave for fathers but even this has now been accepted. Fifteen years later the position of women in the BBC is much stronger and there are now four women on the decision-making Board of Management and Executive Committee with others in strong positions as Controllers, Senior Executives and Heads of Departments. There remains however an imbalance in the proportion of women in senior decision-making roles. I am sure this can be changed, but only if women really want these demanding appointments. Many outstanding women prefer to stay at the level where they feel they can use their talents without destroying their private lives, and several years of child-rearing makes it hard to catch up on the career ladder. So many women have caring responsibilities at home with children or older relatives that it is difficult for them to accept the pressures and long or irregular hours that broadcasting demands of them.

The most exciting part of radio and television is actually making the programmes and personal aggrandisement or large salaries are not as important to many women as a fulfilling life. I am reassured by the young women I meet today who intuitively accept their new status and feel free to choose their own career paths without automatically deferring to a male establishment as I had done for too many years. No longer could a BBC mandarin express an opinion of 50 years ago that 'No woman would be accepted as authoritative enough to read the news!'

Ruth Sims RGN Cert Ed FRCN OBE
Group Chief Executive Officer, Mildmay Mission Hospital
Chairman/Chief Executive, Mildmay International

Ruth's role and responsibilities include identifying need, developing and overseeing high-quality, cost effective palliative care services, including education and training in the UK, and in the developing world, that are an appropriate response to the needs of adults and children with advanced HIV disease.

Ruth represents Mildmay nationally and internationally and is the principal advisor to the Board of Trustees of the charity, especially in areas of policy and strategy. She is accountable to them for the achievement of the aims and objectives of the subsidiary companies within agreed budgetary limits.

Ruth has been the recipient of a number of awards and scholarships. Her selfless work particularly with HIV positive children in Uganda is a labour of love and commitment.

Ever since I can remember I wanted to be a nurse, I don't really know why, but I was very single-minded about it and never considered anything else. When I was 17 years of age I became a pre-nursing student. From there I went on to train as a nurse, became a Staff Nurse, married a Teacher and then went to Teacher's Training College myself. My real interest was in teaching children with learning difficulties and after a year I became Deputy Head of an ESN (S) school.

However, my first love was always nursing – caring for people who were sick and when my own children were grown-up I went back into nursing, this time as a Community Nurse. From there I became a District Nurse, then an Assistant Director, until I was offered the post of District Nursing Manager for Southend Health Authority. During that time I had specialised in the care of patients with cancer and lectured on malignant wound care. I really longed to be able to help those patients whose lives could so easily be ruined by disfiguring lesions, and I felt it a privilege to work with terminally ill patients. However, not long after I became District Nursing Manager, I really felt God was leading me to move in another direction. The reason I say I felt God was leading me, is because as a Christian I would pray and seek God's guidance for my life both for major and minor decisions. In this instance I felt God was guiding me to apply for the post of Matron at Mildmay. Mildmay was a community hospital in East London and it didn't seem to make much sense to me at the time.

The interest I had in Mildmay was because many years earlier I had completed my nurse's training there. When I saw they were advertising for a Matron, I felt more than just interested, I felt that I should take it further and find out more about the post. I went for an informal interview, only to learn that the night before they had decided to create a wing of the hospital as a hospice for people living with HIV/AIDS, which was to be Europe's first. This was so exciting for me because I saw caring for people with AIDS as an amazing challenge. I had only dealt with two or three patients with AIDS in Southend Health Authority, but they had presented all sorts of issues that we, as nurses, had not looked at before, so I felt this would be a very exciting, new, pioneering work which I would love to be involved in. It now made more sense! Over a period of 5 years I was promoted from Matron to General Manager/Director of Nursing, and then to Chief Executive.

I have found a number of aspects of my life and work very satisfying – to be allowed to share with a patient who is dying – a very significant and important time of their life. Being able to work with people who have been marginalised, who have a multi-systems disease, the like of which I have never encountered in all my nursing life. Being able to make a difference and improve the quality of life of people who are suffering stigma, discrimination and prejudice. I have always enjoyed management because there is no right way of doing things and you can be really creative. Finally, the work in the developing world. It has been satisfying because despite the overwhelming size of the problem of HIV/AIDS in Sub Saharan Africa, to be able to develop something that is relevant, culturally sensitive and improves the quality of life of people living with HIV/AIDS, has given me enormous job satisfaction – particularly as this has been brought about by the employment of many local people in the areas of clinical services and training.

In the area of health care, the last few years it has been difficult witnessing first hand the 'haves' and the 'have-nots of this world'. To realise the significance of which part of the world you are born in, particularly if you are a girl, and to what family. I have seen so much of this situation – especially with HIV/AIDS, where, in the developed world, people living with this disease have care and treatment. In the developing world, where the problem is so much worse, people just can't afford the treatment that they need, treatment that would help them. AIDS is unique in the way that it commonly affects several members of the same family at the same time and this is increasing poverty to the extent that children, especially orphans, are suffering extreme distress through lack of care and attention. I find this really difficult.

The person who has influenced me most in my life is Jesus Christ. Although I have obviously never met Him face-to-face I feel I know Him in a very real and personal way. Since becoming a Christian, as a teenager, I have been increasingly influenced by His life and teachings. Allowing Him to be Lord of my life is still, at times, a challenge and a struggle but He has never failed me. He has been creative with the pain and brokenness in my life and given me the courage to accept challenges and take 'risks' in faith, e.g. deciding to treat all sick children at the centre in Uganda free of charge whilst only having a few pounds with which to fund their treatment... within two weeks a donation of £50,000 was given for the purpose and funding is ongoing. I simply could not do what I do now without Him as I believe my strength is in, and through, Him. Giving my life into His control has resulted in opportunities and privileges I could never have dreamed that I would, or could, have been involved in.

As a professional I was greatly influenced by the late Richard Wells – who, when I first met him, was a Clinical Nurse Specialist at the Royal Marsden. He was part of a circuit of people lecturing and talking about HIV/AIDS in the early days of AIDS in this country. At that time I was researching malignant wound care and joined the circuit to lecture on that subject. I thought he was so impressive and articulate, he had such a compassion and understanding for people living with HIV/AIDS. He really had the ability to make people see things differently. When a colleague and I were going to undertake our study he helped us so much even though we were two perfect strangers to him. I think that if it had not been for Richard our work would not have gone ahead in the way that it did. We lectured all over the UK and went to Europe and America. We conducted annual wound care workshops for Smith and Nephew and had a booklet on the subject published by the Royal College of Nursing.

Through this came the realisation that if you apply for awards and scholarships, take a chance and have a go, it is surprising what you can achieve. Richard was a real encourager, he made us believe in ourselves. I therefore think that, in many ways, professionally, the late Richard Wells was the person who influenced me most.

Funny incidents in my career, there were a few of them! The first ward I went on to was a male ward and I was asked to put some flowers into a vase. I went out into the sluice where the vases were kept and picked the first one that I could find. I put the flowers in the vase and went and stood them on a table in the ward – all the patients started to hoot with laughter but they wouldn't tell me what they were laughing at. The vase of flowers stayed there for two or three days before I realised that I had put them in a glass urinal.

Another funny situation was when my hair went bright orange. Again, as a student nurse, I went to a school of hairdressing (because it was cheap!) to have a perm and they decided to give put some highlights in my hair as well – however with the combination of the perm, the highlight lotion and the learner, I came out with an orange head of hair! I went back on duty and the Ward Sister and the men on the ward were hysterical with laughter, they just could not hide it. I was told that Matron was going to do a round any minute so the Ward Sister suggested I should hide behind the oxygen tent, where the patient had the curtains drawn round. I did and had my back to the curtains as Matron opened them and looked in. She didn't say anything and I didn't turn round, but after she had left the ward she sent for me. As I stood outside the door I felt I had to think of a strategy because I thought I was probably going to be asked to leave as she would not approve of coloured hair let alone bright orange! I thought hard about what I could say and decided that the best thing might be to cry because perhaps then she might be less severe. I went in and immediately started to cry. It did the trick, she had enormous sympathy, so much so that she sent me off to a hairdresser she knew in Bond Street, gave me the money to go and have it put back to mouse brown. It was toned down – but even they could only tone it down slightly. It took a time for my hair, and my pride, to recover from this incident.

The most traumatic incident in my career was I think the first time I ever saw anyone dead. I don't know why, but I had always been afraid of seeing a dead body and I was well into my second year of training before I was suddenly confronted with this situation. I deliberately absented myself anytime that I thought I might see a dead body. Even when my mother died, I realised she was going to die very soon, so I left her while she was still alive.

I was a student nurse and had been looking after a young man of 34, he was very sick. I went off for my coffee break but when I returned Sister told me that he had died – we hadn't expected him to die so suddenly. She asked me to go in and see to him. I went outside to the sluice and I tried to pluck up the courage to go in but I couldn't, and I didn't know what to do. In the end I went up to Sister and I said to her 'I haven't ever seen anyone who is dead and I am frightened'. She said, 'That's OK nurse, let's see to things together'. We went in there and I spent most of the time I was washing this patient and preparing him with tears pouring from my eyes. In fact I think they were probably tears of relief as much as anything because I don't know quite what I had been expecting but it certainly wasn't as bad as I thought it was going to be.

Having said this, I am still not keen on seeing anyone who has died and will avoid it whenever I can, although nowadays I do not shirk the responsibility.

My greatest personal challenge was facing up to the fact that my marriage had irretrievably broken down whilst there were four children, the youngest of whom was seven, to be cared for, and realising that, because of circumstances, I was the one that had to leave the family home without my children. The decision to go and leave them was the most difficult decision I have ever had to make in my life. However, from that experience of separation, I have been able to use my understanding of how it felt to be separated from your children, to recognise the need for mothers with AIDS to be together with their children when one or more of them was going to die. As a result of this the Family Care Centre at Mildmay in Hackney was developed.

As a professional it is a challenge I still face, and that is making a difference in the lives of people living with HIV/AIDS in many parts of the developing world. Poverty is so great, people do not have enough to eat and there is no money for treatment – treatable diseases are often not being treated and there is no real alleviation of pain.

Trying to improve the quality of life and provide care in those settings is an enormous challenge, but one that I, along with all others who are involved in this, am not prepared to ignore. We really have to look at ways of improving the quality of life of those who are suffering in this way and to look at a creative way of responding to their needs. I suppose the challenge is feeling impotent, and the fear is that you might decide that there is nothing you can do. There is always something you can do – the creativity is in finding out what it is and how to do it.

My greatest personal achievement I feel is to have gone from a situation of brokenness, as a mother separated from her children, to have developed a close, warm, loving, caring, communicating relationship with all four of my children, who are now adults.

In my professional life to have led the development of a comprehensive range of palliative care services for adults and children living with AIDS, both in the UK and in the developing world has been what I would consider my greatest achievement.

I am especially privileged to have developed the Family Care Centre and the Nursery for children of HIV positive parents here in the UK, and to have led the development, in Uganda, of The Mildmay Centre, the Mildmay International Study Centre, a Mobile Clinical Training Team to take training to the rural areas, and the current development of two Day Care Respite and Rehabilitation Centres for orphans with AIDS, 0–5 years and 6–13 years. To be able to see the difference that loving acceptance by caring, well-trained, health care professionals can make to people who are suffering is a great motivator to further development.

Although I was a deputy head teacher at 25 years of age, until the time that I was separated from the rest of my family, I did not really see myself as a career person, I was not ambitious at all. I was happily married for 22 years, married and had children at exactly the time I wanted to, spent time with them whilst having a small part-time job while they were little, which I really needed to give me space and something else to think about besides babies.

I thoroughly enjoyed being with my family, having come from a broken home myself, I had some insight into what had been missing in my life, i.e. demonstrations of love and affection from my parents. I therefore think I took advantage of the opportunity to learn what not to do. Having been sexually abused as a child, having been adopted – which I didn't know about until I was 18 years of age, plus a few other traumas like that, I think that the effect of that sort of deprivation and abuse is that as an adult one finds it very difficult to make lasting relationships. I think abuse leaves one feeling vulnerable, not having a lot of self-confidence and not feeling that one can make relationships work and, in my case, this was the biggest effect of my difficulties as a child on my adult life. I do believe that if my plea to the doctor for help when things started to go wrong, had not been responded with 'its your age, you've had a hysterectomy, you'll be fine soon, you are just having a funny five minutes', and there had been a few of the right sort of questions asked, then my ex-husband and I might well have been helped to resolve our problems.

Having had a happy marriage, despite the hell of divorce and separation, I am so glad that I married and have children. At the time of separation from my children I really put my all into work so that I didn't have to think about things that hurt me, and I am quite convinced that is one of the reasons why I was able to be offered promotion and eventually get to the Chief Executive Officer grade. I worked 18-hour days when I was developing Mildmay's services, I had the time to give, and I didn't have competing priorities. Considering the hours I worked, and continue to work, I do not think I could do this work in the way that I do at present without damaging a marriage, or whilst caring for dependent children,

If I could change one thing for women it would be that women all over the world would have equality of status and equality of opportunity with men, from birth right through their lives.

My advice to women is to work at being a good communicator. The importance of good communication cannot be underestimated. In both personal and professional relationships understanding will be enhanced, conflict minimised and solutions to problems identified through open communication. A breakdown in even one relationship, which is not resolved, can result in stress, which can be destructive and may have a profound effect on all aspects of ones life.

It is also crucially important to know your limitations and know when you can't do something and when you need to ask for help from someone who has more experience than you have in that area. Sometimes it is more important to know what you can't do than it is to know what you can do.

Over the next 20 years for women in the UK I think that we will see more women in senior positions, positions of influence and authority. I think that it will be made easier for women to pursue their careers whilst at the same time being able to take a real part in the bringing up of their children. Moves will be made to ensure that women will be rewarded for their efforts on a equal basis with men in similar positions.

In the developing world there are already increasing numbers of women in positions of authority, and education is the key to further opportunities. As the importance of education for girl children is recognised, more women will ultimately be eligible to take up senior positions where they can influence policy and decision-making and improve the opportunities and openings for women.

Sadly I think the impact of HIV/AIDS will reduce many of the gains as increasingly more girls and women are forced to care for sick family members in hospitals and in their homes. However, women are resourceful and I believe they will rise to the challenge.

If I was at the start of my career again would I choose the same profession? Yes, because I have enormous job satisfaction and I am very fulfilled in the work that I do. The rewards are far greater than any contribution I could ever make.

Rita Sussmuth PhD
Politician, Prasidentin des Deutschen Bundestages, Bundeshaus, Germany.

In terms of protocol, the speaker of the German Parliament is the second most important person in the republic, after the president. Rita was much more than a figurehead: she was the voice of conscience in Chancellor Kohl's Christian Democrat Party, speaking out repeatedly on the need for conciliation with Jews and Poles, and putting a firm demarcation line between the party and the nationalist right wing. She champions women's causes, pleads for a softer drug policy and addresses the problem of AIDS and family dilemmas.

Rita has had a long and distinguished academic and political career. She studied romance languages, literature and history at the Universities of Munster, Tubigen and Paris. She followed this with postgraduate studies in science, sociology and psychology at the University of Munster where she was awarded her PhD. From 1985–1988 she was Federal Minister for Youth, Family and Health Affairs. Since 1986 she has been the Chairperson of the CDU's Federal Women's Union as well as being a Member of the CDU's steering committee. From 1988–1998 Rita held the position of President of the Bunestag.

Work is very important for all of us. We need to satisfy our basic needs and that includes being free from fear, having a safe roof over our heads, being able to sleep in peace, have enough food for ourselves and our families and being gainfully employed in work which helps us meet those needs as well as providing us with a feeling of worth and dignity.

The career we choose is important for many reasons. Work gives us a sense of our worth and status in society. This is good in some respects but also dangerous in others. For example, a wife and mother may choose a lower paid job with flexibility because it allows her to care for her family. She may be capable of much more but she is limited by the opportunities around her. We know in Germany every second mother has a job outside of her home.

Work also has a role in providing men and women with an opportunity to be fully integrated into wider society. Women who are working exclusively at home may feel isolated and undervalued. Some women opt for a compromise by caring primarily for their families but also opting for an honorary position, which provides flexibility. Although this can be a satisfying choice in my opinion a 'real job' is quite different. I feel if a woman wants to pursue a career she should not be discriminated against.

I know we worked hard in government to change things, yet the sad fact remains that women still on average earn less than men. We have found women climb the career ladder more slowly than men and there are only 5% of women in senior management positions in large corporations. This begs the question of why?

Women who are proactive and take the lead in enterprise can often earn three times as much as men. Women are known to be good senior managers taking a holistic approach to caring for their workforce.

It sometimes feels like women themselves are reluctant to pursue a career and often this is due to the pressure of their families and partners. Women today are still largely responsible for the provision of domestic arrangements and the detailed care of children. For some there is still the feeling that the career of the man is more important than the woman.

It is important that employers provide good maternity arrangements, career breaks and facilities for families if women are to be encouraged to develop their hidden talents. Flexibility in respect of both time and location if women are to be fully integrated into the world of work. Home working with appropriate technology is a wonderful opportunity. It also has environmental benefits including a reduction in workday traffic and noise.

For our younger generation of women it is important we improve the development and training opportunities open to them. It concerns me that young women with excellent grades still find it hard to obtain an apprenticeship place.

Young women should not be pushed towards stereotypical jobs like office work, hairdressing, etc. Girls should be encouraged to consider engineering, information technology, etc.

Although I may sound a little pessimistic, change has taken place over time. In 1961 a doctor said: '... a mother with children under 15 years of age is not supposed to work outside of the home... her job is to look after her family.'

This raises other issues for women. The value of the work done by men and women during a week is nearly identical. The fundamental difference is that for a woman working at home her 50+ hours receives no pay. Family is a high priority for most of us but there needs to some equity in the way resources are allocated to men and women.

The Christian Democrat's are now in opposition. As a young teacher, long before I entered politics by joining the CDU, I worked day and night to help realise Brandt's broad vision. That really was a new start.

Helen Suzman DBE BCom
South African Politician (1953–1989) and Human Rights Activist

Helen entered her political life during what was to be a turbulent period in the history of South Africa. She fought for her beliefs and the hope of a better South Africa for all people. For many years she was a lone voice in Parliament representing the non-apartheid views of the Progressive Party. Her tireless work has been acknowledged globally and she has been very generously endowed with Honorary degrees by various universities including her own Alma Mater as well as the University of Cape Town, the University of Natal and the University of Rhodes in South Africa; She has 24 degrees from other Universities including Oxford and Cambridge in the UK and many of the top universities in the USA including Harvard, Columbia, and Yale. In 1978 Helen received the UN award for Human Rights and was twice nominated for the Nobel Peace Prize. Her Majesty's Government in 1989 honoured Helen when she was made a Dame of the British Empire and by South Africa when President Mandela presented her with the Order of Merit (gold) in 1998. Helen served South Africa as an MP for 36 years, 13 years as the only sitting member of the Progressive Party and 6 years as the only woman in Parliament.

My title at the present time would not be 'a woman at work' but a 'retired woman who worked for many years'. I first worked as a statistician for the War Supplies Board during World War II and for 8 years from the end of the war as a lecturer in Economic History at my Alma Mater, the University of Witwatersrand. In 1948, the United Party, headed by General Smuts, went out of power and was succeeded by Dr Malan's National Party which had supported Germany throughout the war and whose election platform was apartheid and race discrimination. I thought our family should emigrate. My late husband had good degrees from the UK and USA and would easily have obtained a job in his profession. He, however, was not in favour of leaving and I was ambivalent as I was hopeless at domestic work, could not cook and envisaged a starving family of myself, my husband and two young daughters. So we did not emigrate.

As I wrote to a friend at the time, if one remained in a country ruled by a racist government, one had to do try to do something about the situation. Political activity was the obvious choice, and my interest had already been roused by my membership of the South African Institute of Race Relations, a non-governmental organisation strongly opposed to racism, and to the oppressive measures against black citizens which existed even before the apartheid regime, such as the pass laws. These laws restricted the mobility of black persons, enabling them to be employed mainly as migrant workers, who were prohibited from bringing their families with them to the urban areas. I prepared evidence for the Institute against the pass laws, which was presented to a Commission of Inquiry into the migratory labour system that had been appointed by General Smuts. This task further stoked my interest in politics. I suppose if I had to say what had influenced me in my choice of careers I would have to look back to my schooldays where I was taught important basic values by the head nun at the convent I attended; apart from respect for human rights, she taught me punctuality and to be a very bad loser, for she chastised the pupils with her ever-ready ruler if we lost a hockey match. I think that was useful in my political career in a country where the elections were based on the Westminster system of 'first past the post'. In other words, you had to win, it was no good coming second. That was something I understood right from the beginning of my career. I was also much influenced by Professor Hansi Pollak and Jules Lewin who both made clear to me when I was a student the tremendous disadvantages suffered by Black, Coloured and Indian people as a result of race discrimination in South Africa.

I entered the political maelstrom in 1953 when I was elected as the Opposition United Party MP for Houghton in Johannesburg, a constituency which Americans would call a 'silk stocking district'. It was a position I held until I decided not to stand in the 1989 election. I was, therefore, a Member of Parliament for 36 years. In 1959, 11 United Party Members of Parliament, including myself, broke away from the Party because of its equivocal attitude on the apartheid issue and formed the Progressive Party. There was an election in 1961 in which all my colleagues were defeated. I remained the only member of the Progressive Party for 13 years and was also the only woman member for 6 years during that time... As the only Progressive Party member in Parliament for 13 years I had to deal with every important issue that arose in the House. It was, of course, very hard work, but I was far too busy to be sorry for myself, though I often wished that I had someone with whom I could exchange a joke or two when strange things were said in parliament. Such as, on one occasion when the Minister of Bantu Administration, an elderly gentleman named De Wet Nel, announced that members should be very careful what they said in Parliament because only the other day he been in the Transkei and had seen a Bantu on a bicycle with a Hansard under his arm. In 1971, seven Progressives were returned to Parliament and we formed a stalwart little group opposing every apartheid measure introduce by the Government and the numerous measures that undermined the rule of law.

I had to cope with my own personal position of having to attend Parliament in Cape Town – 1,000 miles from my home in Johannesburg for five or six months each year, leaving the family of my two daughters, aged 10 and 13 while I attended sessions. I was fortunate, however, in that they were healthy girls who were happy at school and they had at home a resident physician in the shape of my husband and a conscientious Dutch housekeeper and surrogate parents, my father and stepmother, to look after them. I did not have the guilt many working mothers appear to have, possibly because I am an extremely independent person myself having lived through a childhood without a mother who died when I was born.

Although human rights, race discrimination and the rule of law were my main concerns as a Member of Parliament, I participated in every debate, which affected women. I played a major role on the Select Committee, which recommended changes to the laws, which denied rights to women married in community of property. Although the legal rights of women have advanced considerably since I entered Parliament and gender discrimination is prohibited under the new Constitution adopted in South Africa in 1996, many disabilities remain for women living in rural areas under traditional chiefs, a conflict which will eventually have to be resolved by the Constitutional Court.

I think I can say with justification that I was a respected Member of Parliament, very careful to be factually accurate and following the principle of 'seeing for myself'. I did not use newspaper reports or hearsay as the basis for speeches in Parliament. I used my position as an MP to gain access to resettlement areas and squatter camps, and to visit prisoners and detainees. It was on the basis of first hand knowledge that I made my speeches in Parliament, very well reported, I may add, by the English-language press. It was also during this time that I visited Robben Island and first met the former President, Nelson Mandela, forming a friendship, which has lasted since 1967.

By and large, I enjoyed my career as a Parliamentarian. I look back on my career with pleasure though I wish I had stayed in Parliament for four more years so as to witness the changes, which I had advocated all those years, becoming a reality.

Since leaving Parliament in 1989 I have, *inter alia*, written my memoirs, *In No Uncertain Terms*. I served as a member of the Independent Electoral Commission, which supervised South Africa's first democratic election in 1994 and as a member of the South African Human Rights Commission for 3 years. I am an Honorary Life President of the South African Institute for Race Relations and of the Democratic Party (Originally the Progressive Party) of South Africa. However, at 82 years of age, I have resigned from all other activities except a few education trusts.

These days I spend much time reading. I play bridge and look after my menagerie of three dogs, a Labrador and two Shihtzus. I write the occasional article or letter to the newspapers and carry on a fairly extensive correspondence with friends and former colleagues in South Africa and elsewhere in the world. There are too the wonderful game parks to visit in South Africa and I have a very nice apartment at one of our superb seaside resorts, Plettenberg Bay.

Finally, apart from observing with disappointment some of the unpleasant features of life in South Africa such as the alarming unemployment rate of 30% and the high incidence of violent crime, together with a good deal of nepotism and corruption, I have to say that South Africa is a beautiful country with a wonderful climate and rich natural resources. It is of course, of enormous satisfaction to me that despite my complaints against government policy in certain respects, I am deeply relieved at the disappearance of all the heinous laws of the apartheid regime which I opposed with such vigour during the time that I was a woman at work.

I rejoice at South Africa's readmission to the comity of nations, to the UN and to the Commonwealth, its membership of the Organisation of African Unity, and its leading role in the Southern Africa Development Community. Of course, like all South Africans I thoroughly enjoy our renewed participation in international sport, where we seldom lose!

The profiles

Joanna Trollope OBE MA (Oxford)
Novelist

Joanna is a much-loved bestselling novelist of global renown. Her books often explore the fortune and misfortunes of the middle classes in England. They are contemporary novels dealing with modern relationships. Her books have included The Best of Friends, The Brass Dolphin, The Choir, The Spanish Lover, A Village Affair, *and* The Rector's Wife *to name but a few. A number of the novels have been adapted for television including* The Choir, *1988, televised in 1995, and* The Rector's Wife, *1991, televised 1994,* Other People's Children *had just been filmed for the BBC. In 1980 Joanna was awarded the Accolade of Romantic Historical Novel of the Year.*

Joanna is currently Vice-President of the Trollope Society, a member of Council for the Society of Authors, Vice-President of the West Country Writers' Association, Patron of Gloucestershire Community Foundation, Founder and Co-Trustees, The Joanna Trollope Charitable Trust; and she is a Member of the Campaign Board of St Hugh's College, Oxford. Joanna was also a member of the Government Advisory Board for the National Year of Reading 1998–1999.

I was prompted to take up my career as a writer by a desire to communicate and a strong belief in the importance of narrative in human relationships. As a result it has been particularly satisfying to receive feedback from readers. The reader response has been vital and it has proved to me that the communication is working and a need is being at least partly met.

On the downside having achieved a significant measure of success the exposure of a public profile is hard because of the intrusive media attention which is often inaccurate and at times curiously judgmental. There seems to be a difficulty in accepting middle-age, middle-class success. The results of this in my personal life have at times been very traumatic. There have been legions of amusing incidents during my career usually resulting from people feeling they know me intimately and are therefore free to say exactly what they like... which they then proceed to do.

My children, I guess, have been my greatest influence as indeed have been the effects and responsibilities of parenthood. On the professional side I have been strongly influenced by editors; present and past, also past writers; especially nineteenth century novelists including the real Trollope.

One of the greatest challenges I have faced as a person has been overcoming emotional vulnerability and anxiety – except that I think I never entirely will, and this is part of the creative process! As a professional it has been important to be steady and persistent – best sellerdom took 20 years to achieve.

My greatest achievements? I think they are simply the affection of my family, my friends and my readers.

Marriage has been very important in my life (I've been married twice though I'm now single), and my children have been vital. I am very glad to have been married, and I am now glad and relieved to have freedom. I am doubtful that any successful career can operate without a knowledge of human relationships.

If I could change one thing about the world for women it would be in the First World, less pressure to perform perfectly at all levels. In the Third World, freedom from continuing barbaric oppression and exploitation.

My advice to other women would be; in the first case — there is more time — i.e. life — than you think and therefore less hurry.

It is hard to predict what will happen to women over the next 20 years. I wish I knew. It depends so much on the development of relations between the sexes, as well as on practical matters like government support.

Would I have chosen the same career path if I was at the start again? Absolutely. My career as a writer has given me more personal satisfaction than I could have dreamed of and I hope some reader satisfaction too.

Catherine Walker
Fashion Designer, Chelsea Design Company Ltd.

Catherine Walker is the fashion world's contradiction. A Greta Garbo figure in a world of hype, famous for being private, hugely successful in couture which is most fashion houses lost-leader. Perhaps the greatest mystery to many is why she never exploited her 16 year relationship with Diana, Princess of Wales whose image Catherine was instrumental in creating.

Catherine Walker is French and was educated at the University of Lille and Aix-en Provence where she took a doctorate in aesthetics. She moved to London in 1969 where she met and married an English lawyer who tragically died in 1975 leaving her with two baby daughters. She began her career in 1976 selling her designs from a basket in the Kings Rd, Chelsea. She spent the next 20 years teaching herself the skills of couture and forming a traditional couture studio in Sydney Street, Chelsea. In 1995, Catherine found she had breast cancer and in typical fashion told her staff it was a 'hiccup'. And that it would be 'business as usual'. Despite Catherine's enigmatic and modest manner she is gradually being recognised as one of the great talents of our age.

I am the co-owner of the Chelsea Design Company Ltd and as the designer, I am responsible for producing two collections a year. I became a fashion designer by accident. After the sudden death of my first husband, John, I started to sew as a kind of therapy which by its nature was introspective. This 'inward looking' approach to fashion was the opposite to what most people expect from fashion designers who are supposed to be a little more forthcoming if not downright extrovert, but it led me to an interest in the technical side of creating garments which in turn lead to couture.

Professionally, I have found it most satisfying working with a team of highly skilled technicians. One area, though, which has been a challenge, is the fact that my handwriting is very different from the English way of approaching fashion. In addition, because English is not my natural language I have often felt trapped without the words to express myself in a profession that above all requires precision, so I use a sketching pencil and shears instead!

The person who has been the greatest influence on me is the photographer John French. He used to tell his models to imagine they had a string attached to their heads stretching to the ceiling. It elongated the body and when I translated this into my work it was as if a light had come on. On the business side, my partner has had to teach me everything.

On a non-professional note I have had to be an influence on myself. I am blessed/cured with a body that overreacts to tiny stimuli both physical and emotional. So I have had to learn to listen to myself and learn my own lessons the hard way. In an odd way the person who has had a strong but beautiful influence on me was my great Uncle Achile. He was a typical Provencal eccentric with a long white beard. He would declare his love for me each day and write me poems one of which I have translated here:

Petite princesse lointaine
tu reves de bouquets de fleurs,
de sonorites, de couleurs,
de mer bleue et de vastes plaines…

Tandis qu'aux heures incertaines
dans le soir gris tombent nos pleurs,
tu ne reves que de bonheurs;
Comment les saisir a mains pleines,

Comment les conserver? surtout,
comment garder, supreme atout
l'enthousiasme et la jeunesse?

Ah! pour que nulle heure, des jours
a venir, jamais ne te blesse;
En toi, garde un immense amour!

Achile Sevin, Aix en Provence, Juin 1960

This is my translation into English:

> Little Princess far away
> You dream of flower bouquets,
> Of sounds, of colours,
> Of blue seas, of vast plains…
>
> While during uncertain grey hours
> Of evening our tears fall,
> You dream only of happiness
> and how to seize it with open hands,
>
> How do you cherish it? Most of all,
> How do you keep it, this supreme asset of
> enthusiasm and youth?
>
> Ah! So that no hour of any day
> ever comes to hurt you
> keep your heart full of love!

My work is filled with humourous incidents. A few stick in my mind – the bride who would only try on her dress for fittings *inside* a plastic bag to keep it clean; the cerise bias-cut satin dress – for a man; the 94-year-old couture client having a fitting next to a 14-year-old client; the satin column dress for a 6-foot-tall, nine month pregnant bride… I could go on!

The greatest professional challenge I have had to face was treating the Princess of Wales as a real person at all times rather than an image or an icon. I found that the effect of my work with Diana was that is attracted the good and the bad and also placed me in a pigeon-hole in many people's minds. I am only now finding that I can escape that pigeon-hole and start to design with the freedom most designers enjoy.

In my personal life, the two greatest challenges I have had to face are: being widowed with two baby daughters, and in recent years suffering from breast cancer. Any serious trauma has consequences in one's life far beyond their immediate impact and today I am still reacting and learning from them.

My greatest personal achievements are my two beautiful daughters Naomi and Marianne who have helped keep me young at heart.

I feel my greatest professional achievement is yet to come.

The impact of family and relationships on my life is enormous. I am very emotional and all human encounters affect me whether positive or negative. I have been married twice and when my first marriage was abruptly ended by the death of my husband, it was a tragedy in so many ways; I was sad that I didn't have the luxury to get to know his bad sides as well as his good and to get closer in the process.

Women have a greater emotional responsibility in the world than men, it would be good for men to know how different women are in the first place so that they can view the difference with respect and pride.

If I could pass on one piece of advice to other women it would be, do everything you can to look after yourself and keep your heart young and full of love, spoil yourself the best way you can and never stop dreaming.

The age of childbearing can now be delayed to allow women to start a career. I think this will remain the same over the next 20 years, and maybe more women will be coming back to work after having children. I hope women will have more control over their lives and will use this freedom, but not at the expense of themselves, and in turn, at the expense of their families and society.

I would never have chosen fashion designing as a career, but I am pleased it happened accidentally.

Lynn Wallis FISTD
Artistic Director, Royal Academy of Dancing

Lynn has made an outstanidng contribution to the world of Dance having worked with most of the key figures over many years. Her current role is as the Artistic Director, of the Royal Academy of Dancing. She is responsible for setting and maintaining the standards of dance training world -wide. Lynn is a Fellow of the Imperial Society of Teachers of Dancing.

Greek dancing was in the curriculum at my school and when I was 10 years old the teacher suggested I should take ballet classes, as I appeared to derive great enjoyment from movement. As soon as I started to learn classical ballet I realised this was what I wished to study and follow as a career. I took private classes with that same teacher and after only six auditioned for the Royal Ballet Lower school. Having had very little study I obviously didn't know very much and had to follow almost everything that I was asked to do in the audition class. I had an interview with the head of the school and whilst waiting for this in the corridor was thrilled with the buzz going on all around me and I was in awe of all the dancers passing by me. The excitement in the atmosphere was, I was sure radiating from the creative environment of which I knew I wanted to be a part. I was accepted into the school, but on returning home and realising what an enormous financial burden it would have put on my parents for me to be a boarder, I opted to study locally and re-auditioned for the upper school being accepted at age fifteen. I was moved into the graduate class after my first year and our daily class teacher was Dame Ninette de Valois. Although I was somewhat terrified, in retrospect, consider myself extremely fortunate to have studied under the very person who formed the Royal Ballet and indeed other companies around the world, some of which I was to find myself linked with in the future. At the end of my first year I appeared in a Character dance demonstration for the annual school performance at the Royal Opera House Covent Garden. To this day I remember vividly the excitement of taking my first step onto that famous stage, the magic was almost overwhelming.

After 3 years training, I joined the Royal Ballet Touring Company and embarked on my career as a professional ballet dancer. The life in a touring company was a hard one, the dressing room became one's home for weeks on end and there was much to be learnt living at close quarters with others around you. It was a matter of respecting one's colleagues and working together for the common end. This was an education in itself; one, which I believe, gave me a firm foundation to deal with everything that life was to hold in store. There were challenging and stimulating times of studying new works and new roles not to mention the occasional trips overseas. One of the most exciting of these was a tour on which Dame Margot Fonteyn and Rudolph Nureyev joined us. There was also an enormous amount to learn about the profession on a day-to-day basis. I really hadn't appreciated what went on backstage to ensure the smooth running of the performances and how intricate the planning and liaison between the departments had to be. This whole aspect of the work became fascinating to me and I began to spend my free hours observing technicians and wardrobe personnel at work, as well as watching others in rehearsals. It made me realise that in fact I wanted to move beyond being a dancer and become more involved with the creative process, to assist in preparing young people for their future in the theatre. It seemed that the timing for my transition couldn't have been more perfect plus I was fortunate in having someone who believed in giving me the opportunity to achieve my desire. I went to speak to Barbara Fewster who was then Principal of the Royal Ballet School and had also taught me as a student in my first year. I explained to her what I wanted to do and she entrusted me to the position of Assistant Ballet Mistress to succeed Joy Newton who was taking early retirement the following year. Barbara started me on my new path, inspiring and guiding me as a young and inexperienced young teacher. In preparing the students to be members of the *corps de ballet* the work entailed not only teaching them sections of the classical repertoire but also appreciating dance as a whole, the discipline of working closely with others, perfecting technique, musical awareness whilst allowing for the development of artistic interpretation. It was a big task and an enormous learning curve for me also.

In addition to these classes I was to produce the school performances at the end of each year. This opened up even more challenges as it involved everything from teaching the selected ballets, to organising rehearsal schedules, liasing with the theatre staff, the conductor and orchestra. It was somewhat like a huge jigsaw puzzle – the pieces had to be sorted and organised, time being of the essence in order to build and complete the final picture. If one piece were out of place the whole thing would fall apart. But this building process was to me one of the most fascinating and challenging aspects of my job. Over the years I was fortunate through these performances and the ballets that were being performed to receive guidance from great choreographers and producers including Sir Frederick Ashton, Sir Kenneth MacMillan and Sir Peter Wright. It was always extremely nerve-racking when they came into the rehearsal room, as I was acutely aware of the responsibility of reproducing their works both in the choreographic sequences and their intent.

A further window of opportunity opened up as I was invited to reproduce some of these same works for various organisations overseas. My learning curve continued as I was faced with different working practices as well as understanding the various cultures and customs of the countries I visited.

The first place I went as a guest was to Canada, teaching for a Summer School. This started a connection with the National Ballet School in Toronto and one that was to change my life significantly in years to come as it was there that I met Erik Bruhn, the world renowned dancer. He had created a ballet for the boys of the National Ballet School and we subsequently asked him to come to London to stage the same work for the Royal Ballet School. I worked with him through this and then again, at his invitation, as his assistant on his production of *Giselle* for the Royal Swedish Ballet. Then came the change and once again Barbara Fewster gave me encouragement to proceed. Erik invited me to go to the National Ballet of Canada to become Artistic Co-ordinator alongside Valerie Wilder who was already in place as Artistic Administrator. I packed my bags and set up home, loving every minute of the new life and the challenges that it held in store. The years working with Erik were truly wonderful. I was to learn a great deal from his expertise and met many world renowned artists and choreographers whom at the beginning of my teaching career I would never had dreamed I would ever have met. The dance world was deeply saddened when Erik passed away. However, he had recommended to the Board that should he not be able to continue with his work, the management of the Company should be left to Valerie and myself. Realising the enormous task that we had on hand we asked Glen Tetley who had had a long association with the Company to become Artistic Associate. We worked closely for 18 months but then it was time once more for my life to change. I returned to London and resettled, happy to spend time with family and friends and taking on freelance work with the National Ballet of Portugal and La Scala Milan. After 2 years I joined English National Ballet as Deputy Artistic Director and was back again to the touring life. My responsibilities covered a wide range including mid-scale touring, English National Ballet School and the Education unit but although not looking for a change after 3 years I was approached by the Royal Academy of Dancing to become Artistic Director. The work I am involved in with the Academy is diverse and every day one faces new and different challenges in a world that is fast changing and ever demanding. My travels with the Academy have taken me all over the world and it seems that wherever I go there is someone I know from years gone by. Past knowledge of the cultures and customs in the countries in which we operate and having worked with people of all ages and at various levels of training have, I believe, helped me considerably in my demanding role.

To be asked about my greatest achievement, I would respond by saying I would hope I have helped young people to fulfil their dreams through the education and enjoyment of an art form that is all embracing. To see a student or professional achieve their aim has been the most rewarding part of my time as an educator, whether it has been a child who may find that dance is their best way of expression or a professional portraying a role to their own satisfaction. I consider myself to have been extremely lucky in my career and perhaps to have been also in the right place at the right time. The opportunities for fulfilment have been multi-fold and if given the choice I would do it all over again. But above all family, friends and colleagues without whom I know I would never have had the courage to face the challenges, have given me support and encouragement. There are so many insecurities that one faces in life but through communication I truly believe they came be overcome and for me dance has been my way of speaking.

Hanna Gronkiewicz-Waltz LLB MA PhD
President of the National Bank of Poland

Hanna Gronkiewicz-Waltz has been President of the National Bank of Poland (NBP) since March 5, 1992. During her 6 years at the NBP, she has been instrumental in strengthening the independence of the central bank and has assisted the dynamic growth of the banking sector, developing a clear-cut licensing policy. It was during her term of office, in 1995, that two historic reforms of the Polish banking system were carried out – the redenomination of the zloty and the move to a managed float of zloty exchange rates. She is a leading proponent of anti-inflationary policies. Hanna has faced the double challenge of being a woman in a predominantly mans world but also a very young woman. Hanna was 39 years old at the time of her appointment as President.

In 1975, Hanna graduated with distinction from Warsaw University Faculty of Law and Administration. Her Master's thesis was in the field of international public law. After graduation, she began work at the same faculty as a member of the academic staff in the Department of Comparative Administrative Law and National Economic Management, part of the Institute of Legal and Administrative Science. In 1981, she defended her PhD thesis, entitled 'The role of a sectoral cabinet minister in managing the state economy (legal aspects)', obtaining the degree of Doctor of Legal Science; the thesis was published in 1985.

In 1989, she served as an expert adviser to the Polish Sejm and Senate on questions of public and business law, with particular reference to banking law and the successive amendments being made to banking legislation. Hanna has specialised in banking law since 1983, particularly as regards the legal position of central banks. In 1993, she defended her thesis for the degree of doctor habilitatus; entitled 'The central bank – from a centrally administered economy to a market economy: legal issues', the thesis contained a series of proposals for changing Polish banking legislation. She is the author of over 40 academic publications, including monographs, and co-author of a textbook on administrative and business law.

Hanna is not a member of any political party. In 1980, she was a founder member of the NSZZ Solidarity trade union branch at her faculty, and in the years 1989–92 served as branch chairperson. Hanna has received numerous awards, including ones conferred by the British commercial journal The Central European *(in 1995 and 1998) and by the weekly newspapers* Zycie Gospodarcze *and* Warsaw Voice. *The American monthly* Global Finance *has included her among the best central bank governors of the world on three separate occasions, in 1994, 1997 and 1998. In 1998, she won the Kisiel Prize. In 1990, she was awarded the Silver Cross of Merit for her contribution to local government reform in Warsaw. In 1997, the Primate of Poland decorated her with the medal 'Ecclesiae populoque servitium praestanti' – for Distinguished Service to Church and Nation. The same year she was honoured for her services to the co-operative banking movement. In 1998, the NBP Management Board awarded her the Decoration for Distinguished Service to Banking in the Polish Republic.*

Banking has been a passion for me I was prompted to take up this work because of my academic interest in the challenge of transforming the economic system. I was also very excited about having the opportunity to implement some of my own ideas. I had been researching for 8 years a new model of the central bank at Warsaw University.

I have found it very satisfying to be able to lead on the arrangement of procedures and regulations of banking activity. For me as a professional, being in the position to strengthen the banking sector was very creative and fruitful. It was quite a challenge however, being in the position where I had to protect the independence of the central bank. Prior to transformation, independence did not exist for the Bank in Poland.

I can't think of one individual more than any other that influenced me as a person but in terms of my professional life the Heads of the biggest central banks, e.g. Alan Greenspan, Chairman of the Federal Reserve System have been a profound influence

The funniest incident in my career was at the time of the voting in Parliament about the Presidency of the NBP. I heard from one of the politicians that it was definitely not a good move that the candidate for the position of the President of NBP was a woman and not only that a young one!

The most traumatic situation I have had to deal with in my career was when I had to announce bankruptcy of the bank. Nothing can describe the feelings I had during that very traumatic period.

My greatest challenge, as a person has been remaining immune to stress. Banking at this level is highly stressful and being able to remain calm is an invaluable asset. It has also been a challenge to ensure I selected good associates to take forward our work and that we were able to co-operate and work as a successful team.

My greatest achievement without a doubt has been 26 years of marriage and my wonderful daughter. I got married when I was studying. My husband has been a very positive influence on my life; he supported me during a battle for presidential office. I can not imagine how I could cope with stress at work without my family support.

If I were able to change one thing about the world for women it would be that boys would be brought up to be unselfish so they can be the positive, supportive, potential future husbands families deserve.

If I were able to pass on one piece of advice to other women it would be what I always tell my female students 'a good husband who does not suffer from any complexes is the key to their future happiness and a positive career.'

It is my sincere hope that more and more women will hold responsible positions in society. A well-educated woman who has the appropriate resources and support is equal to anyone. I am satisfied with the life and work I have chosen. I would make the same choices again. I have always enjoyed my work, at first with my students and now at the bank. It gives me a lot of satisfaction.

Mary Warnock
Philosopher and Life Peer

Baroness Warnock has worked for most of her life as a university teacher. She read Classical Honour Mods, and 'Greats' at Oxford, with 2 years of school teaching in the middle, because of the war. She took a degree in 1948 and a further degree in philosophy (the then recently invented B Phil) in 1949. Baroness Warnock married in July of that year and joined St Hugh's College, Oxford, to teach philosophy in the October. She stayed there until September 1966, when she left to become Head Mistress of the Oxford High School GPDST. Baroness Warnock came back to university and continued teaching philosophy in 1972 and stayed until 1985 when she became Mistress of Girton College, Cambridge. In the same year she became a Life Peer and joined the Cross Benches (Independents) in the House of Lords.

I do not really think of myself as a career philosopher though I wrote quite a lot of books on philosophy; but I have always been interested in other things, especially in education at all levels, and I always contrived to do things other than teach philosophy, much as I enjoyed that. I think my natural habitat was always school rather than university, and I think I enjoyed most the 6 years I was at the Oxford High School, though in other ways the 1960s and early 1970s were terrible times for people with teenage children as we, and the Oxford High School parents had.

I do not feel that I made many choices in my life. I never had any doubt, from childhood onwards, that I wanted to be an academic. I was tempted to take up Greek History rather than philosophy while I was still an undergraduate, but my friends were mostly philosophers, and it seemed more fun to settle for that, though I loved Greek History. But I think I probably knew that I was not scholarly enough to make a success of it. In any case, I knew by that time who I wanted to marry if I could, and he was a philosopher.

I have been incredibly lucky all my life and I believe that there is a tremendous amount of luck or chance in the way people's careers develop. I had the luck to get involved in school education while still at St Hugh's by becoming a university member of the County Education Authority, in charge, eventually, of the Music Committee of that body, and I enormously enjoyed that. Then it was lucky that I became Head Mistress, though I never thought that I would be appointed (nor should I have been: I had no formal qualifications), because that led to other things, such as my becoming Chairman of the Government Committee of Enquiry into the Education of Children with Special Needs, from 1974 until 1978.

It was through my being a Governor of a school in Surrey that I met the man (Sir Brian Young) who later became Director General of the then IBA (Independent Broadcasting Authority); and he recommended that I became a member, in 1972. I remained a member of the Authority until the early 1980s and I think I enjoyed that work more than anything I had ever done before or since, though it hardly counts as part of my career. Again, it was preposterous that I should have been asked to join the

Authority because I hardly ever watched television, and I listened only to Radio 3. I had never heard a commercial radio station since the days of Radio Luxembourg in my childhood.

I suppose that philosophy teaches one to look at everything with, if possible, a fresh eye and to examine all one's prejudices; and this means that one can learn new things, and tackle new subjects quite easily. Certainly, the most difficult new subject I had to tackle was the biology I had to learn when I became Chairman of the Government Committee of Enquiry into Human Fertilisation and Embryology. I had had a totally science-free education, though I picked up a bit as a member of the Royal Commission on Environmental Pollution. Anyway, chairing this Committee (1982–1984) was probably the most difficult thing I have ever done, because people's passions run so high, and I had to persuade the Committee that we ought not simply to express our feelings, but to produce a policy which Ministers could use. There were bad moments, and I was not a very popular Chairman, particularly for forcing the Committee to report within 2 years, as required, but on the whole I greatly enjoyed it. I could not possibly say what the funniest thing that happened to me in all these years was because there were so many things that I found funny, rightly or wrongly.

The part of my career I enjoyed least was being Mistress of Girton, but this was not the fault of the College. It was because I never had any life in Cambridge because I rushed back to Oxford every weekend in term, and was not there in the vacations unless I absolutely had to be. I never therefore felt a properly Cambridge person, though I became very much attached to the beauties of the city, and to Girton itself.

I have always been absorbed in my close family (this includes one of my sisters as well as my husband and five children). I could have survived, I suppose, if I had never got married, but I would hate to have been married and not had children. Working in a university is the very best possible job to combine with children, though even that was difficult at the beginning. We had to employ nannies, and it was some time before we settled down into a succession of good nannies who stayed until they got married. The worst aspect of early married life was fearing the nanny would leave, and this was made worse by our friends sometimes thinking that because we had a nanny we could easily look after their children while they went on holiday. Of course this made the nanny leave.

I do not think that this kind of difficulty, or the worse difficulty ,when some member of the family gets ill, will ever go away for women. My advice to women would be 'try not to feel guilty' and 'try not to be too serious about the fact that you are a woman.' If I could choose one change in the world for women, it would be that they might be expected to be as much interested in men's appearance (when newly arrived at a job for example), as men are in women's.

Rosalind Wright LLB
Director of the Serious Fraud Office, London

Rosalind was appointed Director of the Serious Fraud Office in 1997 having developed a distinguished legal career, first working in private practice in as a barrister at Common Law Bar, Chambers of Mr (later Mr Justice) Morris Finer QC, then as a Legal and Senior Legal Assistant in the Director of Public Prosecution's (DPP) Office dealing with major crime in the Metropolitan Police area, specialising in major fraud prosecutions in England and Wales. She then became Assistant Director in the DPP's Office followed by Assistant Director of the Fraud Investigation Group (London). Rosalind then went on to take the position of Head of (disciplinary) Prosecutions and Deputy Director Securities and Futures Authority (formerly, the Securities Association) followed by the challenge of General Counsel and Executive Director, Investor Protection, Legal and Policy Department, Securities and Futures Authority (SFA).

I have been a prosecutor since 1969. Looking at this statement in stark print, it comes as something of a shock. Not only because 30 years of prosecuting are in themselves a very long time to be engaged in such a restricted area of law but because at the stage when I embarked on a career in the law, I would have regarded the very notion of a life dedicated to accusation, of trying to prove guilt and bringing people to 'justice' with horror.

My first pupillage was under the wise, liberal and enlightened guidance of the late Paul Sieghart, a man distinguished for his humanity, his love of civil liberties and of justice, as well as for his intellect. Through him, I learned to love the law and being a lawyer as a means of liberating others, of enabling people to put forward their side of the story, of demonstrating injustice and putting things right.

As an idealistic young barrister, I naturally thought one could only achieve such ends as counsel for the defence, standing up for the rights of those wrongly accused, the unfortunate victims of the 'the system', whether in a criminal or a civil context. Falling, more by chance than by design, into the arms of the Director of Public Prosecutions (or rather his Office) after 5 years in private practice where I had tried, with varying degrees of success, through appearances at many magistrates courts and county courts in the London area to demonstrate the virtue of my client's cause, I found to my astonishment, that victims were to be found on both sides of the criminal fence. That there could be moral justification and professional satisfaction in representing the rights of victims of crime and seeking redress for them through the criminal process. That there was intellectual satisfaction in constructing a case, supported by cogent evidence to prove that someone who thought they had covered their tracks was guilty of massive deception. That one could act as champion of the poor, the dispossessed, the weak and the gullible by prosecuting those who took unfair advantage of them.

I had joined the DPP's Office, at the end of 1969, because I thought I was becoming something of a public embarrassment at the independent Bar. As a member of a set of chambers whose members were enlightened, liberal, kind and encouraging, I could have had no better start to a career as a barrister. There was plenty of interesting work, including four exciting and at times terrifying years, acting as junior to a senior member of our chambers, Peter Pain QC, instructed to represent a doughty, very elderly, retired Colonel and his wife, the next-door neighbors of the formidable and alarming Dr Barbara Moore, the marathon walker and vexatious litigant, in a protracted boundary dispute which took us into courts of every conceivable kind and at every possible level; I think only the Coroner's Court was left out and that probably only fortuitously. I had by then married and had two babies in quick succession. My husband, a young junior hospital doctor, earned very little; I barely broke even. Proper full-time childcare was well beyond our budget. I left the babies with my long-suffering parents whenever I had a case outside London. Otherwise, I took them with me to chambers, where I breast-fed them, having ordered my good-natured (male) room-mates out for the duration (they were squeamish and I was overly modest); and to court, where I left them with the Matron who had charge of the women prisoners or, in the county courts, with the kindly girls in the court office. They would baby-sit while I represented my clients next door, anxiously looking up at the slightest sound of wailing from outside the court-room, usually produced by someone else's baby or by passing traffic in the street.

I achieved renown in the courts of Acton, Uxbridge, Shoreditch and the City of London, as 'that woman barrister with the babies'. It was not how I had expected to establish my reputation at the Bar.

I joined the civil service because I needed a regular income and a flyer detailing vacancies in the legal civil service caught my eye on a Middle Temple library noticeboard one day. With a regular, though fairly limited income (my first annual salary at the DPP was £1,250), I could pay for help at home. The babies settled into a routine, away from the excitement of the courts and I embarked on a prosecuting career as an employed barrister, first at the DPP, later working for the Securities Association (which became the Securities and Futures Authority) bringing disciplinary cases against brokers and dealers, and then back to mainstream financial crime, at the Serious Fraud Office.

In the 30 years that I have prosecuted, I have seen life from a very skewed, but not necessarily false perspective. I have seen human nature at its worst; people who have murdered their own children and those of complete strangers; people who have lied and cheated and robbed and blown people up with bombs. I have also seen some very brave people, who have been prepared to risk their own safety to attend court as a witness to give evidence and help to secure the conviction of those who had harmed many other people and could do so again and again unless stopped and taken out of circulation. I have been privileged to work with people of the highest integrity, in the law on both sides, in the police force, and with colleagues in the civil service and in regulation who never seem to achieve public recognition but who continually demonstrate astonishing intellectual and ethical qualities of which the general public is, I am convinced, completely unaware.

There have been some fascinating cases, not all of which were brought to court. There was the international conspiracy, hatched over three continents, by a ring of multinational crooks who chartered a huge oil supertanker, 'The Salem', off-loaded its cargo secretly at Durban and then scuppered the empty hull off the West Coast of Africa. The intention was to make a vast profit by selling off the oil in breach of the sanctions then in force on supplying oil to South Africa and at the same time, to perpetrate a massive fraud on Lloyd's of London, by claiming for the loss of the cargo and for the hull of the tanker. No prosecution proved possible in England and Wales for jurisdictional reasons, though some of the conspirators were brought to justice in the USA and in Greece. In another case, there were protracted enquiries into the affairs of two Lloyd's managing agents who had enriched themselves at the expense of Names on their syndicates; the money trails led us to Switzerland, where the authorities, mindful of the Swiss banking confidentiality laws then strictly applied, felt unable to give us the full co-operation we needed and delayed the progress of the investigation until it was too late to amass a case to support an request for extradition of one of the main protagonists from the States. These were frustrations which make the job an infuriating as well as, more often, a very satisfying one. The irony is that disparities between jurisdictions and the requirements of local laws still operate to frustrate enquiries and prevent trials of serious offences taking place. Little has moved on, despite lip service paid at innumerable international conferences of prosecutors and law enforcement agencies to the value of international co-operation in the fight against major crime.

Cases which have resulted in a successful prosecution have been the result of a good deal of luck as well as hard work, which goes into everything we do. It is often forgotten that the purpose of a trial is to try the evidence; to allow the defence to test the testimony of the prosecution witnesses; to put forward their side of the case and then to let the jury make up its mind as to whether it is 'satisfied so that it is sure', or, in the phrase less commonly used in court now, 'beyond reasonable doubt', that the prosecution has proved that the accused is guilty of the offence charged. What goes on in the minds of the jurors in any individual case is impossible to discover with any accuracy, though intelligent guesswork, from the demeanour of the jurymen and women during the course of the trial, by counsel and the court staff often accurately predicts the result. Cases which the prosecutor thought a dead cert, with overwhelming evidence to support the charges, occasionally result in acquittals. It is tantalising not to be able to ask the jury why they came to the conclusion they did, leading to not unreasonable speculation that factors other than the evidence weighed on them; factors such as the impression a sincere-looking defendant made in the witness box, or the persuasiveness of his counsel, or, conversely, counsel's incompetence which may have made the jury feel sorry for the defendant.

The job is occasionally frustrating; it is always fascinating and a great privilege. I think I have been very fortunate to have had the opportunities in life I have had; to have three healthy daughters, grown to adulthood, a loving and supportive husband of 34 years, three grandchildren and a career which has kept me on my toes and constantly exhilarated are bonuses I could not foresee when I started my career at the Bar, but I am eternally grateful for all of them.

CHAPTER 4
What qualities and coping mechanisms do these women have to achieve?

Andree Le May

It is clear from the contributions of the women included in this book that they have achieved high levels of success in their careers. Success for them is often described as multi-faceted, ranging from financial and/or personal fulfilment to commitment to getting the job done well in partnership with family, friends and colleagues. Many of the women link success to an ability to juggle a variety of roles and responsibilities both within and outwith the work arena. However, this juggling may result in feelings of overload with which they have to cope; for some this can only be done by working longer and harder, for others it means finding time for themselves and others outside the demands of their working environments. Alongside this there is often an implicit assumption that to succeed may, in itself, provide a mechanism for coping with the pressures that often accompany work and success for women. This chapter, using the profiles in Chapter 3, focuses on the qualities, which these women have or need to have in order to succeed, and the coping strategies, which may help them to keep a balance in their lives in order to achieve their goals.

What is striking about these women's profiles is their great energy and passion for what they do, despite in some cases a somewhat serendipitous arrival at their chosen work pathway. For many of them the key to their achievement has been getting a 'fit' between work and their lives outside work, coupled with an ability to find a unique niche in their work which partners their passion, interest or knowledge. Although some give the impression that their careers just 'happened' to them many identified key initiators – personal circumstances, role models, interest or knowledge about the area of their work. Alongside these qualities their ability to capitalise on things that appear to 'just happen', has allowed them to realise their vision and match that with the appropriate level of risk needed to achieve their goal(s). Their tenacity to follow things through, linked to the desire to achieve and an ability to juggle and balance many elements of their lives, has undoubtedly contributed to their success.

However, despite the influences of chance on their careers and the easiness of their story-telling these women have, either inherent or learnt, qualities which they have used to push forward the boundaries of their achievement. Many are highlighted in the profiles as each woman tracks her career trajectory; others are not evident in these accounts but can be found in other writings, which centre on women and work. The qualities which leap out from the profiles include the ability to juggle, the foresight to seize the moment, the opportunity to have and apply vision to their work niche and the skill to sustain that vision through working with others and developing themselves, not only against goals using reflection as well as activity, but also against appropriate role models. The work opportunities presented to these successful women have allowed them to capitalise on their qualities, find the best match between themselves and their careers and to develop others alongside them. Many of the women profiled value the opportunities for creativity and variety afforded within their work and the possibilities which these offer for sustaining interest and revitalising challenges. These in turn may provide the impetus to continue when things get tough as well as providing, for many of them, a sense of achievement and the opportunity to acknowledge that, in the main, they 'wouldn't change what they did'.

There is a growing literature on women at work, which focuses on the qualities needed for success. Some of these qualities are neither unique to women nor to those who work but form the basis on which many of us move our lives forward. They revolve around the ability to have vision, set realistic goals and work towards attaining them. In order to do this we need to know where we are going, how we are going to get there and how we will judge our success at some point in the future. The qualities associated with this process centre on the ability to be future orientated with realistic vision and being able to reflect on and evaluate progress towards the goal(s) which we set. In conjunction with these, women are often viewed as having greater emotional responsibility for the world and it may be the combination of this with other qualities within and outwith the workplace that makes women's contribution unique. This is not an uncommon view and this capacity has been explored by Arlie Hochschild in her study of emotional labour. Hochschild (1983) suggested that women do more 'emotional managing than men' often in conjunction with work associated with 'affirming, enhancing and celebrating the well-being and status of others' and frequently accomplished in what appears to be a seemingly effortless way. This latter quality would appear to relate directly to success and its interpretation by others.

Having vision and the ability to set and attain personal goals may not however be enough; the challenge is targeting these skills in order to match qualities to opportunities. Maddock (1999) studied women managers and found that success was often linked to their ability to have a collaborative focus to their work, be that through working with others or through the central focus of their business (e.g. providing support for others in the community or within institutions). The necessity to collaborate enabled these women to be seen as innovators within their working environment, whose prime goal was to make things better in some way. This quality innovation, is presented as an ability to handle uncertainty, fit together pieces of information and present a fresh perspective and is also evident in some of the profiles presented in Chapter 3.

It is clear from both Maddock's (1999) research and the women reviewed in this book that success does not fit within a tidy picture, neither is there a magic formula which guarantees achievement. Success is essentially unique to each person and each context. However, what is becoming more apparent is that success necessitates flexibility and a blend of certain qualities including the abilities to be 'tactical and strategic, thoughtful and reflective, sometimes passive and sometimes very determining' (Maddock, 1999, page 9). These form a mosaic of qualities which can be at the opposite ends of a continuum, each may be needed on specific occasions to achieve success within the workplace which facilitates a balance between work and the rest of life. Selecting which quality(ies) to harness would appear to be a central tenet of success.

Coping with the variety of situations in which women find themselves requires us to draw on the array of qualities outlined above and in the contributions found in Chapter Three. Of increasing importance within the work arena are those situated along the strategic-tactical and thoughtful-reflective continua; and the ability of the respondents to capitalise on these may in fact be a cornerstone of their success in driving forward their own agendas. Often the ability to use these qualities appropriately is the result of a unique blend of our own qualities, the culture, in which we work and live, and the role models, which we have been exposed to. There can be little doubt that organisational cultures provide a variety of milieux in which to shape and test ourselves and our roles. Some cultures are empowering and supportive whereas others are restrictive. Against these possibilities it is interesting that many successful women have decided to 'go it alone' or are in such a senior position that they are able to shape the culture of the organisation in which they work. In these cases they have the potential to facilitate others' development through charismatic leadership and acting as role models as well as having considerable control over their working lives.

Having an appropriate selection of qualities needed to succeed provides only half of the story. The unique and multi-faceted challenges faced by women at work mean that whatever qualities are apparent they need to be coupled with a battery of coping mechanisms in order to survive. Many respondents seemed to cope with the myriad of demands placed on them by showing tenacity in their ability to work harder than others, work over the odds or put in extra effort to prove their worth, hence the frequently described wonder-woman image. Several writers on women at work would agree with this view, as indeed would many working women. Other women work in a different way being able to lay down more prescriptively the boundaries of their commitments preferring to work within these rather than risk the consequences of over-commitment.

It is apparent, however that the balance needed between 'work' and 'life' is hard to achieve, frequently incurs a cost and therefore involves some degree of sensitive but active management.

All of us find it difficult to keep control of things from time-to-time whether we work or not, for those who combine agendas it is increasingly important to evolve a number of ways to cope with the challenges and frustrations on the road to achievement which go beyond working longer and harder. These coping mechanisms reflect the variety of situations in which women find themselves and include mechanisms for coping within the workplace, within our out-of-work lives and between the two. In many ways women who combine worlds need to possess the extraordinary qualities of the chameleon, being able to shift and blend to a kaleidoscope of different demands. This not only presents its challenges and potential conflicts but also provides a variety of rewards.

The women featured in Chapter 3 however, do not seem to dwell on the potential for conflict between their different worlds but have been able to blend achievement with support from close friends, family and colleagues – the linkage between success and supportive partners is highlighted by several respondents. This, coupled with clarity of purpose and control over their vision, may be the two most important means of coping for many working women.

Confidence in the vision that women have maybe, in itself, one means of coping with the path towards it, however, to move vision into reality often means convincing others of its value and many women see themselves, as Maddock (1999) suggests by quoting Cynthia Cockburn, 'as agents of change', the 'managers of tomorrow'.

Alongside this, being able to be in control is of paramount importance to success. For many years psychologists have described the ability to exert control over life events as a central factor in our ability to cope, describing two distinct personality types – those who consider external factors as controlling their lives and those who feel themselves to be in control. Being in control may present in different ways and be reflected in the way we interact with and work alongside others, in short our ability to work in partnerships and the leadership style(s) which we adopt; these may be linked to our portrayal of the 'manager of tomorrow'. However, being unable to control events may mean that women lack the precision for achievement. Maddock (1999) suggested that 'Many women are proud to being able to handle multiple pieces of information at any one time and of being holistic. However, within the work environment focused on very narrow targets, a scatter approach can be ineffective and viewed as indicating lack of confidence' (page 45). In the main, clear focus with accompanying strategies to achieve success and feelings of being in control may be the more fruitful although more challenging path to tread.

Often coping within both the 'work' and 'home' contexts is characterised by an image of juggling. Managing multiple roles both within, outwith and between the work/home interface needs careful management to prevent burn out and frustration. In order to do this and survive many woman have learnt a new skill or coping strategy – to juggle. This juggling is hard to define, save through the natural image of 'keeping many balls in the air at once', but it can certainly be seen as an important part of coping and success being closely linked to achievement as well as maintaining physical and mental well-being. However we define juggling it appears to relate to our own individual, and thereby unique, blend of support needed from, and in many instances willingly given, by others in order to keep everything on an even keel. Although successful juggling can be viewed as constructive and is seen as a positive asset, juggling can also be used to facilitate some of the more negative aspects of the 'coping through working harder and longer' routine which many women feel is a necessary accompaniment to their success. In these instances the notion of juggling may take on a more negative value in which survival rather than balance is the prime goal. The value of constructive juggling cannot be under-estimated and can be clearly seen in the results of a long-term study of health within the American community of Framingham (Haynes and Feinleib, 1980). This research focused on a large group of working and non-working women (married and single) and men to establish their susceptibility to heart disease. The findings showed that working, married women had an increased risk of heart disease when compared to their single counterparts but for married working women with children the incidence of heart disease rose with the number of children. Their overall conclusion suggested that women who worked experienced more daily episodes of stress than either non-working women or men. If these results have currency elsewhere then it would seem to be very important to consider ways of promoting more constructive juggling with accompanying levels of support to minimise the negative effects of stress. In support of this a more recent study in the UK undertaken by Cooper and Lewis (1993) found that married, working women, who lacked active husband/partner support were at the greatest risk of stress. These findings emphasise the need for sophisticated constructive juggling, in a partnership, which is mindful of its protective as well as pragmatic functions.

Maddock (1999) refers to the 'strain of womanhood' (page 102) in which women experience difficulties in 'branding' themselves within the work arena – finding their style – with minimal need for compromise with their vision. She emphasises the influence of role models in this process suggesting that women in the workplace often identify with juniors or clients (emphasising the 'collaborative' nature of their style) whereas men on the other hand pattern themselves on the boss adopting a more straightforward, targeted style. This is an interesting observation which, when coupled with a consideration of working styles and the eclectic preferences of women within this, begins to challenge our view of success and takes us back to the profiles which emphasise the 'non-generalisability' or uniqueness of success. Success to one woman may not be constructed in the same way as it is for another. This, of course, further complicates our lives since we need to find role models that equate with our own image of success. There would therefore seem to be great merit in considering the potential for matching role models' ability to, and strategies for, coping with the road to and the results of achievement with our own visions of success. Many women reading this chapter will be able to identify their own successful and unsuccessful attempts at role modelling.

Coping can also be facilitated by recognising the importance of looking after oneself; so many of us neglect this and focus on trying to look after others because we are 'absent' at work and feel the need to compensate for this. Whether this is the case or not it is important to find more time for ourselves. There are, of course, many ways of doing this through leisure and related activities, added to these it may be useful to consider how to use those moments which are seemingly 'unproductive' to best advantage and to savour them rather than feel frustrated by them; we all recognise the potential of a cancelled meeting to catch up or take a break from the usual pattern of our day but few grasp it with enthusiasm.

In conjunction with these more individual mechanisms for coping many strategies have been adopted by organisations with a view to reducing problems associated balancing work and home life. These include the use of flexi-time, working from home, maternity and paternity leave, and targeted training and development. These have been met with varying degrees of approval and resultant success. On a more strategic level however, governmental policy is increasingly focusing on the creation of family-friendly working environments and policies. These aim to enhance our ability to realistically combine work and family commitments in an attempt to get a better fit between our working and our family lives. There are many critics of the various approaches used, however, if they add to our own battery of individual coping skills and help to create opportunities for achieving a greater balance in life then they can only be a welcome addition to our working lives.

The profiles in Chapter 3 together with other published information suggest that achievement is an intricate tapestry comprising opportunities, qualities, luck and an ability to balance work with daily life; getting this right is an obvious challenge to all of us that can be rewarded richly in a variety of ways. The challenge for many women centres on finding out 'how to act' in their particular worlds – work, home or both, how to capitalise on their inherent qualities and develop others and how to cope with the resultant strains that this complex reality necessitates.

CHAPTER 5
Is success worth it?

Professor Anna A. Maslin

Is success worth it? In many ways this is a loaded question. What does the question mean and can there really be an answer? Looking at the accounts of the highly successful women who participated in this book it is obvious that the majority have worked very hard to achieve success and majority have taken pride and pleasure in their accomplishments.

Success as we have already explored can be multi-faceted including material, physical, emotional, psychological and spiritual dimensions. For many, success in its most obvious form is material. When asked, Honor Blackman, suggested;

'The value of material success is that it frees you in many ways. It enables you to take time and make choices, including the kind that bring a great deal of satisfaction but very little money.

But this freedom also involves a constant pressure to make the right choices followed by the anxious desire to be as good or better than before in order to maintain the success.

Artistic success often goes hand in hand with material success but sometimes what the general public considers memorable may have required no great effort. On the other hand success to the artiste may mean a difficulty triumphantly overcome. The fact that probably no one else was aware that there was this challenge makes it the more satisfying.

Risks must be taken and the difficult and the unlikely tackled so that we are able to develop because it is those challenges that make a career satisfying.'

How we spend our time is a useful indicator of where our priorities lie. The musician 'Sting' interviewed by Parkinson on the BBC seemed to support this view when he said;

'I thought success and happiness were the same thing but they're not. At my most successful I was most unhappy. My happiness is now my wife and family'.

Annette Benning, 41, the hugely successful actress, the wife of Warren Beatty and mother of four children said 'If I never make another movie, that would be okay with me... I don't have to worry about the separation other women have to endure when they go back to work... I bring my kids with me and that keeps me sane. Sure there are days when I am totally stressed out and things are insane. But most of the time I say "Yeah, well, this is my life and I'm lucky to have it"'.

Some are not so lucky, the *Sunday Times* reported the tremendous difficulty facing Aisling Sykes, of being in a high powered job with City Bank JP Morgan and feeling she had almost no time to be with her young children when they were awake during the week. One of the points at issue seems to be that if a person is making a substantial salary an employer may feel they have the right to make calls on their time which extend far beyond the normal. Men have tolerated this for many years; whether they should have is another question.

Family-friendly working policies for men and women are important for maintaining the fabric of family life. This case like many others raises the question of whether this kind of career/material success is worth it? The late Countess Elizabeth Longford argues strongly for women to choose careers, which are compatible with family life, i.e. where you can largely work from home or where your hours are flexible. To achieve this, society as a whole needs to ensure changes take place in the way we think about work so that options of this sort are not only available to the highly motivated or privileged.

Dame Rennie Fritchie clearly outlined her experiences as a portfolio worker, which has been very successful for her. Dame Rennie's advice is to accentuate the positive; 'Anyone who works in a flexible way offers a range of additional benefits to an employer and to colleagues and sometimes it is important to make sure they recognise it. For example, making statement like "Because I'm not here all the time I bring objectivity to this issue" or "Because I do a variety of jobs, I don't get stale and keep my energy and enthusiasm up" and so on. There are many many good things that happen as a result of working in this way. We need to recognise them; then we need to draw them to the attention of others in a positive way.'"

Glenys Kinnock clearly articulated: 'There is still much to be done to ensure conditions are conducive for women to combine work with family commitments – after all, working mothers, rather than fathers, still bear the primary care responsibilities of their children, and nine out of 10 lone parents are women. Many more men are, of course, taking a full role in the home – although I have never met a man who has complained about the difficulties of combining a family and a career!

Mothers of young children who wish to restart work after maternity leave must be offered the necessary measures to facilitate their return to the workplace. It is to be hoped that the gradual moves we have seen recently, towards the provision of crèches and family-friendly policies, gain momentum.'

Covey, 1999, noted: 'What matters most is how we respond to what we experience in life.' What has been interesting in many of the personal accounts is the fact that the women who have enjoyed their success are often well-organised, highly motivated and tend to be able to turn a problem into an opportunity. We cannot always control what life will throw at us but we can control our response to it.

Catherine Walker, who designed so many of Diana, Princess of Wales gowns came into her successful career through sadness: 'After the sudden death of my first husband, John, I started to sew as a kind of therapy which by its nature was introspective. This "inward looking" approach to fashion was the opposite to what most people expect from fashion designers who are supposed to be a little more forthcoming if not downright extrovert, but it led me to an interest in the technical side of creating garments which in turn led to couture… In my personal life the two greatest challenges I have had to face are: being widowed with two baby daughters, and in recent years suffering from breast cancer. Any serious trauma has consequences in one's life far beyond their immediate impact and today I am still reacting and learning from them.'

Successful women also seem to have a knack of recognising an opportunity. These women are able to visualise an outcome and work towards it by taking carefully calculated risks, recognising that change and constant re-evaluation are a part of the process. They will see the project through to a successful completion. It is this process and the achievement of the result that gives these women a feeling of success. Marla Salmon illustrated the point: 'My career path is a reflection of multiple forces, rather than a conscious decision at any one point in time. It has been profoundly shaped by my early rural childhood experiences in a family led by a general practitioner father and nurse mother who believed that people should be of use to others around them and their larger community. Enhancing the health of people – and enabling others to serve in these ways – became a compelling commitment for me and a way to "be of use." My actual career choices do not reflect a linear, planned path. Rather, there are themes that reflect my commitment to being of use, an evolving understanding of what is important to me personally and professionally, what I believe and value, what I am good at doing, and what I've wanted to learn along the way. These themes have expressed themselves through shaping the ways in which I have acted on the many opportunities that have presented themselves along the way.'

Many of the women who have been very successful and have enjoyed their success seem to have been driven not so much by the need for recognition but by the desire to do well and fulfil their potential. Anita Roddick illustrated this when she said; 'It wasn't only economic necessity that inspired the birth of The Body Shop. Women, when they want to earn a livelihood, usually earn it through what they are interested in or what they are knowledgeable about. I had a wealth of experience to draw on. I travelled, and I spent time in farming and fishing communities with pre-industrial peoples. My travels exposed me to body rituals of women from all over the world. Also the frugality that my mother exercised during the war years made me question retail conventions. Why waste a container when you can refill it? And why buy more of something than you can use? We behaved as she did in the Second World War, we re-used everything, we refilled everything and we recycled all we could. The foundation of The Body Shop environmental activism was born out of ideas like these.'

Ruth Sims also illustrated the point: 'Trying to improve the quality of life and provide care in those settings is an enormous challenge, but one that I, along with all others who are involved in this, am not prepared to ignore. We really have to look at ways of improving the quality of life of those who are suffering in this way and to look at a creative way of responding to their needs. I suppose the challenge is feeling impotent, and the fear is that you might decide that there is nothing you can do. There is always something you can do – the creativity is in finding out what it is and how to do it.'

Success doesn't come exclusively from the desire to be powerful. For success to have meaning there is this need to believe in yourself, to be as well educated as possible, to have an even temper, to be able to work hard, to be able to delegate and to be able to prioritise. Prue Leith a master at handling a significant number of projects at once stated: 'One quality, which has helped me to achieve success, has been the ability to find good people and delegate responsibility to them. It is important to hire people who are better than you are and not to feel threatened by them. You do need to keep control and know exactly what is going on but staff need the freedom to grow, to solve problems and to surprise you. It is important to be fair, to be honest and to be up front. I feel it is vital to be part of the solution not just the person who finds or creates the problem. For me it was important to develop family-friendly working policies so I was able to keep the best staff. Flexibility and good maternity leave arrangements at work is important. Companies need to concentrate on what is essential. Companies need to concentrate not only on client's needs but staff needs. Companies are organic living creations. If all the company stakeholders, including staff, are not content the company will become unhealthy.'

It is hard to work out whether high levels of self-confidence precede the ability to succeed or whether it results from the success. The ability to turn a problem into an opportunity is a major contributor to a person's perception of their success in a given situation. Jane Manning the opera singer clearly feels her individuality and self-confidence even when she behaved against the norm were of value to her. 'Personally, privacy has always meant a great deal to me. I never had it as a child or young adult. I spent much time at home, my every movement monitored by caring parents, especially my mother, whose relationship with her own mother had been exceptionally close. I was expected to conform and never really did. I suppose it was inevitable that I should end up in a profession where eccentricity is the norm, and I always felt more comfortable with individuals who were a little out of the ordinary. At school, I was deemed to be so lacking in public-spiritedness that I was never made even a sub-prefect – the only person in my form to be overlooked. I was a late developer and now realise this to be an advantage. To be allowed to be myself was quite a battle, but when I spread my wings and went to Switzerland, I discovered that I could function very well in the world at large, and that unnatural regimes such as school or college are not the real thing! My freedom was hard-won but I treasure it.'

There is little doubt that for the majority of the women in this book that education was seen as central to their success. Dame Cicely Saunders advice is simple: 'If I could pass on one piece of advice to other women it would be educate your children, especially the girls.'

This recognition of the value of education spanned the both the experiences of women from developed and developing countries. Kegalale Gasennelwe from Botswana in her hope for the future stated: 'I believe women will become more educated and as such will be more critical thinkers and visionaries. Women will occupy higher positions than now and be involved in decision-making at high levels. Because of their foresightedness they will develop programs to alleviate poverty and enhance the health status of their families and communities and the world at large. Because of their kindness and wisdom women will use of rational thought rather than physical strength. As a result there will be fewer wars and prosperity will abound.'

In this book as with the SBH cohort, Oxbridge in particular had made a significant contribution to providing opportunities for a women to enter into a man's world. It is obvious from the group of women participating that a significant number benefited from an Oxbridge education. Victoria Harrison clearly noted: 'Of course I enjoyed Oxford, but I now see that an Oxford education also offers opportunities for making 'contacts'. Some of my contemporaries eagerly grasped these, but I did not – though I made a number of friends for life. And Oxford gave me more self-confidence and an analytical approach. One of my Oxford tutors (male) gave me freedom to write my weekly essays on subjects that interested me, instead of cramping me into an inflexible programme of teaching, and this increased my enthusiasm and helped me to do well in my final examinations: a first-class Oxford degree in physiology then obviously opened doors.'

This desire to share education with others and measuring success by the ability to enhance opportunities for others, this comes out again clearly through a number of the contributions. Christine King, Vice-Chancellor of Stafford University strongly stated; 'I have a particular commitment to offering opportunities to people who might otherwise be excluded from Higher Education, whether because of physical disability, social and educational background, age or any other barrier. What is so thrilling about working in Higher Education is that we see our students develop intellectually and personally and know, as they graduate, that one way or another they will make a difference to the worlds they enter.'

Valarie Bragg likewise agreed: 'In my professional life interaction with the students has been most satisfying – talking to them, listening to them, earning their respect, treating them as young adults, watching them grow and mature, and leave for exciting careers ranging from entrepreneurs, business people or on to Higher Education.'

Subject choice for a potential career has been an issue for some of the women in this book. Rita Sussmuth espouses the modern view: 'Young women should not be pushed towards stereotypical jobs like office work, hairdressing, etc. Girls should be encouraged to consider engineering, information technology, etc.' Jan Peters shares this view and her current role is to co-ordinate government and national efforts to increase the participation of women in science, engineering and technology: to increase the uptake of science and related subjects at GCSE, NVQ, A Level and degree; to stimulate and facilitate increased levels of networking and co-ordination between organisations promoting science, education and technology for women in the UK and world-wide; work across the public and private sector to ensure the progression and promotion of women to senior levels and ensure that the UK benefits from the contribution of women on public committees and policy-making bodies.

But as a younger person Jan herself had difficulty in pursuing the subject/career of her choice herself. 'As a teenager I was put off engineering by among others my mother who told me it was dirty and not for a person with allergies. Then I was stimulated to pursue scientific journalism to pursue environmental interests following an article on marine biology in the *Sunday Observer*. I studied for a science degree driven by the sense that one needed a qualification to be able to write with authority and my careers advisor recommended general science degree, based upon the subject I most enjoyed at A level.

Driven to further study following my degree as the only job options appeared to be quality control; and having the sense that I still didn't feel able to write with authority on any specific subject; focused my interest in electronics, properties of materials and microscopic order of atoms in crystals. My Masters project on semiconductors proved to me that engineering wasn't about being dirty – in fact semiconductors are made in such clean environments that the scientists/engineers need to dress up to keep the environment clean.'

Some of our slightly older contributors expressed the same view for example Qhing Qhing Dlamini: 'When I completed High School in 1971 in my home country, Swaziland, I wanted to study for an Engineering degree. However, my teachers and family all thought that I should study Medicine. I still put down Engineering as my first choice and Medicine as my second choice, when applying for a scholarship from the Government of Swaziland to pursue my university studies. When I went for an interview for the scholarship upon obtaining my High School graduation results, the all-male Scholarship Selection Board was simply appalled that a female could think of studying Engineering. Without even giving me an opportunity to justify my first choice of studying Engineering, they emphatically informed me that they are granting me a scholarship to study Medicine, which is what I did.'

For success to be worthwhile it does appear to require some planning for most people. It would seem that to be successful, in the round, you have to take a conscious decision where to concentrate your efforts based on your own priorities, i.e. work and family, work and hobby, work and work. Many of the women in this book combined work and family but some have taken a conscious decision not to marry and/or have a family. For some marriage and a family were just not possible. Margaret Anstee commented: 'In my generation it was virtually impossible for a woman to combine a highly peripatetic career such a mine (I moved to some new part of the world on average every 2 years and was constantly on mission travel) with marriage and a family. Apart from the practical difficulties, until as late as 1971 it was strict Foreign Office policy to insist that a woman resign irrevocably on marriage no matter who the prospective husband might be, or whether he was ready to follow his wife to the ends of the earth.'

Jane Manning described her experiences in opting for marriage but without children:

> I have been very happily married for 33 years to the composer, writer and broadcaster Anthony Payne, after a whirlwind romance of only 3 months (another happy impulse!). We have no children, a mutual decision. My career blossomed at just the time when a family might have been planned. I'd also had some rather off-putting experiences with badly behaved toddlers! We put off thinking about it until we realised we didn't really wish to change our lives so radically. Although aware I have missed many important experiences, I don't regret this – one can't do everything, and our ensemble of young musicians, Jane's Minstrels are a happy alternative family – with much more in common with us, I think than our own children might have had. So I haven't missed out on close contact with young people.(I was in fact engaged to a local man when I left the Academy, but discovering that my teaching job meant rather more to me than the relationship, broke it off just in time.) I can honestly say that I never experienced the overwhelming maternal urge described by friends, and, despite having many close friends whose children are a joy to them (and whom we also enjoy) I've never wished to change places with them.

Reading the accounts it is easy to see individuals vary in their feelings about deciding or being unable to have a family. Some are very happy, others less content. One of the most moving accounts comes in the words of Dame Cicely Saunders who was 83 years of age at the time of writing and who had dedicated her life to her work: 'Personally it was a challenge remaining single until 1980. I feel my greatest achievement as a person was to have been loved by three men from Poland, marrying the third and helping all to die fulfilled and at peace. My work did have a profound impact on my life. I did not find it easy to be single but I could not have done it all if I had been married. Nor would I have met so many people to love.'

The majority of women in this book opted for family life and appear to find it enhances their enjoyment of any success they achieve. Margaret Kartomi, academic/musicologist simply said: 'My greatest challenge personally has been bringing up a beloved daughter and my greatest achievement has been being a good wife and mother.'

Rabbi Julia Neuberger echoed this with the words: 'My greatest achievement has been to have two children, apparently reasonably well-adjusted, who as adults seem to like spending time with their parents, despite our busy and chaotic life styles. As a professional, I think my greatest achievements have lain in moving on to the next thing without – I hope – leaving the people I worked with before feeling I had simply abandoned them.

Family is hugely important to me. I have been married to the same man, Anthony, for the last 26 years, and we have a close family relationship, close also to our two mothers and my three brothers-in-law and their wives, and we live near the two mothers who were both widowed 3 years ago. I have a strong sense of family – and a strong sense of familial duty as well as pleasure.'

There is also a view which comes through the book that successful women with balanced work and professional lives tend not to over socialise. Sarah Doukas from Storm summarised by saying '... most of my closest friends date back to my childhood and I've made an effort to keep these friendships intact. My early relationships are important as they keep me level headed. I don't really socialise within the business and this gives me a more balanced outlook about the business and prevents me from being obsessive about it."

There can be little doubt that success for many, is seen as worthwhile, when it is seen through the eyes of their parents. Many of us are heavily influenced by our parents whether it is because they instilled in us the feeling we could achieve, or whether it was because they ensured we had a good education, or whether it was because of the human values they were able to share with us. Lisa Perry recounted; 'It is only now, as a mother, that I more fully appreciate what a loving, selfless and dependable woman my own mother is. As a child I knew safety, security and love. Happiness and laughter are my overwhelming memories. My parents have given me a belief in my own abilities and talents, a sense of optimism that the world can be a beautiful, inspiring place, a knowledge that although bad things happen and people do bad things they can also be kind and caring. I also have the security of knowing that wherever life takes me my parents will always endeavour to support, encourage and love me. They are certainly the two people who have influenced me most.'

Many of us had parents who did not have the advantages of education they made available to their daughters and the achievement of a successful life and career for many is their way of saying thank you to their parents. Dame Margaret Anstee clearly felt this to be true: 'As will be clear from what I have said already a happy childhood and supportive parents were key factors in my later development, as was the fact of being an only child – had there been more children it is doubtful, given my family's very modest circumstances and rural background, that I would have been given the chances that I had. In personal terms it was enormously important to me to fulfil my parents expectations. Sadly, they did not live long enough to see all my achievements but they visited me in South America when I was already a successful Chief of Mission. Through me they were able to travel abroad (my mother had never been abroad, my father only on active service) and I was able to provide for the material comfort of their later years. I know that they felt that their considerable sacrifices on my behalf had been worthwhile.'

Victoria Harrison likewise shared: 'During my school days my parents encouraged me: taking an interest in my homework, testing me on factual information, and paying for extra tuition in areas which the school didn't cover. I was better at learning anything involving a logical sequence than at memorising things, and I remember my mother drumming history dates into me to ensure that I did better in the next examinations in history, one of my less good subjects, though I later married a historian. My father was also ambitious for me, and encouraged me not to drift away from the natural sciences – though at that time it might have been easy for me to move, as so many girls then did, into the arts and humanities. I was not pushed unduly.'

Nafis Sadik, Executive Director, of the United Nations Population Fund echoed similar sentiments: 'I was born into a conservative Islamic family in Pakistan. I had wonderful parents. My father was a very capable and gifted man. He held the positions of finance minister and former vice-president of the World Bank. He was unusual in that he did not share the common view that women must always marry and raise children. My father had great vision. He believed it was important to educate both girls and boys. As you will appreciate that was not a common view in our part of the world at the time. Our wider family was not pleased and voiced their concerns about my going to college and then my being faced with the prospect of work.'

There is little doubt that success is more meaningful when it is shared and many of the women found the support of their husbands as being profoundly important. Several suggested it was important women took this into account when they were choosing their life partner.

Shared values, true friendship, emotional support and encouragement can make or break the relationship and the ability for the partners to flourish. Lorna Muirhead shared the view: 'Without doubt family life has been the bedrock on which I have built my life. It is the single most important thing to me. The proverb "to be happy in the home is the ultimate aim of all ambition" is my mantra. I acknowledge that my experience of family life has been very fortunate and that in spite of the best efforts some families and some marriages break down and that is a tragedy. I am extremely fortunate to have married a scientist whom after 35 years I respect and love and hope to spend a long retirement with.'

Hanna Gronkiewicz-Waltz feels advance planning is important: 'If I were able to pass on one piece of advice to other women it would be what I always tell my female students "a good husband who does not suffer from any complexes is the key to their future happiness and a positive career".' As does Sandra Dawson: 'I believe women should have a choice as to whether they marry or not and have children on not. Life can be full and productive whatever the choice. I chose marriage and children as well as a full and satisfying career. I hope women who choose a similar path will be encouraged to choose their life partner carefully. It can make all the difference.'

For some there were early broken marriages but often this seemed to precede the woman making a significant progression in her professional life and as SBH noted most in this situation had: '... chosen better the second time around... Many had husbands or partners with complementary work patterns, who had taken a substantial share in childcare. A less aggressively career orientated husband provided a happy resolution for many of these women.'

For professional success to be worthwhile for many women there is the need to adapt career patterns to accommodate child rearing. At present it is becoming more acceptable for women to continue to produce high quality work but using more family friendly work patterns. Victoria Harrison summed up 'I am pleased to have reached my current destination, but I cannot say that I arrived in it as a result of particular ambitions or sustained or coherent planning; it was more a matter of taking opportunities as they presented themselves. I believe that it is important to be flexible, to be prepared to change tack, and sometimes to do something completely different – particularly if trying to co-ordinate two careers in a family. I love my work, but I have never regarded the pursuit of any particular career as overriding. I hope that in future it might be made easier for women (and for men) to achieve a better balance, and to pursue interesting careers without the current macho pressures to work exceptionally long hours to the exclusion of other interests and family life.'

Maeve Binchy, the bestselling novelist when asked her view of whether success was worth it offered:

Is success worth it?

In my case the kind of success I had which was as a popular novelist has been very much worth it. Tiring but hugely pleasing.

I have met thousands of people in different countries, readers who got caught up in my stories and told me their own. That was marvellous.

What was the bad side? The constant travelling, the long journey's to do promotion, cities for one night and up the next day at dawn having to be cheerful and optimistic. Realising you must be nicer to the last person in the line because he or she has waited all that time.

It is lovely getting letters from people but when you have basket after basket to reply to its hard to find time any time at all to write the next book. I think I have been tired all through my fifties since I am not good at delegating and switching off…

As 60 approaches so does a great slowing down.

No regrets about anything, I'd do it all over again if I had the chance but possibly next time round I would try to remember the actual number of hours each day before taking things on.'

Success has got a downside as many of our contributors have alluded to; hard work, long hours, sacrifices and pressures. Helen Suzmann illustrated this when she discussed the impact of her work on her family life; 'I had to cope with my own personal position of having to attend Parliament in Cape Town – 1,000 miles from my home in Johannesburg for five or six months each year, leaving the family of my two daughters, aged 10 and 13 while I attended sessions. I was fortunate, however, in that they were healthy girls who were happy at school and they had at home a resident physician in the shape of my husband and a conscientious Dutch housekeeper and surrogate parents, my father and stepmother, to look after them. I did not have the guilt many working mothers appear to have, possibly because I am an extremely independent person myself having lived through a childhood without a mother who died when I was born.'

One of the other significant pressures of success is that of the public or media on your private life and those of the people you love. Joanna Trollope candidly shared; 'On the downside having achieved a significant measure of success the exposure of a public profile is hard because of the intrusive media attention which is often inaccurate and at times curiously judgmental. There seems to be a difficulty in accepting middle-age, middle-class success. The results of this in my personal life have at times been very traumatic. There have been legion amusing incidents during my career usually resulting from people feeling they know me intimately and are therefore free to say exactly what they like… which they then proceed to do.'

Darcey Bussell likewise recalled; 'Another challenge in my career was when I was still young and I was taken out of the role of Manon although I did go on to perform it successfully the next season. I had been working hard with a Russian colleague and we didn't seem to quite gel. Two weeks before the ballet was due to open he came to me and said he felt it wasn't working between us and because I was the younger artiste I was dropped from my role. The main reason it was so hard at the time was the totally disproportionate press attention I received. The front pages of a number of the newspapers had stories on the Gulf War on one side and me being dropped from the role on the other. It was surreal. How could a 21-year-old ballet dancer equate with the

Gulf War! To add to the bizareness of it all was having to deal with the fabrications some people dreamed up. I felt very alone and I really didn't feel my company was supporting me in the way that they could. No one seemed to want to help me and I was very aware of the injustice of it all. I was young and vulnerable. I was so disillusioned I felt like leaving the Company. Handling negative and inaccurate press is a learnt skill and I think I would have felt better about the whole experience if proper support had been in place.'

The irony of becoming successful is the fact there is the possibility that once you've achieved it you may wish you hadn't. Wheway (1998), recounted a story:

There once was an famous American:
He failed in business in '31.
He ran as state legislator and lost in '32.
He tried business again in '33 and failed again.
His sweetheart died in '35.
He had a nervous breakdown in '36
He ran for state elector in '40 after he regained his health.
He was defeated for congress in '43,
defeated for congress again in '48,
defeated when he ran for the Senate in '55,
and defeated for the vice presidency of the US in '56.
He ran for the Senate again in '58 and lost.
This man never quit. He kept on trying 'til the last.
In 1869, this man, Abraham Lincoln, was elected President of the United States.

I read this illustration at a time when I had unsuccessfully applied for a job. I wondered if the moral to the story was try, try, try again or whether in fact you could be trying too hard. Wheway doesn't go on to mention Abraham Lincoln was assassinated after he achieved his dream. It could be that sometimes we are trying too hard.

Heather Angel who was our first contributor both alphabetically and chronologically summed up by saying: 'The important criterion is to have a vision and to follow it through. Do not falter along the path. If, however, the opportunity arises to make a more interesting or rewarding detour, grasp it and enjoy it. You never know to where it may lead.' Darcey Bussell likewise commented: 'If I were able to pass on one piece of advice to other women it would be to have confidence in yourself. Don't let other people put you down. Believe in yourself. You can and you will make a difference. If you really want to do something you can. It is important to be proud and to have a sense of humour.' Mo Mowlam is of the same opinion: 'One of the most important assets you can have is confidence. The confidence to set yourself goals, and the determination to meet them. The confidence to take the future into your own hands. Confidence in yourself and your abilities – and also in the people around you – is essential, whether it's when you're starting a new job, growing a business, doing the next stage of exams, or even getting into the House of Commons. If you believe in yourself it can make all the difference.'

Jane Showell-Rogers illustrated that it is possible to take control of the opportunities life presents and develop them even slightly later in life: 'I am very much a "people" person, so having a home that was often a hotel or sometimes more like a "soup kitchen" was a real joy (most of the time!). On the other hand, describing myself as a "housewife" was often difficult in a society that tends to talk about people being "only" a housewife: as my husband worked from, and involved our home so much it was never a boring experience, though.

Once the children were settled at secondary school, I began to look for fresh challenges outside the home. I was keen to find ways of serving our local community and became interested in the Magistracy. I had one or two friends that were Justices of the Peace, and they encouraged me to apply. I have been a JP for nearly five years, and find that it keeps me firmly in touch with the realities of life. That has been particularly true since I have begun to sit in youth courts.

At around the same time, I was looking for a fresh direction. The idea of going back to being a secretary didn't appeal at all. I was trying to keep up with developments in computing though, and attending a computer course. The teacher suggested I might like to think about teaching adults, and now I find myself teaching the various computer programmes at my local adult education college in Richmond. There is nothing more satisfying that having a student who is scared of the machine in front of them, getting addicted to it and excited by what they can do through it. I see a major part of my aim as being to increase the students' confidence in their skills, so being able to survive in a constantly changing IT world.'

Sandra Dawson underlined her belief like Jane that women at all stages can be successful and make a major contribution when she stated: 'I hope women will have the courage to believe what they would like to do is possible. It is important women don't underplay their contribution if they are returning to work. Women who have been at home have many skills which are valuable, parenting, volunteering, teaching and administration to name but a few.'

Lisa Perry, full-time mother and wife at the start of her child-rearing years commented: 'After 10 years of teaching, counselling, disciplining encouraging, and caring for other people's children, I am now endeavouring to do the same for my 18-month-old twins Jonah and Isabelle. At first it seemed an overwhelming task and I like many new mothers wondered if I would ever again have time to take a relaxing soak in the bath or drink a hot cup of coffee. But as these two tiny, helpless, demanding babies have grown into little people with very different needs and characteristics some structure, routine and enjoyment has once again returned to my life. We begin each day determined to eat, explore, play, rest, clean at least one room in the house, and survive intact until bedtime. Ah bedtime that wonderful, peaceful, precious time. And I thought teaching was hard work!'

Sally Magnusson, broadcaster, journalist, wife, mother of five children, in her contribution to this book likewise echoed the superwomanly feats that go into any mother's ordinary working day as she neared the end of her account she recalled: 'And then you look at them (your children), squealing with delight, their faces ruddy and their eyes bright, and you think there is nowhere else in the world you would rather be, and its worth it, and you don't care that the biggest decision you make today is whether to have eggy soldiers or Dairylea sandwiches for tea. This is it. This is life.'

Virginia McKenna summed up her contribution by saying; 'Fulfilment is a very personal thing and, I suppose, depends on ones expectations. I have found it in the light of an African dawn, the hand of a friend, the love of my family, the eyes of a rescued animal, a walk in the wood in winter, beautiful music. It just needs an open heart and an open mind. In a world with so much to see and wonder at and try to understand, how can one ever be bored?'

If success is measured simply in terms of seniority, salary and status then it can be very hollow. If success is measured, in values that endure, and in values that an individual perceives as being truly important to them, then that success can be a wonderful thing.

Part Two: Tips for Women at Work

Chapter 6
Preparing yourself

Professor Anna M. Maslin

Well you've decided now is the time! Time to make a move at work, time to go back to work or time to start looking for work. The thought of taking such a big step can leave you with a queasy feeling in the pit of your stomach not to mention a number of sleepless nights. Life changes no matter how big or small can range from making you feel really excited to stressed beyond belief.

We may be making a change for a number of reasons. We may need to earn more money to support our children. We may need to give our brains a much-needed kick-start. We may want to use our talents for the benefit of mankind.

When preparing yourself you need to focus on a number of issues. Part two of this book concentrates on a number of key areas many working women will find useful to have thought through. These will include, applications, CVs, interview techniques, salaries, Individual Performance Reviews, personal presentations, managing home, work and time, issues with childcare, dealing with the unexpected, stress, bullies, and even a little on flexi-working and working from home.

Whilst I fully support the fact that education is one of the key factors in enabling a person to have the tools to succeed I am assuming that the majority of people reading this book are at a point in their lives where they want to find a satisfying job with the qualifications, skills and expertise they already possess. In some cases a woman will be in a position to undertake a degree or professional qualification which will involve the investment of substantial time and money but for many it may not be possible at this time. Even if you do not have a vast formal education you can optimise the skills you have on offer to make yourself as attractive as possible to a future employer.

One of the key ways you can prepare yourself is to take the time to quietly consider a few questions. Buy yourself a small notepad and have a quick brainstorm.

- What formal qualifications do I already possess?
- What informal qualifications do I have?
- Do I have any particular skills or talents?
- What do I enjoy spending my time on?
- Would I prefer to work with my head or my hands? Or both?
- Will my health stand up to my choice of work?
- Will I be on my feet for long periods?
- Will I be putting a strain on my back?
- Will I be putting myself under a great deal of stress for little reward?
- What would my ideal career be?
- What have enjoyed in jobs I have undertaken so far
- Do I want to take a job, which will allow me time and or money to facilitate me in being able to gain additional qualifications for a career, which will be my longer-term goal?
- What is available locally?
- Am I prepared to travel?
- Is childcare or other responsibilities going to impact on my choice of work?
- Is my partner or family supportive?
- If I died tomorrow what would I wish I had spent my time on?
- What resources are available locally to help me gain information or additional skills?
- Where is the library?
- Where is my local job center?
- Is there an internet facility available locally?
- Can someone show me how to use the internet?
- Is there someone locally who can provide me with vocational advice?
- Are there free basic PC skills courses available in my area for adult learners?

- Am I eligible for any other free or low cost adult educational opportunities?
- Is there vocational guidance at my current place of employment?
- Do I belong to a union that has a careers advice service?
- Do I belong to a professional organisation that will give free advice?
- Is there a government department who deals with the career I would like to embark on?
- Have I considered working for myself?
- If I would like to be self-employed, do I know how to write a business plan?
- Do I know who to talk to, to get advice?
- Do I know someone trustworthy who is self-employed who will share his or her experiences honestly?
- Do I have the facilities, i.e. premises and equipment to set up a business?
- Do I know a trustworthy accountant?
- Do I have the support of a good bank?

Shirley Conran back in 1977 observed:

> 'Careers advisory officers all made surprisingly similar comments on mistakes that women make when they want to go back to work.'

Here are 14 of them:

Mistake 1

'She really made her biggest mistake when she stopped work and assumed that, because she was bringing up children, she would never have a job again.'

Mistake 2

'She assumed that she'd never want a job again.'

Mistake 3

'Never assume that because you're interested in children when your own are young that you have a universal interest in children that will last for life. It rarely does... If a mother wants to start a new job working with children I'd advise her to wait. If she plans to teach 4-year-old infants, she should wait until her youngest is at least 8 years old – then see if she still feels the same way about 4-year-olds.'

Mistake 4

'She isn't practical about her own abilities... She isn't realistic about the opportunities available... She's too romantic.'

Mistake 5

'The majority of women returnees, I see underestimate their competence and abilities. A woman needs to be a bit more confident. She needs to make a conscious effort to be positive: she mustn't cop out by saying she's shy or hasn't any self-confidence. The family attitude can make or break a woman in this frame of mind: a condescending or tolerantly amused attitude can be crushing.'

Mistake 6

'The Queen of the Hearth syndrome... The woman who thinks that running a home for a few years automatically equips her to take on anything without training or experience.'

Mistake 7

Again indicative of a Queen of the Hearth. 'She thinks she's always right... Nobody is allowed to contradict her... She won't fit into other peoples established work pattern and wants to do everything her own way... This is the hardest thing to get a woman to realise about herself. But you've got to see how the system works before laying down the law to other people.'

Mistake 8

Especially when there are teenagers in the office – and there generally are: 'If you treat teenagers as children (because they're not much older than your own) then you're in for trouble.'

Mistake 9

'She's so used to being on her own and not working to a set routine that she finds it hard to accept a timetable and stick to it.'

Mistake 10

'When a woman starts work again she tends to underestimate how much time it takes to run her home in the way she's been doing it. It's often a good idea to have a dummy run a week or two before you start the job.'

Mistake 11

'Perhaps the saddest mistake that a woman can make is not giving herself the best chance, taking the first job she's offered, not finding out what is available or what she's suited for and never taking advantage of the good free help that's offered in career guidance and training. Over half the women I see don't know what they're good at and don't really know what they want.'

Mistake 12

Is made when she goes after the job. 'Few women know how important it is to present themselves properly when being interviewed for a job or think in terms of the employer's reason for their meeting. She can be her own worst enemy if she goes on about wanting to take time off to take the children to the dentist: what an employer is least interested in is when you're not going to be there. Wait until you have the job and have proved how valuable you are, then people are generally prepared to make concessions, within reason.'

Mistake 13

Not doing anything (and whining on about it) because there is no immediate opportunity that is exactly right. This often indicates lack of guts, fear of competition, fear of the world outside... and fear of being turned down by some of the people some of the time. Everyone who succeeds has risked failure.'

Mistake 14

'Giving up to easily.'

Although Shirley Conran wrote this 25 years ago the principles remain largely the same. Although the comments are a little dated in part there is a basic truth, which remains applicable even today.

Women at Work

Chapter 7
Cracking the CV

Tom Storrow

The *Curriculum Vitae* or CV seems to generate a surprising amount of concern and mystique. Its sole purpose is to get you onto a 'longlist' (the preliminary selection of candidates for further assessment and discussion) or a 'shortlist' (the final selection of candidates for formal interview and/or other assessment) for a particular job[1]. Entry to one of these lists gives you an opportunity to sell yourself and your skills and attributes and to find out more about the employer and the post. Thus, the CV has something of a 'key to the door' nature and so it is important to get it right to enable you to progress towards the job you want.

However, the bookshelves of the management and personal development sections of my local bookstore seem to have plenty of volumes on how to write this fabled 'perfect' CV, so why bother writing a chapter on CVs for this book, apart from the fact that we wish to provide you with a range of practical tips all under one cover?

Well, I happen to believe that a CV is a personal statement. As such, it should reflect the style and personality of the candidate as well as describing their suitability for the specific post for which they are applying. For this reason, I will not attempt here to set out the 'perfect' CV, as this will be quite different for different individuals and especially for different posts. I believe that the idea that there is a perfect standard CV, regardless of the individual, the post and even the industry, is for charlatans and the gullible.

Let me illustrate my point.

My own background is in the public sector, especially the National Health Service (NHS). In the NHS, for senior professional posts and for almost any post above supervisory level, employing bodies will tend to do the following:

- Advertise the post openly in vacancy bulletins and probably in the national, local or professional press inviting potential applicants to send for an Information Pack.

- In the Information Pack provide a Job Description/Role Specification and a Person Specification, plus information about the department or organisation and often background information about the location/schools/house prices, etc.

- Shortlist candidates against the criteria set out in the Specifications.

- Interview candidates before a panel, possibly also asking them to make a presentation, undergo psychometric assessments, etc.

- Take up references and often make informal enquiries (although the validity and fairness of this may be very questionable) about the candidates.

Other, non-public sector, industries often rely upon very different approaches. The following being a reasonable example of such an approach:

- Advertise the post, asking potential candidates to send in their 'resume', or for senior posts use recruitment consultants to search out candidates and obtain their resumes.

- Review the resumes received, longlisting those candidates felt to be worthy of more detailed contact.

- Begin an interview/meeting process, during which more information is given to candidates about the organisation and more information is sought from the candidates about themselves (again this may involve panel interviews, psychometric assessments, presentations, etc. at the later stages).

There can be further, very different approaches. My own experience in joining the company for which I work now involved neither CV nor resume – the company Chairman knew me well, sounded me out about joining them over a glass of beer and made me 'an offer I couldn't refuse' a few days later! Conversely, I have a number of friends and colleagues who made their first contact with their current employers by sending in a CV 'cold' and asking whether there were any suitable vacancies, rather than responding to an advertisement.

Obviously, there are numerous variations upon and permutations of the themes I have outlined very briefly above, but the simple point that I wish to make is that different industries and different employers will require and expect different responses and thus different CVs from potential employees. Thus, the only 'perfect' CV can be the one geared perfectly towards a given post with a given employer in a given industry at a given time.

Having said that, I think that there are some principles and some alternatives that are worth considering, and some questions that you can ask yourself in preparing your own perfect, customised CV. I have based the principles and suggestions that follow upon my own research and reading and especially upon the recruitment and personal development experiences that I have had and seen in the NHS and other industries. These are set out below, not in any order of priority and certainly not to be followed slavishly, but rather as points for consideration, reflection and even challenge, which I hope you will find helpful before you complete your own CV.

Information Packs, phone calls and advance visits

In most parts of the public sector – and in some other sectors – there is a custom of providing Information Packs to respondents to the job advertisement, and often visits or telephone contacts are offered and indeed encouraged for senior posts. This is not done out of politeness, but usually because public sector employers in particular are bound by rules of equality of opportunity and openness, as well as the normal equality legislation. Thus, they want to ensure that prospective candidates fully understand the requirements of both the post and the organisation and respond to these in their application. Further, this approach can help to 'sell' a post or organisation when there are real recruitment shortages. Additionally, of course, it can also provide some initial contact and thus 'first impressions' of candidates.

(As I indicated above, this is not the case in all industries, and many use the process of asking for a 'resume' in order to get a quick overview of potential candidates before deciding on a longlist who will be contacted for more detailed discussions, interviews and assessments. There is more on this 'resume' style of CV to come.)

However, if you are already in the public sector and want a change or promotion – or if you want to get into the public sector – do not just send in a standard resume, having failed to make contact or obtain the Information Pack. That would be almost a guarantee that you won't even make the first-cut of shortlisting. Indeed in our public sector orientated Recruitment Division, we would not bother looking at the CV of someone who had not sent for the Information Pack, as such a person would be quite unable to respond to the specifications.

The 'full CV'

Most public sector and some other employers will expect more than a one or two page 'resume'. They will expect you to have made contact when the position was offered, and they will particularly expect you then to have addressed the key issues in their Information Pack.

These issues are usually reasonably obvious, being summarised in the requirements covered by the Role and Person Specifications. At the very least, they will also expect some reference to their organisation in the CV, even if only on the front or title page! However, some employers ask for a statement of what you can do for them, and failure to answer this will almost certainly consign your CV to the wastepaper bin. Even if they do not ask for it explicitly, consider adding a section anyway on why you want this particular post and what skills and experience you will bring to it.

There is no such thing as a 'right' length for this type of fuller CV. It has to be long enough for you to provide the evidence of the qualifications, experiences and skills that enable you to meet their requirements and to tell them why you are the candidate they need, without being boring or pedantic. Perhaps something in the order of three to five pages would be acceptable, but this always must be a matter of personal judgement, based on the impression you want to create and the employer's requirements. For example, medical CVs can be much longer, because prospective consultant surgeons and physicians need to set out in some detail their training, special interests, research and publications.

Obviously, if they ask for 'no more than three pages', then you fail to follow the instructions at your peril – there's more on dealing with such instructions later. However, an obvious tip is not to forget how much room for manoeuvre you can create on the apparent length of a document by playing with the margins, borders (if you have them), font size and style.

Think about the order in which you present your CV. A fairly standard approach is to use about half of the CV to give personal and contact details, qualifications, membership of professional bodies, names and addresses of referees and an outline of your employment history (with just a couple of lines under the recent posts giving a flavour of what they were, scale of responsibilities, etc). The remainder can then cover key skills and experiences, based clearly on a response to the requirements of the Role and Person Specifications. In these pages, don't be afraid to use the headings from the employer's Role and Person Specifications. By doing so, you can help them to do the shortlisting, which they will probably appreciate – especially if they have lots of applicants – whilst you are also saying, 'Look, I meet your requirements, don't you dare not shortlist me!'

The main alternative is to give the information about your skills and experiences under the headings of each of your current and previous posts (in reverse chronological order, i.e. starting with current job and working back). Make sure that what you write is about your experiences and achievements, not just a potted version of the job description for each post you have held. Employers want to hear what you achieved in the job, not just a list of the duties you were supposed to perform.

If you follow this latter approach, then remember to 'taper' the list of posts, giving less and less detail of the jobs and the experiences, as you go further back, as employers are usually more interested in what you have been doing in the last three – five years than what you did 20 years ago. A good example of this 'tapering' is quite often seen in CVs of senior managers in professions such as nursing. Effective CVs in these cases will often bring together in summary form a series of junior posts from early in the individual's career. This can be done partly to save space (there really is no need for potential Directors of Nursing to list out the full details of every Staff Nurse job they held in the 1970s) but also because the summary statement can have much more impact.

For example, completing the career history by saying something such as, 'Between 1975 and 1989 I held clinical posts at Staff Nurse and Ward Manager levels in Medical specialties in hospitals in London', is a clear statement that says 'I've got some real clinical/professional experience and credibility.'

In organising your experiences for the CV, again remember what the employer has told you they are seeking. This may mean that you have to be brave and leave out or heavily edit experiences of which you are very proud, but which unfortunately are not relevant to this post. It may also mean 'talking-up' other experiences which are a little thin, but which are important to this post. However, this does not mean fabricating or grossly exaggerating experiences or skills – there is more on this presently.

Having suggested a split of about 50:50 between personal details, education, career history, etc. and skills, experiences and what you have to offer, do think about the order in which this information is presented in your CV. For example, let's say that your CV will run to four pages. If you put your personal and contact details and career history on page one, followed by a two-page skills and experiences section, finishing with the page of education, memberships, referees, etc. this will mean that employers can get into the 'meat' of your real experience more quickly. It is probably better to do this – especially if you are demonstrating that you meet their specifications clearly – than forcing them to read through all of the personal and background stuff before getting to what they really want to see.

In tailoring your CV to the Role and Person Specifications for the job, remember that you may be able to influence the later interview processes, by leaving 'hooks' upon which questions could be hung. For example, you may tell them what you did in a specific situation, but not how you did it – saving that for later!

The physical appearance of your CV

When it comes to the physical assembly of a fuller length CV, remember what usually happens to CVs in the Personnel Department or at the Recruitment Consultants – i.e. that they are pulled apart and photocopied if they are to be reviewed by several people or if there is to be an interview panel. Thus, if you have a multi-page CV, do not use those forms of binding that will require your CV literally to be ripped apart for copying – what will the edges of each photocopy sheet look like? Consider instead one of the simple slide-and-clip folders/binders that look good but can easily be taken apart and reassembled.

Similarly, do not use strongly coloured paper, which is likely to show up as dark grey when photocopied. One of the most striking CVs I've ever seen was beautifully set out and printed onto red paper. It was stunning, but it had to be retyped by a junior clerk as it produced a photocopy of black print on a dark grey background! The retyping was not perfect and obviously this had some impact on the CV, but this effort was only made for the candidate because she was excellent; otherwise the CV would have been consigned to the reject pile. I suggest using either standard A4 white or at most a cream coloured paper (as this is pleasant on the eye in original form but will also photocopy well). Also, try to use a good quality paper, rather than the flimsy paper out of the office photocopier!

The 'resume CV'

As I indicated earlier, there are some employers who will want the two-page (or even one-page) resume type of CV, either because they have adopted the recruitment approach of making contact and sharing more information after seeing the CV or because they believe that everything they need to know can be summarised in just two pages. This type of CV has been a standard in the USA for some time, not least, as Max Eggert has observed, because of the strong equality legislation there, which has led to the exclusion of almost all personal information.

This type of CV inevitably will have to be more standardised and perhaps less customised to a particular post. Clearly, you can still edit some of the key skills and experiences within the confines of two pages, to try to match what you know about the post, the employer and/or the industry, but much of the CV will have to be of a fairly standard format and content, in order to keep it short.

The resume format usually comprises the following:

- A brief 'profile', describing you and your skills and attributes.
- Basic personal and educational details.
- A brief career history – probably no more than 4–5 lines per recent post.
- An outline of key skills, experiences, projects, etc.
- A brief statement of intentions/ambitions/why this post (if appropriate).
- Referees (if appropriate).

It is probably only the fourth and fifth points that you may want to customise a little – remember that usually the purpose of a resume is to have it to hand quickly to open up a dialogue with potential employers or even to use as an introduction to employers to whom you wish to write and send a CV 'cold'.

Profiles at the top of your CV or resume

Here I must confess to a personal prejudice. I rarely read profiles, because I find too many of them difficult to take seriously.

The concept of the profile is particularly linked to the development of the two-page resume mentioned previously, in which there is little space to write about personal style and motivation and so the 'profile' is used. In these circumstances, the profile clearly can be very helpful.

Unfortunately, however, in my experience the profile often appears to become an anonymous jumble of mock-American management-speak. For example, I would suggest to you that there is little point in writing something like, 'A highly-motivated, self-starting, experienced and people-focused senior manager with a particular strength in project and performance management'. Unfortunately, I've seen quite a few like that. There is little point in writing it because no one would ever describe himself or herself as anything much different to this. (Can you really imagine anyone writing the opposite: 'A poorly-motivated, slow, inexperienced sociopath, with particular weaknesses in project and performance management!')

Hence, the profile is too often reduced to platitudes and buzzwords. Personally, I'm more interested in the provision of evidence of real achievements, and would rather give over the limited space to that instead of unsupported self-promotion.

In addition, I have a second prejudice to confess – and this shows my age and my tendency to pedantry! The example I've written above is not written in English, as there is no subject or verb. I have an allergy to such damage to the language. I also have a fear – perhaps irrationally – that it may be easier for people to tell me lies when they write in such an impersonal style that they could be referring to anyone.

However, profiles can be helpful in saying something about style and approach in a succinct way, so perhaps it is best to focus on this, and to try to write it in English. For example, 'I am a very experienced and enthusiastic NHS/HR/Production, etc. senior manager, with a good track record of project and performance management at both Board and local service levels. My personal style is based on developing relationships and trust, and I am particularly motivated by change and strategic management issues.'

Having shared some of my prejudices with you, I should remind you that some of these observations and suggestions are highly personal and you might agree with me and want to use some of them or you may violently disagree. That's fine; as I said at the outset, a CV is a personal document and must reflect you, not me or some other writer.

Use of the first person

My comments above also raise the issue of the use of the first person singular (I, me, etc.) in profiles or in the main body of the CV. Some people say that you should describe yourself in the third person (he, she) or anonymously (a highly motivated manager, etc.), so as to avoid starting every sentence with 'I' and thus running the risk of appearing self-centred.

I would certainly agree that you should not start every line of a bullet-point list of posts held or achievements with 'I did...', 'I held...', etc. However, in a body of text, my own preference is always to write in English, using the first person, but using the great and wonderful variety of the English language to help avoid repetition. For example: 'I worked at... In my particular experience there was... The leadership of the project was offered to me... We delivered...', etc. In some circumstances, the use of the first person plural (we, our) can also be very powerful as an indicator of personal style, if the employer is seeking a team player and leader. However, remember that its overuse might give an impression that others led and you were only a part of a project. To get a balance, I like phrases such as, 'I led XYZ and we achieved...'

Honesty is the best policy

I mentioned previously the need to edit your skills and experiences to the job requirements. Leaving things out or playing them down if they are not very relevant is fairly easy and straightforward, if sometimes painful. A little more difficult is the issue of 'talking things up'.

It is one thing to make the most of a particular skill or experience and to talk and write quite a lot about something that perhaps you have only done once or twice. However, it is quite something else to claim to have qualifications, skills or experiences that you do not have. You might think that this is 'fair game' if you can get away with it, but I suggest that it is not only dishonest but also foolish, often leading to unhappy appointments, based on either deceit or an inability to do the job properly. Further, if you do this and you are found out, it may well be that you will have given your employer grounds to dismiss you. Even if you are not found out directly, you run the risk of it becoming clear in due course that you cannot actually do the job. This is likely to create stress for you if you try to hide it; or a different type of stress if your managers can see it and feel the need to take action!

I can understand people sometimes being desperate to get a job and perhaps feeling prepared to take a risk. However, if you not in a genuinely life-or-death situation, then why run the risk of losing your job/career or putting yourself under stress for the sake of a pay rise or a grander title?

Further, I always recommend to my personal development clients that they should be themselves throughout a recruitment process. If they do this and the employer likes what they see, then that is great, potentially leading to a perfect match between the person, the post and the organisation. If they do this and the employer does not like what they see, then I would suggest that this is also great – who really wants to be a round peg in a square hole, placed there because they pretended to be a square peg?

Personal details

There is some debate about whether or not to include personal interests, hobbies, and other commitments. Some people say that you are applying only for a job and that there is no necessity for this to be linked to your personal life. Others say that employers like to know something about the 'whole person' – particularly as senior and executive-level jobs can be so all consuming that they inevitably impinge on your personal life anyway; and many jobs today require a degree of mobility and flexibility that our parents would have thought ridiculous.

My view is that unless you feel very strongly, or you know that this employer would frown upon it, why not err on the side of putting in something brief about you as a person, your interests, etc. Remember that it is possible to use this to your advantage, by demonstrating that you can combine a successful career with other aspects of your life, and/or that you are respected in other walks of life, being a school governor, trustee of a charity, honorary lecturer, or whatever. However, if you think that mentioning your personal circumstances, as a female will cause problems with a particular employer, then perhaps you need to ask yourself whether you really want to work for them.

There is also some debate about whether to include your age or birth date. I know that some employers might be seen as 'age-ist', but if they shortlist you then they will at least be able to estimate your age when you meet them, so omitting your age from the CV is only delaying them finding out your likely age. Further, my experience is that when candidates exclude their age or birth date, employers and recruitment specialists are usually curious and so always try to calculate the age from the dates of qualifications, degrees, etc. Thus, my feeling is that it is usually pointless excluding your age.

A different matter is whether to mention family commitments. Unfortunately, some employers will be wary of women with a young family, assuming that they will take more time off. Others might have realised that they need to be flexible and supportive in order to fill their vacancies and so will offer part-time work, flexible contracts or crèche facilities. If the employer appears to be the latter camp, then you can probably mention children or other commitments in your CV or at interview, if you wish to do so. If they appear to be in the former camp, then I'd probably leave out such personal details.

Preparing the raw material

If you are in the type of industry that requires the resume approach to CVs, it is fairly easy to keep your CV up-to-date and ready to use. You should decide upon a format with which you are comfortable and prepare a slightly longer version than the classic two pages – perhaps having a long list of skills and experiences that you can edit down quickly for a particular post or employer. This basic 'raw material' resume can be reviewed every few months, so that you can add in to the long list new experiences, qualifications, etc.

It is a little more difficult if you will have to prepare a more thoroughly customised and extensive CV, but the same principle applies. Keep your standard two pages of personal details, qualifications and career history as up-to-date as possible. For the rest of the fuller CV, I recommend keeping a paragraph or two on each of your key skills and experiences, and updating and adding to these every few months – this might run to several pages, but don't worry about it; this is your 'catalogue' of CV material, from which you will choose the best items as you need them. It is surprising how quickly we can all forget a really interesting or important experience, when our jobs require us quickly to move on to a new project, target or assignment, so keeping these notes is really helpful. It is then much easier to read through all of these paragraphs and edit them down to fit a particular Role and Person Specification, than to start with a blank sheet of paper.

Do what they ask and make yourself easy to deal with

I mentioned earlier the use of the employer's own headings and specifications – playing their own words back to them, which they may find flattering, and organising your CV to fit with the specification or schedule against which they are selecting candidates for interview, etc. My colleagues in our Recruitment Division rejoice when a candidate follows the headings given to them, as it makes the assessment of that CV much easier. Think about it for yourself – you set out a specification of your requirements and instructions about how to respond, then you get 100 responses to plough through, many of which have not followed your instructions, but some of which have; towards which candidates will you be most sympathetic?

Sometimes, employers ask for unusual things. I remember once applying for a senior post in the NHS where the organisation asked in the Information Pack for candidates to apply in the form of a letter to the Chair covering the five key headings of the Person Specification, with a brief CV appended. I spent a Sunday afternoon following these instructions, stripping down my public service-style CV to look more like a resume and writing a letter. My letter was very straightforward; it comprised seven paragraphs. The first paragraph stated my wish to register my application for the post. The last paragraph provided a very brief summary of my reasons for being interested in the post, my hope that the letter was clear and helpful, and my hope that I may be able to expand upon it at interview. The five paragraphs in the middle were simply one to each criterion in the Specification, giving a brief example or other evidence to show that I could meet their needs. The letter ran to about two and a half pages, with the normal letter headings and layout. To cut a long story short, I was longlisted but didn't take things beyond that point. However, I later asked the HR Director for some feedback on my application. She told me that I was one of the first people on the longlist – not because I was an early applicant, but because I had done exactly what they asked and provided the evidence to show that I met their criteria. I was amazed, as the post was not really in my field, and I said, 'But, surely, everyone did the same, didn't they?' Her reply was, 'Tom, don't be so naive – hardly anyone followed the instructions!' I guess that the longlisting for that post did not take too long!

Some things to avoid

In addition to not following basic instructions, there are some other gaffs to avoid.

- Sending in a paper copy of your CV with either a 'Post-it' note or a small sheet of lilac-coloured paper instead of a more formal covering letter probably won't go down too well – I've seen notes stuck on, just saying 'Re – your ad in last week's XYZ'.

- Don't put crucial information about your candidacy into the covering letter without also putting it into your CV – unless it is asked for, as in my personal example. Often, in larger organisations the covering letters don't make it to the interviewers, being set aside in the HR or photocopy office.

- If you use a standard CV – especially of the resume style – do print it off fresh each time you use it, on decent quality paper. Fourth-generation photocopies never look as attractive as an original. The worst example I've ever seen was from a very senior person, who really should have known a lot better. He sent in a 17-page standard CV, which had obviously been photocopied over and again. It was completely unedited and unstructured for the job (a CEO position!) and the ancient photocopying meant that many pages did not line up properly. It was a very interesting read – his life and career story, in effect – but he didn't make it to the shortlist.

- Don't try to be funny – unless you know your audience personally very well indeed and know that they will appreciate the joke.

- Unless it is specifically requested, it is probably better not to include photographs of yourself or gimmicks such as images from Clip Art. The former, unfortunately, can be used critically (unless you are incredibly photogenic), as employers may make judgements about you from your appearance in the picture, which you are not there in person to correct. The latter can look tacky and give an impression that you're desperate to show off your computer skills – or, worse still, that you need to fill up empty space because you have nothing useful to say. Obviously, as with many of these principles, there may be exceptions. For example, in a 'creative' industry or job, something unusual or even artistic might be appreciated. Think carefully about whether this employer/position is one of those exceptions, before you do anything that might otherwise be written off as gimmicky.

- Avoid the commercially available off-the-shelf CVs that are around. I've tried to make it clear that I think that CVs should be personal, customised statements. If you use a pre-prepared CV, you will risk cutting across all of this advice around customising your CV to yourself and to the industry/organisation. I suggest also that you will not be sending in your CV, even if it has some of your details in it, but in reality someone else's. You also run the risk of the employer recognising the version you are using and being less than impressed.

Finding the right job opportunity

In this chapter, I have assumed that you might be preparing your CV, resume or application form for a specific post, or at least for a specific organisation or industry to which you may send your CV speculatively (what I've called sending in a CV 'cold'). However, in this final section, I want to say a little about looking out for these opportunities and positioning yourself.

I have stressed several times the importance of being yourself and looking for a post that matches your skills, experience, ambitions and style. Thus, if you are already into a profession, industry or type of job, then the two basic approaches you need to consider if moving onwards and upwards are keeping in touch with the posts being advertised and seeking out organisations with possible vacancies that are not yet on the open market.

For the first of these two approaches, you need to find out what are the standard publications, newsletters, vacancy bulletins or websites in which the type of posts you are seeking will be advertised. If you are really actively seeking a move, then you may need to consider taking out subscriptions to professional or trade journals, to ensure that you don't miss out. Additionally, you may need to spend time regularly visiting either general employment websites or the websites of specific organisations, in order to keep in touch.

Once you spot an opportunity, remember to find out all you can about the post and employer – either by sending for information packs or by doing some research of your own. All of this will support your customising of your CV to ensure that the employer believes that you have something to offer.

If you are considering sending in a CV 'cold', I would still strongly suggest doing the research and homework. Employers and recruitment companies receive many such 'cold' CVs. You therefore need to ensure that yours does not just get discarded or filed away. So, you should consider what they are likely to be looking for (again, from trade journals and websites, find out what are their big issues at present and think about how you can help them with these) and how can you best demonstrate that you have something unique or desirable.

If you are not even at the stage yet of looking for specific posts or organisations, perhaps because you are thinking of a complete career change, you need to start your research and homework even further back. You need to think in the way that a school-leaver or new graduate would. Ask yourself some of these questions:

- What do I really enjoy doing?
- What am I good at doing?
- Am I prepared to train/retrain – with the possible consequences on earnings in the short-term?
- Do I want responsibility or leadership roles or am I happy as a team member/worker?

- What sort of career development opportunities do I want – do I want a straightforward 'job for life' or am I looking for a position that could take me upwards and outwards?
- What do I want/need in terms of salary and benefits?
- Do I have/want geographical limits on where I work?
- Do I need a job that gives me a particular work-life balance?
- Then finally, where might I compromise on the balances between enjoyment, satisfaction, pay, geography, career and other life issues?

My strong advice is to find the type of support that school-leavers and graduates have in terms of careers advisers. Obviously, this does not have to be a formal career adviser, but could be provided by family members, friends and colleagues. However, do not forget the potential availability of specialist careers advisers at your local Employment Centre or at a recruitment company or agency. Further, don't be afraid to approach people in the type of professions, jobs or organisations that may be of interest to you. My experience is that they are usually flattered to be asked to talk about their jobs, careers or professions and will often give you much more time than you might have imagined. In one of my former roles as a hospital manager, I was approached many times by students, members of the public and members of the hospital's clinical and support staff about careers and opportunities in hospital management. I don't think that I ever turned down anyone who asked to have time to talk these things over with me.

Further reading

As I mentioned at the start of this chapter, there are plenty of books telling you how to prepare your CV. I'm wary of some of them, for the reasons I've already stated. However, I would recommend the following very accessible and easy-to-use books. They include more examples and model layouts than we have space to give you here, they are published in the UK and they do not try to preach only one way of preparing a CV:

Eggert, M. (1999) *The Perfect CV* (London, Random House Business Books).

Howard, S. (1999) *Creating a Successful CV* (London, Dorling Kindersley).

Notes:

[1] I'm assuming here that we are considering professional, technical and managerial posts, for which the use of a CV as the means of imparting your personal, educational, professional and other information is likely. For clerical, manual and other such jobs, the use of a pre-printed application form telling you exactly what the employer wants and where to put it on the form, is probably more likely. Having said that, at least some of the suggestions in this chapter could usefully be applied to an application form.

Chapter 8
Interview intelligence

Tom Storrow

Interviews can create all manner of nervous reactions – not least amongst those doing the interviewing! I can think of many situations throughout my own career, particularly when fairly junior staff were involved on either side of the interview table, when it was unclear who was the most nervous, interviewer or interviewee.

Why is this so? My guess is that this may be one of the most formal yet personal interactions that people have at work. Obviously, much can be riding on the interview for all concerned and everyone wants to look and sound good. If you haven't had much experience as interviewer/interviewee, it can be a potentially nerve-wracking time.

In this chapter, I shall concentrate on trying to provide some tips for the interviewees, but some of the observations and suggestions may be equally valid for those of you doing the interviewing. Similarly, I have tried to focus on recruitment-type interviews, but again some of the comments will be applicable in other interview situations, such as those for appraisals, research or even investigations or disciplinary matters.

My tips are based on a mixture of research of the varied literature, personal experience, observation, and – I hope – some common sense. Some of them will seem very obvious, having been stated in every guide to interviews since God quizzed Adam and Eve on the whereabouts of that apple, but they do bear repetition. Others may seem almost crass, and you will think, 'Surely no one would ever do that!' However, unfortunately, all are based on real examples of bad practices as well as good.

I'll start with some general comments that could apply to virtually any interview format, but as I go on I will try to describe some of the different formats and some specific things that you can consider for each. The final section touches on some of the different interview settings and some issues to look out for before and after the interview itself.

Interview tips

Influencing the interview through your CV

You can start your influencing of the interview when you prepare your CV. As indicated in the last chapter, full CVs should always be tailored to the post or industry, based upon your research about them and then deploying carefully your evidence, experiences and skills. However, this can be done in such a way as to suggest areas for expansion and follow-up at interview. Leave 'hooks' on which the panel can hang some questions. For example, on some notable experiences tell them briefly what you achieved, but do not tell them how – save that for the interview.

This is much easier with the shorter, resume style of CV. Here, you will only have space to give a very basic outline of the jobs you have held and your skills and experiences in them – this should always be developed at the interview and meeting stages.

Presentations at the start of an interview

Many of the more formal type of interviews – especially in the public and academic sectors – now start with a presentation, so remember some of the key tactics for good presentations:

- Keep to time – there is nothing worse than over-running badly and having the Interview Panel Chair stop your presentation. For a 10-minute presentation, aim to finish in say nine to nine and a half minutes, and rehearse this.
- Avoid jokes as part of your 'warm-up' – they rarely work.
- If you are allowed visual aids, such as PowerPoint or overhead projector (OHP), then use the minimum number of slides, each with the minimum number of words on them – in such a pressured situation you want simple reinforcement and summarisation, not complex lists or analyses. Similarly, I suggest avoiding the fancy 'transitions' on Power-Point, as they can distract from the simple messages of reinforcement and summary that you are trying to get across in a limited time.
- If you are using an overhead projector put the slides into protective covers, to make them easier to handle.
- You should never use paper 'windows' over parts of an OHP slide, and nor should you ever try to cover parts of a slide with a loose piece of paper – if you need to reveal a slide's contents in stages, then you have put too much information on it (obviously, this is much easier to handle with a PowerPoint presentation).
- Rehearse the physical side of the presentation aids – setting up and using the

PowerPoint projector or OHP. (Incidentally, for my own presentations, I now tend to take my laptop, assuming that the venue will have projection facilities for PowerPoint, plus OHP slides as back-up, and printed copies of the slides in case both technologies fail! The worst case of PowerPoint failure I've seen, with the candidate struggling on and on to try to get the system and his own presentation working, went on for 17 minutes, by which time any attempt to continue was only wasting everyone's time.)

- Face your audience, not the screen, and make eye contact with all of them from time-to-time. Try to avoid using notes, other than perhaps a single card with your 'prompts' on it – and certainly avoid reading your presentation word-by-word. All of these things will help you to make more eye contact and to raise your head from out of the notes and slides.
- Try to use the 'rule of threes' – basing your presentation around three broad themes, each with three sub-points.
- Remember the old teachers' adage: (a) tell them what you are going to tell them, (b) tell them, and (c) then tell them what you have told them.
- The use of the last two points could give you a simple format to follow in a 10-minute presentation – a few seconds with an introductory slide to tell them of your three key themes; a maximum of three minutes on each theme, covering three sub-points for up to one minute each, and with a slide for each theme (the slide should have just three lines on it, one for each of the sub-points); 20 seconds to summarise and tell them what you have told them, with a repeat of your introductory slide (total nine – nine and a half minutes).
- If you are prone to fidgeting whilst on your feet making presentations, then you must prepare yourself to try to stop this. I usually tell men to take their keys and change out of their pockets before they go into the interview room. Women are much less likely to have pockets full of keys and money, but they can just as easily fidget with their jewellery – so dress carefully. Other points about body language are covered later in the chapter.

The same broad rules and structures will work for other types of recruitment presentations, such as those to groups of potential colleagues, stakeholders or staff.

Entrances and where and how to sit

The first thing to be aware of here is to manage your entrance to the room. Try to think about whether you are likely to be greeted at the door and offered handshakes, or alternatively just told to come in and take a seat. If you don't know how they will handle this, then be prepared for anything that might face you as you enter, so that you can concentrate on eye contact and positive first impressions, rather than being surprised or looking around for what to do. Similarly, leave bags and cases outside if at all possible – as you enter, you should be focused on the interviewer(s) not on where to leave your bags.

In the main part of a formal interview, try to sit where you can make eye contact with each panel member without having to move much more than move your eyes or your head and upper body. If the chair they have given to you is too close to the desk or table, then move it back a little as you sit down, so that you can see everyone without moving too much. Do not move your seat to face different members of the panel at different times through the interview (I've seen that done four or five times!). Further, never put your elbows on the interview desk/table (I've seen that done three times – on each occasion, the interviewers shrank back from the invasion of their – or least the neutral – space).

If you are in a boardroom, meeting room or someone's office, you will have to take the chair set out for you. However, if you are around a coffee table or if there is just you and the interviewer in a meeting room, then try to pick a seat where you will sit across a corner of the table from the interviewer, rather than on opposite sides of the table. This can feel more comfortable; perhaps a little more like a discussion between colleagues.

Body position and gestures

There are plenty of writers much better qualified than I am to write in detail about body language or non-verbal communication. However, as an experienced interviewer and interviewee, perhaps I can suggest a few basics to look out for.

The first thing to try to do is what is often called 'positive listening', when you make eye contact with the person speaking to you, and smile and nod at appropriate points. This is remarkably effective in getting people to be positive about you and to pay you more attention. Try it out in a meeting or at a smallish lecture – you might be surprised at how much the speakers will start to focus on you, as they receive signals telling them that you are interested, supportive and attentive.

Next, think about your posture. You need to be comfortable, so that you won't be wriggling in your seat after 15 minutes, but you also need to look alert and attentive. As I said in the first section, I've seen this carried to extremes, with candidates placing their elbows on the table or on their knees as they lean forward and try to look intense and engaged. This usually looks at best rather false and at worst will give signals of aggression ('invading their space') to the interviewers. Think about where you put your feet as well as your hands. Shuffling, bouncy feet can be a real indicator of nerves, whilst obviously your hands can be a real help or hindrance. Try to keep your hands fairly still and usually together, using them occasionally if you want to give a non-verbal signal of emphasis, balance, etc. Clearly, wringing hands, playing with jewellery, flailing arms or tightly crossed arms all give fairly obvious signals.

If you are in a boardroom, you may be able to hide nervous feet and hands under the table for at least some of the time. If you are in an armchair or round a coffee table, this will be impossible, so you must be aware of your own nervous habits and try to control them.

Listen carefully to the questions

Listen carefully to the questions that are being asked of you and let the questioner finish the question. This doesn't just mean that you should appear to be listening through the 'positive listening' signals – you really need to hear what is being said and asked. In particular, you need to be aware of falling into the trap of hearing and responding to a 'trigger word' in the first line of a question by telling them everything you know about it at great length. As I cover in more detail later, don't be afraid to clarify a question or take a few seconds to think about your response.

Is the interviewer listening?

Remember the concept of something I've heard called 'mental noise'. Often, after someone has spoken – for example, in asking you a rather complex question – they will be re-running their own words in their head for a few moments, asking themselves, 'Did I phrase that correctly?' During this time, they may not be listening to you as intently as you might wish. So, if you are confused by the question, pause and ask politely for clarification – to help you and them. If you are not confused but you are concerned with whether they are listening properly, start your answer with a brief 'holding statement', such as, 'That's an interesting question...' or 'Yes, I did read the report on that matter...' (Obviously, you can also use this tactic to buy a few moments thinking time – but don't over-use it, as interviewers will quickly get wise.)

How should I answer 'big' or wide-ranging questions?

If you are asked very wide-ranging questions, try to give 'headline' answers, which demonstrate that you know and understand the issues, but through which you can then invite them to ask you to expand. For example, if you are asked about a major or even rather philosophical subject that we will call 'XYZ', you could begin by saying something such as: 'XYZ is a very big issue in our work and I'm sure that we could all give a lengthy lecture on it. However, to me, the key components of XYZ are ABC and the key financial components of this, DEF and its training implications, and GHI and the marketing issues.' (You might add a few more words on each of these.) You can then ask the interviewer, 'Would you like me to expand on any of those points?'

Again, don't imagine that they want to hear everything you know on a subject in great detail – demonstrate that you understand the big picture and then see if they want you to go into more detail. Also, allowing them to ask you to expand makes them feel that they are in control of the interview, when in fact you are!

How should I answer 'closed' questions?

On the other hand, you need to avoid one word or other extremely brief answers, unless these are very obviously called for. Sometimes, of course, interviewers are not very skilled and they ask you 'closed' questions, such as 'Racial discrimination in employment is wrong, isn't it?' Really, there should be a single word answer to this. However, if you think that they really meant to ask you, 'How would you go about handling an apparent case of racial discrimination within your department?' then you may again need to seek clarification about what they really want from you. This is much better than stunning them with a one word answer when they expected two minute's worth of considered response, or vice versa.

Use real and personal examples

Whenever possible, deploy some personal evidence and experiences in order to show that you have done more than just 'read the book'. For professional and managerial posts, it is particularly important that you demonstrate, through both an intellectual understanding and some real experience, that you can do what they need you to do. Concrete examples in which you are personally involved are always the best evidence – it allows them to get to grips with a real example and provides you with the comfort of being on some home territory upon which you can easily expand if needed.

Use positive words and statements

Try to use positive and active words and statements. For example, it sounds much better to say, 'I can deliver this project, based upon my previous experience with XYZ', as opposed to 'I think that I will be able to deliver the project as I once did something similar'. As I said in the CV chapter, never tell lies or claim something that isn't yours – the costs of being discovered are too great and the risks of being stressed by a job that you shouldn't really be in just aren't worth it. However, it is quite reasonable for you to stress the positives and to try to answer gaps by referring to alternative experiences or how you have handled and coped with a similar gap elsewhere.

Another good example of always staying positive lies in the classic answer to the old fallback question of tired interviewers, 'What are your weaknesses?' I learnt a long time ago that this is one of the easiest questions to answer, as long as you are prepared for it. Don't go for some glib answer such as, 'I suppose that my weakness is being sufficiently arrogant to believe that I don't have any other weaknesses!' Pick something that has been a weakness in the past, mention this and then go on to say how you have learnt to cope with it and turn it to your advantage. For example, 'Well, early in my career, one of my bosses used to tell me that I could appear rather driven and thus tended to judge others by my own standards. I came to realise that people can have very different motivators – and of course a range of other responsibilities outside of their career – and I began to do a little studying around this. It's helped me to explain what I want more clearly and to investigate what support my people may need to help them deliver it. That original feedback has been very helpful in improving my abilities as a manager.' Think of your own version of this and use it – you will rarely be asked for a second 'weakness'. (If you are, give a very quick second answer, such as: 'My numeracy skills are a little weaker than my written work, but I've learnt to handle this through close working with my departmental accountant colleagues.' You will almost never be asked for a third!)

Language

Do some research into the type of language that is commonly used at the organisation and think about how and whether you can fit in with this. By language here I mean the organisational jargon or their manner of speaking.

Are they very formal, referring to people by their titles and surnames or are they informal, using all first names? Are they very strong on technical jargon? Are there any current organisational buzzwords or issues that everyone will be talking about? (This tends to happen in my field, the NHS, where new policies or reports are immediately referred to by an abbreviation or by the name of the person who chaired the committee producing the report – I'm sure you can think of examples from any organisation.) Will informal or 'street' language be frowned upon or encouraged?

You might find that you can use slightly different styles of language depending upon the setting – for example, being more formal in the boardroom but speaking (still under control) a little less formally in a one-to-one with a potential colleague.

Dress

Dress codes for interviews have to reflect the type of post and organisation involved. It is probably best to go for standard business attire for most professional and managerial posts, although there will be exceptions to this – perhaps, for example, if you are applying for a job with a creative or computing company, where dress might be much less formal.

The obvious rules must be to check out what appears to be the dress code in that organisation, but if in doubt you should go for a 'default position' of smart business wear. Generally, darker colours appear more sober and professional, whilst very bright colours usually look like the wearer is trying to make a statement. Jewellery should also be smart and understated.

Remember that most managers doing the interviewing are likely to be of an age, background or seniority that may have a bearing on their impressions of you. Similarly, the post for which you are being interviewed may have particular requirements in terms of appearance. For example, an applicant for either a Receptionist post or a new Partner post with a firm of county-town lawyers who turns up with nose-rings, pink hair, a bare midriff or wearing combat gear might not impress!

For more on appearance and personal presentation, see Chapter 5.

Preparation and 'question-spotting'

It is quite possible to prepare for an interview in much the same way as we all did for our exams at school, by 'question-spotting' (and also by 'panel-spotting'). You should be able to work out some of the most likely key question areas from any Role and Person Specifications made available to you, and/or from any visits you have made to the organisation, plus other intelligence gathering. For example, if numeracy and financial management appear high up the Person Specification, whilst budget management is a key part of the Role Specification, then you really should expect some questions about your budgeting experience and your numeracy. (You may also find that they will wish to carry out assessments of your skills through formal tests as part of the selection process). Similarly, if there are less tangible issues that do not appear openly in the Specifications, but which are obvious on a visit and which the organisation fairly readily admits, such as issues around team-working, a merger or new technology, then again you should expect and prepare for questions on this.

Similarly, look at who will be on the panel. This is probably easier in the public sector, where the panel membership is likely to be made known to you. Try to find out about their particular interests or pet subjects. Both of these will enable you to predict at least some of the questions, so that you can prepare your answers.

Pauses and silences

Don't be afraid occasionally to pause for a few seconds for thought, and don't panic when you do so. Used carefully, a pause for thought can make you look thoughtful and considered. However, I'm sure that most of us think that a few seconds silence in an interview feels like several minutes and this can easily panic us into saying something (anything!) to fill the space.

If you are really struggling to say something, use the 'holding statements' I mentioned earlier and/or ask politely for some clarification. For example, you can say, 'That's a really big question for our whole industry/me/our profession, do you want me to give you my personal impressions on the subject or to discuss the current national policy position?' Something like this will again give you some thinking time, but it will also allow you to find out exactly what the interviewer was looking for, without you appearing either too challenging or ignorant.

If you really don't know the answer to a question, then it is always better to say so, rather than holding a really prolonged silence – or, worse still, waffling on and proving that you don't know the answer! In my experience, interviewers tend to be more impressed by someone being honest than by someone trying to con them!

Aggressive interviewers

I'm sometimes asked how to handle an aggressive interviewer. I think that the first issue to decide is whether this aggression is a role that the interviewer has been asked to play, for example to test candidates' resilience under pressure. This might be acceptable for some posts.

However, if you think that this isn't a role that they are playing, then you need to think about how much you want the job and whether you are prepared to accept aggressive and/or patronising questions and comments. If the employer/company accepts or even encourages aggressive, patronising or possibly discriminatory behaviours, then you will just have to accept this and respond either in kind or as positively as you can, if do you really want the job. (In these circumstances, Martin Higham recommends imagining the interviewer sitting in his or her bath!) Otherwise, withdraw from the selection process and look elsewhere.

Any questions for them?

Often, at the end of an interview, you will be asked if you have any questions. In a larger, formal interview setting, the best answer is something like, 'No, thank you, I've had the opportunity to clarify the things that I needed to clarify before the interview. Thank you for inviting me to come along today'. If you haven't had the opportunity for discussions and clarification, then either you haven't tried hard enough, or if you have tried but they haven't answered, then you need to ask yourself, 'Why?' and 'Do I want to work for such an organisation?'. Never, ever produce a list of questions you want to work through – it makes the panel's hearts sink!

It may be more appropriate for you to ask questions in a less formal, perhaps one-to-one interview, where a genuine exchange of information is being sought. If you are in one of these settings – perhaps – at an early stage in the process or with a less formal employer, then you should have prepared a few key questions that are important to you.

However, if you are asked whether there are any additional or closing comments that you wish to make, then don't pass up this opportunity in any setting. Max Eggert recommends that you have a 30-word statement prepared about yourself to use in these situations, to sum up your abilities and why they should appoint you. You should certainly have something ready for these opportunities and combine them with a brief and pleasant 'thank you for inviting me' sentence. Remember that first and last impressions really can make a big difference, and a good closing statement can leave the panel/interviewer with a favourable impression as you leave.

Salary negotiations

You should not introduce pay negotiation into an interview, unless you are in the type of one-to-one final interview where pay is clearly part of the agenda. If you are in a panel interview situation and the pay/package is an issue for you, then you should raise it in principle before the interview, and then discuss it after an offer has been made. Apart from anything else, once an offer has been made, you are in a much stronger position to negotiate, as the organisation is unlikely to want to let you go and start the recruitment process all over again!

Some specific interview types and events around the interview itself

Interview and assessment settings

I can think of many different types or settings for a recruitment interview, such as:

- A formal interview (i.e. you and them on opposite sides of the boardroom table or at least a large desk) before a panel of senior mangers and assessors.

- A formal interview before just one or two senior managers.

- A formal interview before the owner of the company on his/her own.

- An informal (i.e. 'round the coffee table' version) of most of the above.

- A series of two or three shorter, 'criteria-based' interviews, in which you will be seen by different small panels or individuals who will each be looking at different criteria from the employer's specifications for the post.

- Longer, probably less formal interviews with recruitment consultants who have been retained by the employer to search out or assess candidates for a final shortlist.

- Meetings, presentations and interviews with potential colleagues, staff, Board members or other 'stakeholders'. These can range from presentations to a large number of colleagues and/or staff to apparently informal one-to-one 'chats' – but all should be regarded as part of the interview and assessment process.

- Apparently 'social' interactions, including the traditional 'trial by sherry'.

All of these types – and I'm sure that you will be able to add several variations or new types – of interview or assessment should be regarded as requiring you to be 'on parade'. I've seen people blow their chances by saying or doing something inappropriate in an off-guard moment during apparently more informal or social events. For example, a male candidate who took off his jacket and tie and drank mineral water from the bottle during a fairly formal 'trial by sherry'; and a female candidate who said something rude about one panel member to another during an informal one-to-one.

Handling the 'social events'

Before moving on to touch on some other potential aspects of the selection process, I'd like to say a little more about these apparently social events. As I've already said, you should regard every part of the face-to-face contact as being part of the assessment – and this should even include asides made to the person showing you in and out of the interview room or to and from Reception (don't forget how important the opinions of the MD's secretary may be!).

Being 'on parade' means that you should try to avoid eating or drinking during most of these events – apart from at sit-down meals, although even then I'd aim to eat as little as politely possible. Be very wary of buffets and drinks – carry round a plate with a sandwich on it and keep a half-glass of water in your hand in case you need a sip, but otherwise plan to eat after the event. The dangers lie, of course, in spilling/dropping things and in being asked questions whilst you have a mouth full of vol-au-vent.

I extend the eating and drinking cautions into the interview room itself. If possible, avoid drinks and biscuits – again, other than a half-glass of water. Full glasses, cups and saucers and biscuit crumbs have an amazing ability to empty themselves all over candidates at the worst possible moment. For example, be careful of small bottles of sparkling mineral water – I once saw an unchilled bottle go off, in the hands of the candidate trying to open it, like a champagne bottle on a Grand Prix rostrum! Similarly, even if the coffee or tea offered to you doesn't spill, the slightest hand tremor can be exaggerated by a cup and saucer, suggesting a nervousness that you want to hide.

Other potential parts of the assessment process

However, there can be other stages to a selection process as well as the interview itself and these social events. I have mentioned already the use of assessment techniques such as tests and profiling, but these are worthy of further consideration.

Tests of numerical, verbal and non-verbal reasoning and ability, plus personality questionnaires are used for some senior, professional or technical posts. Sometimes these are combined together with interviews and group exercises into an Assessment Centre. The purpose of this multi-faceted approach is to obtain a wide range of possible evidence about the candidates' abilities, style, experience and potential.

If you are going to be asked to undertake either a full Assessment Centre or some tests and profiles alongside a more standard interview, then this will normally be made clear to you in advance. This should allow you to prepare yourself, at least of the level of gaining some familiarity with the techniques to be used.

If you are already inside a larger organisation, you may be able to get access to some of the standard tests, exercises and profiles from your in-house training or human resources department. If you do not have such support, you can access many examples via the internet. For example, my colleagues often use the tests and profiles developed by Saville and Holdsworth Ltd (SHL), one of the major suppliers in the UK – you can find out about them, their techniques and samples via the SHL website.

It is important to remember that some of these techniques are tests, whilst others are not. The numeracy papers, for example, will test your abilities, usually giving you a percentile score against a comparable cohort of managers or operatives. On the other hand, personality questionnaires do not have right and wrong answers – only your answers. They are designed to ask you to give preferences against a range of statements or issues, with the collated answers indicating your style, motivations, attitudes and so on. Most of the major personality questionnaires are sufficiently well designed and validated to detect attempts to skew the profile or give a false impression, so don't be tempted to try to give answers that you think the employer wants. As in the CV and the interview, be yourself – if they like it, that's great and if they don't then that's great as well.

Occasionally you may also be asked to participate in group exercises. These may take the form of a debate or discussion by candidates around a series of issues or options. Usually, they are again used to get an indication of style, listening, influence and decision-making. The best tactic is simply to participate positively, being aware of the impact that you have on others and the task assigned to you. Remember to consider what the assessors might be looking for; it might be power and persuasiveness or it might be skills in involving others and reaching a consensus.

In conclusion

Do remember that when your CV has 'opened the door' to a prospective employer, you then have to go through the door and sell yourself, showing them why they should appoint you. Everything that you say, do and wear can have an impact on the overall impression that you make, so think carefully and ensure that the version of you that they see is a well-prepared, true and positive one.

Further reading

As in the case of CVs, there are plenty of books around to advise you about presentations and interviews further and in more detail than we can here. Two that I have found helpful and accessible are:

Eggar, M. (1999) *The Perfect Interview* (London, Random House Business Books).

Higham, M. (1983) *Coping with Interviews* (London, New Opportunity Press).

CHAPTER 9
Salaries and individual performance reviews

Jennifer Parr

Introduction

It has to be said that I never considered myself an expert on salaries and individual performance reviews. Like many of us, when faced with the opportunity to move jobs or go for that next promotion I found the conversation with prospective employers to determine the salary very awkward, and I always wished that there was some quick advice, a formula to follow, or time to research it properly. I'd get through the ordeal, and emerge with a sense of achievement or 'I should have gone for more' feeling. Likewise in my experience appraisals differ from organisation-to-organisation, and significance from role-to-role. I have never been offered training or advice on preparation. Therefore, the whole experience can become quite confusing, and meant that my performance in the appraisal was not likely to be effective.

In my endeavour to produce some tips for you, I have learnt an immense amount about the traps and trends that we as women share at national and international levels. Hopefully in compiling this, we will all be enlightened and forewarned. It should also allow us to become more aware of the context that we find ourselves in, and therefore more competent in our quest to avoid them.

Salaries

Legislation and policy

'The Equal Pay Act (1970) requires women to show that they do work or are work rated as equivalent by a job evaluation scheme, or work of equal value to that of a male comparator'. At the turn of the century, 30 years after the Act, women are still receiving £250,000 less than equivalently qualified men over their career (Walsh, 2000). David

Harper suggests that the Kingsmill report on women's employment and pay (Dec 2001), does not go far enough to overturn ingrained discriminatory practice as there is a reluctance to legislate for change.

The gender pay gap – women and unequal pay

Perhaps naively, I had assumed that the world was fair, and that regardless of gender, I would be remunerated according to my ability and performance. After all, this is the twenty-first century. However, there is a gender pay gap, which is hugely complex, resulting in women earning only 82% of the average male salary when engaged in full-time work, and only 61% when part-time. The gender pay gap is analysed at national and international level, and the contributing factors here in Britain cannot be assumed to be the same in Europe, America or the developing world. I don't propose to unravel the full picture, but rather to whet the appetite by providing insight into the gender pay gap, which will inform your preparation in the context of any prospective job.

The *Final Report to the Women and Equality Unit* (Anderson *et al.*, 2001) endeavoured to understand the causes of the gender pay gap. These are in summary:

- Women have less work experience than men, and more part-time experiences, which are rewarded less favourably.
- Part-time working is overwhelmingly concentrated amongst women.
- Women tend to spend less time commuting than men, possibly due to the predominance of caring being accomplished by women, employed in part-time roles, and taking up employment nearer to home. This may lead to a higher incidence of lower paid women in an area, driving down the wage for women-concentrated jobs.
- Female-dominated occupations are often the lowest paid.
- Undervaluing of women occurs through appraisal systems, reward systems, retention measures, wage setting practices, and valuation of 'women's work'.

Public sector employment provides evidence of a smaller gender pay gap. Women earn 92% of their male counterparts average salary when in full-time employment compared with 72% when part-time. Teaching and nursing are pre-dominantly female dominated professions and are provided by the public sector. Women in the private sector tend to earn between 3 and 5% less than those in the public sector.

Unpaid labour

What is 'work' then? Many definitions have been used over time. In the 1930's Margaret Reid developed the third party principle to account for what constitutes domestic production. That is those tasks, which a third party could perform for pay (cited Benería, 1999).

Benería (1999) describes the complexities of the debate over unpaid labour, and argues that internationally governments do not collect accurate statistics or effectively acknowledge the contribution made by those working part-time, or in unpaid contexts. The result on an international level is that the Gross National Product (GNP) of countries is not accurate. This is an example of the consequences of ignoring the contribution of women and their labours. She divides the contribution of unpaid work into three areas:

1. *Subsistence sector*

The estimation of backyard rural household activities like cultivation of vegetables as well as those of subsistence production in agriculture, forestry and fishing. Women's unpaid agricultural labour is highly integrated with domestic activities (Benería 1999, p.290). This is more prevalent in developing countries, with the resulting effect on the inaccurate calculation of GNP.

2. *The household economy*

Assessment of the contribution of domestic work is totally excluded as it falls outside conventional definitions of work. As women provide most of the domestic work, this exclusion affects predominantly women.

3. *Volunteer work*

These tasks are not directly linked to the market, it is often of a professional nature and increasingly provided by women, and those with particular social characteristics.

The Cabinet Office report showed that women do take more time out from conventional paid work than men, and on average have 4 years less work experience than men. It appeared that absence from the labour market for 4 years significantly affected the returning salary, however there was no real effect for periods longer than 4 years. Women were particularly affected if they were absent from the labour market for more than four years if the reason was to undertake further education, whereas their male counterparts were unaffected.

A study undertaken to assess the effect of childbearing (twins) on married women's labour supply and earnings concluded that in the short-term, childbearing does reduce women's participation in the labour market. Surprisingly, the impact of unplanned births on labour market participation has begun to decrease over the longer term (Jacobsen *et al.*, 1999).

Negotiating salaries

As mentioned earlier, I found the salary negotiation element of a job move quite awkward, perhaps I felt it was a bit 'bad taste' to talk about money. As a result I have fallen into all the traps of what 'not' to do over the years. I was always puzzled about when was the right time to bring it up and how much should I go for.

On one occasion, throughout the interview process, the only thing I knew about the salary was what it said in the advertisement, which led me to believe that the company would offer a fair salary. When it came time to have the discussion, I was naive and unprepared to negotiate. I had been led to believe I should be grateful for the job, I accepted less than I was worth and the experience set the scene for the forthcoming employment. My self-esteem was directly affected by the outcome, and therefore my personality and performance as well.

Chastain (1980) starts her book, by suggesting in the preface:

'… by negotiating, women stop discriminating against themselves and increase their earnings in the process'.

What is negotiation then? Negotiation is not a confrontation, but it is a dialogue between two parties (at least) to agree some mutual accommodation. When you negotiate, the outcome should be a win-win situation for both parties.

Chastain devotes a whole book to the topic of negotiation of salaries and although it is now over 20 years old, it's value is very current, and its concepts fit closely with best practice.

How to get the best salary

Choices

Easily the most important thing to remember about negotiating a salary is that you must do it. There is really no choice. This is part of the process for men and women to advance themselves and there is no reason why women should allow men to get all the spoils.

Certain choices are available about how and when to do it. Chastain advises to wait until the end of the interview process, and when you are sure you have a job offer, as by this time, you will have had an opportunity to learn about what is important to the employer, and you can use this to demonstrate how you meet their requirements. Even if they raise it with you earlier, it is best to avoid the discussion until you have a chance to really appreciate what they want. She also suggests:

- Make the first offer. This lets the employer realise your expectations of salary.

- Don't accept straight away, as you may need time to reflect, and possibly come back with more questions regarding other benefits.

- Don't appear too eager. They must feel that they have worked hard to get you.

- Never undertake salary negotiation over the telephone, and I would extend this further to include more recent developments in technology, like email. Whilst it may feel more comfortable for you to be separated in time or place, it does not facilitate the nuances of communication that you need to be aware of. It is more in your interest to be face-to-face, as the employer is less likely to feel comfortable offering a low salary, if you are there in person to respond. Make an appointment to discuss the salary when the time is convenient to you, and when you have had ample time to prepare mentally.

Practice and preparation

Even if you are not interested in the actual job, it is really helpful to get some practice without the added pressure of ruining your chances with the one job you really do want. Apply for a variety of jobs, and attend one or two interviews. Try to get as far in the process as possible, and practice the salary negotiation phase to gain familiarity.

A few years ago, I was looking to change jobs, and I went to a prestigious recruitment company to help me. Throughout the process I was coached at every stage. They also provide quite a lot of background information about the prospective employer, and can help you to identify a suitable salary range. They also provided some tips about presentation, both of myself, and throughout the interview. This included posture and how to appear interested but not aggressive. To demonstrate this, they conducted a mock interview, and judged me on my performance including non-verbals.

I was advised to do four things, all of which will influence how well you will do when it comes time to negotiate that salary:

- Prepare a written summary of myself demonstrating how I matched their requirements both in the job description and the brief I had been provided. Using the same terminology and phrases helps them visualise you within their organisation.

- Ask them if they had any concerns about my experience, or fit for the job in question. This gives them an opportunity to raise any last issues with you but more importantly, it provides you with the chance to reconcile their concerns and reinforce your strengths and match.

- Ask for the job! After all, you have already got them to confirm that they have no concerns about your experience, and therefore demonstrated that there is no reason why you should not be employed.

- Write a letter to them after the interview stating how you really benefited from the opportunity to meet with them, re-confirm your interest in the position, and reinforce your match with their specification.

These were unnatural behaviours for me as I would never normally be so aggressive to get what I want. But if it is not me demonstrating my worth to the prospective employer, then it will be my competition. Two of the hardest things to do involved handing over the summary at the end of the interview, and asking for the job. I have done this three times in my career and have got the job each time. It helped the interviewer see several things about me.

- The quality of my work
- My dedication to get what I wanted
- How closely I matched their requirements.

By the time it came to talking about money, they really wanted me, and could not see how others they had interviewed would help them achieve their aims as effectively.

Prepare answers to likely questions or situations. Put yourself in the situation of the employer, and focus on what they feel are essential qualities. The job description will provide this information, but consider other personal qualities to assist you to calculate your value to the organisation.

Practice the conversation using role-play, anticipating and preparing their objections to the salary you perceive to be reasonable. This helps you become more comfortable using the words, hearing yourself speak in a positive objective way about your strengths rather than focusing on your weaknesses.

Deciding your value

Undertake some benchmarking. Find out about other organisations with similar roles. You could explore this in the interview, or contact other organisations directly. Determine what the salary ranges are for the role, and how the role you are applying for differs in its scope, and responsibility. Assess the ranges both within the private and public sector, as we have seen there are marked differences in salaries between the two.

Calculate the amount you need to earn in order to live in the manner that you intend to. This should be the lowest salary you would accept. Hopefully this will be somewhere within the salary range that you are anticipating.

Chastain has advice about how to pitch your price. She says to pitch it higher than the top of the range, in order to give you room to negotiate. The exact amount should be anywhere between 5–20% higher but this is a personal choice. Both parties need room to be flexible. You must expect to accept less than you ask for, and they must expect to pay more. Both of you must in the end feel that you have negotiated, and neither should feel that they have lost face.

This is where your earlier preparation comes to fruition, as you have not only already established their likely objections, but also answered them and developed your rationale for a higher salary, and why you are value for money to them.

Other elements

There are other factors, which will affect your decision about salary, and also about the suitability of the job for you. You must consider how are you going to advance in the future, both in terms of role and salary. This will involve a certain amount of research.

How the salary is structured

There is evidence to show that women are more likely to work for small employers, (Anderson *et al.*, 2001), are less likely to belong to a trade union, and as a result are unlikely to benefit from collective bargaining.

You may find that there are automatic annual increments which you are entitled to regardless of your performance, within a pay scale, or conversely you may be put on a salary which will not increase until you re-negotiate, or change positions. If this is the case, when you agree a salary, also agree a review date, and ensure that this is confirmed in writing.

How are increases negotiated?

Are increases based on your performance and linked to an appraisal system, or does the organisation achieve this through collective bargaining with trade unions, or through job evaluations? Again, agree a date for an appraisal when you accept the position.

Identify reward and incentive schemes

Some organisations conduct Performance Related Pay (PRP) schemes. These should be non-discriminatory, and use formal systems to ensure equity.

Contact the trade union

They will be able to advise you about the type of salary structure, and may even be able to give you advice about salary ranges.

Promotion (pace and prospects)

Pudney and Shields (1999) stated that in the NHS, male nurses are promoted faster than their female colleagues, which amounts to up to £48,000 additional earnings over a career.

It is therefore imperative to identify how other individuals have progressed. What are the prospects of promotion for you, how quickly is this likely, and how are promotions accessed. You could always speak to individuals who work there to appreciate their experiences, and also identify where the previous post holder has moved to.

Chastain makes a very valid point about negotiating future increases. Never dismiss the power of your current and day-to-day performance as a tool to negotiate that next salary, which she calls 'on the job negotiating'. Achieve maximum visibility within your role, as every positive stroke will be useful especially if you are dealing with senior colleagues. Undertake small challenges to lead projects, and utilise every opportunity to demonstrate by example your value to the organisation. This does not mean telling everyone how wonderful and indispensable you are, but making your contribution to the output of the organisation valid, especially with higher-level exposure.

Individual Performance Review (IPR)

Individual Performance Review (IPR) is one form of a personnel-based appraisal system, which is used widely in the public sector. Significantly women view their success differently from men in self-appraisal in that they are less likely to attribute it to their own ability.[4] The authors suggest that this influences the perceptions of the woman by male colleagues, and possibly provides barriers to progression (Andersen *et al.*, 2001). It is therefore necessary to appreciate the purpose, and process of IPR, in order that the disadvantages, which exist, are minimised, and maximum benefit can be obtained.

Purpose

There are several types of appraisal, which include competency-based and 360-degree appraisal. Whilst some forms of appraisal are purely organisation-based, Giddins and Turner (1995) suggest that appraisals typically comprise elements of both organisation and personnel-based approaches. They state the purpose of an appraisal system as being four-fold and based on the feedback loop:

- Set standards
- Monitor performance
- Compare performance with the standards
- Take action to improve.

Redman *et al.* (2000) categorise the outputs of the IPR system as those summarised in Table 1.

Appraisals often follow the yearly business planning process, and form part of the objective setting of the organisation. This process normally commences with the executive objective setting, and then cascades through senior managers and so on. Your place within the organisational structure will determine the time of the year when your appraisal will occur. The Labour Research Department (LRD) state that unions do not like links between appraisal and pay, however increasingly IPR does link performance review with PRP. It is important to differentiate between the two however, and prevent any discrimination through arbitrary treatment of employees (LRD, 1990).

Most systems of appraisal will ensure that there is a formal process of preparation and review to achieve this. Ensure you are aware of anything your organisation provides to assist you and your employer to conduct a fair appraisal. The LRD also states that there should not be any negative consequences for you, if you are absent, for example, on maternity leave, jury or service or union activity.

Commonly an IPR will follow a pre-determined process within the organisation. There are several stages of the review:

Table 1

Output	Explanation
Management Control	The setting and measuring of work objectives.
Employee Motivation	Enhanced job satisfaction and motivation as a result of face-to-face performance review. * 66% of subjects in their study felt that the IPR contributed to improved job satisfaction and motivation.
Training and Development (Personal Development Plans)	The identification of training and development needs following performance review, as a result of clarifying strengths areas of development and specific objectives to achieve the development requirements. * Although this is often discussed, this may be undertaken in a vague manner, and more emphasis placed on setting work objectives rather than developing a personal development plan. * Often due to budgetary constraints employees were encouraged to find alternative development sources than costly courses.
Rewards (PRP)	Commonly IPR is linked to Performance Related Pay (PRP). If this is the case, the IPR would result in a rating of an individual's performance, which would determine the reward, gained. * The respondents did not favour the link between IPR and PRP. One of the criticisms was due to PRP being team dependant, but individually based.

Stage 1

Preparation

- Reflect on your experience of appraisals, as this will assist you to put it into the context of your current organisation and appraisal system. This will also enable you to determine if you need any further explanation or training in the current system.

- Training should be provided both for you (the appraisee) and the appraiser to ensure that both of you are adequately prepared about the purpose, process and expectations of each role.

- Ensure that you agree a date for your review and the date is not re-scheduled. The existence of this will help you identify the commitment of the organisation to the appraisal system in place.

- You should consider and utilise any feedback provided by your manager regarding your performance within the previous year when performing your self-assessment.

Thinking about your Personal Development Plan

- Consider what you believe are important achievements for you in the next 12 months. This may be to develop further skills, for example: negotiation, or people management.
- Attempt to decide what you want your next role to be, and any shortfall in your current skills. You may wish to meet managers of roles similar to one you wish to achieve, and discuss areas of development that will assist you in getting there.
- Some organisations and trade unions offer career counselling.
- Human resource departments can inform you of the essential criteria of your desired roles, and some can even provide assistance to demonstrate pathways to develop the skills and competencies required for individual positions.

Pre-interview self-assessment form

- Many organisations assist you in your preparation of an appraisal by providing a self-assessment form.
- This may provide questions and prompts to assist you to focus. It is generally not mandatory to share this with the appraiser. Common themes in this form could be:
    - Satisfying aspects of the role
    - Objectives achieved most and least successfully
    - Training and development undertaken.

Time should be provided and utilised to complete the self-assessment, prior to the review interview. This should be completed as it assists you to organise your thoughts and focus on your achievements and areas for development. Without preparation, the interview may not achieve what you require. It is also particularly difficult to identify areas of weakness, examples, and then identify ways to develop improved performance in the area without adequate consideration.

Chastain (1980) suggested writing a memo to the appraiser prior to the appraisal. This would provide evidence of your achievements since the last review, future desires for your career, and some areas that you would like to discuss. Some of these areas may be covered in the self-assessment form used, however any opportunity to prepare the appraiser, and focus their mind on your strengths and achievements should be used especially if the IPR is linked to PRP.

Stage 2

Face-to-face interview

This interview should take as long as required to be able to cover all aspects of the IPR. It can last anywhere between 30 minutes and 2 hours.

It is helpful to view the IPR interview as an opportunity to have positive quality time with your manager, where positive and negative feedback can be provided.

An output of this interview is a report. This is discussed, agreed and signed by both parties. If you do not agree on the report the organisation should have a process in place to manage this. You should be made aware of the procedure during the organisations IPR training. At the very least, the disagreement should be recorded (LRD, 1990)

The form is retained by both parties, and objectives and personal development plan forwarded to human resources.

It is not always a natural behaviour to objectively review your performance. You may find it hard to openly discuss your strengths, or weaknesses. Again, it is advisable to attempt to predict the nature of the appraiser feedback in order that you are not surprised. Chastain (1980) comments that some women find it impossible to do this without crying. If this is something that you may do, develop a strategy to deal with it. Identify trigger situations, reflect on previous experiences and attempt to identify alternative ways to approach the situation. Chastain suggests that you may be able to become detached and analytical, or alternatively acknowledge the feedback, and suggest that you have some time to consider it, and arrange an alternative time to discuss. However, you should develop your own way of engaging with these situations.

The interview should produce an objective setting element. Both you and the appraiser should have previously considered appropriate objectives for the forthcoming year. Your objectives should be able to demonstrate your contribution to the organisations overall goals. You will be able to identify likely objectives set by your manager/appraiser by reviewing the expectations of you at different levels. These would include:

- The organisation's mission statement, values and business plan
- The local department objectives
- The manager's objectives
- The key result areas of your job description or job role.

There may also be other un-stated expectations of you and your role, which you should also capture.

Personal development plan

The actual interview should produce a personal development plan, which you both agree. The thinking and research you have undertaken in the preparation phase will inform you, and enable you to influence the direction of the development plan.

Managers will always be more interested in development, which does not have a direct financial cost, and so always suggest a combination of ways of achieving development. Some of these may include:

- Shadowing others who undertake roles similar to that which you are interested in for your next role.

- Secondments to other departments, or acting up into a role vacated by sickness, holiday or maternity leave as some examples.

- A request to take a lead role on a committee or group which may develop your profile within the organisation or expertise in a particular area, and which may utilise skills which you want to further enhance.

Rating or PRP

If appraisal is linked with PRP, the interview will also generate a performance rating. This will determine your performance related pay. Some criticise PRP as often it is a team-based award, but with an individual recipient. More commonly these days, the calculation involves an individual, department and an organisational performance rating.

Stage 3

Mini review

This is held to follow up the IPR and may be held anywhere between 3 and 6 months later. It is helpful to undertake these mini reviews, as they can identify problem areas and generate development plans to overcome any shortfall. There should be no nasty surprises in the actual IPR, as feedback should be continuous.

Summary

Legislation supports the espoused theory of equal pay and employment opportunities for women, however women in the public sector earn 3–5% more than colleagues in the private sector, and women generally earn only 82% of the salary of their full-time male colleagues.

The causes of the gender pay gap are varied and complex, however not justifiable. By becoming aware of the causes, women can actively develop strategies to counter them.

Every element of your performance will be useful to you when negotiating your salary. This includes:

- The application form and documentation.
- Interview preparation, performance and follow-up.
- Job performance and appraisal.
- Aim for a win-win situation when negotiating a salary. Prepare in advance by rehearsing conversations, obtaining feedback and putting yourself in the situation of the employer to identify likely questions and obstacles. Postpone conversations about salary until you are prepared, and ready to discuss it.
- Acknowledge that women discriminate against themselves by not making the most of, and openly acknowledging their contribution to their success and the success of the organisation. Modesty will not get you that pay rise, promotion, or high PRP rating.
- Research the role and benchmark the likely salary range. Identify your acceptance threshold, and pitch your salary 5–20% higher than the top of the salary range you have identified.
- Research salary progression mechanisms in the organisation and how they relate to your role. That is, IPR, automatic increments, collective bargaining, or promotion. Negotiate a review date at the same time as your starting salary.
- Do not avoid appraisal. This is your opportunity to influence the direction of your role, objectives, personal development and rewards.
- Seek and accept any opportunity to be trained in the appraisal process used by your organisation prior to undertaking the review.
- Prepare for the IPR, including providing an evaluation of your past, current and future performance in advance of the review to promote your strengths. You should not be disadvantaged due to any absences.
- Review the outcome of the IPR, and dispute it if you do not agree with it, as documentation will be kept on your personal file.
- The appraisal interview can be an opportunity for you to become more focused, motivated and improve your job satisfaction.
- Develop strategies in advance to deal with any anticipated negative feedback, and any negative emotional responses that you might experience.
- Ensure that you have access to a follow-up review to measure your performance against the baseline of your performance in the actual appraisal interview and implement any changes required at this time. Agree this date at your IPR interview.

References

Anderson, T. Forth, J. Metcalf, H. and Kirby, S., (2001) *Final Report to the Women and Equality Unity*, Cabinet Office, September.

Benería, L. (1999) 'The enduring debate over unpaid labour' *International Labour Review*, Vol 138, No. 3.

Chastain, S. (1980) *Winning the Salary Negotiation Game.*

Giddins, G. E. B. & Turner, J. E. (1995) 'Personnel appraisal', *British Journal of Healthcare Management*, Vol 1, No. 2.

Havard, B. (2001) *Performance Appraisals* (London. Kogan Page).

Harper, D. (2002) 'Balancing the Pay Scales' *People Management* 10 January, p.17.

Jacobsen, J. P., Pearce, J. W., & Rosenbloom J. L. (1999) 'The effects of childbearing on married women's labour supply and earnings' *Journal of Human Resources*, Vol. 34, Issue 3, Summer, pp. 448–74.

Ka-Ching Yan, F., Redman, T., Snape, E. & Thompson, D. (2000) 'Performance Appraisal in an NHS Hospital', *Human Resource Management Journal*, Vol. 10, No. 1, pp. 48–62.

Labour Research Department (LRD) (1990) *Performance Appraisal & Merit Pay.*

Pudney, S. & Shields, M. A. (1999) *Gender and Racial Discrimination in Pay and Promotion for NHS Nurses* Discussion Paper No. 85, December.

Walsh, J. (2000) 'Employers Urged to Mind the Earnings Gap' *People Management*, 16 March, p.14.

Chapter 10
Personal presentation

April Brown and Anna M. Maslin

We are now in a very image orientated world. Everyone wants to make an impression and they hope it will be a positive one. There are so many resources available now from magazines like *In Style, Vogue,* and *Harpers* all trying to give us the benefit of their wisdom. We even have the stylists now who offer all sorts of advice and constructive criticism. The Trinny and Susannah phenomena play tribute to this. It's often hard to develop your own style because many of us have never had the objective advice or the funds to really sort ourselves out.

This chapter is not meant to be didactic or patronising. April and I have both worked at senior levels nationally and internationally. We have had to be appropriately dressed in, for example, Europe, North America, the Far East, Middle East, African Region, South Asian Region, etc. We have had to meet Ministers in government and people living in absolute poverty. We have had to travel for 36 hours on the go and then appear straight off a plane tidy and ready to give a presentation.

We have prepared this chapter for any woman who may be embarking on a return to work outside of the home. Only you can decide what is best for you but these are just some thoughts or tips, if you like, which although they may seem obvious can be very helpful in making the right impression.

Hair
Regular cuts and care are essential. Many women look dated because they haven't altered their hairstyle for 10 years or more. A good cut can take 10 years off a person. Don't be tempted to trim or colour your hair without professional help. If you can't afford a salon find a friend who has these skills or use a hairstylist who will come to your home or offer to be a model at a local salon. If you take the model option remember you may sit in the chair for several hours, it will be inexpensive, but the result can be excellent.

Conditioner seems obvious, but the new products now available can massively improve the appearance and manageability of hair. We sometimes aren't aware of all the options available today that can make the haystack on our heads look a little more, although not exactly the same as, the glossy mane of Claudia Schiffer.

Remember to keep a small comb or brush in your handbag, at work, etc. again, if we want to avoid the above mentioned haystack look.

If time is really limited, hairstylists can advise on low maintenance styles. Remember Jordan in *I'm a Celebrity. Get me out of Here*. She opted for corn rows, knowing washing; blow-drying, etc. wasn't going to be a possibility for a number of days in the jungle.

Remember dry shampoo can be really useful if you are stuck for time. Again, a spare in the office can be helpful.

Cosmetics

What can we say? Magazines will give you more advice than you will know what to do with. Take advantage of the advice available at cosmetic counters in major department stores. Often the consultants will apply make-up for you and the cost is either free or minimal and even this is often waived if items are subsequently purchased. Remember you don't have to purchase everything they recommend. In fact you don't have to purchase anything at all. Just say a warm thank you and give yourself time to think before you buy. Often good quality, lower priced brands, can give you a really good result. Again with skincare, you may find good-quality lower priced options are very good. Usually the simple brands which are hypoallergenic are a good choice.

As with hairstyles, try and keep up-to-date, with seasonal colour changes even if you only change your lipstick.

For those women with darker skins, at last, there are a number of cosmetic houses that provide make-up which compliment the range of skin tones. These cosmetic companies tend to be found in large department stores in main cities for example, London, Birmingham and Manchester.

Remember to discard mascara after 6 months as bacteria can develop and may cause eye infections.

Try not to share make-up with friends as this can encourage bacterial spread, which may lead to skin breakouts.

In hot climates, some lipsticks have a tendency to melt, so keep them in the office fridge during the day and the kitchen fridge when you are at home. You may laugh but you wouldn't if you had red wax all over the inside of your handbag.

You may require two different foundations during the year, as skin tones may darken during the warm summer months.

Clothes

If it's available see if it's possible to make an appointment with a fashion adviser. This service is increasingly available in department stores and often the advice is free of charge. The adviser will assess your requirements, give you some honest feedback and then will be able to advise you on the following:

- What current styles might be good for your life and body shape
- What colours are fashionable and more importantly what compliments your hair and skin tone.

Remember the stylist is offering you an opinion, you don't have to take it. If you really feel uncomfortable with their advice just move on. It is worth remembering though that sometimes a suggestion with a little modification can work well.

Additional considerations

- Modern, washable suits are available and can be really helpful. They save time and money. These versions from companies like Next and M&S can be lovely quality.
- Trousers can be great but you need to check if they are acceptable in your work environment. Always remember to get the length right to make a professional impression.
- Skirt lengths vary all the time. If you have good legs great but if not choose a style that enhances your shape. A good strategy is to check the shops and catalogues and choose one that is current but flatters.
- Shoes, again another area where trends change faster than you can keep up with. Good fashionable shoes will make you look up-to-date and feel good. Very few of us can afford large numbers of pairs so again look at what's in and choose your footwear with style and comfort in mind. I know many supermodels appear to arrive off flights in sky-scraper heels looking fantastic. For many of us, we will not be travelling first class and will not have porters to carry all the luggage, so low heels in a contemporary style will often be a better choice.

Care for your clothes

- Store clothes correctly on hangers. If you travel take your own hangers. How many times do you get to a hotel to find they have only given you three!
- Ensure that hemlines are intact and not worn or frayed. Keep a mini sewing kit from hotels in your handbag and at work.
- Iron and press clothes carefully. If you haven't got the time pop a suit on a hanger and let the steam from your shower ease out some wrinkles. If you use a dryer just put shirts, etc. straight on hangers to minimise the ironing load.

- Observe the advice on the wash care label. Seems obvious but unless you want your little sister to benefit from your cashmere jumper better safe than sorry.
- Keep your wardrobes and cupboards tidy. Again, today there are so many storage options just pick one even if it is all the same size stacking boxes from a supermarket. If your clothes are organised you will know what you have and what you need.

Shoes and hosiery

As we said look carefully at what is available in shops and home shopping catalogues. Remember it is best only to wear new shoes as second-hand can damage your feet even if it is a pair of cute Mary Jane's from eBay.

- Be careful not to wear heels that are too high. Heels can improve leg shape and of course provide additional height, but if the heel is too high your feet and your temper will suffer, not to mention your posture.
- You can take or leave this as you will, but many suggest your shoe colour should match the colour of your handbag or briefcase.
- Ensure that shoes are kept clean and well-healed. It has been said many a man (or in this case a woman) has been judged at a job interview by the state of their shoes.
- Wear tights or stockings that match and compliment the shoes and clothes that are you are wearing.
- During the summer months many women have struggled with the should she, shouldn't she wear tights. Our view is don't suffer in the heat but do look after your legs. Not all of us are blessed with naturally dark skin or an even skin tone. So take advantage of the range of self-tanning creams that are available to provide a little colour. Cosmetic tights can now be purchased; they have a fine denier and will even out the skin tone.
- If sandals are worn during the summer, then treat yourself to a pedicure each month or every two weeks if possible. Alternatively learn to carry out a pedicure at home. It may seem frivolous but it does all help in trying to make a professional groomed impression.
- Many of us commute into work that can involve quite considerable distances. You may not want to follow the American trend of wearing trainers during the journey to work but there is quite a lot to be said for having some flatter shoes for travelling and then changing into some heels when you reach the office. This serves the dual purpose of being kinder to your feet and alternating heel height which is good for your legs.
- Again not rocket science but always keep a spare pair of tights or stockings in your handbag and at work.

Handbags

There are a number of options now for carrying your personal affects. It's just a question of deciding your budget and making a choice. Even if you can afford it, it is worth thinking twice, three times or more if you particularly have your eye on a bag that costs the equivalent of the down payment on a flat. Expensive bags look good to everyone including thieves. Why put so much temptation in someone's way and yourself at risk. If you are traveling in economically deprived countries remember to choose your bag, watch and any jewellery with consideration.

- Carrying a bag in your hand is often preferable to shoulder bags as these can spoil the line of your clothes. Shoulder bags can exacerbate a poor posture and damage your shoulder if you are carrying too much.

- Black is the colour that is easy to manage and goes with most things. Again, we are making the assumption here that you may not have the time or money to manage a dozen bags. We don't.

- Clear out your handbag each month, remove any rubbish and restore order. The unwanted items could be adding extra unnecessary weight. A simple tip is buy some plain make-up bags or colour co-ordinated children's pencil cases to use as mini filing in your handbag.

- New technology such as laptop computers are very helpful, but unfortunately accompanied with their wires can weigh in total up to 8kg. Bearing in mind what we have already said about shoulder bags and damage to your shoulder we often use the smallest trolley suitcase to carry laptops and heavy presentations. You may be asked if you're going on holiday but you can feel smug because you're not in pain! A small suitcase is preferable to carrying numerous bags which can look like you are back-packing rather than attending a meeting.

- Never use shop carrier bags to carry documents, invest in a briefcase.

Jewellery

Here are some thoughts:

- Some suggest you don't mix gold and silver – decide which metal you want to wear. However, if you have a gold wedding or partnership ring on your hand then aim to keep the choice of metal consistent for that hand.

- If you have pierced ears, then make an effort and wear earrings. Double and multiple piercings can be a bit of a problem if you want to achieve a professional image. If you do have multiple ear piercings just try and keep your jewellery simple. Usually large hooped and drop earrings are best for outside work unless of course your workplace is quite arty.

- Decide what you are going to wear and avoid wearing everything. As a guide:

- Earrings, rings, bracelet.
- Earrings, necklace, rings.
- Avoid wearing ankle chains. Although they can be very attractive they don't scream take me seriously.
- Purchase jewellery you enjoy but remember as with all things less can be more.
- Good-quality and reasonably priced costume jewellery is now readily available, so updating your look can be quite affordable.
- Jewellery should compliment not dominate you.
- Pearls are soft and classical. If they suit you they can be very attractive.

Nails

- Whatever nail length you choose keep nails clean and neat.
- If you have problems with growing your nails, extensions are an option but think it through carefully as they are expensive initially and will need three weekly refills which cost both in time and money.
- Moisturise hands.
- Either learn how to manicure your own nails or make frequent visits to a nail technician. Nail technicians have grown in popularity and can be found along most high streets and shopping centres and so the cost has reduced. Some companies can provide a manicure in less than 60 minutes and so can be booked in at lunchtime.
- If a nail is broken or needs trimming, then file it with an emery board. Don't use a metal board or scissors as this can weaken the nail.

If you decide to manicure your own nails then follow these basic tips:

- Don't manicure your nails in a rush, it won't be successful.
- Remove old polish.
- Use a cuticle remover solution and push back and trim the cuticles.
- Shape the nail using an emery board.
- Buff the nails if you wish to remove fine ridges.
- Use a base coat, to ensure that the nail varnish adheres and to prevent staining of the nail itself.
- Use two–three coats of nail colour.
- Use a top coat to protect the colour.

- If time is at a premium and you can't sit still for long then use a nail drying spray. This will ensure that the nails are hard to the touch within five minutes.
- Once a nail is chipped, remove the paint from all the nails and restart the process.
- As a general rule, nail varnish will only last three to four days before it needs to be redone.
- If you don't have the time or inclination to paint your nails, then just ensure that they are clean and neatly filed.
- If your nail bed is large or you have long nails, then darker colours can work well. If however, you have short nails or a small nail bed, then lighter colours are more appropriate.

Perfume

There are many fragrances on the market with more being launched each week. However, only certain perfumes will suit your skin chemistry. Spend time at the perfume counter, but be careful not to sample more than four in one day as your nose will become confused. It is important to have the perfume on your skin for at least 30 minutes and then smell it again to make sure that it suits you. Body heat can also slightly change the fragrance. As a general rule:

- Autumn/winter/cold climates. Use more intense fragrances, musk, spicy, woody tones.
- Spring/summer/warm climates. Use floral and fruity tones.

After a while you will discover what fragrances best correlate to your mood and personality.

Think twice before applying perfume before you fly, other passengers may not be as keen on your choice as you are.

Travel

Even with the advent of the digital age and express communications, international business travel may be part of your working life. If so, then here are some practical tips about how to make the most of yourself while you are in transit.

You may think travelling light is impossible but again unless you are travelling first class with a number of porters in tow you may want to reconsider, especially when you consider excess baggage payments are not cheap.

Always think carefully about where you are going and what you will be doing. If it is an economically deprived country and you are working out and about with the local population you will want to dress in a way that doesn't cause offence. A simple long black skirt, white T-shirt and flat black shoes can go almost anywhere. The same would be true of camel trousers and a white T-shirt or black trousers and black T-shirt and flat shoes. In very hot climates, a long dress which comes down to the ankles is both cool and modest. Again, simple black works well in most areas.

In general, pack a matching suit combination, which may include jacket, trouser, skirt and dress. You can last for several days with this by just changing tops or blouses. Always pack a simple black dress that doesn't crush for the unexpected reception or dinner. You can pick these up cheaply on eBay.

- Pack two pairs of shoes, high and low.
- Decant shampoo and lotions into small bottles.
- Save the free samples from magazines for travelling.
- Buy mini size versions of hairspray and shower gel.
- Instead of folding, roll tops to reduce creasing and avoid ironing.
- On arrival hang creased clothes in the bathroom, as the steam from the bath or shower will help to eliminate some of the creases.
- Take advantage of the hotel laundry facilitates if you can afford it, if not just wash your smalls in the sink.
- Pack a travel iron.
- If you are flying on a long haul route, you may wish to wear more comfortable clothes in-flight and then change towards to the end of the flight if you are required to attend meetings as soon as you land.
- If you are travelling from a cold climate to hot or vica versa layers work well. Using the black trousers and T-shirt example, start off with tights, trousers, T-shirt, cardigan and light jacket which can be easily rolled up. Keep a pashmina in your hand luggage. As you move towards the warmer climate remove the surplus. It really works.
- Remove make-up and contact lens if you are flying for more than six hours. Keeping make-up on may dry out the skin and skin needs to be moisturised during the flight. Purchase a water spritz to freshen your face in flight.
- Drink plenty of non-carbonated soft drinks to reduce the effects of dehydration and to improve the appearance the skin.

Chapter 11
Managing time

Andree le May

Managing time is one of the most essential and yet difficult elements of our lives to get right. This paradox has always puzzled me since on the face of it time management seems quite straightforward – after all we only have a finite amount of time so you'd think that it would be relatively easy to decide what to do with that time and simply use it in that way – that however is rarely the case! The trouble is that, because we all have different components in our lives – work, home and our lives outside both work and home, we are presented with many competing demands on that finite amount of time and this competition leads us into a constant juggling act.

As I write this I am wondering how good I really am at managing time – some would say superb since I usually do what I commit myself to on time, some would say hopeless since to 'deliver on time' I often borrow time from one part of my 'life' and lend it to another. A good example of that is today – as I write this opening paragraph it is six o'clock on a Thursday morning, I have taken the day off work to get my hair done, buy Christmas presents whilst the children are at school, collect cushions from a shop an hour's drive away and generally to relax before going to watch my daughters in two dance displays during the evening! At the moment the children are asleep, the dogs are also asleep having been walked, watered and fed – all is quiet, save the gentle sloshing of the washing machine, and I have grabbed an hour of writing so that I will meet the deadline (now too rapidly approaching) for this chapter. If I'd started writing three weeks ago, just before I moved house I could have had an extra hour's sleep today – but then I needed to use that time for packing boxes! I expect many of you are nodding your heads all too knowingly – some of you are thinking that that sounds OK – she's worked out her priorities, bargained and juggled with time and made some sacrifices along the way – but generally that's fine because the jobs are getting done; others of you are thinking 'she's mad!' and are about to stop reading this chapter and rush out to buy one of those slim books containing handy hints for time management and send it to me! But seriously, the most important thing is, that crazy as it might seem to anyone other than myself, I have learnt to manage time in a way that best suits my life as it currently is, and perhaps that is the real secret of time management – getting a 'fit' between what you want and what you can (or have to) do. The trouble with that is that we aren't just managing our own time since the main demands on our time are made by other people and the ways in which they manage their time will impact greatly on our ability to use our own time effectively.

Time is undoubtedly an important resource to which we individually assign a particular value, for some it is the central element in the management of our lives – everything is always done on time, to time; whereas to others it is simply something that calmly passes by. One thing that is certain though is that time cannot be replaced or reversed (Adair, 1987). This chapter then is really about helping you to consider how you can get that best 'fit' between what you want to do, what is demanded of you and how much time you have to do it in. In order to try to do this I have chosen to identify key elements of successful time management and describe some exercises that you might find useful in helping you to become more aware of your time management strengths and weaknesses. But before we do that let's try to define time management.

Defining time management

There are surprisingly few general definitions of time management – perhaps because it is obviously and simply about how we use time. There is however a general agreement that time management is about using time to our best advantage. In other words time management is not simply about getting a job done within a given time – it is about doing it well, with the appropriate amount of effort being spent and enjoying doing it and its ultimate outcome. In order to do this La Monica (1994 p.283) suggests, 'The time management process focuses on managing the self so that the ratio of effort to payoff is high'. When payoff outstrips effort we start to feel frustrated and pressured and we stop enjoying what we are doing even if we meet the deadlines set for us.

Some suggest that the focus of our use of time can be divided into components – for instance La Monica (1994) writes, within the context of management in general, about two categories of time – speciality time and managerial time. She describes speciality time as time which 'involves responsibilities which have to be accomplished alone' whereas managerial time 'involves some level of interaction between or among people' (page 283). This, although used by La Monica within a management framework, can help us to understand a fundamental component of time management – that some tasks are done by ourselves (and therefore are perhaps easier to arrange and time manage) whereas others are done with other people (and are therefore more complicated to arrange and time manage).

Highlighting some of the key elements of successful time management

There are many books about time management and this section draws on some of these texts in order to highlight the key elements of successful time management. It should however not be read in isolation from some of the strategies that you have already devised to best manage your own time.

Good time management seems to focus around three important actions:

- Identifying what to spend time on and how much time to spend on it.
- Identifying and working with competing demands on time.
- Evaluating how time has been used and considering how it could have been used more effectively.

Each of these, together with some strategies for helping you to work with time, is discussed as follows.

Identifying what to spend time on and how much time to spend on it

If time management is about getting a job done well within a specified time, devoting an appropriate level of effort to that job and enjoying doing it then the first element of successful time management must be to decide what to spend time on. In my experience this requires a degree of ruthlessness coupled with the ability to negotiate not only with others but also with yourself about how you spend time, as well as the ability to say no without feeling guilty.

In order to do this it is important to do a bit of future gazing. Adair (1987) suggests planning long, middle and short-term goals as an important facet of deciding what to spend time on. Knowing what you want to achieve – and of course doing that from a 'whole life perspective' so that you can think about the ways in which each of the different goals impact on each other – is however not as easy as it sounds. Although each of us probably has some long-term goals that we want to achieve it is hard to decide on a timeframe for achieving these since there are so many expected and unexpected things that might get in the way. But this shouldn't deter you from trying to think of the most important things for you to achieve in every facet of your life and then working out when you want to do this by. Once you have decided on these long-term goals the next thing is to work backwards and see what needs to be done towards reaching these goals and allocate times to each of them. Try to do this now using the template for looking ahead in Box 1 as a way of ordering your thinking.

Box 1. Template for looking ahead

Goal to aim for.

Time by which goal needs to be achieved.

Once you have done this and decided to stick with these goals you need to ruthlessly consider whether or not to do anything that isn't important to these outcomes and review them regularly to check if they are still feasible and desirable. In reality however, this is of course easier said than done but at least it's somewhere to start from and to refer to periodically when you feel that you are deviating from the route that you set out on.

Identifying and working with competing demands on time

Looking into the future may also have led you to identify things in your day-to-day life which compete with each other and therefore stop you managing time as effectively as you could – some things may be described as positive consumers of time (things you have to do and/or enjoy) whereas others are time wasters and do not have to be done – recognising which is which will help you with your daily time management.

Whilst our ability to reach long-term goals is always in the back of our minds we are more likely to be worried by the day-to-day management of time – given that lack of time is often one of the things that is highlighted as causing stress and anxiety. In relation to day-to-day time management Adair (1987) has proposed some useful tips for managing time at work that could equally be applied to other areas of life. Firstly he reminds us of the value of planning the day through drawing up a daily list of:

- What you have to do (therefore identifying the things which conflict in that list).
- What you will do with any free time (either planned or unplanned, for example through the cancellation of meetings).

Drawing up these lists is fairly straightforward, the tricky bit is to set time limits for each of the jobs and then to prioritise them into those that have to be done today and those which can wait (and thereby become the ones that have to be done tomorrow!). One way to prioritise is to start with jobs that will have benefit to you (or others) but can be completed quickly; another useful tip is to clutch together similar jobs (e.g. making telephone calls or answering emails). The other trick is to delegate work to others – so time thinking about how this can be done is time well spent. Adair suggests that this list making helps us to use time effectively but he also warns against turning into a 'time fanatic' (page 63) who is so smug about her management of time that she drives others (perhaps less able at time management) to distraction by spreading handy tips on using time to best effect!

In addition to the use of lists to allow us to make the best possible use of time Adair suggests that we focus on the quality of time as well as the quantity of time. To help to do this you need to identify the times of day when you feel at your best and those when you are at your worst. You are probably thinking that this task is easy – but you might be surprised at how poorly you know yourself – so ask someone you work with to help you. Once you have identified your good times keep the difficult jobs for then.

At the end of each day check back over your list, review the things that you have done 'to time' and those which you have been unable to achieve and why. This will help you identify competing priorities and unrealistic allocations of time to various tasks – after that start to think about tomorrow's list.

List keeping is, for me, a great way to keep a check on what I'm doing and still have to do but it is easy to leave out several important features of living when you draw up a list focusing on completing tasks so in addition to the content of your list remember to allow enough time for:

- Rest
- Relaxation
- Thinking.

Evaluating how time has been used and considering how it could be used more effectively

Although as Adair (1987) rightly says you cannot manage time that is past, it is always worth evaluating how well you have used your time. One way to do that is to identify critical incidents during which you have either managed time well or badly and think through how the good bits of your time management could be transferred to other instances and the poorer bits improved upon. Consider yesterday and use the template in Box 2 to help you identify critical incidents and think about them in relation to your personal management of time.

Box 2. Thinking about how I manage time.

Critical incident (s).

Examples of good time management and related actions.

Examples of poor time management and related actions.

Factors which impact on our ability to manage time well

Adair (1987) highlights several common time problems – at the top of his list is ourselves because we are essentially time wasters! He suggests that we have developed highly skilled strategies for putting things off, failing to delegate things to others, ineffectively managing other people and not really knowing what we, ourselves are meant to be doing. Being aware of this is an essential element in good time management.

Within the workplace there are many factors which impact on our ability to manage time well – they may be linked to us or to others. Three of the main ones are detailed below:

1. The increased use of email to communicate with people has meant that we spend a long time reading and answering a mountain of emails instead of memoranda. Interestingly most of us give this process high priority because our

email correspondents expect almost instantaneous answers – long gone are the delays associated with postage – and the resultant feeling that there was time to think before replying! Although email has reduced the mountain of paperwork there are some tips that used to be applied to paperwork which are just as useful to apply to electronic communication – these Adair refers to as classifying mail (electronic or in paper form) for action, information, reading or binning (either electronically through deletion or literally in the waste-paper bin). He advises also having a way of identifying information that you want to leave alone for a bit – either to think through or cool off about – and having a strategy for doing this.

2. Meetings are often viewed as time wasting especially when they start late or over-run or you feel that you are not the right person to contribute to the area being considered. Adair (1987 p.94–95) describes strategies for managing meetings effectively – suggesting that there are five types of meeting – and that each should be used appropriately to ensure your own and other's time management is not impeded by inefficiency.

- A briefing meeting is where instruction surrounding the undertaking of a task are given.
- An advisory meeting on the other hand is essentially about exchanging ideas and information.
- A council meeting is characterised by decision-making based on consensus with associated accountability.
- A committee meeting is one in which representatives from particular groups meet to make decisions about common concerns.
- A negotiating meeting is one in which representatives of different interests get together to resolve differences and identify a way forward.

Knowing the sort of meeting that you are attending or facilitating means that you can lay down ground-rules and manage allocated time appropriately. Adair also suggests always asking if a meeting is necessary to call or to attend and reviewing each meeting's usefulness regularly.

Delegating to others – or managing people is an important element of managing one's own time and much emphasis is placed on this by Adair (1987). However, it is also important to actively acknowledge that delegation will impact on other's ability to manage time as well.

Conclusion

Managing time is an essential element of all of our lives. In order to do this well we have think about our priorities in life, how these impact on or compete with each other and in relation to these and other people's priorities plan how to manage the time available to us most effectively to suit our needs and lifestyle.

References

Adair, J. (1987) *How to Manage Your Time* (Guildford, Talbot Adair).

La Monica, E. (1994) *Management in Health Care* (Basingstoke, Macmillan).

Chapter 12
What about the kids?

Sue Harrop and Sue Miller

Introduction

One of the most significant considerations for many women wanting to return to paid work after having a family is the organisation of their children's care. While there will inevitably be some additional 'juggling' to do when trying to balance the roles of mother with employee, reliable, good quality, accessible and affordable childcare is recognised as being one of the most important factors in allowing women to return to work.

Until fairly recently finding suitable childcare to allow women to work had been left entirely to families to sort out. However, in 1998 the current Labour Government published the document *Meeting the Childcare Challenge*. In the forward to this document, Tony Blair wrote:

> We also want to ensure that families have access to good quality childcare. This matters to us all. To our children who deserve the best start in life. Good quality childcare – whether from parents, informal or professional carers – is vital to them growing up happy and secure in themselves, socially confident and able to benefit from education. To the many parents – especially mothers – who are unable to take up a job, education or training opportunities because childcare isn't available. To businesses, who suffer when skilled and talented people are unable to take up work.

The Government subsequently produced a national strategy designed to address the issue of childcare and to create affordable and accessible childcare for over one million children by 2004. The strategy recognised that people needed help and support to get appropriate childcare. This childcare needed to be flexible, inclusive, able to respond to all children's needs, respectful of special needs and cultural diversity childcare was viewed as directly related to parents', and particularly mothers', ability to get to work.

In addition the Government introduced Working Family Tax Credit and Childcare Credit as a means to support families on lower incomes to be able to afford childcare and made it the responsibility of employers to help employees to make application for these through the Inland Revenue.

As a result of this and other government initiatives, there has been a growth in the amount and type of childcare available, although it is recognised that having choice in childcare still depends on where people live, their income and employment status.

How do I feel about involving someone else in the care and education of my child?

There have been huge changes in society's views of what constitutes good mothering over the past hundred years. While women have always worked outside the home, out of necessity, nowadays many women choose to work for other reasons. Views about whether this is right or wrong have developed and been challenged by the practice of individuals and the various evidence of the impact having a working mother has on children's development.

The notion that women have the right to paid employment contrasts strongly with a view that going out to work, and particularly following a career, is somehow an indication of selfishness and irresponsibility on the part of women. This has led to concerns that the pendulum may have swung too far the other way so that it may now be frowned upon in some quarters for a woman, particularly one who has been well educated and trained, to stay at home and be a full-time parent.

Whatever your views on this, it is important that you come to your own decision about how you and your family want to live your lives and think through carefully the various options. What suits one family may not suit another and if you feel that you are simply doing what is expected of you and not what you believe in, it is quite likely that you will not be comfortable with your choices.

It is therefore important to know what you feel and to have the opportunity to really think about what you want to do, what you can afford to do and why you are doing it. How do you feel about involving someone else in bringing up your child? What are you going to work for? Money? Fulfilment? To maintain your identity? Status? Company? All of these?

It's probably worth considering before discussing childcare the extent to which you could achieve each of these either by not working, by working part-time, or by working full-time.

What do the people closest to me feel about it?

You are going to need the support of at least one or two of the following people: your partner, your family, and your friends. Their attitude towards your decision will be very significant not only in terms of how you feel about them, but also yourself. If they are negative about the decisions you take it is quite possible that you will have these undermined.

We know that previous experience can have a considerable influence on our values and beliefs about childcare. Coming from a family where the women have always had paid employment can bring as much of a pressure to conform to this model as one where mothers have stayed at home.

Whatever you decide to do, it can be very helpful to rehearse and try to understand with your nearest and dearest the implications of not having you available for childcare duties. This can be particularly an issue if you want to return to work when your family has grown accustomed to you being at home. You will all need to talk about what the impact will be on the everyday domestic help you need to organise as a family. Some women consider what jobs they currently do that they could contract out either to other family members or to a paid worker. It can help to think through how other members of the family may need to alter their days, ways of working, their view of their role in the childcare scenario and the family. Think about sorting out ground rules such as who is doing what tasks in the home and considering what the impact of you working out of the home might be on the time and energy you will have left to be available to your family in it. Remember through this that your family may be very proud of the fact that you have a paid role outside of the home as well as the role you have in it.

How will I know/what will I do if it's not working out?

Whatever childcare arrangements you make, there is inevitably going to be some additional juggling involved in your family life and this can create stress. Taking regular health checks on yourself, your child and the rest of your family is crucial. It's important to have time for you. This will be a benefit not just for you, but for your family too. Listen to your children and listen to yourself.

Research has shown that worryingly high numbers of working mothers have no personal time that they can describe as being strictly for themselves. They may not give themselves permission even to have a medical appointment during the day.

If you find you are unhappy with the way your work-life balance is going, perhaps you are missing the children or do not enjoy feeling rushed or as if you are doing nothing well. Perhaps the situation is leaving you feeling less than comfortable about your performance as a parent, as a colleague, as a friend, as a partner. For many working women it is their friendships that they find suffer or their hobbies and their capacity for fun that reduce when they work. This can be very counterproductive, both for your emotional well-being and that of your family.

Trust your feelings. If you are feeling unhappy, this does not have to be a reflection of all areas of your life. Try to trace these feelings back to find their source and achieve a work-life balance that suits you.

What choices do I have?

If you still want to go ahead with finding childcare while you work, there are a number of choices

We are talking here not about crèche settings that parents typically use for short periods when they are doing an activity themselves such as shopping or sport, nor about playgroups or school nurseries run by education authorities which children typically attend for two hours a day (although remember that some playgroups can now offer sessional childcare of up to four hours).

These sorts of services would not be described as full-day care and generally they do not provide enough cover on their own for working mothers. They may incorporate these services as a part of what they use but 'wrap them round' with other support.

Although also generally not for more than two or three hours a day, we have included Out-of-School Clubs here because they cater for older children so may in fact be the main care provider after the school day.

Bear in mind that you have an increasing right to ask at your own work interviews about family-friendly approaches. Does your employer have childcare facilities, flexi-time, home working?

And remember, it's not just you that makes this decision, it's your partner and your child. They all need to be involved. You all need to be happy.

The choices you have for full-day care are as follows:

- Unregistered care
- Care in your own home
- Care in someone else's home
- Care in a group setting
- Out-of-School care.

Unregistered care

Options

Family member

Could be one of a number of different people: grandparents, sister, brother, member of your extended family. They will typically live quite close to you.

Friend

Again, they will usually live nearby and will probably have their own children that they look after and that your child knows and are therefore available at home. Some parents fit care by a friend around registered care such as a childminder, for example having a friend collect your child from school, but dropping your child off at a childminder who will look after your child until you get home from work. If this care takes place in your home or theirs, and there is no payment involved, then this is an entirely private arrangement and there is no registration necessary.

How do I find out what's available?

You are going to know these people and will have seen them with their own children or with yours.

How do I know if it's a good-quality service?

You will have a feeling that this person has a similar set of values and beliefs, and way of working to you and that you and your children are happy with them. You know they like your child. You have observed them with their own children and yours. Trust your feelings and take note of how your child gets on with this person.

How much will it cost?

It could be that there is no cost, but experience suggests that you really have to speak completely honestly about this and make sure that if this family member or friend wants payment they can tell you.

If they get paid in their own home or yours and are on any benefit or pension then they are breaking the law. They are not even supposed to receive 'in kind' payment such as gifts or flowers. Other registered carers may learn of such arrangements and you or your family member or friend could be reported to the authorities for receiving illegal payments.

Positives

- You know the person and have confidence in them.
- Can be very cheap.
- Can constantly renegotiate childcare needs if you are going to be late or work different times or are going on holiday.
- Generally family members are happier to look after an ill child than paid carers might be.
- May be a fulfilling role for other members of the family, for example, recently retired and still young at heart grannies.

Negatives

- Not everyone has this option.
- Can lead to tensions and even destroy previous good relations if resentments build up.

- You need to be sure that this person does not resent you going out to work while they are at home.
- Payment can be a contentious issue and difficult to discuss with someone who is a family member or friend.
- Can be difficult to lay down your expectations with a family member. They may discipline your child the way they did you, but you may not necessarily want this to happen to your child.
- You lose some of your separateness from your parents if they get too involved with your children.
- People get older and grandparents may just not have the energy to look after the child.

What do parents say?

Jenny: 'Financially it's the been the best solution for me, but it's not straightforward because although we've got the same values, we still have to negotiate lots of things.'

What do children say?

Billie (3 years): 'I like going to my Gran's because she gives me treats.'

Verdict

Good solution if you're on a tight budget, and you've got family or friends nearby, but requires lots of honesty and openness to avoid resentment.

In your own home

Options

Au pair

An au pair is typically a young person, more often than not a female, who wants to come to another country to learn a language and is prepared to work for their keep by caring for the children of the host family. They will expect to live in your home, receive board and keep and a small allowance. In return, they can be expected to carry out some basic childcare duties and to oversee the care of your children while you are at work. Often they will not have childcare qualifications, but may have some informal general babysitting experience.

Nanny

Nannies are qualified childcare workers who may live with you and your family or may travel to work from their own homes. You can expect them to have the capacity to undertake the full range of childcare and education roles, particularly with young children.

How do I find out what's available?

There are a number of agencies that advertise widely in yellow pages or through your local authority's Children's Information Service (CIS). Many childcare magazines will carry adverts for nannies and au pairs as will local colleges that offer childcare courses.

How do I know if it's a good-quality service?

Although there are moves to develop a voluntary Code of Practice for recruiting agencies, this is currently the least well-regulated form of paid childcare. You should ask for references, a full employment history and carry out an interview, but none of these approaches is foolproof.

References have their limitations. It's a good idea to ask if you can phone up and talk to someone who the person has worked for in the past. With au pairs you are probably going to have an unqualified, inexperienced woman who may at best have had some babysitting experience. They may have good social skills and be resourceful, but you cannot expect them to necessarily know a great deal about children. Once they are in post, you may want to spend some time at home with the au pair to reassure yourself about her capabilities. Watch how your children react and if appropriate, ask them how they feel about the person caring for them. You should have a contract that may be drawn up through an agency to clarify roles and responsibilities.

Nannies and au pairs can find life in someone else's home quite stressful. If they are living at a distance from their normal home base, you have to take some responsibility for developing their social networks.

How much will it cost?

If the person is living in your home, you can expect to pay tax and national insurance because you are employing them. You also have to pay for their food.

For prices contact your local nanny agencies through yellow pages to get a feel for fees. If you want to have the person checked for criminal records or social service checks you would have to pay for this.

Positives

- Your child is familiar with their own toys and surroundings.
- You can leave a child in bed if you need to go to work very early.
- The nanny or au pair may be able to do household jobs.
- Your child plays with and gets to know local children, thus making own networks.
- Can look after children of different ages.
- Could have consistency throughout childhood if nanny stays with your family for years.
- If you move house, a nanny might move with you.

Negatives

- Have to share personal home space with a stranger.
- House will be untidy, children will be there all day.
- Other people's children may come into your home while you are at work.
- May be a short-term contract, cannot depend on it being consistent. Au pairs will definitely be expected to be a short-term temporary arrangement.
- Need to be careful not to ask too much of them and to spoil the relationship.
- May have to teach childcare skills if young/inexperienced in childcare.
- You are employing them so the responsibility of being an employer falls to you; you have to sort out National Insurance, holidays, etc.
- You may be responsible for finding a network of support for the person.

What do parents say?

Annie: 'My hours are so irregular and I often have to work very late, way past the hours a nursery would be open. With two children under five an au pair or nanny were really the only options as it meant that I could leave the children asleep if I had an early call, or that they'd be able to be put to bed at a reasonable time if I was late. The house isn't that big and you do lose some privacy and it does feel odd to come home sometimes to a house full of children you don't know that have been invited in. But at least it means we've always got a babysitter and that's eased things for us if we need some time to ourselves.'

What do children say?

Finley (4 years): 'I like Anna. She plays with me and makes me my lunch.'

Verdict

Good option if your hours are irregular, but be prepared to share your space and perhaps have to invest in training.

In someone else's home

Options

Childminder

Childminders are self-employed people, generally women though sometimes men, who care for children in their own homes. They have to be registered with Ofsted (Office for Standards in Education), which is now responsible for registration, inspection and quality assurance. The CIS in your local authority will be able to supply you with a list of names and details for childminders in your area. Strict regulations govern how many children they can take and at what ages. Childminders are inspected and have to meet certain standards of care and safety in their homes, often more than you would expect in a private house. Childminders often have their own children at home too and are doing minding as a way of making some extra money while at home. They will generally take children from birth and may also have some children in their care who they just collect from school and in this way they act as an after school service.

Childminders are now being encouraged to adopt a more educational approach to their care role, and in some areas childminder networks have been set up to facilitate sharing of equipment but also so that if one of the network is ill another member can cover for her and still take your child. Some networks can deliver early years education to Ofsted standards. Childminders and parents are expected to draw up a contract between themselves, which sets down the expectations and arrangements on both sides. Experience suggests that time that is spent getting this right reduces tensions and misunderstandings later.

How do I find out what's available?

Each local authority will have a CIS with a list of all the registered childminders in their area and they can very often say who has availability and from which schools if any they can collect children.

How do I know whether it's a good-quality service?

Often word of mouth is a good way of hearing about what a childminder is like. If they are popular and well liked and respected by other parents is this because they are a good service? You can ask to see the inspection reports, which Ofsted produces, on each childminder that they register. Childminders are now inspected once a year. This visit involves an inspection of the house and a consideration of whether they are a fit person to care for children. They will have been police and social services checked as are the other people that live with the childminder who will have been police cleared if over 16.

They are expected to keep records of accidents and of children's attendance and also of any medical treatment they have had to administer while your child was in their care.

You will want to know whether their home is a child-friendly environment. You have to go on your own gut reaction to this, but look at the quality of the environment, the play space available, the toys, whether they take the children on outings. Now childminders can take up to 10 books out from a local library and many local authorities have toy libraries that can lend toys suitable for children with special needs. There is also training available for childminders. Some areas have childminder networks. These allow groups of childminders to meet, the children they mind to play together and this provides opportunities for cover if your childminder is ill, as your child may be able to go to another minder in the network that they have met and know. A childminder network will have a quality assurance kite mark.

How much will it cost?

Costs vary, depending on where you live. Individual arrangements are made with the parent if they wish the childminder to provide food, in which case the parent would be charged, or if the parent supplies this and the childminder just prepares it. Charges would also reflect whether the childminder or the parent supplies nappies. If this is the only child your childminder intends to care for and there are some changes that need to be made to the house to fulfil the conditions of registration, you may need to talk about who pays for this.

Everyone is now entitled to the minimum wage so you must pay this or be breaking the law. Most childminders do not earn enough to have to pay National Insurance or pensions.

Think about things like car seats, cots and buggies. Petrol costs, checking driving license and car seats are all important if you are asking the childminder to take your child in a car. New childminders can apply for a start up grant from the local Early Years Development and Childcare Partnership (EYDCP), but after that they need to find out what services there are available. You may have to take responsibility to ensure they have things like cooker guards.

Many childminders will charge a retainer of half their fee over the child's holiday, though separate arrangements would need to be made by you to cover the childminder's holidays and any sick pay.

The National Childminding Association (NCMA) is the national organisation for childminders that sets standards for childminding and advises the Government about policies relating to them.

Positives

- Child becomes part of a new family.
- Can be relatively cheap.
- Relaxed and informal – more like home.
- Opportunity to develop a close relationship between child, parent and childminder.
- Can look after a range of ages from same family.
- Child can stay with a family for a long time.
- Usually local so can pick up from school.
- Newly registered childminders must, since the introduction of the childcare strategy, have a basic training as part of their registration and have access to further training.

Negatives

- Have to take child to and from childminder's home.
- Difficulties if childminder is ill, and generally they will not take your child if they are ill.
- The unstructured informality may not suit parents who want something more 'educational'.
- Generally not formally qualified, but experienced as parents.
- Childminders tend to work alone so you might feel that your child would be quite isolated.
- Your children may not necessarily get on with the childminder's own family or other children that attend.
- The regulation is relatively light touch and you have to make a personal judgement about how the person will behave when you are not around.
- One person becomes the main carer after you.
- For first time parents, having your child making such a close relationship with one other person outside the family could be quite threatening.

What do parents say?

Sue: 'I looked long and hard for a childminder I really felt I could trust. I felt comfortable with Lucy instantly. In fact, Kate now has two families, and regards Lucy's children as surrogate brothers and sister.'

What do children say?

Kate (9 years): 'I really love Lucy's house. It's fun because she's got Daisy who is my age and I can play with her.'

Verdict

Works well if there is a professional level of relationship between the parent and the childminder, trust and respect on both sides for the contribution each is making to the child's care. Can go wrong if ground rules not established at the beginning and kept to and if not having regular reviews of how the situation is developing.

Group settings

Options

Full-day care

Can be run privately, on a voluntary basis or by a local authority. Should be open every day, and take children from between six weeks and five years of age. Opening hours can be from 7.30 till 6.00 p.m. There are some moves to have settings open for longer and over weekends in certain parts of the country. Generally able to offer full- or part-time places. Caters fully for needs for meals and sleep.

Staff generally hold a childcare qualification. There will be a range of activities, often with outdoor play and they may take children to activities.

Some have particular early childhood philosophies, for example, Montessori or Highscope and policies relating to areas such as equal opportunities and special needs.

Some large employers run their own childcare nurseries for staff, though not many, and this is something that the Government would like to see expand. Some employers find a local nursery and pay to keep some places open there on a regular basis for their staff.

How do I find out what's available?

Information about group daycare settings is available through the CIS, yellow pages or by word of mouth.

How do I know whether it's a good-quality service?

You have to decide what you think a good setting needs to have and then look for that. Trust your own feelings. In general though, it should be registered through Ofsted and this will mean that, like childminders, it is regularly inspected. Ask to see the Ofsted report, which will be available in the setting itself or over the web.

When visiting, take your child with you and see how they react. Ask yourself:

- Will your child be safe?
- Will they be happy?
- Will they have consistency – what's the staff turnover like?
- Will the setting reflect the society they live in?
- Will they be able to stay there for a long time because it has after school provision?
- Will it provide early years education? If it does there will be a reduction in your fees because the setting will get a grant from the Government to cover this.
- Does it have extras like music, language, and dance?
- Is there evidence of staff training and qualifications via certificates, etc. on display?
- Does it have a key worker system?
- Do the children have visits and trips, for example, to the local library? What are the arrangements for these?

How much will it cost?

This depends on the area, though normally fees are per day. Cost will depend on the number of sessions and the age of your child and in general fees are higher for babies where the ratio of adults to children has to be the greatest. The CIS will be able to give you an indication of fees in your area and what these fees cover in the way of extras such as food and nappies. Some people will get reductions in fees because of their personal circumstances or means, or because they have more than one child attending.

Positives

- Stepping-stone to school: children get used to being in a group.
- Qualified staff.
- Long opening hours.
- Cover for staff illnesses possible.
- Number of adults involved so do not have to rely on one person.
- Can see through all of pre-school childcare needs.
- Some actually will let you do a mix and match with a local education setting so your child does not 'miss out' on an educational place.
- You may feel more reassured that in these settings there are more checks and balances of care possible.
- Quality assurance schemes exist for settings and you can ask if the setting has any 'kite marks'.

Negatives

- Catering for needs of a group means more likely to have routines: set times for meals, outings, sleep times and this can feel less flexible than a home setting.
- This can effect the settings capacity to fit in with the individual child's rhythms.
- At the end of the day, private settings are businesses that have to make a profit and this will require the owner to balance paying for training, qualified staff and resources.
- Staff work shifts and different children may attend at different times. Your child may not always see the same children or adults each session.
- For some children, going to the same place for several years can feel institutionalised.
- Your child may mix only with children of their own age because the setting is organised like this.
- Typically more expensive than other forms of daycare.

What do parents say?

Claire: 'I felt I could trust my child's key worker and be reassured that my child is safe because there are lots of checks and balances. I could always rely on the nursery to be there.'

What do children say?

Thomas (4 years): 'I like all the toys and Kelly's my special worker.'

Verdict

For people that work long hours and in inflexible and demanding jobs, this provides reliable long-term group care for pre-school children. You can choose whether it's near where you work or where you live.

Out-of-school care

Options

Out-of-school clubs

This is childcare for a child that is wrapped around the normal school day. It can be before school, after school, breakfast time and holiday play schemes.

It provides something different from school; a place children can play, do activities or homework and chill out. Parents have to book their child in, and pay on a sessional basis.

How do I find out what's available?

The CIS in each local authority will have lists of available registered out-of-school care. They would know if there is a pick up service that will transport a child from a school that does not have out-of-school care to one that does.

Asking at your local school or playgroup or nursery will also tell you if they offer any hours over and above their core time.

How do I know whether it's a good-quality service?

You need to do a visit when the setting is operating. When visiting consider whether the setting will be able to provide for the needs of your children that they are likely to have at the time they are there.

Settings have to be registered through Ofsted if caring for children under 8 years of age and you can ask to see the Ofsted reports. Ask if staff are qualified, particularly in play work areas and that the activities are appropriate for the age and the time of the day they are looking after children. Does it fit the children's natural rhythm? Can they relax if it's after school? If it's breakfast time, is it a chance for them to wake up properly? Does it offer an environment if they need to do homework that's appropriate? Are there computer facilities if they need them?

Will your child feel comfortable with the other children and be able to do what they want to do? Will your children be picked up and then brought to the setting? Will they get the sort of meal that they need? Will they be able to cope with the additional time they will be away from home?

If you are considering holiday play schemes ask whether they are offering a variety of appropriate activities that will keep children stimulated and happy all day? Is it a safe environment? Are they checking who comes in and out have a legitimate reason for being there? Are there appropriate arrangements for children's safety when they are taken out of the setting? Are risks properly assessed and responded to with older children? Have they got a quality assurance kite mark?

How much will it cost?

These clubs are paid for on a sessional basis. Costs will depend on the age of the children and the length of time they are there.

Positives

- Can be relatively cheap.
- Local.
- Very often children will be with their friends from school.
- Siblings can be looked after together.
- Can have play opportunities and visits you cannot give them.
- May have homework club where they could get support with schoolwork.
- Flexible.
- Lengthens the time that you can stay at work or start work in the morning or over holidays.

Negatives

- Can make it a long day for young children.
- Keeps child away from their home-based activities.
- Not a home environment and children do get a longer period away from home.
- Can be problematic for older children who feel they could cope with being more independent and having more of a say about how they spend their leisure time.

What do parents say?

Jackie: 'I can pick Hannah up from the school and know that she's been looked after safely.'

What do children say?

Hannah (10 years): 'It means I'm safe out of school. It's fun and there's lots of people you can play with. My mum can stay at work extra hours until she feels she needs to come and pick my sister and me up.'

Verdict

Good option particularly if you are on a tight budget. Out-of-school care is becoming easier to find in local areas as a result of government support.

Who can I talk to for advice? Where do I go from here?

Apart from friends and family, some of who may have vested interests and certainly their own perspectives on what children need, there are a number of organisations and websites you can visit:

Children's Information Service
www.childcare-info.co.uk

Kids Club Network
www.kidsclub.co.uk

National Childminding Association
www.ncma.org,uk

NDNA
www.ndna.org.uk

Need a Nanny?
www.dfes.gov.uk/nanny

Choosing a Childminder
www.childcare-info.co.uk/childcare/childmndr

What is an Out-of-School Club?
www.tameside.gov.uk

Daycare Trust
www.daycare trust.org.uk

Office of Standards in Education
www.dfes.gov.uk

Yellow pages

Chapter 13
Dealing with the unexpected, stress and bullies

Catherine Gaskell

Introduction

Being the target of bullying in the workplace and the subsequent stress associated with this can have a major impact on the well-being and health of working women. This chapter explores bullying behaviours in the workplace and gives practical advice on how to cope if you are being bullied. It uses anecdotal experiences of women who were targets in their workplaces and it includes theirs and others top tips for surviving the experience. The chapter concludes with 25 tried and tested stress-busting antidotes and a list of helpful websites and reading for further advice support and information.

Many of the facts in this chapter can be attributed to examples and experiences on the UK National Bullying Advice line.

- Definitions of bullying
- Bullying behaviours
- Why are you being bullied?
- Who is getting bullied?
- Three women's stories
- Surviving the bullying experience
- Twenty-five best stress-busting tips
- References, website's, further reading.

Definition of bullying at work – taken from *Bullying at Work* by Tim Field (1999)

Bullying occurs when one person, typically (but not necessarily) in a position of power, authority, trust, responsibility, management, etc. feels threatened by another person, who is usually (but not always) a subordinate who is displaying qualities of ability, popularity, knowledge, skill, strength, drive, determination, tenacity, success, etc. The bullies have conditioned themselves to believe that they can never have these qualities, which they readily see in others.

The definition used by the Manufacturing Science and Finance Union (MSF) is 'Persistent, offensive, abusive, intimidating, malicious or insulting behaviour, abuse of power or unfair penal sanctions which makes the recipient feel upset, threatened, humiliated or vulnerable, which undermines their self-confidence and which may cause them to suffer stress.'

NASUWT (Career Teachers Organisation) define it as: 'The unjust exercise of power of one individual over another by the use of means intended to humiliate, frighten, denigrate or injure the victim.'

The Bully-online website defines bullying as 'behaviour which consistently undermines another's confidence, reducing feelings of self-worth and self-esteem.' Whatever definition of bullying you choose, it is a process where an individual in the workplace is systematically undermined, discriminated against, and treated in a way that hinders their delivery of work objectives.

Most people say they know when they are being bullied though recognition may not always occur at the time of the incident.

Descriptions of 'bullying behaviours' include:

- Constant or destructive criticism.
- Marginalisation – being left out of decision-making.
- Humiliation – in front of peers or junior staff.
- Being given the silent treatment.
- Excessive monitoring of performance and outputs.
- Being starved of resources often hand-in-hand with being overworked.
- Work being increased or removed.
- Being isolated and excluded from the inner circle/decision-making.
- Ridicule/or ideas and success stolen.
- Unrealistic goals or deadlines being set.

This list is not exhaustive. Bullies can use and find a range of these and other behaviours to intimidate, belittle and destroy the confidence of their targets. Bullies are often described as being behaviourally immature, rigidly short-term in their outlook and constantly interfering, dictating and controlling. People who bully do so to avoid facing up to and dealing with their inadequacies. Other bullying tactics include using sarcasm, insults and personal comments, ridiculing ideas and managing performance in a negative and punitive way, controlling and dominating the target with threats of sanctions or the loss of their employment. Bullies also may work in pairs or groups and can thrive in certain environments.

Symptoms of bullying – in the workforce.

Bullying which occurs over a prolonged period of time can have a number of effects on your life. Like the effects of stress it can have psychological effects on your confidence and as well as physical effects on your health.

Some psychological effects of bullying collected by Carolyn Ashton (1999) include:

- Shattered self-confidence.
- Impoverished interpersonal skills.
- Impaired communication skills.
- Increased sensitivity.
- Sense of unworthiness.
- Unusually strong feelings of guilt and shame.

She goes on to list the physical symptoms of stress induced by bullying:

- Excessive constant tiredness, listlessness, and fatigue.
- Headaches/migraine.
- Loss of sex drive/libido.
- Excessive or compulsive picking or scratching.
- Poor skin quality, irritations, e.g. athletes' foot/psoriasis.
- Disturbed sleeping patterns.
- Unusual hormonal changes.
- Unsettled stomach from butterflies and trembliness to being sick.
- Irritable bowel syndrome.

Most victims of bullying in the workplace would claim they could distinguish between bullying behaviours and being robustly managed. The purpose of management includes concepts such as resource control, goal achievement, optimisation or production and can be attained either by individual effort or teamwork. The concepts of bullying are much simpler and revolve around the bullies need to control others. The ultimate purpose of bullying is for gratification of the individual and survival.

Why does bullying and harassment happen?

According to *Conflict Management Plus* organisational factors may be cited as contributing significantly to bullying.

- Adversarial, highly competitive organisational culture
- Structural or cultural change.
- Long hours culture.
- Increase of external/market pressures.
- Collusion/avoidance – particularly at senior level.
- Lack of support for people experiencing and delivering bullying behaviours.
- Physical and emotional resources limited or drained.
- Low commitment to equality of opportunity.
- Inadequate interpersonal skills training.

Possible signs of a bullying culture in the workplace

- High staff sickness and turnover.
- Weak human resources department – unwilling/unable to tackle bullying in the work force.
- No policies and training on harassment, equal opportunities in management.
- Obvious nepotism and established favourites.
- Dictatorial and controlling management style prevalent.

The bullying bosses test – is your boss a bully?

According to Sandi Mann (2002) writing in *Managing your boss* some signs that you may have a bullying boss included in the following behaviours. Read through this list and tick off.

How many do you experience regularly?

Your boss is prone to exploding angrily	☐
Your boss picks on you and others unfairly	☐
Your boss humiliates you in front of others	☐
Your boss pressures you into doing things you don't want to do or doing things their way	☐

Your boss has power over you – they can fire you if you don't do what they want.	☐
Your boss constantly ridicules you	☐
Your boss belittles your achievements	☐

You do not need to experience all of these behaviours to realise you are being bullied. These behaviours constitute bullying if they are continued rather than one off. Other behaviours can also be apparent with a bullying boss but the main purpose of them is to reduce your confidence in your abilities, create anxiety and stress and hit on your self-esteem. They also can leave you feeling isolated and losing confidence in your performance and abilities.

Who gets bullied?

The UK National Workplace Bullying Advice Line statistics for the period of 1 January 1996 through to 31 January 2002 state that workplace bullying is a global phenomenon. The top four groups as recipients of bullying behaviour are teachers, nurses, social workers and workers in the charity/not for profit/voluntary sector.

Ninety percent of cases involve a manager bullying a subordinate, 8% are peer to peer bullying and 2% are subordinates bullying their manager. Over 50% of reported bullies are female, probably due to the fact that teaching, nursing and social work have higher than average percentage of female managers. The only apparent difference – (according to the Bullying advice lines respondents) between male and female bullies is that females make much worse bullies than men. 'Bullying is not a gender issue' it claims – bullies may prefer same-sex targets on the basis one knows one's own gender and weak spots. Intelligent bullies also like to remain outside the provisions of the Sex Discrimination Act.

Why me: Are you a victim of bullying?

Maree was a successful assistant to a popular team manager in the health service who was abruptly removed from their post and replaced by a new manager who bullied Maree. She believes she was targeted for her perceived loyalty to her former boss.

> 'On the first day my replacement manager lined my colleagues and me up and asked us openly to pledge allegiance to her – it was a crazy situation. I couldn't do it. From then on she targeted me and undermined me at every opportunity.'

Maree believed she experienced bullying due to her new manager's insecurity and need to control the team. Over the following months she described being split off from her peers, her responsibilities shrinking, feeling 'left out of the loop' and being told less and less information – which left her feeling that she was no longer part of the team.

According to excerpts from *Success Unlimited* Maree may have become ideal 'bully fodder' because of trigger events.

- Re-organisation.
- She had a new manager appointed.
- Obvious displays of affection and respect or trust from co-workers.
- Refusing to obey an order – in this case a public pledge of allegiance.

Personal qualities that Maree displayed and bullies find 'irresistible' include:

- Popularity
- Idealism
- Competence
- Being slow to anger
- Honesty and integrity
- Being helpful
- Trustworthy and trusting
- Sensitivity
- Giving and selfless
- Difficulty saying 'No'.

Jane realised she had been bullied only after she had left her position as a personal assistant. 'It was my second position, and I was young and naïve and eager to please. My boss was an older male and made personal and derogatory remarks about my physical appearance. I was to hurt and embarrassed to say anything. He commented on my nose and mouth and said I looked like a boxer, as my nose has been broken as a child. I was very sensitive to this and other personal comments. I don't know why I put up with it.'

Jane displayed further personal qualities that bullies find 'irresistible' such as:

- Tolerance.
- An inability to value oneself whilst attributing greater importance and validity to other people's opinions of oneself.
- A strong forgiving streak and desire to think well of others.
- Low assertiveness.
- Internalising anger rather than expressing it.

Jane found it hard to believe she was being bullied and had concluded the behaviour was light-hearted if unwanted office banter; she claimed she felt awkward about challenging it at the time and felt she would be labelled as insensitive, naïve or not able to take a joke. Jane's solution was to leave this position and only years later is she able to label her experience as 'bullying'.

Sandy would have described herself as both competent and confident. Moving to a new senior position within the health service, she joined a newly merged organisation. She was popular with her peers and looking forwarded to the challenge of her new role. Her bullying experience started from her first performance appraisal – where the feedback was so negative as to be both undermining and belittling to her former confidence and personality. She described feeling 'gagged' when contributing in meetings and later described ' it was as if what I contributed was of no value'. She was soon asked to attend fortnightly performance monitoring meetings – where she felt routinely criticised and picked about on her performance in the privacy of the 'bullies' office.

Sandy described becoming aware that her external perception as a manager was being undermined as she was excluded from information and was finding herself not being invited to relevant meetings. Members of her team were given time privately and exclusively by the bully where her performance was discussed. Not unexpectedly her profile internally and externally as a competent manager began to diminish.

Sandy began to doubt her own competency and abilities. Her staff appeared to know more than she did about strategic decisions. Questions about her ability to lead her team began being circulated and 'subordinate to manager' bullying began to surface.

Sandy felt she was targeted because of her initial confidence in her own abilities. She was seen as a highflier and therefore was perceived as a threat. She also described herself as popular and likeable with a number of friends in her peer groups at work. Sandy also believed her questioning style was seen as insubordinate and disloyal.

Sandy had unwittingly become bully fodder by some of her behaviours:

- Refusing to join a clique/showing independence of thought.
- Being popular with colleagues/customers/clients/patients.
- Challenging the status quo, especially unwittingly.

Bullying can occur at any time in ones career as shown by the experiences of Maree – middle manager in an established team, Jane – a junior member in an established team and Sandy – a senior member in a new organisation. Each one of them was subjected to bullying behaviours of varying degrees by events that triggered bullying and the bullies need to 'bully and seek control'. Bullies are predatory and opportunistic and you can happen to be in the wrong place at the wrong time. However, some behaviour's can trigger and worsen bullying and qualities that the victim possesses that contributed to this may be the ones that conversely make the victims initially popular.

These include:

- Slowness to anger
- Giving and selfless nature
- Difficulty saying 'No'

- Diligent, industrious
- Tolerance
- Strong sense of humour
- Quick to apologise
- A strong desire to be reasonable
- High coping skills.

Why do women put up with it?

Carolyn Ashton (1999) cited 'there are a number of reasons why bullying behaviour is often tolerated in the workplace…'

Lack of recognition – Women may be anxious to name what is happening to them for fear of being ridiculed or labelled oversensitive – particularly if the bully is older, well established and respected. CJ described an experience where a subordinate became bullying and intimidating in front of her eyes. 'He lowered his voice and made derogatory comments about my management style and made me feel physically threatened. I had been trying to give him feedback on his performance in which others had found him intimidating and he turned it on me. This pleasant, gentle, professional middle manager became an aggressive rude and a threatening ogre in my office. Speaking to peers afterwards they found it hard to believe my experience, as he was normally so differential and much older than me. He'd taken early retirement and commenced a much junior position in all areas of customer relations, afterwards I understood his move down the ladder.' Under pressure his bullying nature became apparent.

For some bullies they are able to hide their behaviours so well the target reporting them is initially disbelieved, however, bullies rarely strike once, and after some digging a history of similar behaviours is usually unearthed.

Professionalism – People and especially those good at their jobs/take pride in their work and try hard to avoid criticism and attack. They may feel walking away is letting the bully win. This professionalism can cause women to remain in the work environment to keep trying to prove their worth.

Financial incentives – As the sole or equal breadwinners, women often need to work to support their family's expenditure. Therefore confronting the bully especially if they have hiring/firing powers is too high a risk for the family.

Loyalty and commitment – To ones place of employment, if the job was enjoyable before the bullying, hope is often placed in the fact the bully may leave, change or find another target.

Desire to care for those in ones charge – (e.g. patients, inmates, children) or junior staff. Women often feel the need to protect and care for others and this may be tapped into by the bully and used against them.

The support of colleagues – Having a 'bully' in the office can be the focus for negative energy. Teamwork can develop to support the bullied or to share experiences and commiserate. Being the current target can generate more support and this in turn can build peer support (in some, not all cases) making it hard to leave the area/workplace.

Bullying *vs* Harassment

At present if you are being bullied and you are white, British, able bodied and the same gender as the bully you are not covered under discrimination law. There is very little protection in legal terms afforded to those who experience bullying in the workplace.

The Protection from Harassment Act (1996) has influenced employer's awareness and accords emphasis for the first time on the targets perception of harassment rather than the perpetrators alleged intent. Harassment and bullying differ in several ways, though there is much overlap.

Harassment often has a physical component and may include intrusive contact both physical but also intrusion into personal space and possessions. There is focus on the individual due to differences such as gender; sexuality and offensive vocabulary may be used to belittle the victim publicly. Harassment takes place in and out of work and the harasser may occur for peer approval, i.e. to prove a macho image.

Bullying in the workplace is often more subtle and is usually exclusively psychological, based on trivial criticisms and allegations of under performance. It is the far more secretive act carried out behind closed doors without witnesses, the victim may not even realise they are being bullied until much later. The typical workplace bully will lack social and interpersonal skills. They may realise their reputation as a 'difficult to work for' boss and believe this is due to them being a perfectionist and demanding high standard's which the target simply cannot meet.

What can you do if you find you are being bullied?

In asking a group of women this question the most consistent response was 'tell someone about it!' Women in general find sharing experiences whether good or bad a helpful exercise and part of that is to validate the feelings you are having.

Speak up!

This depends on what you intend to do about the situation. Sharing your experience with a work colleague can be a way of ensuring others note what is happening to you but only if the colleague is unlikely to side with the bully or repeat the behaviour. If the bully is the boss, speaking to your Human Resources department in confidence, your Trade Union representative or if your employer has a whistle blowing policy – seeking out the designated lead for your areas are all possibilities. It's also a good idea to have a witness or representative with you so you can clarify what you said and any information/advice given to you. Keep notes of the dates and times you spoke to management about your experience.

Best tip

Keep detailed written notes of all conversations with the bully and who and when you approached people or professional organisations for help. These may be vital pieces of evidence if you decide to take up a grievance with your employer at some stage.

Speak to the bullies line manager

This is a high-risk strategy. It can and has stopped bullies in their tracks but if the bully is senior and established and has a close relationship with their line manager it is not an advisable strategy. If the bully has a history of bullying and the organisation wants to 'shed' them you may find yourself central to the case and your views will count. If the bully is not aware of the impact of their behaviour on you – having a manager speak to them about your perceptions has in some cases been effective.

Talk to peers outside of the work situation

They may not be able to help directly but you can offload to them and friends can help balance the situation. It's easy to become sensitive and overly focused on your experiences. You need to create a work-life balance and getting perspectives from others outside of the workplace especially if you work in a specialist field can be an advantage at times.

Reduce contact time with the bully

If possible try and remove yourself from 'target practice.' Avoid the bully but not your work responsibilities. Keep communication clear and if possible communicate in public or by email and keep all your records. A clever bully will be aware of the ability to keep and forward emails so their behaviours may be curtailed. Ensure you clarify information they give you and ask for written feedback. You may not get it – but they may be more wary if they know you keep records of requests. Keep focused on the job. Stay very polite.

Take care of yourself

Being the target of a bully can seriously affect your health. This is the time to review your diet and alcohol intake. Ensure your diet is high in vegetables and fruit, that you take lunch breaks and leave work at a reasonable hour. You may find your sleep patterns are affected and this in turn effects your productivity and alertness at work. Make sure you switch off from work stress by turning mobile phones and pagers off where possible. Also try not to take work home with you.

Best tip

Use the journey home to unwind so once at home the bully doesn't 'come too'. Ensure you have a routine that enables you to leave work problems at work – leave your briefcase at the door, mobile switched off and change out of work clothes.

Seek counselling

If the bullying behaviour impacts on your self-esteem and confidence or you develop physical symptoms such as – insomnia, panic attacks, phobias, avoidance of situations, ruminations or depression, consider seeking professional help. Your occupational health department can refer you and there may be confidential schemes attached to your company. Alternatively your Union may provide a counseling or advisory service. Your employer has a duty to ensure your health and welfare under the Health and Safety at Work Act (1974) More recently a discussion document *Managing Stress at Work* (1999) indicates that if advice is not followed by employers on a voluntary basis then the HS Executive may introduce a statutory 'Approved Code of Practice' which would make employers liable to a criminal prosecution.

Best tip

Don't let life become unbearable through bullying and cumulative stress before asking for help. You are worth more; your health is worth more – treat yourself well and expect everyone else to do so to.

Assertiveness training

Consider if your manner is allowing the bully to intimidate you. Are you allowing the bully access to you because you are compliant, tolerant and overly helpful? Consider taking assertiveness training and ask trusted friends for feedback on your demeanour and whether you are falling into the target zone because of being too nice.

Sometimes you have to walk away

At the end of the day remember it's 'only a job'. As Maree decided after feeling undermined by her new boss and made to feel devalued – leaving her position was a positive option – 'so I wasn't left mentally and physically exhausted.' Maree joined another organisation that appreciated her skills and helped restore her confidence.

Knowing when to walk away is an important choice – don't compromise or sacrifice so much because of bullying behaviours you can't enjoy your job or position. Choosing to leave can be an act of assertion and enable you to move to a more positive environment. Working should be a stimulating and financially rewarding part of your life – if being targeted has reduced this – remember you don't have to stay and suffer.

Best tip

Sometimes you may choose to walk away. You can only fight so much. Know what your limits are and start accumulating 'Get out of hell money', enough so you can leave if you have to – when you need too. Having some financial padding can enable you to leave an unworkable situation.

Stress management

Working as a woman outside of the home – though often rewarding, demanding and challenging can when combined with our other roles of partner, carer, daughter, lover friend, and parent – make us feel overwhelmed at times. Whatever role you are in, you will at times, feel that you are doing a disservice to another role or barely covering all the bases.

Stress has been described as 'The gap between what you want and what you actually have!' Most of us can identify the physical symptoms of stress – we have experienced panicky feelings through to insomnia and anxiety attacks. Most of us are able to identify that stress in our lives is a combination of events in our work or private lives that makes us feel overloaded.

Below is a compilation of stress-busting ideas to help when the going gets tough.

Twenty-five best stress-busters tips

Take a holiday

Your perspective can become terribly narrowed when in a crisis. You envision you are in a long dark tunnel and you ruminate and relive the events that are bothering you. A holiday can radically blow away the clouds and allow your perspective to come back. Never underestimate the affect of tiredness on your moods.

Try something different

Be an experience mercenary. Visit a local art gallery, go to the theatre, and take a day off mid-week. Change your hairstyle/lose weight – change can help reduce the feeling of being in a rut – and get you out of your routine.

Say 'No'

Don't keep doing what you've always done – when you feel overwhelmed take control in other areas of your life:

- Send supermarket cakes to the Scouts end-of-year event.
- If you are having friends/family over dinner, tell them to each bring a course, don't be the martyr in the kitchen.
- Don't volunteer if you don't want to – decline elegantly.
- Hire a cleaner – keep your weekends free and pay someone to do your ironing.

Start a journal

Writing down your progress and keeping a record of feelings is one of the best ways to keep centred in a crisis. You can note your feelings and coping strategies and realise how far you have come.

You can also list patterns and record when your experiencing problems how you feel and what helps. Journaling is a powerful way to record your coping strategies and experiences.

Talk

Especially good for the 'counsellors' in us – out there. If you are the fixer, sorter, problem-solver type who is often leaned on, it can be liberating to offload and swap roles. Find a trusted friend and spill the beans. Allow yourself to receive support.

Volunteer

Like to try something different? Volunteer for something you want to do, not out of guilt or social pressure. Mentoring is a popular area where your experiences can help adolescents in a range of situations. Share your knowledge and increase your confidence and competence quota at the same time.

Don't always be nice

As Kate White writing in *Why good girls don't get ahead but gutsy girls do!* She advocates that women should not always follow the rules. White advocates just because its never been done before doesn't mean you can't do it, and just because someone says you shouldn't doesn't mean you can't.

Consider cutting corners, saying no, saying yes, and not waiting for the perfect time – jump in – ready or not!

Read

Reading can be a way of immersing yourself in a different space for a while. It can be an avoidance but also a way of recharging your batteries. Reading can be a way of having experiences and developing your knowledge whilst not leaving your home or role – it can also give you private time and be used as a people excluder when commuting! Don't underestimate the power of a good book to lift your mood and take you out of yourself. Consider joining a library or starting a book circle where you review books with a group of friends.

Music

Loud music whether opera, rock, R & B or even Christmas carols can blast the cobwebs out and be therapeutic. Trying to feel down when listening to Aretha Franklin belting out 'Respect' is difficult. Use music on that home journey to help bring closure to the day.

Baking or cooking

For some women this fulfils the need to nurture and is relaxing. Whether you're a 'goddess' or simply god-awful in the kitchen – cooking can be pleasurable if it's done at your leisure, uninterrupted and for your enjoyment. Some women feel it can bring a sense of achievement also.

Spend time with children

Either yours or borrow some! Their irreverence, need for attention, sense of silliness are all absorbing. Children can help blow away the storm clouds – especially if involved in a physical activity – a long walk, take them swimming or visit a zoo. Do something that needs your full attention and arrange your day so you can give it. Bliss!

Exercise

Not one of my favourites – but if you're a gymphopbic like myself – long walks in bracing weather are a great way to lift the blues or ruminations. Exercise increases endorphins, a natural stimulant, which helps to raise your mood by increasing positive hormones.

Balance

Are you doing too much? If you're reading this you probably are! Slow down – learn to drop a few of the balls you're juggling. Your health and state of mind being in balance are more important that 'sweating the small stuff' as Anthony Robbin's, writes 'It's all small stuff.' Take a holiday minus your work phone – and leave work on time consistently.

Treat yourself

The usual suggestions of candles/baths/massage – have been well documented and used in the last 10 years. Find what you enjoy doing and do it. Favourites collected include shopping on your own, buying books, a good cappuccino and a trashy magazine or a quickie manicure, lengthy facial and trying out lots of new cosmetics!

Feng shui

A lot has been written about the principles of feng shui. In Lillian Too's book *Feng Shui at Work* (1999) she advocates designing your workspace to promote health and well-being, reduce negative energies and enliven your environment.

Using plants with rounded leaves, sitting your desk in the most appropriate corner, using light to attract energy, using mirrors correctly all help to make a more harmonious and stress free environment in which to work. Consider making your work environment as pleasant as your home to reduce stress in this area.

Try therapy

When your mood is not coming up, or if you feel your self-esteem/confidence is in your boots or you have contemplated self-harming or have suicidal thoughts – consider getting professional help. Life is not to be endured but enjoyed.

Set goals

Set 'small, smart' goals to get you through when the going is tough. Each tick can be therapeutic which is why the smart 'specific, measurable, attainable, realistic and time-orientated' goals are so important. Even in the worst situation try and move forward, whether on the work front or making a date to see friends. Goals can also be rewards for completing difficult tasks.

Reward

Depending on your budget – treat yourself. From a manicure to a ticket to a concert. Or buy time – have a friend take the kids and you return the favour, use this time to shop, plan and take a weekend break or simply read but make it a positive experience.

Study

Is there something you want to know more about? A subject you want to look into – a qualification, you must have! Studying is a focus that enables some women to learn new skills and change direction. Or develop a hobby or interest further. Local universities and further education colleges offer night classes, which are often short and provide a taster in a range of subject areas.

Renovate

Think about the rooms you live in – do they serve a purpose? Does the colour scheme soothe or motivate? Is an ambience created? Find your style and stick to it. Develop a sample of styles by ripping out colours/details from home style/lifestyle magazines and devise your stratagems for creating an environment you want to come home too. Think about colour/texture/smell – in your new environment.

Donate

You know the rule – if it has not been out of your wardrobe for a year – out it goes – permanently! Do not keep clothes that you need to lose 5lbs to fit into. They remind you of a slimmer you! Instead most high streets have a plethora of charity shops to donate too. Unclutter and be altruistic at the same time.

Garden

If you do not have a garden – try a window box. Growing something from seeds or cuttings is very rewarding and can be therapeutic. It needs a little time, some attention and can result in a creation, whether it is an entire flowerbed or a group of well-fed African Violets.

Change

Small is good when already under stress – so moving house is not advisable, but you could change your hair colour, the coffee you drink, the café you have lunch at, your route to work. Variety can lift you out of a rut and help stop ruminating and dreaming of what you haven't got.

Sleep

Lack of sleep or sustained periods of broken sleep is one of the best ways to lose perspective. When you are tired it is easy to feel run down, make mistakes through lost concentration and generally feeling like the world is against you. A good nights sleep is essential to remain balanced. Use lavender oils on your pillow or a few drops distilled into carrier oil and rubbed onto temples before bed.

Count your blessings

You are a woman, with great potential, courage and self-worth – going through a difficult period – but life is still great!

References

Ashton, C. (1999) *Bullying and Harassment in the Workplace*. Notes from seminar held on 15 June, London.

Conflict Management Plus. Issue 9, handout.

Field, T. (1999) *Bully in Sight*. (UK, Success Unlimited).

Mann, S. (2002) *Managing your Boss in a Week*. (UK, Hodder and Stoughton).

Robbins, A. (1989) *Unlimited Power*. (UK, Simon and Schuster Ltd).

Toos, L. (1999) *Little book of Feng Shui at Work*. (UK, Element Books Ltd).

White, K. (1999) *Why Good Girls Don't Get Ahead... But Gutsy Girls Do*. (UK, Century).

Useful Websites

www.successunlimited.co.uk/bully/

www.suzylamplugh.org/home/aboutus

www.stress.org.uk

www.isma.org.uk

Bullying online (the website of UK National Workplace Bullying Advice Line).

Useful Publications

Andrea, A. (1992) *Bullying at Work*. (UK, Virago).

Covey, R. S. (1994) *First Things First*. (UK, Simon and Shuster).

Goleman, D. (1996) *Emotional Intelligence*. (UK, Bloomsbury).

Harrold, F. (2000) *Be Your Own Life Coach*. (UK, Hodder & Stoughton).

Kinchin, D. (2001) *Post Traumatic Stress Disorder*. (UK, Success Unlimited).

White, K. (1998) *The 9 Secrets of Women Who Get What They Want...* (UK, Century Random House).

Chapter 14
Work-life balance
Flexi-time and working from home

Professor Anna M. Maslin

We all sometimes feel life is getting out of control. None of us have unlimited time and yet many of us feel as if we have unlimited responsibilities.

The Government in the UK is committed to helping us all recognise that work-life balance is a real issue and one where staff and employers need to work together to improve the situation. The aim is to raise employer's awareness to the business benefits of helping employees create a better balance between work and the rest of their lives.

Options, which could be available, are:

- Flexi-time which give people the choice about exactly what their actual working hours are. Often built into this are either core hours or core days when people agree to meet together on corporate business.
- Staggered hours where employees are able to start and finish at different times.
- Time off in lieu where employees and employers agree time can be taken off at a mutually convenient time for extra hours worked.
- Part-time work. This is work, which is less in hours than full-time employment. Some people define it as less than 30 hours a week.
- Job sharing where two people share one job and divide the pay, holidays and other benefits. Each person is employed part-time but together they cover a full-time post.
- Home working. This allows an individual to work all or part of their time from a homework space.

Home working

I guess the reason I am writing this section is because I have now worked from home at home for the last 7 years after the birth of my third child. My office is in London, my home is in Bournemouth 100 miles away and I travel a great deal for work.

Home working has meant for me that I don't have to get up every day at 5.00 a.m. and come home at 8.30 p.m. It means I can see my children in the morning and have dinner with them in the evening. It means that although I still have to have childcare I can be physically close if I'm needed.

I think for home working to be successful there needs to be a number of elements in place. These include:

- A boss who is supportive and trusts you.

- An employee who is trustworthy and gets their work done (if a person didn't work at work they won't work at home).

- An employee who does not need to have people around constantly to feel valued.

- A suitable work environment. I have an office at home with phone, fax, PC, etc.

- Regular hours or a way of being contacted at all work times. If you are working at home you need to be available.

- Good childcare. Working from home may mean you can drop the children off at school or collect them but you will not be able to look after them during work hours. The children need quality attention and your attention needs to be on your work.

- A reliable messaging service. Whatever suits use. If you don't have a secretary a remote access answering machine or other messaging service that you check regularly.

- Regular updates. People need to know what you are doing verbal or written, regular updates are important.

- Flexibility – both the employee and employer need to be willing to compromise. In my work I may be away from home overseas for a week or so at a time, because of this I appreciate being able to work from home days either side of a trip so that my family get to see me too.

Home working isn't for everyone but I think it is becoming more widely recognised as a valid and effective way of improving working lives for many people particularly now housing is so expensive in many major cities. For me home working has been an excellent way of achieving a healthier work-life balance.

For further information visit:

www.dti.gov.uk/work-lifebalance

Flexible Working Arrangements
Equal Opportunities Commission
Information advice including publications
Tel: 0161 833 9244
www.eoc.org.uk

Flametree
Information and advice
Tel: 020 7376 0618
www.flameree.co.uk

Flexecutive
Experts in the field of flexible working
Tel: 020 7636 6744
www.flexecutive.co.uk

New Ways to Work
Information advice and publications
Helpline: 020 7503 3578
www.new-ways.co.uk

Parents at Work
Information, advice and publications
Tel: 020 7628 2128/3578
www.parents@work.org

Chapter 15
A personal view...

Heather Angel

Working for yourself

As the sun dips towards the horizon, a huge white ice arch becomes suffused with a pink glow. In front of this amazing backdrop hundreds of emperor penguins huddle together as the temperature plummets to -30°C. It had taken me almost 2 weeks to reach this part of Antarctica in an ice breaker and several hours trudging over the ice to reach this spot, but I knew this moment would live with me forever. As I savoured the pristine wilderness, I reflected that had I chosen another path as a career I would never have experienced this magical moment.

By the time I married Martin (a fellow zoologist) at the age of 23, I presumed I would carve out a career as a marine biologist for life. After all, I had a zoology degree and had been doing marine biological research for 3 years. I never dreamt I would abandon my love for the marine world and develop an even greater passion for photography. Yet, it was only a few years later that I took the plunge to work as a freelance wildlife photographer.

Why work for yourself?

The prime reason why most women work is quite simply to earn money to survive, or to help support a growing family. Work can be so much more pleasurable if you are lucky enough to find a job that you relish. But not everyone can be so lucky. Working for yourself is an option that deserves consideration for doing what you enjoy when you want to do it.

Without a job specification in black and white, how do you decide where to start? Life's path is a plethora of crossroads; arguably never more so than when debating what to do when contemplating working for yourself. The most obvious springboard may be a life-long interest or hobby; but it could equally well arise from reading an article or even overhearing a chance comment on the radio or on television.

A good starting point is to jot down what you enjoy doing (although in reality it may prove not possible or practical to develop this into a way of earning money). One lady I know began catering for friends' dinner parties and within a few years had developed a most productive business branching out into commercial as well as private catering with her own distinctive van. If you enjoy writing, overheads are minimal when starting up as a freelance writer; although it will help if you are computer literate.

But working for yourself is by no means a bed of roses. I have listed the pro's and con's (see below) from my own experience of working as a self-employed photographer for 30 years.

Pro's

- You will be your own boss
- You can choose your own work schedule
- You can work around the family
- You can work at what interests you
- You can dress as you please – except when meeting clients
- You can stop working when you choose.

Con's

- You have to generate the workload and work out priorities
- No guaranteed monthly salary
- You will have to learn how to keep necessary records (both income and expenditure) so that profit and loss accounts can be assessed at the end of your tax year
- Learn how to say no to social invites which clash with your business demands
- You will need to set yourself goals
- You will have to learn – and learn fast – how to sell yourself and promote your business
- You will need to look ahead to the future
- If you become ill, you will not have an income unless you take out an insurance policy.

Feasibility study

Having a dream is one thing, but how do you make this become a reality? Before you take the plunge, here are a few queries you should ponder.

- What type of business appeals to you?
- Can you identify who would want to buy your product or use your services?
- Have you researched a gap in the market that you could fill?
- Have you discussed your aspirations with your partner, family or friends?
- Will you need a bank loan or other funding to get the business started?
- How will you promote your business?
- Have you set yourself 6-month and first year achievable turnover targets?
- Have you costed your expenses for the first year?

If you covered the last two points, then it will not be too difficult to produce a written business plan, which is essential for obtaining a bank loan.

Time-savers

Whatever path you choose to take and however you achieve the launch of a business, you then have to think constantly of ways and means of achieving your goals. This is always tougher when you are a sole trader; whereas if you decide to go into business as a partnership, you do at least have someone else to bounce ideas off and to discuss the way ahead. Balancing a budget is important, but so is being organised and thinking ahead of ways and means of saving time.

Nothing annoys me more than wasting time standing in queues – whether it be in a supermarket, a bank or at a railway station. So here are a few ways in which I avoid queues.

- Shop late (or very early) in a 24-hour supermarket to avoid check-out queues.
- Avoid going to a bank at lunch-time, when the staff are reduced and full-time workers converge on banks.
- Book rail tickets over the 'phone or on the internet. They will either be posted or can be collected from the station.

Whenever I go on a train or plane journey, I make sure that I utilise the downtime to the full by having a thick pad and plenty of pens (less weight than a laptop and quicker for me to input) packed in my briefcase the night before. This is how I write most of my articles and books and also jot down promotion ideas. I am fortunate in having a PA who deciphers my scribbles and inputs them into a computer.

Organise your day

As women, we are fortunate in having the ability to multi-task, which is a huge asset whether working for a company or for yourself. Whether you live on your own or have a family, it is essential to organise your time efficiently, to slot in the essential domestic tasks – such as shopping, cooking and transporting children – into your working day.

I chose to write this 'personal view' on Good Friday, a day when I knew both the 'phone and the fax would stop ringing and I could ignore my emails (I get between 15–20 a day).

Much to my husband's merriment, I have always been an avid list maker. Firstly, this helps not only to make sure I don't miss one of the many deadlines set me daily, but also it enables me to prioritise the jobs. Secondly, it gives me great satisfaction to cross off each job as it is completed.

My list today reads:

- Write copy for *Tips for Women at Work*
- Edit and caption elephant pictures from Botswana
- Compile two digital lightboxes for a US client
- Call USA re hummingbird workshop
- Scan new pictures to upload on website.

At first glance this list may appear rather daunting, but the last three tasks are not at all time-consuming. Digital lightboxes are compiled by going to my website, selecting relevant images for each client, who is sent an automated email for them to pull the images up on their screen from my server. Scanning slides is now much less time-consuming because I can scan them in batches of five at a time. After putting them in the holder I press two buttons and then revert to another task, returning after they have all been scanned to correct the colour and add the correct file name.

Promoting yourself

Some people shy away from promoting themselves; but if you are going to make a success of working for yourself it is essential that you let people know you exist and what you have to offer. Chapter 2 is devoted to how to write your CV when applying for a job. Once successful, the CV is invariably moth-balled until you decide to apply for another job, when it is hastily updated.

From experience as a self-employed person, I know how just how essential it is to keep my CV constantly updated, because I never know when it will be needed. So as soon as I return from an overseas trip, have a new book published, do a TV interview or an exhibition is staged at a new venue, my CV is updated. During the first four months of 2003 I cannot recall how many times it has been dispatched around the world. It all started in Beijing in February when an exhibition of my work opened. I was besieged by the press, and many glossy magazines wanted to produce features on my work. A call to my office (I have a mobile I can use from China) ensured my CV was emailed to each publication. Since then, I have been asked to lecture and run a week's workshop in Singapore and the organiser needed my CV to help him promote the event.

Another useful way to promote yourself is to take note whenever a client expresses pleasure and satisfaction with your work, ask them for a quote to use on a leaflet or on the internet (when you get your own website).

You only have to walk past the magazine section in a newsagents to appreciate just how many titles are now published. It would be difficult to think of a topic that does not have its own specialist magazine. While most magazines have regular writers, there is always scope for getting free publicity in the news pages. We regularly send off press releases to the photographic press. These used to be in print form, but now we send them as an email. Essentially you need a punchy eye-catching title, a few paragraphs of copy and, preferably, a relevant photo. The following release appeared (with a photo of the puffin) in every magazine we emailed with all my contact details (which have been omitted for publication here).

PRESS RELEASE

Winning Puffin

Heather Angel has won the Animal Antics category in the prestigious International Photography Awards organised by the US magazine *Nature's Best*.
Her winning shot depicts a puffin in flight with legs and tail askew in an Icelandic gale.
Angel relates the story:
"In July 2001 I went to Iceland specifically to take puffins in flight. Strong winds are normally bad for photography. One day when a gale was blowing I almost turned back, but on climbing up to the cliff top I noted virtually all the puffins were hunkered down against the persistent wind. Not a promising start to a photo session! Suddenly an extra strong gust of wind blew a puffin off the cliff and it hung hawk-like just above the ground with its legs and tail askew. I was able to take several frames before the bird descended out of sight."

Safety aspects

In recent years, several women have approached me regarding the safety aspect of my job, which takes me to remote parts of Britain and around the world. I usually reply with the following advice:

- When venturing to a remote place on your own, make sure someone knows where you plan to visit and at what time you expect to return.

- Carry a mobile phone.
- If possible, arrange to meet a local contact who knows the area.
- When travelling abroad remove all jewellery and don't flash expensive cameras in towns and cities.
- Don't carry a conventional handbag abroad; it is too tempting.
  I distribute my money, travellers cheques and credit cards in different places, which I am not going to divulge here!

Conclusion

Before you start your own business, talk to as many people as possible, so you will be aware of some of the pitfalls at least. Once you have made the decision to work for yourself, embark with enthusiasm, it is very likely that you will be rewarded with your efforts and be forever grateful that you took the plunge. I am a firm believer that life is what you make it.

Reference

Burch, G. (2003) *Go It Alone: The Streetwise Secrets of Self Employment* (London, John Wiley & Sons).

If you have access to the internet and use a search engine such as www.google.co.uk to search for self-employment UK several useful websites appear. Notably a most helpful one from the Inland Revenue www.ukonline.gov.uk/startingupinbusiness which gives advice on record keeping, with a help-line number for newly self-employed; also a free appointment can be arranged with the Inland Revenue's Business Support Team.

Dame Lorna Muirhead

Introduction

Choice is the word of the moment and many modern women are fortunate that they can exercise it in many ways.

Now reaching the end of my professional life, I belong to the first generation of post-war women who, having the benefit of a good education, went on to pursue a career, married, had a family, and then had to make decisions about how career and family could co-exist.

In my early working days, midwifery, which is my profession, was largely the prerogative of single women who like many others in the NHS, gave unstintingly of themselves to their work. It was very rare to find a married midwife; in fact I was the first one to be employed by my hospital in 1965. Now, over 50% of midwives are married and many have children.

My children were born before the days of statutory maternity leave, therefore, if women had babies they left paid employment, raised their children, usually until school age and then had to decide if and how they were going to return to the workplace.

The need to earn money was not a prime consideration. Lifestyle was more modest and mortgages obtained taking the salary of the husband into account. This meant that the woman's income was not needed to support the basic essentials of living and although money was not in abundance, it was perfectly possible to exist on one salary, unlike today's lifestyle which, though more opulent, often requires a joint income to support it.

It could be said that I had far more choice of whether to return to paid work than many women do today. When I see the pressure on some of my younger colleagues trying to maintain a home and family, whilst having to pursue a full-time job, I sometimes wonder if today's women have been liberated.

When my children were of school age I thought long and hard about what I now wanted from my life which seemed to me to be like a jigsaw, with many pieces making up the whole picture. I loved family life and I valued my profession, so in common with many other women I decided I would try to have both. I became a part-time midwife. This left me enough time in between my days on duty to fulfil my role as housekeeper, wife and mother.

Advantages of a part-time career

I had a job I loved and was mentally stimulated. I relished the companionship of my colleagues and was making use of my training. Most of all I had an identity. I also had time to have a large input into my children's lives and I was able to manage my domestic commitments. For the first few years I was happy and fulfilled; lucky I thought, to have the best of both worlds.

Disadvantages of a part-time career

The prevailing attitude of many employers and indeed of some colleagues, was that part-time workers were simply at work to earn 'pin-money'. We were not really ambitious or indeed as dedicated as those who worked full-time, and unlike our full-time colleagues, had no need of professional development, nor promotion. Therefore, we were simply used to provide a service. To be fair, some part-time workers fitted this stereotype, but I was not one of them.

Whilst at work I gave 101% of myself to the job. I kept professionally up-to-date and over many years helped pioneer innovative practices and techniques in my ward. I wrote chapters in midwifery textbooks and was a frequent lecturer at statutory study days and refresher courses for midwives. I was politically aware and professionally informed and engaged in local politics through my local branch of the Royal College of Midwives, where in turn I became it's secretary, chairman, press officer and steward. As an articulate women who hates controversy, but loathes injustice even more, I was able to support colleagues through disciplinary and grievance procedures, becoming an advocate for those midwives less able to defend or speak for themselves. No, I was certainly not at work just for the pin-money.

Problems for me

Coping with the lack of career progression for part-time workers was one of the most difficult tasks I had to face. It wasn't that I wanted promotion for itself, but I felt I had more to give than I was able to do in the position I held. It is true that my clinical skills were valued and that I had much satisfaction from looking after pregnant women, but it is almost impossible to influence anything from the shop floor. Eventually, when those in senior positions retired, there were many part-time midwives who had the ability, and qualifications which would have made them eligible for promotion, but the fact that they were part-time prevented them being considered. The result was that those much younger in the profession, and more importantly, often of little proven track record were promoted above those who had both. Some of these women were very able, others were not.

I became increasingly frustrated by this. I needed to influence the politics and policies of my profession which had to be left to others. I tried to keep these feelings subjugated and learned well the mantra that women could not have everything in life and that I was lucky to have home, family and career and for many years this had to be enough. Had I just been there for the money I would have simply got on with the job and left promotion to others.

Problems for my employers

Having a subordinate who is able, aware and challenging is not comfortable and I know that though I was respected I was often viewed quite rightly as a thorn in the side. I asked questions about many things, which subordinates were not encouraged to do, and I had strongly held opinions on many professional issues. The wool could not easily be pulled over my eyes. I had been round the block too many times. This was no-one's fault it was just how the system worked. Many other women must have felt as trapped as I did. Personally, I had a very good relationship with my employers and, off the record, they often asked for my professional advice and opinion, and even more surprising they usually took it. I gradually learned to accept that this was how things must be. But today, with over 50% of the workforce now part-time, creative ways must be found to harness their abilities to a career structure, not only to fulfil their potential but also to meet the needs of the profession.

Personal experience

Aged 50, my children grown, my obligation to my parents happily discharged, and encouraged by my husband who has always believed that children and marriage had prevented my reaching my professional potential, I was now free to take on a new professional challenge. However, 50 in the workplace is ancient and really I had missed the boat. It is customary now-a-days to study for a degree to further a career. This is not what I wanted to do, by the time I had a degree what opportunities would there be for someone approaching their mid-fifties? Nor did I want simply to increase my working hours as physically running round a busy labour ward, working even more shifts and unsociable hours, was not appealing. However, I did want to do something for my profession which remained a passion.

I decided that my forthright opinions which for many years had been expressed in my workplace with limited influence, might be better elsewhere, where they may have more effect. With this in mind I decided to seek election to the Royal College of Midwives (RCM). RCM is the largest and oldest midwifery organisation in the world and concerns itself with the professional and employment needs of the UKs midwives. Much to my delight I was elected to Council, joining midwives from all over the UK to debate, discuss and give direction to midwifery. I relished the informed debate, became far more politically astute, and far less parochial. It was the beginning of one of the most exhilarating chapters of my life and I consider it to be the best professional move I have ever made. This was my time, those years between 50 and retirement. All the frustration and disappointment I felt as a result of lack of career advancement vanished. My election to Council, where I had the opportunity to influence things, I valued all the more because it had been a long time coming.

Totally unexpectedly, and as the result of a chance remark by a member of Council, I stood for election as President of the RCM in 1996 and to my great delight was elected for a 4-year term of office, after which I was re-elected unopposed for another 4 years.

The presidential role is an ambassadorial one, and doing it, I represent the country's midwives at home and abroad. To say it is the most wonderful position is an understatement. As well as fulfilling all my professional needs, it allows me to indulge two of my passions, eating and talking for midwives! I have discussed, debated and dined with royalty, members of both governments, colleagues from associated professions, such as doctors, nurses and health visitors, as well as midwives from throughout the world. It would be very difficult not to be inspired by it all.

Conclusion

In the year 2000's New Year's Honours List I was awarded a DBE and became Dame of the Most Excellent Order of the British Empire for services to Midwifery – I was absolutely astonished, and have barely stopped levitating with joy since. Of course it was the presidential role which caught the eye of the Prime Minister, but I like to think that the work I did for 30 years, directly looking after pregnant women, which represents the work most midwives do, was that which was really being honoured. I also like to believe that if a still part-time clinical midwife from Toxteth can find herself in such a wonderful position, anyone can. Women, today, who for many years may have had to put their own needs to one side whilst juggling responsibilities, need to believe that their day will come.

It would be presumptuous of me to advise others how to organise their working lives, whether working full- or part-time. Women are good at finding their tailor-made solutions. However, my experience of many modern women is that they ask too much of themselves, risk becoming exhausted in the attempt, and have absolutely no time for themselves. Perhaps the reader would like to consider this quote, which though I still struggle with, I wish I had found earlier in my life 'Give commitments sparingly and honour them completely.'

Rosie Barnes

I had my first job at 15 – a Saturday job as a shampoo girl in a local hairdresser. I earned about 7s. 6d. (old money – we are talking about 1961) with the odd extra sixpence tip from kindly elderly customers. I learnt what hard work was and I learnt how not to be 'put upon'. My friend who was doing the same thing arrived very early, as requested, on the Saturday before Christmas and worked until 9.00 or 10.00 p.m. When she arrived home, exhausted, with not a penny more than the usual 7s. 6d., her mother was so incensed, she insisted she went straight back to demand overtime payment. More in fear of her militant mother, I suspect, back she went, and got her extra payment.

It has always been one of my principles that 'if you don't ask, you don't get'. I'm neither a greedy nor a militant person, but I will not be exploited. However, in that frantic rush of getting the ladies of Radford, a poor area of Nottingham, suitably 'glamoured' – a local expression – for Christmas, the salon owner may not have given a thought to his long-suffering shampoo girl. The pitiful payment for her endeavours may have simply been an oversight. It could of course have been a blatant exploitation. However, the principle proved effective. My friend did ask and she did get.

Subsequent Saturday jobs in Pork Farms – a local chain of pork butchers – was followed by holiday jobs with them, soon to be followed by my first big breakthrough. My large extended family was a 'Player's' family. My Dad and several of his brothers and sisters worked at John Player & Son, the tobacco manufacturers. Indeed, my Dad met my Mum when as a 13-year-old, she was sent to work on his cigarette machine. His first memory of her was that she was too small to reach the machine and he had to fetch her a box to stand on. One of my maiden aunts, who had what they certainly thought was a far more prestigious job in the Player's offices, 'spoke for me'. In those days, some 40 years ago, paternalism on the part of employers was common. In Nottingham, whole families were often linked to a particular company, Player's, Raleigh (bicycles) and Boots being amongst the major local industries. So when I was 'spoken for' and subsequently offered a holiday job in the No. 3 factory canteen, it was regarded by all, including me, as an honour. The work was hard, physically tiring and the hours long. A normal day was 8.00 a.m. to 6.00 p.m., but it was paid for on a proper basis. The overtime rate was 11/2 times the hourly rate for evenings and double time at the weekend. In spite of paternalism, which didn't seem strange or unacceptable to me prior to my university days and the challenging of existing order that came later on in the sixties, Players was, in many ways a progressive company. Women received equal pay to men, the only difference I recall being our cigarette allowance. Men were given fifty cigarettes a week and women twenty.

This inequality never bothered me much, as after a few ineffectual and spluttering attempts with Perfectos, the Player's brand of my choice, I gave up all attempts to become an accomplished smoker. Rather than increasing my sophistication as I had imagined, the watering eyes and choking coughs identified me as a hopeless novice, a fate worse than death for teenagers who are required to appear experienced and nonchalant in every new adolescent situation. So, before we knew it was bad for us, and in spite of a strong desire to appear worldly wise, I did learn to listen to my body. Stiletto heels were in vogue for a while during my formative years, and I have given them up with rather greater reluctance. Being on the small, plump side, high heels seemed to me a far better alternative to cutting back on food and drink. They have had to go, though. To do a long day and to remain focused, you have to be comfortable in your body, so fashion has to be kept in perspective.

Player's and its attitude to women had changed considerably by the time I was old enough to work there. My Mum worked there until she was married, but then, as was the custom and the rules, she was obliged to leave. Player's, like many other employers, did not employ married women. The situation changed with the advent of the war in 1939. The men were called up, and as a protected industry keeping the troops in cigarettes, Player's couldn't meet its commitments without opening their doors to married women. Married women could stay on, but were required to leave when the first child came along, unlike Raleigh who did employ women with children. One of my aunts who took a job at Raleigh after her daughter was born was somewhat frowned upon for reneging on her maternal duty.

I learnt a lot in that canteen, returning during school holidays over several years. We produced drinks, snacks and dinners for several thousand people three times a day, served them, cleared up after them and kept the place clean – and clean it was. The food was simple, wholesome and cheap. If I remember correctly, soup and a roll cost 11/2d. This is all beginning to make me sound somewhat geriatric, but I'll press on! The other thing I remember vividly is the huge number of black people I served, many of whom had fierce tribal markings, as recent immigrants. As a little girl, I only knew white people. It must have been the wave of immigration in the late 1950s and early 1960s that changed the profile of Nottingham people, and the strangeness of these faces made an impression on me. Living in a multi-ethnic, multi-cultural society now seems so normal and desirable, but then, it was a very new experience.

One last point from this era. When I was 15 or 16 years old, I started my summer holiday job on the same day as another girl of my own age, who had left school and was starting permanent employment. We got on well and adjusted together to the other employees, the long hours and the nature of the work. We were two of a kind – carefree youngsters with everything to look forward to. When I returned the following year, I got a shock. She had aged and thickened considerably, and had acquired the world-weary resignation of some of the older women who had been there for decades. The difference between us was pointed. I got to know the older women quite well. They remain rich characters in my life, but the tedium of this kind of work for a lifetime was not for me. I knew I wanted something different and was determined to get it, even though what 'it' was eluded me somewhat.

One tip I was given in my early twenties and which I bore in mind has proved to be a mixed blessing. I was advised never to learn to type, as in the late 1960s, women at work were often sidelined to a secretarial or administrative role. If I wanted a managerial role, I had to be focused, not reduced to typing for male colleagues. Like so many things, it strikes incredulity in the younger generation that such a phenomenon existed so relatively recently, but I can assure you it did. So, learn to type I did not, which probably stood me in good stead for the next 20 years but has been a considerable disadvantage over the last 15 years or so, what with the advent of the computer. So I will learn!

Since leaving university, I have had five entirely different careers, as a qualitative market researcher, a marketing executive, a primary school teacher, a Member of Parliament, and more recently Chief Executive of the Cystic Fibrosis Trust. I have enjoyed them all and feel privileged to have had such a varied and stimulating working life. So what tips would I give to my daughter for example?

Firstly, always be yourself. No-one can be happy if they are not true to themselves and very few of us can keep up a persona that is not really our own.

Secondly, be hard-working and enthusiastic. A few of us get to the top easily and with a minimum of effort by luck or because of amazing talent, but most of us have to graft for it.

Thirdly, be positive. It is easy to write lengthy documents explaining why things can't be or weren't done, and to criticise everyone else's good ideas whilst never having one of your own but then no progress is ever made.

Fourthly, don't be afraid of failure. Take risks, albeit calculated ones. Nothing ventured, nothing gained. No one thought I had a hope of winning the by-election in Greenwich, becoming an MP in 1987, including initially the electorate. But win I did, and handsomely at that.

Finally, be a person who makes things happen. That's what you're paid for!

Linda Conlon

I was genuinely flattered to be asked to write a contribution to *Tips for Women at Work*. The publisher wrote to me stating he thought I was a successful woman who had achieved great things and that I might want to share some of the lessons I had learnt with other women. Who wouldn't be flattered?

I think he (not she!) might have revised his opinion if he had seen me in action a few weeks later having failed miserably to meet the deadline he had given me for submission of copy. So many things had crowded in on me. A last minute invitation to travel to Beijing to lecture on science communication involving much research, endless to-ing and fro-ing between Newcastle and China and conscious efforts to push the SARS alert to the back of my mind. Our own Science Festival – a first for Newcastle – that required not only a great deal of management time but also the reading of several thick, recently published tomes before interviewing the authors on stage in front of an audience. A major event attracting probably the greatest concentration of scientific talent the North East has ever seen, including two Nobel Prize winners. My daughter being admitted to hospital twice in two weeks, in great pain and no one knowing quite what was wrong with her. The peculiar smell from the downstairs loo seeping richly through the house as if a whole team of rugby players had used the facilities after a vindaloo curry. Oh yes, and my son ringing up in the early hours from university to discuss endlessly why the love of his young life had ditched him. Is it any wonder I had forgotten what a wonderful working woman I really was?

As I write this, I am conscious that my own list is one that could be replicated by working women – and working mothers – throughout the country. It's a juggling act that requires keeping so many balls up in the air at any one time that I can only sympathise wholeheartedly with Cherie Blair when she admitted recently to dropping one and making a clanger. Nor am I entirely surprised that recent statistics reveal so-called high flyers are not prepared to sacrifice their careers by stepping off the ladder and having babies – it costs a lot, it's exhausting and they feel that they never quite get back on the right rung of that all important ladder.

Male support in the home is incredibly important. Some women don't have it. I'm lucky enough to have fantastic support at home. But, however hard he tries, my husband is not a mother. He is not hard-wired to feel like a mother and when the chips are down, it's mum that the kids want. I cannot help but smile when I look at a postcard sent to me by a friend showing Fred Astaire and Ginger Rogers dancing divinely. The caption reads: 'Ginger Rogers did everything Fred Astaire did, but she did it backwards and in high heels'. Alison Pearson, the author whose recently published and highly successful novel, *I Don't Know How She Does It* (2002), charts the frantic life of working mother Kate Reddy, believes that '... sacrifice is written in our genes. It's part of the guilt chromosome we inherit from our mothers'.

Even as we move forward into the twenty-first century, I do believe that women have to be, if not twice as good as men, then at least much better than men to get as far as their male contemporaries. Of course it's not fair. The playing field is levelling out but it's still bumpy in places. There wouldn't be a need to publish a book called *Tips for Women at Work* if all was equal, would there?

Like most women, I suspect that I've not followed a life plan. They are fine for those single-minded, totally focused women who cherish a burning desire to fulfil an ambition. I have nothing but admiration for them when they achieve their dreams. But I subscribe to the school that believes life plans are a bit like corsets – they seem like a good idea but in the end they just constrict you.

This is borne out by the fact that I have been a bit of a jack of all trades during my working life, ricocheting between jobs and disciplines – and finally ending up doing something I both enjoy and believe in. I've dabbled in marketing and public relations as an employee and as a freelance operator; urban regeneration and property development; and science communication and running a small business. I firmly believe that you can do just about anything if you have the passion and commitment to make things happen.

It is not easy to offer generic tips to working women. This book does that superbly well and I hope women will use it as a reference guide. Women are very different and what works for some women might not work for others. But from my own experience I would offer the following three guiding principles that I hope will strike a chord with all women.

Try to do something you enjoy and believe in

We spend long periods engaged in work. It's a miserable, demoralising and exhausting experience to do something you don't enjoy or fundamentally just don't believe in. I hated my first job. It was sales driven, male dominated and just not me. From the minute I arrived, I spent all my time plotting an exit. I moved to a job that I enjoyed and to a culture I felt more at home with. Don't be afraid to recognise when you have made a mistake. Move on and do something you want to do.

Don't be afraid to stretch yourself

However much we enjoy a job, it's easy to become cosy and opt for the safe and well-trodden path. We all need a challenge and a change if we are develop. Have a go at doing something that interests you but at the same time scares you! I spent almost 10 years as Director of Corporate Affairs at an urban development agency. It was a fascinating and high profile job but after so long I felt I could do it in my sleep. The opportunity arose to do something completely different – steering a millennium project through from concept to delivery. The two jobs could not have been more different. I was simultaneously terrified and elated! When the project was finally delivered, the sense of achievement I felt was overwhelming.

Earlier in my career, I applied for a job that stated applicants must be graduates with journalistic experience and should hold a clean driving licence. I was neither a graduate or a journalist – I couldn't even drive a car having failed my driving test two days before I sent in the application. However, I thought it was worth a go. Luckily for me, the field was a lean one. I was offered the job on condition that I passed my driving test within six months or they would ask me to leave. I passed and stayed in the job for five very happy years.

Admit what you don't know

This is something women are much better at than men! We find it relatively easy to admit what we don't know and we know when to seek advice. Generally, men see it as a sign of weakness to admit ignorance. They feel they are losing face in a testosterone-charged boardroom. I have found that this ability to admit what we don't know is a very powerful tool in the female weaponry. While managing a huge team of architects, quantity surveyors, engineers, designers, lighting specialists – almost all men – I found the process so much easier to handle when I admitted that I did not understand all the technical detail. They were quick to explain, offer support and, together, we delivered a multi-million pound project on time and within budget – I had never managed anything remotely like it in the past. It's also very useful to be able to ask 'dumb' questions – it's amazing how many people sat round the table want to ask the same questions!

From my experience as both an employer and an employee it's worth acknowledging that you have children. Don't pretend that they don't exist! As an employee, I remember the time that I sloped off to attend my son's sports day. I said that I was going to a meeting but instead I took part in the mother's 100 metres sprint. I came a credible second and got a rosette for my efforts. I proudly displayed it on my chest and returned to work. My boss asked how the meeting went. Very well, I responded. I didn't realise you got rosettes for being at meetings, he said. Being a kind and considerate soul, he gently pointed out that if I'd needed time to go to a sports day event, I only needed to say so. Since becoming an employer, I've tried to emphasise to working mothers on my staff that nativity plays, sports days and birthdays are as important as anything in our business calendar. I've found that if I approve time off openly and up front for these events, then staff will repay this consideration many times over when I really need them to be around to fulfil business commitments.

Finally, I don't pretend to have identified the ingredients that make a successful working woman. There isn't such a magic formula. But I do believe that this book focuses on many of the common issues that we all face. It highlights and offers practical solutions and is an immensely useful reference book. Well worth dipping into when the going gets rough!

Chapter 16
Conclusion

Professor Anna M. Maslin

Tips for Women at Work has aimed to cover a range of topics that many of us find challenging as women in the workplace. *Tips for Women at Work* has given us the opportunity to reflect on key aspects of achieving success in the workplace. It has enabled us to consider important issues around the practicalities of the way we work including psychological preparation, CVs, interviews, salary negotiation, individual performance review, personal presentation, time management, childcare, stress, bullies and work-life balance.

How we spend our time is a useful indicator of where our priorities lie. Achieving seniority and a salary to match may be the dream of some young women but dreams also have a price. Is the price too high – have you negotiated the cost?

People-friendly working policies for men and women are important for maintaining the fabric of community and family life. It is vital that women are aware of what is possible and what is reasonable so that they can benefit from the advances in policy and technology in the twenty-first century. Flexibility at one time was undervalued. Now many employers are able to recognise the value a flexible employee adds to the organisation and business objectives. Flexibility and new ways of working can help to ensure clarity of vision and the ability to approach work with a refreshed mind and body.

For professional success to be worthwhile for many women there is the need to adapt career patterns to accommodate family life. At present it is becoming more acceptable for women to continue to produce high-quality work but using more people-friendly work patterns.

Victoria Harrison summed up in *Women at Work* (2002):

'I am pleased to have reached my current destination, but I cannot say that I arrived in it as a result of particular ambitions or sustained or coherent planning; it was more a matter of taking opportunities as they presented themselves. I believe that it is important to be flexible, to be prepared to change tack, and sometimes to do something completely different – particularly if trying to co-ordinate two careers in a family. I love my work, but I have never regarded the pursuit of any particular career as overriding. I hope that in future it might be made easier for women (and for men) to achieve a better balance, and to pursue interesting careers without the current macho pressures to work exceptionally long hours to the exclusion of other interests and family life.'

Tips for Women at Work has tried to share principles, advice and tips to ensure women gain confidence when dealing with the world of work, whether at interview, appointment or in the workplace. It is hard to work out whether high levels of self-confidence precede the ability to succeed or whether it results from the success. The ability to turn a problem into an opportunity is a major contributor to a person's perception of their success in a given situation.

In *Women at Work* there was little doubt that for the majority of the women education was seen as central to their success. Although in *Tips for Women at Work* we have not focused on education directly that is not because we do not value it highly it is simply that in *Tips for Women at Work* we are offering a practical resource for colleagues in the here and now.

Dame Cicely Saunders advice in *Women at Work* was simple:

'If I could pass on one piece of advice to other women it would be educate your children, especially the girls.'

As editor of this book I would agree.

Women at Work endorsed the view that for an individual to be successful at work it does involve some planning for most people. *Tips for Women at Work* hopefully provided readers with some of those important tools.

It would seem that to be successful, in the round, you have to take a conscious decision where to concentrate your efforts based on your own priorities. Unlike some other studies in *Women at Work* we did find that the majority of women in our cohort did opt for a career and family life. For our group of highly successful women family life appeared to enhance their enjoyment of any success they achieved.

Rabbi Julia Neuberger stated quite simply:

'My greatest achievement has been to have two children, apparently reasonably well adjusted, who as adults seem to like spending time with their parents, despite our busy and chaotic life styles. As a professional, I think my greatest achievements have lain in moving on to the next thing without – I hope – leaving the people I worked with before feeling I had simply abandoned them. Family is hugely important to me. I have been married to the same man, Anthony, for the last 26 years, and we have a close family relationship, close also to our two mothers and my three brothers-in-law and their wives, and we live near the two mothers who were both widowed three years ago. I have a strong sense of family – and a strong sense of familial duty as well as pleasure.'

In *Women at Work* and *Tips for Women at Work* we have looked at work-life balance. There was a view, which came through *Women at Work,* that successful women with balanced work and professional lives tend not to over socialise.

Sarah Doukas from Storm, the highly successful model agency was quoted as saying:

'Most of my closest friends date back to my childhood and I've made an effort to keep these friendships intact. My early relationships are important as they keep me level-headed. I don't really socialise within the business and this gives me a more balanced outlook about the business and prevents me from being obsessive about it.'

Wheway and Ross-MacDonald (1998) recounted a story:

'There once was an famous American:
He failed in business in '31.
He ran as state legislator and lost in '32.
He tried business again in '33 and failed again.
His sweetheart died in '35.
He had a nervous breakdown in '36
He ran for state elector in '40 after he regained his health.
He was defeated for congress in '43,
defeated for congress again in '48,
defeated when he ran for the Senate in '55,
and defeated for the vice presidency of the US in '56.
He ran for the Senate again in '58 and lost.
This man never quit. He kept on trying 'til the last.
In 1869, this man, Abraham Lincoln, was elected President of the United States.'

I love this story. Is the moral to try, try, and try again or whether in fact you could be trying too hard. Abraham Lincoln was assassinated after he achieved his dream. It could be, as I said in *Women at Work* that sometimes we are trying too hard.

We all have hopes, aspirations and dreams. We all need to consider how our lives will have meaning in an uncertain world. Women are amazing. They can achieve great things, they can multi-task and they are often under-valued. I hope *Tips for Women at Work* will have given readers some practical resources in helping them achieve their goal and attain a healthy work-life balance.

References

Maslin, A. M. (Ed.) (2002) *Women at Work: perspectives and experiences* (Newcastle, Northumbria University).

Wheway, T. & Ross-MacDonald, J. (1998) *The Sanctuary for the Mind* (London, Thorsons).